Wisdom from Above

Wisdom from Above

A Primer in the Theology of Father Sergei Bulgakov

AIDAN NICHOLS, O.P.

GRACEWING

First published in 2005

Gracewing
2 Southern Avenue, Leominster
Herefordshire HR6 0QF

UK ISBN 0 85244 642 X

Typesetting by
Action Publishing Technology Ltd, Gloucester, GL1 5SR

Contents

Abbreviations

AB	*Agnets Bozhii*
DZh	*Drug Zhenika*
II	*Ikona i ikonopochitanie*
KP	*Kupina neopalimaya*
LY	*Lestnitsa Yakovlya*
NA	*Nevesta Agntsa*
U	*Uteshitel'*

Foreword

By the Archbishop of Canterbury

Father Sergei Bulgakov was probably the most prolific and the most profound of the great twentieth-century Russian Orthodox theologians; but he had also had the deepest immersion in Western modernity through his early work in economics and philosophy. His immensely wide reading in intellectual history as well as in the theology and spirituality of the early church is clearly in evidence in almost every page he wrote in his maturity. And all of this makes perfect sense of the comparison with Hans Urs von Balthasar which Fr Nichols proposes in these pages.

It is a comparison that also helps us put into perspective the questions that hang around Bulgakov's orthodoxy. His early work was dominated by speculations on the Divine Wisdom, Sophia, which appeared to suggest that Wisdom was almost a divine personage. But as his thought developed, the language of Sophia became more and more a hugely fruitful metaphor for connecting diverse theological themes – creation, incarnation, sacramental life, art, liturgy, the social order. God's Wisdom was understood by Bulgakov as an eternal quality of self-giving which allowed God's life to be lived 'in the other' as well as for the other. God loves his own love, and so loves to see that love reborn – in the eternal Son, in creation, in the Church. 'Kenosis', self-emptying, becomes a governing theme in practically all areas of theology in such a light.

It is one of the many virtues of Fr Nichols' excellent introduction that he makes it absolutely clear that Bulgakov's great works on Christian doctrine, while they freely use the Sophia imagery, are not in any way compromised by some sort of gnostic speculation (which could not be said of every Russian thinker who had used this idiom). What is presented here is a sophisticated and far-reaching scheme of Christocentric teaching that makes the dogma of Chalcedon come alive in all kinds of diverse contexts. As in his work on Balthasar, Fr Nichols digests an immense amount of complex material and summarizes it with complete clarity and exemplary sympathy. As research on Bulgakov by Catholics and Protestants as well as Orthodox grows in volume, it is a great help to have this authoritative, comprehensive guide. I hope it will encourge further study and deeper assimilation of one of the most searching and moving as well as one of the most complex of modern theological minds.

† Rowan Cantuar:

Introduction

By Bishop Kallistos of Diokleia

The present book by Fr Aidan Nichols, O.P., has appeared at exactly the right moment. Unduly neglected in the half-century following his death, Fr Sergei Bulgakov is now becoming recognized in his true stature as a profound and creative thinker. Alike in Russia and in the West, we are witnessing a veritable 'Bulgakov renaissance'. Yet, although during the last ten years at least three excellent studies of Bulgakov have appeared in English, Fr Aidan's work is the first comprehensive and systematic survey of his theology. I trust that many readers of this book will be inspired to turn to Bulgakov's own writing, now widely available in translation.

A number of Balgakov's views have proved highly controversial: his teaching, for example, on the eternal kenosis within the Trinity, on the divine humanity, and above all on Holy Wisdom. While not uncritical, Fr Aidan offers what he describes as a 'benign reading' of Bulgakov's theories, showing in convincing terms that, while daring and at times speculative, Bulgakov was no heretic. On the contrary, we may see him as what the French call a *passeur*, a ferryman, one who enables us to cross frontiers and to unite disparate worlds. Firmly rooted in the Patristic tradition, at the same time he engaged – in a way that only a very few Orthodox have done – with the concerns of Western modernity and post-modernity. His was a vision marked by apocalyptic boldness and by Paschal joy.

'If you are a theologian,' said the fourth-century Desert Father Evagrius of Pontus, 'you will pray truly; and if you pray truly, you are a theologian.' Fr Sergei Bulgakov was exactly that kind of theologian. With all the fullness of his fiery yet humble nature, he devoted himself to his ministry as priest. An eloquent preacher, a spiritual father gifted with prophetic insight, above all else he loved the Divine Liturgy, which – in the words of his bishop Metropolitan Evlogy – he always celebrated with 'fear and trembling'. As he himself liked to say, 'One should imbibe theology from the bottom of the eucharistic chalice.' A notable pioneer in the Ecumenical Movement, he never ceased to grieve over our inability as divided Christians to share together in Holy Communion.

May his memory be eternal!

Bishop Kallistos of Diokleia

Preface

I heard the name of Bulgakov through one of the dearest people I ever met, Dr Nicolas Zernov, who was Spalding Lecturer in Eastern Orthodox Culture at Oxford when I was an undergraduate at Christ Church in the 1960s.[1] Years later, when doing some work myself at Edinburgh on the theologians of the Russian Diaspora, I got a first glimpse of the richness of his doctrinal thought.[2] He was surely the greatest of the Paris School that the exiles established in the years after the First World War. I was reminded of this when sent for review Archbishop Rowan Williams' splendid commentary on a number of excerpts from Bulgakov's corpus, published in 1999.[3]

The chance to turn that 'glimpse' into something more substantial came in 2003–4. When I was in Ethiopia, looking for suitable charitable works of the Catholic Church there for the congregation and associates of Blackfriars Cambridge to support, I was introduced to the Apostolic Nuncio who soon gave his opinion that aid by the English Dominicans in the teaching of theology would be just as useful – especially if it could emphasize *Eastern* Christian thought. This book began life, then, as lectures to the zealous and attentive students of the Capuchin Franciscan Institute of Philosophy and Theology outside Addis Ababa. From most regions of Ethiopia, both Ge'ez and Latin rite, diocesans and Religious, they were the most appreciative class I have ever taught. It is to them that this study is dedicated. I am most grateful to

---

[1] And see J. Pain and N. Zernov (eds), *A Bulgakov Anthology. Sergius Bulgakov,1871–1944* (London, 1976).

[2] A. Nichols, O. P., *Theology in the Russian Diaspora. Church, Fathers, Eucharist in Nikolai Afanas'ev,1893–1966* (Cambridge, 1989).

[3] *Sergii Bulgakov. Towards a Russian Political Theology*, edited with commentary by Rowan Williams (Edinburgh, 1999).

Elizabeth Roberts for making available the sketch of Bulgakov used on the cover of this book.[4]

A word of thanks, finally, to the Editor of *New Blackfriars*, Father Fergus Kerr, who kindly gave permission for the reprinting in the opening chapters of some material originally published in that journal.[5]

Blackfriars St Michael's
Cambridge
St Peter and St Paul, 2004

[4] For its provenance, see below, p. 303, note 31.
[5] A. Nichols, O.P., 'Widom from Above? The Sophiology of Father Sergius Bulgakov', *New Blackfriars* 85. 1000 (2004), pp 598–613.

1

Introducing Bulgakov: his life and work

The aim of this book is to present the dogmatic theology of one of the principal Eastern theologians of the twentieth century, the Russian Sergei Bulgakov.[1] But first we need to know who he was and, as the modern idiom has it, 'where he was coming from'.

His early life

Bulgakov was born in 1871 in a provincial town in central-southern Russia, the son of an Orthodox priest (married, of course: in fact, he came from a long line of priest-ancestors).[2] As a boy he was sent for his education to a kind of minor seminary – common in the Russia of the period – in the province's chief town.[3] These schools provided a good basic education but they were infamous for the strictness of their discipline. Bulgakov hated it, and it was in this context that he came as a young teenager to reject his family religion. In 1884, the precocious thirteen-year-old began to undergo a crisis of faith which endured till 1888 when he declared himself an unbeliever and was transferred to an ordinary civil school for

[1] Strictly speaking, his name should be spelled in its archaic form, 'Sergii', after his priestly ordination. But I have taken the view that, to Western readers, this slight modification of the more common spelling is more confusing than enlightening.

[2] For his life, his own posthumously published autobiographical notebook remains untranslated: *Avtobiograficheskie zametki* (Autobiographical Fragments, Paris, 1946, 1991). The fullest secondary account is also in Russian: L. A. Zander, *Bog i mir. Mirosozertsanie ottsa Sergiia Bulgakova* (God and the World. The World-View of Father S. Bulgakov, Paris, 1948), I., pp. 27–61.

[3] G. Freeze, *The Parish Clergy in Nineteenth-Century Russia: Crisis, Reform, Counter-Reform* (Princeton, NJ, 1983), pp. 102–139. For the wider context, *see* R. L. Nichols and T. G. Stavrou (eds), *Russian Orthodoxy under the Old Regime* (Minneapolis, 1978).

the completion of his secondary education, In 1890 he enrolled at
the University of Moscow. Almost at once he began to take an interest in Marxism.[4]

Philosophy, politics, economics

In the 1890s, Marxism did not imply membership of a particular
political party or even commitment to an actively revolutionary
programme. What it implied was, rather, belief that economics was
the single most important field of study if one wished to understand humanity – and also that man, the human being, was
essentially material, albeit an expression of the nobility and
complexity matter could attain. There certainly *were* revolutionar-
ies among the Russian intelligentsia. But when in 1897 Bulgakov
published his first work – on markets in the capitalist system of
production – it became evident that he was, rather, a 'legal
Marxist', one who looked to bringing about the goals Marxist
economic analysis might suggest within a framework of legality, of
the development of the *laws* of Russia, in a peaceful, orderly way.[5]

By this date, he had also registered the first of a trio of experiences which were to bring him back both to religion and indeed to
Christianity in its Orthodox form. This was in 1894 when holiday-
ing in the Caucasus mountains on the border between present day
Georgia and the Russian Federation. It was an experience of the
beauty of the mountains as somehow more than material – a
pointer to a beauty that transcends matter, *going beyond* it (which is
what the word 'transcendent' means). A few years later, in the
period 1898 to 1900 while he was studying abroad (by this point,
incidentally, he was married), he had the second experience which
led to his re-conversion to the faith. And this was by way of
response to the spiritual purity he glimpsed in a painting of the
Blessed Virgin Mary by the Italian Renaissance artist Raphael
(1483–1520). Known as the 'Sistine Madonna', he saw it displayed
in Saxony, in the city of Dresden's art gallery.

On his return from Germany to Russia, his Marxism was definitely shaken, and his master's thesis on capitalism and
agriculture, which he presented at this time, is generally regarded

---

[4] On the ideological background, see the essays in C. E. Timberlake (ed.),
*Religious and Secular Forces in Late Tsarist Russia. Essays in Honour of Donald W.
Treadgold* (Seattle and London, 1992).

[5] *O rynkakh pri kapitalisticheskom proizvodstve* (On Markets in the Capitalist System
of Production, Moscow, 1897).

as the work of someone already leaving behind a distinctively Marxian viewpoint.[6] The thesis enabled him to gain a teaching post at the University of Kiev and to become professor of political economy at the institute there at the early age of thirty.

So his career took off. He combined teaching economics and politics, writing and editing, especially on issues of philosophy and culture, and practical politics. In 1905, after defeat in the Russo-Japanese war, the tsar was forced by public opinion to allow the setting up of a parliament with limited powers, the *Duma*. The following year, Bulgakov founded a political newspaper and tried to start up a new political party on more or less Christian Socialist lines.[7] In 1907, he was elected a deputy to the Second *Duma*. But if by degrees he had become disillusioned with the Marxist view of man as 'economic man' – man for whom economic and social forms always come first, he was also losing confidence in the idea that constitutional reforms, such as Russia had just introduced, could of themselves change people's lives.

These shifts in his outlook coincided with a change of direction in the aspirations of the Russian intelligentsia generally. They became more interested in the creative powers of the human mind – an interest which, in philosophy, is often connected with the school of thought called 'Idealism'. And they also began to look more sympathetically at religion and especially at the Russian heritage of Orthodox Christianity. Such intellectuals looked for a reform and renewal of the Church. That was partly because they expected so deeply rooted an institution to have some effect in transforming the rest of society.

Bulgakov's own personal development mirrors these trends.[8] He moved from Marxism to Idealism, without, however, denying his earlier interest in the economy and the potential of matter. And then he moved from Idealism to a rediscovered Orthodoxy, without, however, denying his earlier conviction of the importance of human creativity, the uniqueness of the human subject, the person who says 'I'. This happened at an exciting time in Russian cultural and intellectual life, a time historians have dubbed Russia's 'Silver Age'. Of course, we know with hindsight it was not to last. It

---

[6] *Kapitalizm i zemledelie* (Capitalism and Agriculture, St Petersburg, 1900).

[7] For his later appreciation of Christian Socialism, see *Khristianstvo i sotsializm* (Christianity and Socialism, Moscow, 1917). As the title indicates, (Archbishop) Roman Williams' anthology *Sergii Bulgakov. Towards a Russian Political Theology* (Edinburgh, 1999) has much that is to the point.

[8] *Ot marksizma k idealismu* (From Marxism to Idealism, St Petersburg, 1903).

would be swept away by the Bolshevik revolution of October 1917.

Bulgakov made a contribution to the Silver Age while it lasted. He played a part in re-awakening interest in the most passionately religious of the nineteenth-century Russian novelists, Fyodor Dostoevsky (1821–1881), with a lecture on *The Brothers Karamazov*, Dostoevsky's novel on Orthodoxy and atheism.[9] As it happened, just at the time when Bulgakov was giving this lecture in Kiev, the influential literary critic Dmitri Merezhkovsky (1865–1941) was gaining new prominence for Dostoevsky in the literary salons of St Petersburg.[10] Dostoevsky formed the climax of Merezhkovsky's argument that Russian literature could show the world how the principle that ought to animate human culture universally is religious. It was what Merezhkovsky called, following Dostoevsky and the philosopher of religion Vladimir Soloviev (1853–1900), 'Godmanhood'. The West now stood for a false principle of culture, the self-glorification of man, man's erroneous belief in his own divinity, 'mangodhood', whereas Russian literature, culminating in Dostoevsky, pointed to a different principle, the principle of grace – God raising up humanity into union with himself, 'Godmanhood'. At the same time, Russians were also Europeans, heirs to European culture, and thus had a special vocation to show the West how Godmanhood could replace mangodhood as the principle of a new and better humanism, a humanism of grace.[11]

Reconversion to the Church

For his part, Bulgakov emphasized the mission to culture of a Christianity to which he was gradually returning. In his essay 'Tserkov i kul´tura', he wrote:

> There must be nothing that is in principle 'secular', there must be no neutral zone that would be religiously indifferent ... [12]

---

[9] *Ivan Karamazov kak filosofskii tip* (Ivan Karamazov as a Philosophical Type, Moscow, 1902).

[10] C. Evtuhov, *The Cross and the Sickle. Sergei Bulgakov and the Fate of Russian Religious Philosophy, 1890–1920* (Ithaca, NY, and London , 1997), p. 53. *See also* J. Scherrer, *Die Petersburger religiös-philosophischen Vereinigungen. Die Entwicklung des religiösen Selbstverständnisses ihrer Intelligencija-Mitglieder, 1901–1917* (Berlin, 1973).

[11] D. Merezhkovsii, *Tolstoi i Dostoevskii* (Tolstoy and Dostoevsky, St Petersburg, 1906); for this critic *see* J. Chèzeville, *Dmitri Merejkowsky* (Paris, 1922).

[12] Republished in S. Bulgakov, *Dva grada* (Two Cities, Moscow, 1911), p. 309.

To say as much was to challenge the Church quite as much as civil society, for the Church had in effect abandoned its task of being yeast to the leaven of the rest of culture and withdrawn into the ghetto of its own rituals.

> To create a truly Christian ecclesiastical culture and to stimulate life within the gates of the Church, to overcome from within the opposition of ecclesiastical and worldly – such is the historical task for the spiritual creativity of the contemporary Church and contemporary humanity.13

In March 1909, a number of Silver Age intellectuals produced a manifesto, the essay-collection *Vekhi* ('Landmarks'),[14] criticizing their predecessors for placing too much confidence in social and political changes *as such*. To give absolute primacy to social forms goes against the grain of the human spirit and does not lead to that authentic liberation of the people for which the anti-religious revolutionary element hitherto predominant in the Russian intelligentsia had hoped. It was right to look for a transformation of society, but this should be done by including religious conversion – the conversion of the soul – not by treating the latter as unimportant, much less by attacking religion and destroying religious values in people's lives.

In the summer of 1909 there took place the third of the experiences which brought Bulgakov back to the Church. This was the death of his younger son, Ivashechka, at the age of four. At the child's funeral, Bulgakov had an experience he interpreted as an awareness that his child still lived in the life of the Resurrection.[15] This sent him back to re-read Soloviev's writings and to pick out for the first time the importance for Soloviev's world-view of the theme of 'wisdom': the divine Wisdom that is the true soul of the world. Bulgakov would begin to make use of this idea of the Wisdom of God as the foundation and goal of all earthly reality in the writings on economics and philosophy he produced before the two Revolutions of the year 1917, and notably the 1912 work, *Filosofiya khozyaistva*, 'The Philosophy of Economic Activity'. In this book, Bulgakov argues that, despite the hardships of human labour, the economic process 'has meaning because it partakes of the divine Wisdom, *Sophia*, which was present with God at the

[13] Ibid.
[14] N. A. Berdiaev et al., *Vekhi: sbornik statei o russkoi intelligentsii* (Signposts. A Collection of Essays on the Russian Intelligentsia, Moscow, 1909).
[15] C. Evtuhov, *The Cross and the Sickle*, op. cit., pp. 133–137.

creation',[16] a reference to the eighth chapter of the Book of Proverbs:

> When he marked out the foundations
> > of the earth,
> then I was beside him, like a
> > master workman;
> and I was daily his delight,
> > rejoicing before him always,
> rejoicing in his inhabited world
> > and delighting in the sons of men. (vv. 30–31)

The struggle with nature will have joy and beauty as well as pain if we realize that as followers of Christ human beings have a

> hidden potential for perfection [and so must] work to resurrect nature, to endow it once again with the life and meaning it had in Eden.[17]

The most humdrum activities of daily life can be redeemed by the Christian message of the fall and resurrection of man and nature. We have a common task and it is universal resurrection, bringing the resurrection life and meaning into everything.

The coming of revolution

By the time of the two Revolutions of 1917, Bulgakov was one of the best known Orthodox intellectuals in Russia. Not surprisingly, then, he was elected a member of the Russian Church Council which met after the February Revolution in the aftermath of the overthrow of the monarchy and the introduction of a constitutional regime of a liberal kind.[18] This Council restored the office of patriarch, defunct since Peter I (1682–1725) introduced a form of State-directed synodalism on the model of the established Lutheran churches in Germany. It also prepared a number of measures designed to enhance the Church's life in its new-found freedom, measures rendered inoperative by the October Revolution which brought the Bolsheviks to power and within a

---

[16] Ibid., p. 147.
[17] Ibid.
[18] See J. S. Curtiss, *Church and State in Russia: The Last Years of the Empire, 1900–1917* (New York, 1940); A. A. Bogolepov, 'Church Reform in Russia, 1905–1918', *Saint Vladimir's Seminary Quarterly* 10 (1966), pp. 12–66.

short time unleashed a major persecution of Orthodoxy in the areas of Russia where the Red forces had effective control.[19] During the Church Council, Bulgakov was principally taken up with helping to formulate a response to the theological doctrine of certain Russian monks on Mount Athos who had been arguing – in a way vigorously rejected by others – that when the most holy Name of Jesus is venerated, the person of Christ is substantially present.[20] In the course of 1918 Bulgakov was ordained priest and fled Moscow in danger of imminent arrest.

At first he took refuge in the Crimea, a part of southern Russia which, jutting out into the Black Sea, is surrounded on three sides by water. Here the Red Army had not yet penetrated, and its monarchical opponent, the White Army, was in command. Faced with the collapse of a Christian Russia – 'holy Russia' – and the seeming disintegration of the Russian Church (the Bolsheviks were encouraging the schismatic movement called the 'Living Church'), Bulgakov was tempted to become a Catholic, and for some while secretly added the name of the Pope when he was celebrating the Liturgy.[21] At the end of 1922, the Communists arrived in the Crimea, and Bulgakov was expelled as an unreconstructedly anti-Bolshevik intellectual. He made his way through Constantinople to Prague and from there to Paris. This was the route followed by many emigrés escaping from Russia in the aftermath of the October Revolution and the Civil War.

Exile and death

Bulgakov lived in Paris for the rest of his life, from 1925 until his death in 1944. His life there was inextricably bound up with the Russian theological institute, Saint-Serge, of which he was a founder member and subsequently professor, rector and dean. It was in these years that he became – as many would say – the foremost Orthodox theologian of the twentieth century. Although he

---

[19] D. Pospielosky, *The Russian Church under the Soviet Regime, 1917–1982, I* (Crestwood, NY, 1984).

[20] His defence of these monks was published posthumously under the title *Filosofiya imenii* (The Philosophy of the Name, Paris, 1953).

[21] A lengthy manuscript from this period, setting out the reasons for becoming a Catholic in dialogue – actually, polylogue – form was included in the second volume of Bulgakov's collected writings on social and theological issues, *Trudy po sotsiologii i teologii* (Works on Sociology and Theology, Moscow, 1997), and separately published in French translation as *Sous les remparts de Chersonèse* (Geneva, 1999).

had rejected the temptation to become a Catholic and recovered his deep roots in Russian Orthodoxy, he remained very ecumenically minded. The Catholic Church was not yet involved in the twentieth-century ecumenical movement, so Bulgakov's participation in ecumenism was chiefly with Anglicans and (other) Protestants. He attended the Faith and Order conference in Lausanne in 1926. In 1927 he helped found – in England – the Anglican-Orthodox Fellowship of St Alban and St Sergius, and in the years 1933 to 1935 published some remarkable articles in English in the journal of that Fellowship, arguing that Orthodoxy remained in what he called an 'invisible, mysterious communion' with Catholicism. In words with which not all Orthodox would agree, he wrote:

> Canonical divisions ... only prevent the possibility of a direct and unmediated communion in the sacraments and do not destroy their efficacy. The invisible fellowship, therefore, of those who have been separated is not broken. We ought to consider that although we are canonically divided from the Roman Catholic Church, we never ceased to remain with it in an invisible, mysterious communion with one another through visible sacraments, although these are mutually inaccessible.[22]

Daringly, he went on to suggest not only a degree of common sharing in Eucharistic communion by Catholics and Orthodox as a way to supersede what he called the 'heresy of life' that is division, but also the possibility of an experimental Church union between them in a single diocese. He also wanted the Orthodox to consider in what way the 1870 definition of the role of the Pope in the Church might be applicable to the entire Church if not in the same way as in the Western Church. In the 1930s, however, the Catholic Church was quite as adamantly opposed to these suggestions as were most Orthodox.

By 1935 when the last of these ecumenical proposals was penned, Bulgakov was well known among his fellow Russian Orthodox as a dogmatic theologian. This was chiefly thanks to the publication in Paris of the 'Little Trilogy': *Drug zhenikha* ('The Friend of the Bridegroom') and *Kupina neopalimaya* ('The Burning

---

[22] S. Bulgakov, 'By Jacob's Well', *Journal of the Fellowship of St Alban and St Sergius* 22 (1933), reprinted in *Father Sergius Bulgakov, 1871–1944: A collection of articles by Fr. Bulgakov for the Fellowship of St Alban and St Sergius and now reproduced by the Fellowship to commemorate the 25ᵗʰ anniversary of the death of this great ecumenist* (London, 1969), pp. 1–11.

Bush') in 1927, and in 1929, *Lestnitsa Yakovla* ('Jacob's Ladder'). In these he used a theology of the divine Wisdom to throw light on the figures of, respectively, St John the Baptist, Our Lady and the Angels; with Christ the dominant personages in the *Deesis* or Great Intercession scene on the Russian Orthodox icon-screen. Of these books it was particularly the second, Marian study with its substantial appendices on the related themes wisdom and glory in Scripture and St Athanasius the Great (*c.* 296–373), that offered a foretaste of the wider dogmatics to come. An attractive coda was formed by a little book on the theology of the icon, issued in 1931.

Less influential – partly because a far more difficult read – was the philosophical treatise he published in German at Darmstadt in 1927 under the title 'The Tragedy of Philosophy'.[23] Here he aimed to show how all language, thought, being, must be construed in terms of the functions of basic grammar: the subject, the predicate, and the copula: 'is'. These three functions, argued Bulgakov, reflect the three foundational kinds of determination of all thought. And these are: personality or, in the Greek patristic term, hypostasis; its idea or ideal image or meaning, referred to by another highly charged theological term, *logos*; and lastly, substantial being or the unity of being in all its different 'moments'. In this work, Bulgakov's philosophy of language and his metaphysics are shaped by his understanding of the Holy Trinity, though it is also the best place to look for the influence on him of the classical German philosopher Friedrich Wilhelm Schelling (1775–1854).

The combination of the two – the Trinity and Schelling – goes some way to explaining why there was also controversy. Using German nineteenth-century philosophy as an aid to expounding in more contemporary terms the doctrine of the Greek Fathers was increasingly unacceptable to some notable Russian theologians working in the West, especially Vladimir Lossky (1903–1958) and Georges Florovsky (1893–1979). In 1935 two of the Russian jurisdictions, the Church in Exile based in Yugoslavia and the Moscow Patriarchate, charged Bulgakov with heresy. This was for teaching something he strenuously denied, namely that *Sophia*, the Wisdom of God, is in effect a fourth person of the Holy Trinity (which thereby becomes a Holy Quadernity). Bulgakov remained a theologian in good standing with the third of the Russian jurisdictions, his own, the Exarchate of the Ecumenical Patriarchate for Western Europe. This was just as well.

In the years before and during the Second World War, Bulgakov

---

[23] *Die Tragödie der Philosophie* (Darmstadt, 1927).

went on to write his 'Great Trilogy': *Agnets Bozhii*, ('The Lamb of God') in 1933, *Uteshitel'* ('The Paraclete') in 1936, and *Nevesta agntsa* ('The Bride of the Lamb') in 1945. All were published in Paris under the general title of 'On Godmanhood', *O bogoche-lovechestve* – a term we have already come across in the context of Merezhkovsky's literary criticism and shall meet again. He also produced, at the urgent request of admirers and inquirers daunted by the quantity of this original output, a summary of his dogmatics, published in English translation as *The Wisdom of God. A Brief Summary of Sophiology* in New York and London in 1937.

In 1939 he fell ill with cancer of the throat, and struggled with this disease during the War and the German occupation of Paris. In 1944 he managed to complete a final work, *Apokalipsis Joanna*, 'The Apocalypse of John'.[24] Bulgakov died on 12 July 1944 and is buried in the Russian cemetery of Sainte-Geneviève-des-Bois, where his tomb was surmounted by a wonderful sculpted Russian crucifix, a work of the noted iconographer Leonid Ouspensky (1902–1987), in the course of 1945–6.[25]

Bulgakov's project

Bulgakov is a theologian of *Wisdom*. As we shall see, the idea of the Wisdom of God, *Premudrost' Bozhii*, crops up almost everywhere in Bulgakov's thought. So much so that his theology has been called, from the Greek word for wisdom, *sophia*, a 'sophiological theology', a theology of the wisdom of God.

The Old Testament has a number of 'Wisdom texts' which speak of wisdom as a divine power that is active in the world. (It also has many texts which speak of wisdom as a human virtue, whether acquired by effort or infused by God, but these are not immediately at issue here.) The most important ones are to be found in the Book of Proverbs (1: 1–9: 18), the Book of Wisdom (6: 22–11: 1), the Book of Ecclesiasticus (or Sirach, 24: 1–34), the Book of Baruch (3: 9–4:4) and the Book of Job (28: 1–28). Sometimes these texts give the impression that wisdom is essentially divine, that it is

---

[24] *Apokalipsis Joanna* (Paris, 1947). There is a useful overview of Bulgakov's writings in L. A. Zander, *Bog i mir*, op. cit, I, pp. 62–77. For a full list of his writings, *see* K. Naumov, *Bibliographie des oeuvres de S. Boulgakov* (Paris, 1984).

[25] Reproduced in S. Doolan, *La redécouverte de l'Icône. La vie et l'oeuvre de Léonide Ouspensky* (Paris, 2001), p. 66. For the artist, *see* A. Nichols, O. P., 'Leonid Ouspensky and the Love of Sacred Beauty', in idem., *A Spirituality for the Twenty-first Century* (Huntington, IN, 2003), pp. 113–130.

on God's side of the distinction between God and the world, the Uncreated and the created. On other occasions, however, these texts give the contrary impression: that wisdom is a created reality, on the world's side of the distinction between finite reality and God, very much an aspect of the creation rather than the Creator. Because it is not entirely clear from Scripture what these texts are speaking about, biblical scholars find it hard to give a theological account of them.[26] Bulgakov believed he had come up with a solution, and one that could be usefully included within a vision of Christian dogmatics as a whole. So in what follows, I shall describe his sophiology where it relevant to an account of his dogmatics, but not single it out for special attention. However, as we shall see, there are very few areas of dogmatics where it does not enter. And in particular, it is vital to how this Eastern theologian sees the relation between God and the world, the Creator and the creation: the topic which will occupy as at some length in the following two chapters.

---

[26] D. Bergant, C. S. A., *What are they saying about Wisdom Literature?* (New York and Ramsey, NJ, 1984).

2

The Triune Lord and his Nature as Wisdom

Who and what?

The greatest of the names for God in the Old Testament is surely that found in the Book of Exodus, 3: 14. The Lord reveals his name to Moses as 'I am He who is'. Bulgakov begins his theology of the triune God from there. As he points out, this divine name already implies that God is both a personal subject – 'I am He' – and has an objective nature – 'who is'. The distinction between being a subject, a 'who', and having a nature, a 'what', is of course something we are highly familiar with from our own everyday life. You can ask me *what* I am, and I can truthfully reply: a human being, which means someone who has a human nature. But I have not yet told you *who* I am, a quite individual personal subject of that nature called *me*. In the Church's tradition, the Tradition of the Fathers and the early Councils, we are told that the divine personality is three 'hypostases', Father, Son and Holy Spirit. But we are also told that the divine personality has a single, unique nature, shared by no one else. In God there is one being or nature – in Greek, the main language of the Fathers, one *ousia*. In his single unique nature, God is the personal subject of a tri-hypostatic life.

In speaking of God in this way we are using philosophical language to throw light on the revelation given us in Holy Scripture. So Bulgakov regards it as legitimate to offer us some philosophical reflections which will help with this – will help, that is to say, with the way we may need to think about God our Creator and indeed about the human being he has created. After all, I too, on my infinitely smaller scale, am a 'who' existing as a 'what', the personal subject of an objective nature. Bulgakov will, then, be for a moment speaking purely philosophically – which means, in a fashion that may well not be fully suited to talking about God, who after all exceeds all human categories, however open to the infinite we try to make them. With this caveat entered, therefore, what can we say philosophically speaking of the relation of a subject – a 'who', a carrier of personal awareness, a spiritual being – to its 'what', its nature, its objective reality as the kind of reality it is?[1]

There is, says Bulgakov, an unbreakable unity between a spiritual subject, an 'I', and its nature. My nature gives my life as a spiritual consciousness its content, and without it my 'I' would be more or less empty, virtually a vaccuum with almost nothing in it. Without my human nature, for example, my consciousness of my own 'I' would be (as he writes) but a pale candle, a thin and feeble flame. This for Bulgakov is the starting point of all theologically helpful speculation about the relation of nature and person, as much in God as in myself. He calls it 'the initial ontological axiom'[2]: in other words, the very first principle we must get hold of if we are to make any progress in understanding how either God or ourselves actually are. Without nature, person has no real content.

And Bulgakov goes on to say that we can think of how nature supplies the vital content for the life of the personal subject in two senses or ways. In one sense or way, a distinctive nature – whether we are thinking of the divine nature in the Holy Trinity or human nature in me or you – is taken up by the subject in its action. In other words, the resources of that nature are called upon, brought into play, whenever the subject creatively reveals itself. In revealing itself, the subject inevitably shows us its nature, whether what we are thinking of there is God or man. When the Father acts, or the Son acts, or the Holy Spirit acts we discover what the divine nature is like, what it is and what it does. When you or I act, other people discover what human nature is like, what it is and what it can do, for good or evil. That is one way, then, in which the divine nature or our own human nature supplies content, material, for the life of the subject, whether the divine subject, God, or the human subject, myself. But there is a second way in which this happens as well. Nature does not need to be taken up actively by the subject. It may simply be there as a fact, lying immanent within that subject, making the unique 'who' the distinctive 'what' that it is. Even when I am not think-ing of the Father, the Son or the Holy Spirit acting to express the divine nature, that divine nature is of course always present within

---

[1] For a thematic overview of the philosophical side of Bulgakov's work, *see* L. A. Zander, *Bog i mir,* op. cit., I, pp. 181–475, which deals in turn with the key idea of wisdom; then ontology, cosmology, anthropology, ideas of culture and history and epistemology.

[2] AB, p. 112: *iskhodna ontologicheska aksioma.*

them just as a plain matter of fact. And when I am not seeking to
express my own nature, as for example when I am asleep, I do
not cease existing as a distinctively human being. My human
nature still forms me from within even when I am unconcious. So
nature gives the person – the spiritual subject – materials for their
action – or at the very least it lies continuously within the person,
helping to make them what they are.

A nature as a 'world'

Bulgakov now goes on to take a further step. Speaking very generally, that is, without specific reference as yet to the Holy Trinity, to
God, he suggests that in the case of a spiritual subject its nature
exists for it as what we can call its 'world', *mir*. As a consequence of
our nature, the world is for us a certain kind of world. We inhabit
reality in the way our nature indicates. So it is not *that* strange to
say that personality lives in the world *as in its own nature.*[3] The
objective reality to which our nature affords us access is given us *as
shaped by our nature*. A road, say, is something very different for us
from what it is for a goat or a chicken that may happen to come
across it, or for a insect living in a hole in its surface or a weed
pushing it up from below. And the reason for this is that a road
plays a very different role in the life-world of each of these creatures, thanks to the difference of their natures. Human beings, to
take that example again, have access to the world in accordance
with their human nature, which makes possible their distinctive
approach to the reality of things. And by the same token, it is by
means of our nature that the world around us – and that includes
other human beings, other spiritual subjects – comes to share in
my being as the unique spiritual subject I am. So, on the one hand,
'the life of spirit is an active penetration into the world as into its
own nature'. But on the other hand,

> personal spirit ... appears *conditioned,* in its life, by the 'world' or that
> which is not spirit – although when the latter enters the life of spirit
> it can in fact become [part and parcel of] its nature.[4]

In the course of our life, we explore the world but the world also
enters us. And here the sky is the limit. Our human nature is not

[3] Ibid., p. 113.
[4] Ibid., p. 114.

just our own interior spiritual world but, at any rate, potentially, the whole world whose doors and windows lie ever open.

Looking to the image: the human hypostasis as the image of God

Evidently, such personal spirit – my spirit, your spirit – is not the absolute, the Unconditioned, that which exists only in and through itself. It is only the relative, the conditioned, that which exists by way of another. In saying as much, Bulgakov makes it clear that for the moment he is concentrating on the finite, human example of a personal subject existing in an objective nature, not the infinite, divine example – God – which is where his interest is really focused. As he comments, to be so conditioned – to depend on others – is the mark of a creature, whether human or angelic. Human beings, at any rate, never realize their fullness in this life. They exist through a process; they *are* by way of *becoming*. It is not enough just to say they are limited (that would be true of any creature). As we know from the human life around us, things can be more negative than that. Very often, human beings can be paralysed by their limitations. And yet, to look on the positive side, they never lose their selfhood (Bulgakov calls it by a Latin term, their 'seitas') for this is indestructible. Thus they are living images of their divine Archetype – really reflecting him in that positive fashion, yet only being reflections, as the negative aspects make clear. And the biblical revelation confirms this. Scripture says of human beings that we are made in God's image, after his likeness (Genesis 1: 26), a text which is, really, the foundation of all Christian anthropology.

Bulgakov links our being in the image of God not in the first place to the powers or capacities of human nature but to our awareness of being personal hypostases, unique selves. When God breathed the breath of life into the first man, as set forth in Genesis 2, he made him a hypostasis, a personal subject. In so doing he gave him a share in his own eternal, uncreated life. Actually, Bulgakov says rather more than this. He says that the God of Genesis made the created spirit eternal and gave it a consciousness of its own eternity. In some sense, he goes on to add, God rendered the human spirit uncreated like himself, and gave it awareness of its own uncreated being. This is a strange-sounding addition. Indeed, if these words were taken literally, they would be hugely unorthodox. But compare the way that, in the Greek patristic

tradition, the human spirit is often treated as a created participation of the Holy Spirit and the 'place' where the divine Spirit finds
a home in man. It may even be said that man only truly exists to the
degree that he welcomes such participation. In the *Adversus haereses*, St Irenaeus (*c.* 130–*c.* 200) can write:

> The complete man is a mixture and union, consisting of the soul
> which takes to itself the Spirit of the Father, to which is united the
> flesh which was fashioned in the image of God ... When this Spirit is
> mingled with soul and united with created matter, then through the
> outpouring of the Spirit the complete man is produced: this is man
> made in the image and likeness of God.[5]

Bulgakov's words, however, *have* been taken literally by some
readers who concluded thereby that he was a pantheist, denying
the distinction between the Creator and the creature. But when we
realize how Bulgakov says God made the 'created' spirit uncreated
we see, or should see, that this interpretation cannot be correct.
Rather, like a number of the mediaeval mystics, Bulgakov is
seeking a rhetorically powerful way of expressing something he
thinks he finds in Scripture read in the Church's Tradition. The
privilege of hypostatic existence – existence as a personal subject –
confers on human creatures the possibility of sharing the uncreated life of the Trinity.

He goes on to give the other side of the matter, the way in
which we are unlike God. Quite unlike God we humans are flesh
and psyche, as well as spiritual subjecthood. Our nature is carnal
and psychic. We are animals, if not only animals. We are capable
of so immersing ourselves in our animality that people are aston-
ished when someone chooses to address them on their spirituality
and claim not to know what the speaker is talking about. And the
reason we are so capable is that the world of animality, like other
worlds, can enter through our nature into our spirit, via those
open 'windows and doors'. But Bulgakov does not hesitate to add
that we are just as capable of becoming conscious of our essential spirituality as of our essential animality – and that when we
do so we shall find our bond with the natural world strengthened,
not weakened. The more spiritually aware I am, the fuller my
bond not just with the spiritual world of shared human nature but
with the whole of that wider world to which, in its own way, our
human nature gives us access. In other words, the cosmos, the
universe. But this entire discussion of man as image of God has

[5] Irenaeus, *Adversus haereses*, V. 6. 1.

ben intended to give us a 'handle' on the One we fitfully image, the divine Trinity.

The trihypostatic divine life

As has already been said, God is the tri-hypostatic personality who, by an unbreakable bond of his 'who' with his 'what', possesses the divine nature. Before speaking about the relation of the divine personality to the divine nature, Bulgakov wants to say something more about the three persons in God. When he gets into the body of his Christology, he will of course refer to this again, as he will in his book on the Holy Spirit, the second part of the Great Trilogy. But here he wants to introduce his theology of the three persons who are nonetheless one single personal being, our divine Creator.[6] The Lord God is supremely personal because he unites in himself all the modes in which the personal principle can find expression. Not only 'I', but 'thou' or 'you' in the singular, and 'he', 'we' and 'you' in the plural. The Father, for example, can say 'I' about himself, and 'thou' to, for instance, the Son. And he can say 'he' of, for example, the Holy Spirit. Then again, the Father and the Son can say 'we' together or the Father can say 'you' to the Son and the Spirit. And this would work as well for any of the divine Three. God is thus the fullness of personal awareness, a single personality in three mutually related centres. From all eternity he affirms himself in a Trinitarian fashion, which is to say not as a 'unipersonal "I"' but by the affirmation of each hypostasis in the others. The divine personality realizes itself as the 'source of self-renouncing love, entering into ecstasy [goes out of itself to find itself again] in another "I"'. Or again, in another formulation, the triune God is

> the reciprocity of eternally realised love, which decisively overcomes personal individualisation, identifying three with one and yet itself existing from the real existence of these [three] personal centres.[7]

It is as this personal tri-unity, then, that the Lord enjoys his divine nature.

---

[6] For Bulgakov's Triadology, *see* L. A. Zander, *Bog i mir*, op. cit., pp. 24–71.
[7] AB, p. 118.

The relation of God's trinitarian personality to his nature

How does God's trinitarian personality relate to that nature? Bulgakov tries to explain by contrasting God's case with our own. For us, for our personal spirit, our human nature is a 'given', something we find ourselves born with, something we wake up to, something we find confronting us, standing over against us, whether we like it or not. It is also – and this is a complementary truth, the other side of the coin – an 'agenda' set before us, because over time we have the task of making our human nature more and more our own. This we do as through our experience the world enters into that nature – through the 'doors and windows' spoken of above, and changes it as we grow, develop and (hopefully) mature. So for each of us, our nature is both a given, something we are 'landed with', and an agenda, a task or project to be fulfilled. And the upshot of that? The upshot is that the relation between our personal subjecthood and our human nature, however fascinating it may be, is never fully clear to us. As Bulgakov puts it, our 'I' is 'not transparent to itself and remains till the end unsoundable'[8] – like diving down to a depth of water where you never reach the bottom.

With God, however, things are utterly different. With God there can be no question of any prior 'given' which God wakes up to and has to come to terms with. Nor can there be any question of something as yet unrealized about his being, requiring from him an effort of appropriation, an effort to make his nature his own. Everything – but simply everything – in God's nature is utterly clear to him in his personal awareness: utterly clear and utterly realized. This is how Bulgakov understands the words of St John in his first Letter 'God is Light and in him there is no darkness at all' (1 John 1: 5). In God, everything natural is 'hypostatised'. *What* God is is all in the lucid possession of the Father, the Son and the Holy Spirit. Certainly, we must not allow that the Trinity has a nature that includes with it the potential for God to become something more, or something different from what he is now.[9] Certainly, too, we

---

[8] Ibid., p. 119.

[9] Here Bulgakov is demonstrating how removed his theology is from such German Lutheran philosophers of the nineteenth century as Schelling – with whom he shares, however, some general approaches and themes – and Hegel (1770–1831). He rejects Schelling's notion that the world arises from its divine ground in a process of inner (divine) self-revelation; and Hegel's proposal that thinking (the hallmark of divine Spirit) comes dialectically to the discovery of itself. Behind these two there lies for Bulgakov the esoteric figure of Jakob Boehme (1575–1624).

must not think of the divine nature as a fourth principle in God, in addition to the triad of Father, Son and Holy Spirit.[10] We cannot add the divine nature – as, so to speak, the number 1 – to the persons – to the number of 3 – and get the answer '4', for the simple reason that we are not dealing here with comparable categories. Rather we should say that the nature of God is

> perfectly transparent to the divine hypostases and in this measure is identified with them, while however conserving its own existence. The nature is eternally hypostatised in God, as the sufficient life of the hypostases, while the life of the hypostases is eternally bound up with the nature even though they remain distinct from it.[11]

In his single act of self-affirmation God perfectly possesses his nature, each hypostasis enjoying it both for himself and for the others in his own distinctive fashion, whether as Father, Son or Spirit.

How the Father possesses his nature

Now the principle or fount or source of the divine nature as indeed of the whole Trinitarian being, is God the Father. How, then, does God the Father possess the divine nature? For Bulgakov, from all eternity the Father possesses his divine nature only as giving it to the Son. Such Fatherhood, writes Bulgakov, is the very image of love, since

> he who loves wants to possess himself not in himself but outside himself, so as to give his 'I' to this other 'I' in such a way that he is identified with him; [he wants] to manifest his 'I' by a spiritual birth, in the Son who is the living image of the Father.[12]

So the Father's begetting of the Son is the primal act of possessing the divine nature where the Father has his nature by passing it on, giving it away. Bulgakov speaks of this timeless event in extravagant language. He calls it the Father's 'self-devastation', his emptying out of his fatherly being, and an 'ecstasy of all-consuming sacri-

---

[10] Bulgakov commends – for once! – a Latin synod, the Council of Rheims for condemning this way of treating the divine nature, *divinitas*, by Gilbert de la Porrée (*c.* 1080–1154).

[11] AB, p. 120.

[12] Ibid., p. 121.

fice', language which will later be taken up by a Catholic theologian with whom Bulgakov has many similarities, Hans Urs von Balthasar (1905–1988).[13]

How the Son possesses his nature

The divine nature is manifested, however, not just in the Father's begetting of the Son but in the entire tri-hypostatic life, everything that concerns the Father, the Son and the Holy Spirit in God. Bulgakov emphazises the self-emptying character of all the Trinitarian processions. Each involves a sacrifice, or in the words of St Paul in the Letter to the Philippians (2: 7), a 'kenosis', an act of self-humiliation. Just as the Father wants to possess himself only in the Son, so the Son does not want to possess the divine nature for himself. He wants rather to offer his personal selfhood, his 'seitas', in sacrifice to the Father. He is the Word, yes. But that means he is the *Father*'s Word, not his own. Bulgakov does not hesitate to speak of the 'pain' or 'suffering', *stradanie*, of sacrifice in God. How then can he also maintain – with the entire theological tradition – that God is the ever-blessed One, always enjoying perfect beatitude, perfect happiness? He writes:

> This pain of sacrifice not only does not contradict the all-beatitude, *vseblazhenstvo*, of God, but on the contrary is the foundation of this beatitude which would have been empty and unreal had it not been founded on authentic sacrifice, on the reality of suffering. If God is love he is also sacrifice, which makes manifest, exclusively by suffering, the victorious power of love and its joy.[14]

How the Holy Spirit possesses his nature

So far we have heard nothing much about the Holy Spirit but this is where Bulgakov begins to speak of him. The Holy Spirit, he says, possesses the divine nature as the joy of sacrificial love. He is God as the beatitude of the love of Father and Son, its perfect fruit. The 'self-identification' of the Father and the Son is only, writes Bulgakov, 'ideal', only a determination of the divine mind, until it is 'accomplished' in all reality by the Holy Spirit. 'In God there is

---

[13] In the Conclusion to the present study an attempt is made to list some of these similarities.

[14] Ibid., p. 122.

no determination of himself that is not hypostatic.'[15] What he means is: when the Father understands the relation with the Son as a relation of total communion between Son and Father, then at once that understanding becomes real as the person of the Holy Spirit. When the Holy Spirit proceeds from the Father and rests on the Son, or when he proceeds from the Father through the Son, a triumphant testimony is given to the sacrificial exchange which joins Father and Son for evermore. For this sacrificial exchange is what produces the Holy Spirit.

Bulgakov associates the Holy Spirit with truth and beauty. With truth because he is the Spirit of truth (a name given him by Jesus himself in St John's Gospel, John 16: 13), who announces not himself but what the Son says in the Father's name. He is the Spirit of the truth of the Father and the Son, bearing witness not to himself but to their love. What about beauty? In some of the Fathers – for instance, in St Irenaeus – we get the idea that the Father makes beautiful by means of the Spirit what he creates by means of the Son.[16] Bulgakov wants to take this back beyond creation into the eternal Trinity. The Holy Spirit is beautiful because in him and by him the depths of God become wonderfully clear. I take this to mean that the love of Father and Son, the supreme act welling up from those depths, appears in all its glory in the Holy Spirit.[17]

The sophiological perspective

So far we have heard nothing really to speak of about the divine wisdom. Now Bulgakov wants to put all this in sophiological perspective. When he was talking about the relation of being a subject and having a nature, Bulgakov said that for a spiritual subject its nature is a world. The nature enjoyed by a spiritual subject is an entire world, not least because it gives access to whatever other realities there may be for this subject to know. So it will not surprise us to find Bulgakov describing the divine nature as the divine world, the world of God. Sometimes, he says, people who want to be as Trinitarian as they

[15] Ibid., p. 123.

[16] St Irenaeus, *Adversus haereses*: I. 22. 1; II. 30, 9; III. 8, 3; 24, 2; IV. 20, 1–4; IV. 38, 3; IV. 39, 2; V. 1, 3; V. 9, 4.

[17] The 'appropriation' of beauty to the Spirit – as truth to the Son and goodness to the Father – may have been taken by Bulgakov from Soloviev either directly or through Pavel Florensky. If so, Bulgakov's failure to cite these authors probably derives from anxiety lest their much less theologically controlled version of sophiology should tar his with their brush.

possibly can be, who want to say that God is Father, Son and Holy
Spirit and nothing but that, think they are doing the Holy Trinity a
good turn by denying that there is such a thing as the divine nature in
itself. Bulgakov has already agreed that the divine nature is thor-
oughly hypostatized, taken up into the personal life of Father, Son
and Holy Spirit. But to deny there is a divine nature, and restrict God
to the interplay of the hypostases, is not to do the Trinity a favour at
all. On the contrary, it is to minimize the divine being, and reduce
the being of God to what he calls 'an *abstract* [Bulgakov's emphasis]
consciousness of self'.[18] But the Holy Trinity does not only exist 'for
itself', in the wondrous awareness that is the relations of communion
of the three divine persons. It also exists 'by [or through] itself', that
is to say, by reference to the divine nature, the divine *ousia*. Nor is the
divine nature just the power of the divine life of Father, Son and
Spirit. More than this, it is its content – or, as Bulgakov puts it, the
divine nature is the 'absolute content of the absolute [divine] life,
with all its properties'.[19]

   But Bulgakov has an objection to how all this has usually been
discussed. As he says, in the Church's tradition, discussion of the
divine nature – as distinct from the divine persons, Father, Son and
Holy Spirit – has largely been conducted in philosophical terms
which perhaps *become* theological in the contexts where they are
used but are innocent of much in the way of biblical input. He
writes:

> Substance both in the East and in the West is interpreted purely as
> a philosophical abstraction, and utilized to achieve a logical solution
> of the trinitarian dogma ... Such a conception cannot embrace the
> divine revelation in regard to the one common life of the Holy
> Trinity, of God in three persons. The dogma of consubstantiality
> which safeguards the unity of the Holy Trinity, thus remains a sealed
> book so far as we are concerned – for in a religious sense it has been
> neither properly adopted nor developed. The Bible, however,
> though it never alludes to the abstract concept of substance, does
> give us revealed teaching on the life of the triune God.[20]

Now at one level, Bulgakov himself continues the practice of speaking philosophically about the nature of God. We have seen as
much in the foregoing. He never abandons exposition of the 'God

---

[18] AB, p. 124: *abstraktnomo lichnomo samsoznanie.*
[19] Ibid., pp. 124–125.
[20] *The Wisdom of God. A Brief Summary of Sophiology* (New York and London, 1937),
    p. 46.

of the philosophers', using philosophical concepts he finds helpful tools in talking about the nature of God the Holy Trinity. It is just that these tools sometimes come not from the ancient Greek philosophical tradition on which Christian Scholasticism drew from its origins in the later patristic period onwards. Rather, they come from the classical German philosophers of the nineteenth century. Thus we can see their influence when Bulgakov tells us that it is proper to the content of the divine life that in God *everything is understood*, understood not just as an infinite number of different aspects of the divine mind but precisely as the 'interior organic integrity' of all those aspects.[21] In the world of God – in the divine nature – there is, he says, an 'all-unity', a unity of everything as the divine mind knows it. These remarks reflect the concerns of the German philosophers of the late eighteenth and early nineteenth centuries. It should be noted, though, that those philosophers were themselves indebted to the Platonist tradition. For a Christian Platonist like Origen (*c.* 185–*c.* 254), the intelligible realities, *logoi,* which are the models of beings, constitute an intelligible world, a spiritual cosmos that is coherent, unified, in the Word – and for Origen that is, as for Bulgakov, though in significantly different fashion, an eternal creation taking place when the Son is begotten by the Father

But philosophy is not Bulgakov's main emphasis, which is to unite with these reflections what the Bible has to say about the nature and life of the triune God, and indeed, to give the biblical data priority over the philosophical. The biblical texts on these matters have not, he remarks:

> been utilized in trinitarian theology, in particular as regards the application to the doctrine of the substance of God of the biblical revelation of Wisdom or Sophia, and of the Glory of God.[22]

And he goes on to say that

> In this particular respect the liturgical consciousness of the Church is superior to the dogmatic, for the earliest liturgical texts have included such revelation in the text of hymns, lessons, and doxologies. The *lex orandi* bore witness in itself to the *lex credendi.* This witness, however, was disregarded by theology until the middle of

[21] Ibid.
[22] Ibid.

the nineteenth century in Russia, when there were fresh stirrings of
sophiological thought.[23]

This is of course a covert reference to Soloviev.[24]

And this provides him with the transition he needs to the theme
of divine wisdom. When Scripture speaks of the Wisdom of God, it
means not just one divine property among many, as for example
the justice of God or the mercy of God. The Wisdom of God is the
foundation of all the divine properties. It is the divine nature as
containing that all-unity which is the content of the life of God.
And this means not just all the properties of the divine nature but
the archetypes of all created things as well. It means not just the
divine attributes but what many of the Fathers and later St Thomas
Aquinas (c. 1225–1274) called the 'divine ideas', God's creative
idea of everything that exists from plants and animals to human
beings to stars and planets. All this is contained in the 'all-unity' of
divine Wisdom. There is an 'interior organic unity' to all the divine
properties and ideas.

The divine Wisdom is God's own nature, as known first of all to
himself, to Father, Son and Spirit. It is the divine 'world' where
God lives as the Holy Trinity. It is at once the divine life and the
first principle of all created life before it has yet come forth from
God as the cosmos, the created order.

Bulgakov has already described the Wisdom of God as the 'interior organic unity' of the divine ideas. Now he adds that this
'universal and cosmic assembly' of the divine world is best
explained by the *love* of God. It is God's love that assures the coherence of the world of the divine ideas; and it is God's love that binds
this 'world' of divine Wisdom to the hypostases of Father, Son and
Spirit. The persons of the Trinity love the divine Wisdom with the
personal love that is appropriate to them. But there is also a sense,
Bulgakov thinks, in which the divine Wisdom can itself be said to
'love' the tri-hypostatic God.

This needs a bit of explaining. When something impersonal,
such as the divine nature, is the subject of the verb '[to] 'love'', that
verb – plainly – is not being used in the same sense as when its

---

[23] Ibid., pp. 46–47.

[24] S. D. Cioran, *Vladimir Solov'ev and the Knighthood of the Divine Sophia* (Waterloo,
Ont., 1977), and, less dramatically entitled, R. Slesinski, 'Sophiology as a
Metaphysics of Creation according to Solov'ëv', in W. van den Bercken et al.
(ed.), *Vladimir Solov'ëv, Reconciler and Polemicist. Selected papers of the International
Solov'ëv Conference held at Nijmegen, September 1998* (Leuven, 2000), pp. 131–146.

subject is a someone, someone personal, as, for example Father, Son or Holy Spirit. Bulgakov quite agrees. Love in the strict sense is always between persons and thus, in the Holy Trinity, between the hypostases. However, there may also be love in a non-strict sense, what Christian Latinity calls *sensu lato*. We speak, for instance, of self-love, which is only love in an analogous sense. Self-love is not, obviously, love between persons, because only one person is involved. Such natural love of self, precisely because it is not interpersonal, Bulgakov deems an analogy for the impersonal love which characterizes the Wisdom of God. He speaks of divine Wisdom as typified by love in two ways. Not only is the internal order of God's Wisdom marked by love, because the divine ideas fit harmoniously with each other in perfect unity. (Harmony is a sign of love.) More than this, the divine Wisdom exists through *belonging* to the hypostatic Trinity – through *giving* itself to the divine persons, *yielding* itself up to be drawn into their personal life.[25] Belonging, giving, yielding: these are terms of love. And more especially, these words suggest that the Wisdom of God may be best spoken of by feminine metaphors, since in the deepest and most abiding love we know, the married love of human beings, they are words that suggest the attitude of the bride more than the bridegroom. This is the love that is 'in' the divine nature, what Thomas would call *amor naturalis Dei*. And this is what we find in Scripture which personifies the Wisdom of God as *Lady* Wisdom. When the Old Testament thinks of Wisdom as an aspect of the divine, those writers speak of Wisdom very much as 'she'.

So can we sum up so far? The Wisdom of God is the divinity of God – not the personal existence of Father, Son and Spirit, but the living reality of the divine nature they share – the divine nature as a 'world' that is wonderfully coherent in itself (all the divine attributes and divine ideas fitting perfectly with each other), a world that is at the loving disposal of the divine hypostases, on which they can draw, with which, in which and from which they can act. This is the 'something real about God' that corresponds to the 'Lady Wisdom' of the Old Testament.

---

[25] The Wisdom of God is not itself hypostatic. But it is, if the neologism be allowed, 'hypostatisable'. This is the burden of Bulgakov's essay 'Ipostas i ipostasnost'' which, though contrbuted to an academic *Festschrift* long before the storm broke over his doctrinal orthodoxy on the topic of God, constitutes as it were an apologia in advance. Published in *Sbornik statei posvyashchennykh Petru Berngardovichu Struve* (A Collection of Essays dedicated to Peter Bernhardovich Struve, Prague, 1925), pp. 353–371, its contents are summarized and discussed in R. Williams, *Sergii Bulgakov*, op. cit., pp. 165–167.

Wisdom and glory

How does Bulgakov bring in the second biblical theme for the divine nature – the theme of glory? He does so by considering how the Wisdom of God is revealed not only in the Old Testament accounts of creation and inspiration but above all in the Word incarnate, Jesus Christ.

The Wisdom of God belongs to the entire Holy Trinity, and to each one of its hypostases. But we can see, thinks Bulgakov, why St Paul, writing to the Church in Corinth, found a special connexion between the Wisdom of God and the second person, the divine Son. As the apostle says in his First Letter to the Corinthians, Christ is not only the power of God. He is also 'the wisdom of God' (1 Corinthians 1: 24). In the Son there is present not only the whole content of the divine nature which the Father gives him in generating him. In him is present the ideas of all created things, because by him, the Word, 'all things were made', as St John tells us in his Gospel (1: 3). In the New Testament, as in creation, the Father reveals his Wisdom in his Word. Now Bulgakov goes on to stress that 'what is disclosed in the Word, as Wisdom, is *glorious* [his emphasis]'.[26] This is what the Old Testament writers are saying about Wisdom in creation and revelation when they compare it to beautiful trees and plants. And in what concerns the Wisdom of God as Jesus Christ we know how his Transfiguration in glory, reported as a 'one-off' event in the Gospels of Matthew, Mark and Luke, affects his whole existence, his entire story, for the last Gospel writer, St John. 'The Word became flesh, and we beheld his glory, the glory of the only begotten of the Father, full of grace and truth' (John 1: 16). Thus Bulgakov comes to the second source of biblical enlightenment about the life of the divine nature, the theme of the *glory* of God.

When the Wisdom of God is made known it is always accompanied by the glory of God. How does Bulgakov understand God's glory? The glory of God for Bulgakov is God's joy at the vision of his own being in all its beauty. So far as his human creatures are concerned, this glory of God follows on the revelation of the Wisdom of God in his Word. Its effect is to make that revelation in Bulgakov's words 'precious, desirable, joyful'.[27] Just as following St Paul, Bulgakov links the divine Wisdom in a special way to the Word, the Son, the second divine person, so following the Liturgy

[26] AB, p. 132.
[27] Ibid.

he connects the glory of God in a special way to the third divine person, the Holy Spirit. In the Byzantine Liturgy we find the words 'for the kingdom and the power and the glory are yours to the ages of ages', words which, after 1969, are also found in the Roman Mass as well. In this doxology, says Bulgakov, 'the kingdom' refers to the Father, 'the power' to the Son and 'the glory' to the Holy Spirit.

Bulgakov hastens to assure us, however, that, being specially linked as the Holy Spirit is to the glory of God, does not means that the Holy Spirit has nothing to do with God's Wisdom. On the contrary. First of all, we have seen how the Wisdom of God belongs to all three divine persons. But then secondly, in revelation the Son is inseparable from the Holy Spirit. Distinct, yes. Separable, no. The Father is revealed through the Son and the Spirit conjointly. If the Son appears as the Wisdom of God, the Spirit appears, then, as the 'Spirit of Wisdom' That is a phrase which is fully biblical. At the end of the Book of Deuteronomy we hear that Joshua was 'filled with the Spirit of Wisdom' (34: 9); In the Book of the prophet Isaiah, the 'Spirit of Wisdom' is named as the first of the gifts which the Messianic child will receive (11: 2). And in the Letter to the Ephesians (1: 17), St Paul prays that 'the God of our Lord Jesus Christ, the Father of glory, may give [the members of the Church at Ephesus] a spirit of wisdom and of revelation in the knowledge of him'. The divine Wisdom – this is Bulgakov's proposal – belongs to the Son and the Spirit taken together, as a 'dyad', a twosome, in their revelation of the Father.

So, then, for Scripture God

> possesses or is characterised by, Glory and Wisdom, which cannot be separated from him since they represent the dynamic self-revelation in creative action, and also in his own life.[28]

Can we discern a significant difference in how Scripture uses these two terms, 'wisdom', 'glory'? Bulgakov thinks we can. He writes:

> There is no doubt whatever that [wisdom and glory] do differ from each other as two distinct aspects of the Godhead in its revelation: Wisdom, the first, concerns its content; Glory, the second, its mani-festation. Nevertheless, these two distinct aspects can in no way be separated from each other or replaced by one another, as two prin-ciples within the Godhead. This would contradict the truth of

---

[28] *The Wisdom of God*, op. cit., p. 53.

monotheism, for the one personal God possesses but one Godhead, which is expressed at once in Wisdom and Glory.[29]

Finally, Bulgakov repeats his warning against our trying to have a doctrine of God's nature, his *ousia,* that is worked out purely by philosophical theology, without making full use of what the Bible has to say about the Wisdom and the glory of the Lord. As he says:

> If *Ousia* differs radically from the concrete figures which depict the life of the Godhead in Wisdom and Glory, then it becomes an empty, abstract, metaphysical schema.[30]

Now Bulgakov is in a position to give us his Trinitarian Sophiology – his account of how the Wisdom of God is related to each of the three divine persons. Just as previously, he has given us an account of how the divine nature is related in a special way to each of the divine hypostases, so now he hopes to explain how divine Wisdom – the divine nature as the world containing all God's attributes and ideas in their unity – is related to each of Father, Son and Holy Spirit.

Wisdom and the Son

As we have seen, there is for the New Testament a special connection between the divine Wisdom and Jesus Christ. In the Wisdom of God, the second hypostasis is revealed not only as Word but also as Son – which for Bulgakov means the One who, in relation to the Father, is in an eternal attitude of sacrifice. Of course, when we are thinking about the relation to the Son of divine Wisdom we are not thinking so much of the Son's personal relationship to the Father as of his position in relation to the divine world, the world of God – the divine nature as containing all the divine attributes and ideas. But even in that context of the divine nature, we can still catch a glimpse of the *sacrificial* nature of the Son's being. As the One through whom all created things exist, the Son has a special affinity with sacrifice. The Son allows himself to be the place where the divine ideas are expressed, and the instrument by which they will be further expressed in creation. He lets himself be used in the service of the Father as the One through whom God's world is made. He puts himself at the service of the

[29] Ibid., p. 54.
[30] Ibid., p. 55.

Father and the Father's creative plan. That much we can see even without looking into the question of the implications of his generation as the Father's beloved Son. Right from the beginning, the divine world – the world not only of the divine properties but of the divine ideas, the archetypes of all creation – 'is stamped with the seal of the Lamb'.[31] It carried the mark of the self-sacrificing Word of God.

We learn more about the Son's relation to Wisdom if we go on to ask, How is this world of God actually to be known by us? Given that the world of God transcends mere creaturely existence, it can only be made known if from the beginning God has prepared man to have communion with it. We read in the opening chapter of the Book of Genesis that God 'made man in his own image' (Genesis 1: 26–27), and this text, vital for Eastern theology – and indeed for all traditional Christian theology – tells us there is a special affinity between man and God. 'From the origins', Bulgakov remarks, [the Creator] sets up a correlation between the image [that is, man] and the Primal Image [that is, the divine Wisdom as found in the Word, the second divine person]'.[32] When Bulgakov was speaking about what a person is, we already heard how he regards the fact that each of us is an hypostasis, a unique self, as our *being in God's image* – indeed, as an invitation to share the hypostatic life of the Holy Trinity. But now he wants to say that not just our hypostasis but also our nature – our human nature – is relevant to our being in the image of God, after his likeness. The Greek Fathers – indeed, all the Fathers – assert this, and with few exceptions they link it to the Son. There is something in the Son's divine nature that is directly related to our human nature. So, it is not simply that the divine ideas – of which the Wisdom of God is the total organization – exist in the Son and as humans we are founded on one of those ideas, just as are monkeys and butterflies and pepper-trees and papaya. More than this, as found in the divine Wisdom hypostatized in the Son, God was always in some way human, or – if you prefer – God has always had an essential relation with humanity. For Bulgakov, the Wisdom of God as found in the Word, is the 'divine prototype and foundation of the being of man'.[33] The Son is so much the heavenly Archetype of human nature that he can be called – as Bulgakov here does call him – the 'eternal man ... the human Prototype, *chelovecheskii Pervoobraz*, before the creation of

[31] AB, p. 134.
[32] AB, p. 136.
[33] Ibid., p. 137.

the world'.[34] The Wisdom of God as found in the Word is 'the eternal humanity'.

Not only is there divinity, the divine nature, eternally in God. Not only is there the idea of humanity, the idea of human nature, eternally in God. There is also, eternally in God, what Bulgakov calls 'Godmanhood', the union of divinity and proto-humanity ('proto' at this stage) in the heavenly Man, the Word. Godmanhood – or to give *bogochelovechestve* its alternative translation, easier to turn into adjectives and adverbs in English, the 'Theanthropy' – is going to be the leading term in Bulgakov's Christology, his doctrine of Christ, and in his soteriology, his doctrine of salvation, as well as in his anthropology, his doctrine of man. So much for the Son. What does Bulgakov have to say about the relation of the Wisdom of God to the Holy Spirit and indeed to the Father, the remaining two hypostases?

Wisdom and the Spirit

And first, to the Holy Spirit. We saw how the Son carries a special relation to the world of the divine ideas – the archetypes of all creation. He is the 'place' where the divine ideas exist and the instrument through which they came to be. The world of the divine ideas carries his seal: the seal of the Lamb, the self-sacrificing Servant. But equally, since that world is, as Bulgakov claims, following the tradition of the Greek Fathers, 'accomplished' by the Holy Spirit, it must bear the Spirit's mark as well. The Spirit who, Bulgakov argued, is linked especially to beauty, the Spirit who in glorifying the Father and the Son reveals the beauty of their mutual love, also gives beauty to the world of God, the 'pan-organism' or overall organization of the divine ideas, the archetypes or patterns of all created things.

We have seen how the divine Wisdom is hypostatized in the Word and the Word is the heavenly Man, our Prototype. Where the Word is, there is Godmanhood, the Theanthropy, the divine Humanity. How does the Spirit relate to that? Not in the immediate way that the Word does, for the Word – as existing eternally in God – is divinely human in his own person, and one cannot say that about the Holy Spirit. Rather, the Spirit places himself at the service of the Theanthropy that exists in the Word. The Holy Spirit

[34] Ibid.

is as much involved as is the Son in bringing about a divinized humanity but he is so in the way we would expect from what we know of his role in the divine Trinity. In the Trinity the Spirit exists by showing the Son to the Father and the Father to the Son. He is the moment of their mutual love. It would be utterly out of keeping with his hypostasis for him to draw attention to himself. He is not, therefore, working for himself. Instead, he is in the service of the Son's theanthropic work. His role is that of the loving enabler, who makes it possible for the work of the Son to go forward with ease. The Spirit puts himself at the service of the revelation of the Theanthropy not only in creation but also in salvation through the Word.

Just as Bulgakov found certain features of the relation of the divine Wisdom to the Trinitarian persons which made him think that feminine metaphors are especially well suited to speaking about the Wisdom of God, so this quality of the Holy Spirit's work suggests to him an analogy between the Spirit and womankind: humanity in the female gender in the latter's spiritual – not sexual – aspect. Bulgakov took the not unusual view that behind every great man there stands a great woman who supports and enables. Just so the Spirit supports and enables the Son. In the fullness of time the hypostasis of the Son will be revealed to us in Jesus Christ. In the fullness of time also, Bulgakov is inclined to say, the Holy Spirit will be revealed to us in the Blessed Virgin Mary, who is the Mother of Christ and his Bride, and in the Church which finds its centre in Our Lady. Both the Mother of God and the Church which is Mother Church are in the service of the Son, as is the Spirit.

Wisdom and the Father

That still leaves the Father. The Father cannot be defined in terms of the Theanthropy because unlike the Son and the Spirit he does not in a direct way act personally – hypostatically – in the world of divinized humanity, the theanthropic world. He does not appear in his own hypostasis when the Word, his work crowned by the Spirit, expresses the ideas (including the idea of man) in creation. Nor does he appear directly when the Godmanhood of the Word becomes incarnate, with the co-operation of the Spirit, in Jesus Christ. He simply shows himself indirectly in the creation, which was made by the Word and the Spirit, and again, though more personally, in the life of the incarnate Son, who says to Philip, 'He who has seen me has seen the Father' (John 14: 9), because the Holy Spirit draws people to him. The Father is the ultimate source of the Theanthropy but the Theanthropy itself is realized in the Son and the Spirit, called by St Irenaeus of Lyons 'the Father's two hands'. So likewise, the Father is the ultimate source of the divine Wisdom but in its fontal origin that Wisdom, so far as creatures are concerned, is hidden in the depths of the Fatherly *ousia*.

Like virtually all Eastern Christian theologians, Bulgakov has a strong sense of the mystery of God not just in his essence, his divine nature, which is common to all three divine persons, but in the hypostatic Source of the Holy Trinity, the Father. He writes:

> In his personal, hypostatic being, the Father possesses [the Wisdom of God] as ... the mystery and depth of his hypostatic being, in a true sense as his own nature ... which has still to be manifested, and is to be disclosed in the hypostases who reveal him [in other words, the Son and the Spirit].[35]

So far as the person of the Father is concerned, the Wisdom of God lies deeply hidden in his *ousia*, his being. The Father dwells, it seems, in deep darkness. But that can be a deceptive statement. His darkness is the overwhelmingness of his abundant light. But it is an unapproachable light: thus Paul to Timothy: God 'dwells in unapproachable light, whom no man has ever seen or can see' (1 Timothy 6: 16). Yet the Son and the Spirit in their conjoined work of making manifest the hidden wisdom of God, have made the Father known.

---

[35] *The Wisdom of God*, op. cit., p. 67.

3

The World as God's Created Wisdom

As Bulgakov sees things, what he has done by now is to point us to the 'sufficient basis' of the creation. The Wisdom of God is that sufficient foundation, and the creation which eventually issues from the triune Creator – in and with the beginning of time – is consequently marked by 'sophianity', *sofiinost*.[1] It is, or was meant to be, a *sophianic* creation, a creation filled with the wisdom of God.

The motive of creation

Bulgakov begins his account by pointing out that the God who creates from nothing does not do so because he needs the world – meaning by that, through some hypostatic or natural necessity to complete himself in thus creating. God does not need the world in order to be the Trinity. He does not need the world in order to be divine. As we have seen, he is already the fullness of personhood by being the tri-hypostatic God who in his existence as Father, Son and Holy Spirit exhausts all the modes of personhood there are – I, thou, he, we, you. And in his divine nature he is already plenitude, than which nothing greater is possible. No, the world issues from God's creative freedom.

This said, however, Bulgakov is very keen to emphasize that the world's creation was in no sense an arbitrary act, the result of a vast divine caprice. The creation is not just a manifestation of God's power. He calls such an idea blasphemous, an impiety. And the reason is that the God who in no ordinary sense needed the world still in his love longed for it, desired to bring it about from nothing. Here the love of God is the key. In the last chapter, we saw how love is not only the main feature of the interpersonal life of

[1] AB, p. 140.

the trinitarian persons, it is also 'in' the divine nature where the
Wisdom of God is lovingly disposed to be taken up and used by
Father, Son and Holy Spirit.

> God is love and it is the property of love to love and to enlarge
> oneself by love. It is proper to the divine love not only to realise itself
> within the limits of divinity but to over-flow those limits ... It is
> proper to the ocean of divine love to spread beyond its shores ...[2]

Granted the possibility of creation, the divine love by its own inner
character must take up that possibility. God's 'insatiable' love
moves him to go out of himself, to love elsewhere than himself, to
love beyond himself, in the world. So there is a sense in which God
'had to' create, after all. But this is an altogether *sui generis* kind of
necessity. The 'necessity' of love is really, writes Bulgakov, a 'fusion
of necessity and freedom'.[3] The Absolute need have no relations.
But in fact, as we know from revelation, the Absolute is God. And
God can only be understood not in himself alone, but in his relation with the world as well. If God were simply the Absolute all our
theology would be negative theology, saying what God is not. But
God is not just the Absolute. He is God, related by his love to the
world. And so our theology can be affirmative theology, saying
what God is.[4] God is the Absolute who is also the relative or rela-
tional, and this makes him a mystery of whom we can only speak in
apparent contradictions, statements with two sides either of which,
if pressed to a conclusion, would tend to contradict the other . For
Bulgakov the most important of these 'antinomies' or seeming
contradictions is found in the very statement of what the word
'God' means. It means 'the Absolute existing for another: existing
for the world'.[5]

Bulgakov insists that the 'frontier between the Creator and the
creature must be unfailingly preserved'.[6] And yet he can see an
acceptable meaning in 'panentheism', the philosophy which states
that though God is not all things (which would be pantheism) all
things are 'in' God. To make the link between God and the world
just something contingent, with no implications for God's own
reality, looks like magnifying God but it is really reducing him,

---

[2] Ibid., p. 142.
[3] Ibid: *nerazlichimost' svobodi i neobkhodimosti.*
[4] This is the burden of Bulgakov's reference here to the chapter on apophatic
and cataphatic theology in his earlier work, *Svet nevechernii* (The Unfading
Light, Moscow, 1917).
[5] AB, p. 143.
[6] Ibid.

because it is downplaying the fact that God loves the world with the same love as that whereby he loves himself.

Wisdom in nothing

Bulgakov does not think that belief in creation – belief in our own createdness – requires a prior grasp of divine revelation. It is grounded, he thinks, in a 'metaphysical fact' open to everyone to register. While we do in a sense put in place our own personal existence (we decide to be, more or less, the kind of personality we are), we certainly do not put in place our own being as such. When we advert to this, a conviction of our own limits steals over us and, along with it, a sense that beyond those limits our state is given or created. In this common experience we enjoy what Bulgakov calls a 'metaphysical memory' of our creation. However, from this 'metaphysical memory' we cannot move back by further reflection directly to confront or analyse the act of creation itself. The act of creation is a 'limit concept' (he uses the German term *Grenzbegriff*) which sets a boundary to thinking but not, however, to faith. Here Bulgakov cites the Letter to the Hebrews: 'By faith we understand that the world was created by the word of God, so that what was seen was made out of things which do not appear' (Hebrews 11: 3). The ultimate origin of the world is not one of those things than can be known by rational thought. It can, however, be known through the revelation of the Holy Scriptures, in their testimony to creation by the Word in Wisdom.

Still, we do have from our ordinary resources one clue to the wondrous act of creation and that is the human experience of creativity, of the origination of the novel, the new. By his creativity man bears the seal of his divine Prototype. But of course this is a created creativity: it is only the sub-creative action of the creature within the creation. Unlike such creativity as we embody, God's creativity is an absolute creativity that has to meet no conditions beyond God himself. That is why we say, the world was created 'from nothing' – a statement made in Scripture itself in the Second Book of Maccabees (7: 28).

In the Anglo-Saxon philosophy of language, the misleading character of our speech-forms is sometimes demonstrated by asking, so is 'nothing', then, something if God can create from it? Bulgakov treats this as a real question. If by 'nothing' is meant 'absolutely nothing', then the question is certainly an incoherent one. 'Absolutely nothing' is the contrary of 'something'. But by 'nothing' may also be meant 'relatively nothing', and in relation to this second idea the question is far from incoherent. Being in its non-plenitude, being as *becoming*, is indeed 'relatively nothing'. In this sense, when from absolutely nothing God creates the world in a state of becoming, he gives rise to the realm of relative nothing-ness.

God made the world through Wisdom. Bulgakov uses a translation of the Book of Proverbs which at Chapter 8, verse 22 reads not – as in the most commonly used English Bible, 'The Lord created me at the beginning of his work, the first of his acts of old' (RSV), but rather 'The Lord possessed me at the beginning of his ways, before his works of old'. Here the Russian Bible reflects the translations of the Hebrew *qina* to be found in the non-Septuagintal Greek Old Testaments of antiquity. But a few verses later, at verse 30, Bulgakov's Bible is not so different from our own when it tells us that Wisdom 'was at work with [the Lord]': in the English Bible this appears as: 'I [wisdom] was beside him, like a master workman'. Bulgakov uses the Book of Proverbs to make the point that we cannot suppose God to have improvised the world on day one of the creation. The creation belongs with the eternal counsels of God, as the Fathers of the Church recognized when they spoke of the eternal prototypes of created things in the divine mind. The creation of the world does not mean that God decides at the beginning of time what he proposes to do. It means that the pre-existent content of divine Wisdom begins to exist outside God, in time, as well as within him, in eternity. As Bulgakov writes:

> Metaphysically speaking, the world's creation consists in the fact that God has put forward his own divine world not as a world existing eternally but as a world *in becoming*.[7]

Divine Wisdom (with an upper case 'W') has thus become creaturely wisdom (with a lower case 'w') without for all that ceasing to be itself. God has so to speak 'repeated himself in creation': he has 'reflected himself in [the realm of] non-being'.[8] What in the divine *ousia*, in uncreated Wisdom, was an 'all-unity' now becomes in created wisdom an 'all-multiplicity' in the manifold forms of differentiated being. And so we have the world around us, a world composed of 'all creatures great and small' as Mrs Alexander's Evangelical children's hymn puts it. Bulgakov emphasizes that we

[7] Ibid., p.149.
[8] Ibid.

are dealing here with only one wisdom, one wisdom in two modalities, Uncreated and created. Between the eternal ideas in the mind of God and the temporal realizations of those ideas there is the infinite difference which separates the divine from the worldly. And yet the content of both wisdoms is the same.

In the beginning, on day one of the world, in the unique singularity of the first moment of space-time, a hypothetical observer could not of course experience the cosmos in all its wonder. The world was only at the beginning of its development or evolution. As the Fathers of the Church say, the 'seeds' of all things were planted within the creation but they needed time to germinate and grow. This is something of which modern science makes us more aware, but for the Church's theological tradition, it is not exactly news. In founding the world the Wisdom of God is not at first fully actualized there. The Wisdom of God is at first only present in the world's potential. Using Aristotle's (384–322 BC) terminology Bulgakov speaks of the fullness of created wisdom – and thus a perfect reflection of the uncreated Wisdom – as the world's 'entelechy', the final state to which creation is purposefully moving. But that is the final state – as it were the oak tree, whereas at the beginning all we have is the original potential – as it were the acorn. The Book of Genesis calls the world at this initial stage 'earth', and says of it, 'the earth was without form and void and darkness was upon the face of the deep' (Genesis 1: 2). But the eternal divine plan for the completion of the creation, notably in the emergence of personal – hypostatic – beings on earth (namely, ourselves) was already communicated to that other aspect of the creation which Genesis calls 'the heavens' and which Bulgakov, like the Fathers generally, identifies with the holy angels. The angels knew, from the first moment of creation, what course the development of creation was to take.

The work of the Trinity

When treating of the Holy Trinity, Bulgakov has had occasion to mention his theory that the generation of the Son is already a kenosis or self-emptying for both Son and Father, while the Son's relation to the divine idea has a kenotic aspect to it from the beginning. We do not have to wait till the Incarnation to find in God a kenosis as set out by Paul in the Philippians hymn. Kenosis characterized the divine life from all eternity. But now Bulgakov goes on to add that the creation of the world, the positing of the divine Wisdom outside God for the first time, also has a kenotic character to it. And this is by virtue of the divine love which allows the Absolute to become the 'Absolute-relative', that seeming paradox where God, the unconditioned One, accepts relationship with what is not himself. Inasmuch as the creation is simply the re-statement of the content of divine Wisdom, it remains within God's self-definition, and to say as much is to speak of creation on its eternal side. But insofar as creation constitutes outside of God a reality other than God, it is the work of God, and to say this is to speak of creation as found essentially in time, in becoming.

For Bulgakov, as for the Fathers and such influential mediaeval Western theologians as St Thomas and St Bonaventure (*c.* 1217–1274), it is important that the creation is the work of the entire Holy Trinity.[9] In the act of creation, as disclosed in revelation to Christian faith, each hypostasis is revealed in a way congruent with his own hypostatic character, whether Father, Son or Holy Spirit. The Father is the principal or primordial will at work in the creation. He wills the creation by an ecstasy of love, becoming God for the world rather than simply God in himself. He creates the world by means of the Son in whom and through whom all things exist. For the Father the Son is, writes Bulgakov, 'the content of creation, all its aspects and all its forms'.[10] In the creation, the Father sends the Son into the world not as yet hypostatically (that will only happen with the Incarnation) but 'as the words of the Word in this world'. The Son enters the world, even before the Incarnation, in those creative words which he turns into created realities, thus carrying out the Father's will. Bulgakov sees this service to the world by the Son in obedience to the Father as a first sketch of what will happen to the Incarnate Word, Jesus Christ, at the Atonement on Good Friday. The Son is, as the Apocalypse of St John puts it, 'the Lamb slain since the beginning of the world' (Apocalypse 13: 8). If this seems to some readers theologically extravagant, it may be noted that Bulgakov's convictions here were anticipated by John Henry Newman (1801–1890), who wrote of the eternal Son that the 'first act of His *synkatabasis*' (condescension) was creation itself.[11]

---

[9] G. Emery, O. P., *La Trinité créatrice. Trinité et création dans les commentaires aux Sentences de Thomas d'Aquin et de ses prédecesseirs Albert le Grand et Bonaventure* (Paris, 1995).

[10] AB, p. 151.

[11] J. H. Newman, *Tracts Theological and Ecclesiastical* (London, 1874, 1962), p. 202.

He was the Son of God, equal to the Father; he took works upon Him beneath that Divine Majesty; they were such as were not obligations of His Nature, nor of His Person, but they were congruous to His Person, and they might look very like what essentially belonged to Him; but after all, they were works such as God alone could undertake. He was Creator, Preserver, Archetype of all things, but not simply as God, but as God the Son, and further, as God the Son in an office of ministration ... [12]

What, then, is there left for the Holy Spirit to do in God's creative work? Following his earlier account of the place of the Spirit in the triune life, Bulgakov sees the Holy Spirit as that divine hypostasis who invests the work of God the Son with beauty, making the creation in its structure and order a work of art in which the divine Artist can take delight. The Spirit crowns the work of Father and Son with the joy which for Bulgakov is essential to his hypostatic character. He enables the Father to have joy in the creation as the manifestation of his Word, his Son. And he allows the Son to rejoice in the creation as the revelation of the Father. But insofar as the world in its painful process of becoming is not as yet the created wisdom of God in its completed state, the world cannot receive the Holy Spirit in his fulness. Accompanying creation on its laborious path from incompleteness to completeness is the particular way in which the role of the Holy Spirit in creation has its own kenotic side, just as have the roles of Father and Son.

Eternity and time

Before leaving the topic of creation in general and focusing instead on the creation of man, the human being, Bulgakov pauses to think a little more about the relation between eternity and time. This has to be an important theme for him, given the way he treats divine Wisdom – which is eternal – and created wisdom – which is temporal – as one single content.

Time is not of course eternity. In one sense, it is opposed to eternity, and this is how we commonly think of it. But in another sense time is put in place by eternity, has eternity as its foundation and its final cause, the goal to which it is moving. And in this second sense, time only has coherence because it reflects eternity. Bulgakov compares it to a mosaic, where individual moments are like so many individual pieces of coloured glass that, taken

[12] Ibid., p. 197.

together, nonetheless make up a whole. It becomes easier to grasp
this if we realize that what we are talking about is creaturely wisdom
– which is in time – on the one hand, and divine Wisdom – which
is eternal – on the other. Time is full of eternity, and tends to
approach eternity while never becoming eternity, precisely
because these two wisdoms are one. They have one content.

Of the two, however, only divine Wisdom exists in God. Shall we
say, then, that for God time has no reality, that he is not engaged
with temporal realities as such? Is it true to say that for God only
eternity exists? Bulgakov answers with a resounding 'No'.

> The entire Christian religion presupposes for its truth-value the
> reality of time not only for the world but also for God, and the one
> conditions the other.[13]

To treat God's relations with the temporal as merely a human way of
speaking would be to 'shake the entire content of our faith'. It would
mean transforming the biblical God, the 'Creator, all-mighty, living,
merciful, saving', into the 'immobile Absolute of Hinduism in which
all concrete being is snuffed out and the whole world becomes illusion'.[14] It would make nonsense of the Incarnation where earthly
events happened to One who was God. But what about the way that
Scripture and the doctrinal tradition speaks of God's immutability,
his unchangingness? Bulgakov replies by drawing a distinction which
we also find in such modern Western Catholic theologians as the
German Jesuit Karl Rahner (1904–1984).[15] He distinguishes
between God as he who is changeless in himself, in eternity, and he
who can be involved in change in another, in time. He writes:

> In himself, God is eternal by virtue of the divine everlastingness, the
> plenitude of his life, by virtue of immutability, and total happiness.
> In himself, God is eternal by virtue of the divine everlastingness of
> his tri-personhood which is the eternal act of love of the Three in
> their reciprocal relations.[16]

That is certainly a plain statement. But there is another side to the
question which also requires stating. Bulgakov says:

---

[13] Ibid., p. 155.
[14] Ibid.
[15] See, e.g., K. Rahner, 'Observations on the Concept of God in Catholic
     Dogmatics', in idem., *Theological Investigations* 9 (Et London, 1972), pp.
     127–144, and notably at p. 143.
[16] AB, p. 157.

God is also the Creator, creating life *outside* himself and himself living there outside himself. The reality of this world is determined by God. The reality of the *time* of this world is also valid [therefore] for God, since it is his own work, and, taken as a whole, his own 'placing' of himself. Going out of himself in the kenosis of the creation of the world, the love of God puts time in position even for God himself. It brings it about that God also lives in history and shares in this sense in the world's becoming, for the sake of the world.[17]

And Bulgakov connects with this claim the words of St Paul in the fifteenth chapter of the First Letter to the Corinthians about how the Father is in process of subjecting all things to Christ so that in the end the Son can hand over the kingdom to the Father and God be all in all (1 Corinthians 15: 24–28).

Bulgakov emphasizes that in no way does the Creator's relation with time in the creation lessen or limit his eternity. Temporality – the time dimension – is on a different ontological level from eternity, so the two are not in any kind of conflict. Time has its roots in eternity, is nourished by eternity, and penetrated by it. As Plato (427–347 BC) wrote in the *Timaeos* centuries before Christ, time is the 'moving image of eternity'. We can affirm simultaneously, without any contradiction, the unchangeable eternity of God and the temporality of his works in the world.

As the image of God, we human beings carry within ourselves the 'mystery of this union of time and eternity'.[18] For us – and here Bulgakov is thinking especially of human beings who are Christians – eternal life begins already in the life of time.

Man as microcosm

Bulgakov now turns to deal with that special example of God's creative work that is ourselves. Here we get in fuller form his theological anthropology, his doctrine of man. He begins from the affirmation, 'Man shares in the world of God'.[19] That means, of

[17] Ibid.

[18] Ibid., p. 158. This is also St Thomas Aquinas's view, as his metaphor of the soul as on the 'horizon' between eternity and time indicates. See his *Summa contra Gentiles* II, c. 68 and c. 81, and, less accessibly: *Sancti Thomae Aquinatis, In Librum De Causis Expositio* (Rome, 1955), pp. 15–16. The use of the 'boundary' image for the soul is pervasive in Christian Platonism, as is shown in P. Quinn, *Aquinas, Platonism and the Knowledge of God* (Aldershot, 1996), pp. 52–65.

[19] AB, p. 158.

course, he shares in the Wisdom of God, which we have seen can also be called the heavenly Theanthropy, the Godmanhood of the Word. The Wisdom of God can be called the heavenly Theanthropy because divine Wisdom is centred in the Godmanhood of the Word, for the Word is not only God but also, in a special way, the Prototype of man, who will be made in the image of the Word: something that can be said of no other creature. Now because creaturely Wisdom reflects the Uncreated Wisdom, the world which results from God's creative work will be centred on man, the image of God, precisely because the uncreated Wisdom is centred on the Prototype of man, the Word in his proto-humanity. Man is therefore the summing up of the universe. He is the universe in little. He is, as the Greek philosophers and following them the Greek Fathers say, the 'micro-cosm': the entire cosmos in a small (*mikros*) edition of itself. Conversely, we can say, the 'macrocosm', the 'great' (*makros*) universe, has a human stamp to it. As Bulgakov writes, 'it is sealed by the mark of man'.[20] What that means is, in the first place, that there is nothing in the universe which is alien to man. There is nothing in the universe that is out of reach to our understanding, feeling or will. That is already a strong statement, but Bulgakov goes further still when he says that, as the *Hexaemeron*, the Genesis account of the world's six-stage creation, suggests, the universe was made in such a way as to have humanity as its summit – its high point which holds it together and is also, therefore, its effective centre. Bulgakov compares man's relation to nature to the relation between the Word and the Wisdom of God. Just as the Word holds all the contents of the divine Wisdom together in their integrity, so man has to hold together all the contents of nature. In part we do this anyway, because through our bodies we incorporate in our make up all the pre-human stages of life. But in part it is more a task we have before us, to humanize the world by giving the non-human realities a relationship with ourselves. We do that, I suppose, when for instance we climb mountains or write poems about them, sail the seas or write novels about seafaring, explore forests and create gardens where different plants can be brought together, study the animal world or domesticate certain animals by bringing them into a common life with us. (Of course, we also eat not only plants but also animals, but this is not what Bulgakov has in mind! Rather, our future relation with the animal kingdom will be that made known in the lives of certain of the saints.[21])

[20] Ibid.
[21] Ibid., p. 163, n. 1.

The human hypostasis

The chief difference between the animals and ourselves is that the animals have no hypostatic reality. They lack the dimension of personhood. Animals are individuals, and the higher animals can be sharply individualized by their particularities. But they are not personal, which is why they can look forward to no immortality.

We already saw how Bulgakov, in a manner at first sight opposed to Christian orthodoxy, calls man in one sense uncreated. He returns to the theme here, under the heading 'the constitution of man'. By the spiritual principle in him, a hypostatic or personal spiritual principle, man has what the mediaeval Western mystics call a 'divine spark'. Bulgakov is fond of citing Psalm 82: 6, where the Lord addresses humanity: 'I say, "You are gods, sons of the Most High, all of you"'. That same text continues, however, '"Nevertheless, you shall die like men, and fall like any prince"'. Bulgakov calls us 'created gods'. We are created, like any other creature in the universe, and yet we have a special relation with the divine. Scripture calls this our 'imaging' of God. We have already looked at this in terms of the light it can throw on our divine archetype but now we want to concentrate on it for itself.

Despite all the distance that divides the Creator from the creature there is a correlation between the image, man, and the Prototype, the divine Word, and this correlation in a certain sense prepares the way for the Incarnation. In creating hypostases, personal beings, in the form of the angels and ourselves, God has 'multiplied and repeated his hypostatic faces' – in other words, his own reality as the divine tri-hypostatic personality. There is a sense in which we are 'uncreated'. Now, as Bulgakov writes, to reassure those who are worried by this talk of the human spirit as 'uncreated':

> That cannot mean that the sons of God [i.e. human beings] have the same nature as God, namely that they exist by an eternal, personal act. What it means is that, by their very origin, they can have a communion with the divine nature, that they have the possibility of being 'born of God', which is to say really becoming sons of God, sharing in the divine life.[22]

In the way God has created us, he has not only given us hypostases that reflect his own tri-hypostatic reality. He has also made our nature such that it can enjoy solidarity, communion, with the

[22] Ibid., p. 160.

divine nature through the Godmanhood of the Word. Bulgakov indeed goes so far as to say our nature holds within itself two natures, one created, the other divine. When we hear Bulgakov say that man has two natures, one divine and the other created, we have to bear in mind that, by his own explanation, this is a *façon de parler*. It is a piece of rhetoric, designed to wake us up to our divine calling. Nevertheless, for him the ontological possibility of our communion with the divine nature goes right back to the pre-establishment of our humanity in the divine Wisdom. 'The human spirit', he writes, 'was not created in time but in the eternity of God'. This, he insists, is quite different from the idea of a temporal pre-existence of souls, an idea ascribed to Origen of Alexandria, and condemned by the Church in the course of the sixth century. In the Wisdom of God there is a divine idea not only of humanity at large but of each and every one of us as a participation by a human hypostasis in the divine life.

We are on safer ground when Bulgakov speaks of the relation of this to Jesus Christ. The first Adam, as created, as he existed before the Fall, then, was already the image of Christ, an image awaiting its 'integral revelation', *polno raskritie*, and indeed its *svershenie*,'fulfilment'.[23] In the early Church this was the teaching of St Irenaeus, who wrote:

> The Word, the Creator of all, prefigured in Adam the future economy of his own Incarnation.[24]

Our proto-parent, the first father, included within him the image of the Christ who was to come, included it in body, soul and hypostasis:

> not only in his body, image of the sophianic world, not only in his spirit which in a certain sense was heaven-sent, but also in his structure, in the fusion of the two natures (that of mind and that of soul and body) in a single hypostasis.[25]

For Bulgakov the hypostasis is especially important, because it is as *persons* who have natures that in the last analysis we are able to be like, and have communion with, the Holy Trinity – and so not simply because of our nature as such, however sublime the spiritual element in it may be. Of course, unlike God human beings are

[23] Ibid., p. 161.
[24] Irenaeus, *Adversus haereses*, III. 22, 3.
[25] AB, p. 161.

monohypostatic, one-personed, not tri-hypostatic, three-personed. Still, we can in some faint way reflect the Holy Trinity. Here Bulgakov adds a new dimension to what he has said so far. So far, along with the overwhelming majority of the Fathers, he has spoken of the image of God in us as a reflection of the Son. Now, with a minority of the Fathers – and above all St Augustine (354–430) – he wants to add and if of the Son then, in a sense, of the whole divine Trinity. Although as images of God we were made primarily in the likeness of the Son, this is of the Son as revealing the Father. Revealing the Father is always what the Son is doing. So our imagehood of the hypostasis of the second divine person is not without some relation to the hypostasis of the Father, the first. And again, Bulgakov has stressed that the third divine hypostasis, the Spirit, always accompanies and follows up the revelation of the Father in the Son. So there must also be some echo in a human hypostasis of the personal being of the Holy Spirit too. Bulgakov speculates that just as the Theanthropy or Godmanhood in God himself is revealed in history in the Incarnate Word *together with his blessed Mother* – that is how we see Emmanuel depicted on icons: the Mother and Child, so an echo of the hypostases of the Son and the Spirit is found in the fact that the totality of human hypostases is not simply male but male and female. The human hypostasis in womankind reflects the hypostasis of the Spirit in his relation to the Son in whose image, primarily and fundamentally, all human hypostases, whether of males or females, are made. In these ways, then, we can make sense of the statement that man is 'the living image of the tri-hypostatic God in his Wisdom', and not just of the Son alone.

Freedom and the Fall

These exalted affirmations about the human being need now to be modified to take account of the fact that we do not exist, actually, in the paradisal condition of our first father before the Fall. We come trailing clouds of sophianic glory, but we also exist as dragged down by sin. Bulgakov's account of the Fall begins, as surely any account must do, from an evocation of human freedom. The Fall was essentially an abuse of freedom. We only fell in Adam because in Adam we were free.

For Bulgakov, reasonable liberty, the freedom of the rational creature, is the specifically human form of spontaneity. All life has spontaneity to some degree. Animals show spontaneous reactions to events in their environment, and sometimes manifest in this an instinctive wisdom greater than that of human reason. Naturally, for Bulgakov this is because animal existence too, even though it is not spiritual or hypostatic, is sophianic: it originates in the Wisdom of God. In human beings, spontaneity is creative rather than repetitive. And this means that whereas animals only have their life as a species, human beings are makers of history where nature goes beyond itself into culture. This is the evidence that we have a different kind of spontaneity from that of animals – the spontaneity we call 'freedom'.

Our freedom is the freedom of creative self-determination. But though real – all too real – it is not absolute. We lack the power to 'place' or 'position' ourselves exactly as we will. We do have our own 'I', our self-awareness, but this 'I' is embedded in a nature which is given to us, not ours to make up as we go along. One might have thought that the 'I' depends for its self-disposition on God since like everything else about us he created it. But the 'I' is not a thing, and God, who relates to everything as it is in his Wisdom, does not treat it as it if were. Bulgakov expresses this by saying that God addresses his *fiat* – 'Let it be so!' – to the human 'I' in the form of a question. 'Will you let it be so?' God gives us the possibility of our self-positioning aright, but the actual self-positioning we must do for ourselves. Being in the image of God by virtue of our hypostasis has its advantages, but is also has its disadvantages. It opens the way to tragedy as well as to the happy life.

Essentially, the divine question inscribed in our consciousness by our creation in the image of God can have only one of two answers. The first is the answer God desires. Bulgakov expresses it like this:

> In the measure that man sees God as his Prototype, he conceives his condition as created, that is to say he grasps his metaphysical 'unoriginality'. He knows himself as the reflection of the divine sun in a droplet of being. At the same time, in this free avowal that he is only the *image* of Another, of the Primal Image, there is born in him love for this Other, namely, for God, a love which is as it were the seal of the Word, of the divine Sonship: the Son loves the Father, and man, loving God, sees himself only as the image of his Creator from whom he holds his being. He freely positions himself as *image*. He accomplishes the kenotic act of love, *akt kenozisa liubvi*.[26]

---

[26] Ibid., p. 165.

In other words, what God hopes we will do in life is to see ourselves as our own tiny, created-to-scale, image of the Son in his response to his generation from the Father. Unfortunately, there is also a second answer to the divine question, and Bulgakov has a good description of this negative response as well.

> If man turns away from this sun, and rejects kenosis, he will remain alone with himself, conscious of his Luciferian self-positioning, *liut-siferichesko samopolozenie*. In such a case he knows as his proper source and primal image only himself, thus making a god of himself. Thus he transforms his creaturely 'I' into an 'I' that is falsely divine. This is the way of Satan who suppressed love and fell into a solitary selfhood. And in general this is the way of self-divini-sation, samobozhia, a way that is also open to man, precisely because of his character as a self-positioning 'I'.[27]

The divine 'I' is meant to be for man the divine 'Thou'. We are meant to position our own 'I' in relation to this 'Thou', to respond to this 'Thou' as the absolute 'I' that calls us to communion with itself. Unfortunately, we are sometimes deaf, and sometimes disobedient.

The cosmic dimension

Before setting out his understanding of the Fall, Bulgakov reminds us of a factor about the creation of Adam which we need to bear in mind if we are to appreciate the Fall's cosmic implications. According to Bulgakov, the world, the creaturely wisdom, is essen-tially the world of man: it is a world meant from the beginning to find its centre and its coherence in the human race. Man has the same role for the creaturely wisdom as the Word in his proto-humanity has for uncreated Wisdom. So if something goes wrong with man, something will go wrong with the world as well. Man is to be the 'logos' of the world, the one who both understands its order and confirms that order; he is also to be the beautifier of the world, the one who makes it as lovely a cosmos as it can be. That is also a necessary task of man, just as the Word must allow the Holy Spirit to finish the Word's task of being the One through whom all things were made. Now on Bulgakov's reading of the Book of Genesis, in his unfallen condition Adam had not yet achieved those tasks. Outside Paradise there was a non-paradisal world, as

[27] Ibid., p. 166.

Adam and Eve discovered rather disagreeably when they were expelled from the Garden and made to live in it. Bulgakov understands this to mean that Adam was given the project and the power to enter into possession of the world in its sophianity, in its integral wholeness as the reflection of divine Wisdom. But he did not in fact take possession of the world in that way. In the first instance, this is because the task was beyond the capabilities of a single human hypostasis. Only the total spiritual effort of all the hypostases who are to make up the human race from Adam to the end of time could bring it about that the world was fully humanized according to wisdom and thus in its own turn could come to display the wisdom on which it was based. Adam, however, did have the project and the power to pass it on: that for Bulgakov is what is meant when the hagiograph, the biblical writer, says Adam was in Paradise. What would happen with the Fall was that this project was suspended, this power lost, and the way to the full disclosure of the Wisdom of God in the world closed off.

This already tells us quite a lot of how Bulgakov understands the Fall, or at any rate the consequences of the Fall. Bulgakov has an initial, rather simple, basic statement of how the Fall took place. Although from the moment of his creation, Adam could draw on the help of divine grace, he had to ratify God's creative and sanctifying work in him by a free definition of himself – a free act of self-positioning. Having in himself two possible centres for his being, one spiritual and one carnal or fleshly, he made his choice. He submitted his spirit to the demands of the flesh: an ontological event which the Bible speaks of as the violation of a command – the command not to eat of the forbidden fruit in the Garden. Adam thus died a spiritual death. He lost the active potential for Godmanhood. Adam became what Bulgakov calls a 'natural man'. Bulgakov means by that: he became *only* a natural man. Far from beginning the process whereby the whole world would stand forth as sophianic, as the revelation of the Wisdom of God, nature now began to appear to him as merely material in character – rather than a disclosure of the Word. Nature became for him non-sophianic and since it was in him, as the first man, that the creaturely wisdom had its centre and coherence, we can go further and say that nature itself was dragged down with man to his new unsophianic level. So Bulgakov speaks of the creaturely wisdom God had embodied in the world as now a wisdom that had become 'fallen' or 'darkened'.

How Adam fell

Bulgakov also has a rather more sophisticated account of how Adam fell which goes beyond simply saying he submitted the spiritual side of his nature to the sensual. Adam's created reality, while it was still unexplored for him, that is, while he had not yet come to make it his own as God had created it and wanted it to be, was inherently unstable. It carried with it a risk of failure. As the divine Creator, bringing into existence the free human person endowed with the capacity for self-positioning, God had accepted this risk. Indeed it was not the least part of the sacrificial kenosis which divine love took upon itself in making the world. It was possible – only too possible – that the relative nothingness which came into existence with the creature would gain in potency through human liberty. In this case, a rupture could open up in the fabric of the world. Chaos could come upon man, and if on man then on the world as a whole. Chaos could occur so long as man had not yet ratified his being-in-the-image by freely turning his creative powers to the service of his sophianic vocation: so long, that is, as he was not yet living not just in the image of God but also in God's *likeness*. For the Book of Genesis says of man that he was created not just in God's image, but according to his likeness. The tradition of the Fathers of the Church is virtually unanimous in seeing that as a statement not just about what man is by virtue of creation (the image of God). The Fathers see it also as a statement about how man is called to live in order to fulfil his potential for holiness, for being 'like God' (in God's likeness).

Still, the news is not all bad. Of its nature the world cannot regress into total chaos. It cannot fall into total ruination. And the reason is that it embodies the creaturely wisdom. Accordingly, it contains the divine ideas, and those imperishable elements that are the angelic and human hypostases. The covenant of God with Noah in chapters eight and nine of the Book of Genesis confirms from the point of view of salvation history what we would in any case think on the basis of divine revelation as a whole. God promises Noah he will conserve the world in being, and points to the rainbow as the sign of this promise, stretching from heaven to earth. The idea of the world self-destructing is the idea of an ontological impossibility. The world cannot commit suicide, though individuals within it can. As Bulgakov writes:

The world is indefectible, and the ways of God are unsoundable in the accomplishing of his works.[28]

And he adds:

This long and arduous process in which God pursues the accomplishment of the world in the company of man, we call divine Providence, the 'economy', and, at the centre of this journey, the Incarnation.[29]

---

[28] Ibid., p. 171.
[29] Ibid.

4

God and Evil, Freedom and Providence

The topic of God and evil has already been broached (twice) in the theological anthropology which Bulgakov set out in the first volume of the Great Trilogy, *The Lamb of God*. There he needed to refer to the fall in order to get his readers to understand an important part at least of the rationale of the Incarnation. But the fullest account comes in the third volume of the Great Trilogy, *The Bride of the Lamb*. This is where we find the most complete version of Bulgakov's 'theodicy', his account of how the fact of evil in the world can be acknowledged without calling into question the existence of an all-good and all-powerful Creator.

The character of evil

Bulgakov begins this fuller account by declaring his attachment to the traditional Christian view of evil, sometimes called the 'meontic' view of evil, from the Greek words for 'not being', *mê on*. Considered as a substantial principle, a principle of being, evil does not exist. There is no second principle beside God, 'independent, parallel and competing with the good'.

> Oriental dualism, which admits two equal principles, a good god and an evil god, an original light and an original darkness, is quite incompatible with Christianity as indeed it is with sane thought.[1]

What, then, is evil if it is not substance? Bulgakov answers, it is a *state*, a condition, of created being, and more specifically this condition is defined by the absence of something which should be present but is not. He gives us the classical words for this in the

[1] NA, p. 159.

Greek and Latin Fathers. Evil is *sterêsis* or *privatio*. It is 'privation'.

However, as Bulgakov points out, in practice evil does not *feel* like this. In the eyes of the Creator evil may be nothing. But creatures, those who inhabit or compose the creation, are often staggered by its destructive force. If evil does not exist on the higher level of the divine, it certainly seems to exist, judging by its effects, on the lower level of the created world. There is a mystery or at least an antinomy, a seeming contradiction here, with which we must come to terms.

Conditions of possibility for evil

Bulgakov suggests we can readily identify at least one 'condition of possibility' for evil. This condition of possibility, it must be stressed, is not itself evil. Far from it. But it helps us to see how evil might come about. What Bulgakov is talking about is the limitedness and inherent imperfection of created things. Creatures are in a state of becoming – not of being in the full sense of the word. They are also singular and partial and in these senses only enter potentially into the harmonious inter-connexion which should characterize the world as a whole. Each creature, accordingly, is faced with a series of different possibilities. Every creature has to search. No creature is perfect from the start. If a creature does not become a master-piece this may not be due to sin. It could just be a consequence of the limitation and partialness that makes creatures prone to mistakes. Here Bulgakov cites the words of one of Job's comforters in the Book of Job chapter 4: 'Even his angels [the Lord] charges with error' (Job 4, 18b). Even the holy angels, who are altogether strangers to sin, are subject to error and imperfection as a consequence of their creaturely limitations. The greater the capacity a creature has for self-determination in its becoming, for directing itself towards its own goal, the higher the chance it will be subject to serious mistakes, to aberrations. This would have been the case even if evil had never entered the world. Nor is this entirely to be regretted. There is a sense in which it is a wonderful privilege for the creature to be able to make mistakes. It shows that the world of which it forms part is not a robot or a machine but living and sharing in the responsibility for finding and doing God's will. In fact Bulgakov goes so far as to say that our fallible creative activity is a work of the love and condescension of God, who entrusts to the limited powers of the creature a responsibility for carrying out the divine will 'on earth as it is in heaven'.[2]

But if one presupposition of the possibility of evil lies in the way created nature is only in process of moving towards its own perfection, another concerns the subjective rather than objective side of human existence. We do not only *have* a nature; we *are* subjects. And in this perspective it is our personal freedom which is the relevant factor. Our personal freedom holds out the possibility of self-determination toward the good, or toward the evil. Possibly, Bulgakov suggests, the way creation was brought into being out of nothing is relevant here. Only God is total actuality (Bulgakov uses the formula St Thomas Aquinas took from Aristotle: *actus purus*). The free creature is not fully actual and so experiences a degree of what Bulgakov terms 'ontological inertia'. A created hypostasis, whether human or angelic, must use its freedom to shake off this inertia, and not all hypostases do so. Once again, this is not in itself sin, not in itself evil. We all know lazy people who in other respects are rather virtuous. But it may be the basis of an inclination to sin, to evil. Bulgakov also makes a suggestion which comes at the matter from the opposite direction by considering the possible drawbacks to relative ontological fullness, and not just relative ontological emptiness. We cannot help noting that it was the greatest of the angelic intelligences, Lucifer, who led the fall of the Angels. Possibly a relative plenitude of being can also incline a hypostasis towards a sinful state unless it has a spiritual life of a sufficient integrity to counteract this.

At first sight, Bulgakov appears to ascribe to Adam before the Fall a relative ontological emptiness. He follows St Irenaeus in holding that Adam as first created is somewhat in the position of a child. Adam's innocence is initial *naïveté*, based on inexperience, though it is also, says Bulgakov, 'passive holiness', '*passivnaya svyatost'*. By 'passive holiness' Bulgakov means a real holiness but one based on not knowing evil and sin. Bulgakov contrasts this with what he terms 'active, *aktivnaya*, holiness' which comes from conquering evil and sin, and thus going beyond them. To begin with, Adam obeys God by an instinctive response to the inner call of his nature, which, like all nature is of course sophianic, an expression of divine Wisdom. In order to enter into personal self-possession and be able to determine himself hypostatically for

[2] Ibid., p. 161.

God, Adam cannot rest here. There must be what Bulgakov calls 'an injunction aiming at his freedom',[3] a challenge from beyond him, directly from God. The divine prohibition on eating the fruit of the tree of good and evil is precisely this. Adam failed the necessary test, and in that moment, so far as the human – as distinct from the angelic world – was concerned, evil arose. So, and by the same token, did moral good. Moral good is not ontological good, of the kind the Lord recognized at each stage of his work of creation when he looked on what he had made and found it 'very good' (Genesis 1: 31). The good which arose by sheer contrast when evil was first known in the human world was specifically moral: the good that is the norm of ethical striving in accordance with right reason. For Bulgakov, such moral good only makes sense as an alternative to evil. It is, he says, 'a reaction of holiness against sin'.[4]

Bulgakov takes the view, shared by some philosophers, that freedom is by definition uncaused by anything beyond it. If we ask, what is the cause of a free act, the only answer can be, 'the subject of the act is, precisely in his freedom' or, more briefly still, 'my freedom is'. This in turn means that while my freedom may obey the divine law by its own accord – a free accord – with the sophianity of the world, the world's wise ordering by God, it may also act in a way that is anarchic and arbitrary, rebellious and mad. Bulgakov calls this the 'odious privilege' of the free human creature, and it is one that cannot be withdrawn by God, not even in the face of the terrible danger it conceals, the danger of Satanism, the outright, conscious, deliberate rejection of God and godliness. Bulgakov writes:

> The love of God, indeed, manifested in the creation of the world by the principle of the liberty of the creature [he means, the risk such liberty involves for God testifies to his love], sets no term to its longanimity which extends to any sacrifice. Furthermore, the love of God is ready in advance to undertake the redemption to restore the disfigured face of the creature.[5]

So just by virtue of having allowed for the real possibility of human evil, the Creator prepares to become in the future the Redeemer.

As we have already seen in the matter of the two answers that might be given to God's interrogatory *fiat*: by an act of loving

---

[3] Ibid., p. 165.
[4] Ibid.
[5] Ibid., pp. 166–167.

humility every created hypostasis needs personally to accept the creative act of the divine power by which it was brought into being. The creation, writes Bulgakov, is a 'work of love', in the sense of being

> an encounter between the Creator and the created, of the love that gives and the love that receives with gratitude and humility.[6]

By an act of ecstatic love, indeed, the Holy Trinity goes out of itself into the realm of nothingness where it makes to issue new hypostases created in its image: which means to say, hypostases that are bearers of the gift of love. For Bulgakov, writing in a burst of poetry in the last volume of the Great Trilogy, a created person is 'a flame of the Spirit, *yazik Dukha*, of the love of God, which in turn raises up out of nothingness the flame of love on the part of the creature'.[7] At the beginning of the existence of every hypostasis there is the gift of the real possibility of such love, but the possibility is divinely given to creaturely freedom, as a project the person is invited, not forced, to realize.

The comparison with the angels

These comments are meant to be by way of elucidation of the fall of Adam, but Bulgakov is convinced that a consideration of the origins of evil must look at angelic freedom and not just its human counterpart. Unlike St Thomas in the West, he thinks that the sin of the angels need not have happened all at one instant. It could have come about as a result of a 'series of internal events and determinations', of which the outcome was simply incompatible with existence in heaven.[8] By whatever act or process, the angels, as St John says, were 'thrown down' (Apocalypse 12: 9). Bulgakov is thinking of the way that the *final* expulsion of the angels from heaven in the war with Michael appears to come, for the author of the Apocalypse, *after* the Incarnation, as the world moves toward the end of time. However, Bulgakov agrees with Thomas about the essence of the sin of the angels, which was pride. It was false self-love: 'egocentrism, alienation, blindness, solipsism, being overcome by pride'. We see the significance of the pride of 'Satanic non-love' when we realize what such pride was rejecting: namely,

[6] Ibid., p. 169.
[7] Ibid.
[8] Ibid., pp. 166–167: *ryad vnytrennnikh sobitii i samoopredelenii.*

the Trinitarian form of love whereby in the tri-hypostatic, sacrificial loving of Father, Son and Holy Spirit, each person finds itself
no longer in itself but in the other hypostases. Rejecting such love
is not a comfortable condition. The created hypostasis does not
cease to know that it is created, that its being is a gift. It knows that
by making itself its own centre it has usurped the place that rightly
belongs to its Maker. There arises in it therefore envy and hatred
for God, an all-consuming jealousy and, because of the hopeless-
ness of this competition with God, despair. This is quite as relevant
to humans as to angels. Bulgakov quotes the Syrian writer Isaac of
Nineveh (d. *c.* 700): the fire of Hell is the torture of love. It is when
persons created for love have extinguished in themselves a love
that does not cease to be the internal law of their own being. As he
puts it 'Satanic malignity is the infernal face of inextinguishable
love'.[9]

It is a major feature of Bulgakov's theology of the angels, his
angelology, that the angels are partly defined by their relations
with mankind. The word 'angel' means 'messenger', so this is not
an unreasonable conclusion. In his term, the angels are 'synanthropic': in some quite basic and essential sense they co-exist with
us, they exist in relation to us. The fall of Lucifer and other angels
does not modify this position. It simply means that whereas their
'synanthropy' once worked in our favour, now it works against our
interests. Thus the fallen angels become demons and the demons
tempters of men to evil. Admittedly, their enterprise is a hopeless
one. As Bulgakov says:

> Satanism is an adventure that is going nowhere. Created by God and
> belonging to God, the world will return to him.[10]

But meanwhile, on the way, the evil angels can do a great deal of
damage. Their story is the prologue in heaven to that of the human
fall, the fall of man. Human evil is connected to angelic evil but it
must also be distinguished from it. Thanks to the clarity of their
intellects, the sin of the angels is deliberate, direct revolt against
God, and as such it is sheer evil, pure evil. Human evil begins in a
way that is more complex, less conscious, less intense. As the
Genesis narrative teaches us, it contains large elements of decep-
tion, illusion and error. In the first stage of their collusion with
angelic evil, our proto-parents, the ancestors, were naïve and igno-

[9] Ibid., p. 170.
[10] Ibid., p. 174.

rant. But then in a second stage they showed what Bulgakov calls 'frivolity and curiosity' which was not at all innocent, because these vices showed the way 'filial love and confidence [towards God] were already growing cold in their hearts'.[11] That still leaves open the question of the immediate source of Adam's disobedience to the divine command – a command which Bulgakov supposes was either directly infused into his awareness by God or transmitted through the angels. For Bulgakov, the immediate source of man's disobedience was Adam's thought that

> through the elements of the world he was going to be capable of raising himself to the highest degree of spiritual life and knowledge.[12]

In the words of the tempter to Eve, 'you will be like God' (Genesis 3: 5). But in fact the opposite happened. Man's awareness of his own spirituality became darkened. The balance between the flesh and the spirit was disturbed. Man became a victim to death as we now know it.

We have seen how at this moment man is introduced not only to evil but to the moral good. In *The Bride of the Lamb* Bulgakov makes it plain that moral good is not just a matter of striving virtuously to observe various values in human life, which is the impression that could be gained from *The Lamb of God*. Rather, moral good is an attraction to the ontological good which from now on will be at war with evil in human history. Fighting on the side of the good – both ontological and moral, then – is the power of Theanthropy, Godmanhood; fighting against it is the evil which now acquires in man, in the world, a creative force of its own. Bulgakov points up the big difference between evil in the realm of the angels and evil in our own world. Evil in the realm of the angels affects only their own persons. But with us it affects our nature, and our human environment, so that from now on every human being who enters the world (the question of the Most Pure Virgin does not arise at this stage in Bulgakov's work) is infected by evil and assimilates it, making it his or her own. Through our common human nature, all new human hypostases suffer from original sin.

---

[11] Ibid., p. 175.
[12] Ibid., p. 176.

Original sin

A number of modern Eastern Orthodox theologians are rather
sceptical about original sin.[13] Quite often they maintain that it is a
specifically Western theological doctrine, deriving from the work
of St Augustine who has never been as influential in the East as in
the West.[14] But Bulgakov is not of their number. Not only does he
have a high doctrine of original sin. He also gives it great prominence in his dogmatic scheme. In fact he calls it 'the axis of the
Christian doctrine of salvation'.

> With the fall of Adam in Paradise, the entire human race fell. It was
> redeemed by the New Adam, Christ.[15]

The Church's doctrine of salvation starts out, he says, from the
following premises.

> First, the unity of the human race in Adam and the loss of its origi-
> nal condition. Secondly, the common nature, weakened by sin,
> inherited by all human beings, as well as the personal fault of each
> one through his or her sharing in sin; thirdly, the redemption
> accomplished by Christ with the restoration not only of the first
> created man, Adam, but of each man in whom original sin is effaced
> by Baptism.[16]

This summary is identical with the common Catholic doctrine in
West and East alike. To this doctrine, writes Bulgakov, numerous
liturgical texts bear witness. To reject it would be to call into question faith in the redemption, which the Church has defended
'jealously' since Augustine's quarrel with the Pelagians.

   This is not to say, however, that he is unaware of the difficulties
some of his Eastern colleagues have felt. The Greek Fathers have

---

[13] See for example Father John Romanides' work, *To protopaterikon hamartêma*
(Athens, 1989, 2nd edition).

[14] For the difficult relationship so far as the Russian Church is concerned, *see* M.
I. Tataryn, *Augustine and Russian Orthodoxy: Russian Orthodox Theologians and
Augustine of Hippo. A Twentieth-Century Dialogue* (New York and Oxford, 2000).

[15] NA, p. 178. For Bulgakov's theology of the fall see also *Kupina neopalimaya*, the
Marian volume of the Little Trilogy, at pp. 21–76. Bulgakov's acute lack of
sympathy for later Scholasticism's theology of the fall derives in part from a
degree of confusion about what is 'normal' before the fall and what is 'natural'
then, as well as a tendency to assume in the Latin Scholastic authors an opposition between nature and grace.

[16] NA, p. 178.

their own ways of speaking of the reign of sin in post-Adam humanity and sometimes these are less radical than Augustine's. Bulgakov
shows the limits of his acquaintance with Latin theology when he
says that after Augustine all later Western theologians were
committed to the view that original sin was for the descendants of
Adam a personal fault. But St Thomas Aquinas, to take just one
example, says clearly that in the children of Adam original sin is
called 'sin' only by way of an analogy. On the other hand, says
Bulgakov, something like Augustine's doctrine is necessary if we
are to do justice to the Church's practice of baptizing tiny infants.
A further problem, though, is that for modern evolutionary
thought the origin of our species presents no empirical evidence of
a state of original perfection. What Bulgakov is seeking, evidently,
is a theology of original sin which will go beyond Augustine while
retaining the basic thrust of the North African doctor's teaching.
How does he frame this?

He is brisk with the supporters of evolution. There is no problem
with the notion of evolution as such. It fits with the notion that the
'seeds' of creaturely wisdom planted by God are developing in
purposive stages. But by itself the evolution of the animal kingdom
could only produce an 'anthropomorphic animal'. It could not
produce man. The human spirit is not, then, a product of evolution but 'bears the mark of the Eternal'. Issuing from God, it
'comes to inhabit a form of organic life brought [by the evolutionary process] to the maximum of its relative [animal] perfection'.[17]
The appearance of a 'theomorphic' – God-like – spirit in the first
human creature is a mystery. It occupies a hiatus in the causal
chain of nature. It is not a matter then, for empirical investigation.
If known about, it can only be by other means, from other sources.
There is, then, no reason to rule out the claim that Adam enjoyed
an initial spiritual perfection. Indeed, the opposite is true. There
is every reason to rule that claim in. A unique event took place
when Adam came to be. The moving, purposive life of nature –for
which the foundation is of course created wisdom but here
Bulgakov calls it in a Platonist phrase 'the soul of the world' – was
in an extraordinary moment hypostatized as Adam. Animal nature
became hypostatic. It became in Adam a person. The Fall, then, is
in some kind of time, but it is not in empirical time. It is in a time
which, like the act of creation itself, established the limits and character of the world now explored by scientists and indeed by
common sense experience. As a meta-historical moment, it takes

17 Ibid., p. 191.

place on the threshold of our world, as the world of human expe-rience is coming to be. Using the philosophical language of Immanuel Kant (1724–1804), Bulgakov calls Adam's perfection and fall an 'a priori' of history: in other words, these are truths you need to get hold of in order to understand man in history as we know him to be. The upshot is, then, that Bulgakov agrees not only with Irenaeus but also with Augustine: the father of our race, though childlike, enjoyed a wonderful plenitude and harmony of being, which he lost for us. The myths of a golden age of human-ity which various cultures possess may well be obscure memories of that. So there is also a sense in which when Adam fell it was not only from relative ontological emptiness. In another sense, he was relatively ontologically full.

But how do we experience original sin now, then? For Bulgakov it is a reality for the human species as such; it works in and through our species with a mysterious power; it has entirely concrete effects. Like everything else about a species, it is something that modifies the quality of life and being of each and every individual who belongs to that species. Since the first Adam was the created prototype of our species the harm he did human nature in his own person affected our nature too, like a sort of hereditary illness. But given the closeness of the bond between nature and hypostasis, it could not affect our nature without to some degree damaging our persons as well. Bulgakov proposes that each created person, when he or she comes into the world, as a hypostasis about to be united with human nature, ratifies this fall of Adam – at any rate in the sense of consenting to receive this sick human nature derived from the first parent. This is a theologically unnecessary concept – unnecessary because Bulgakov fails to realize that celebrating infant baptism for the washing away of the guilt of original sin does not necessarily entail ascribing to the new born child personal guilt in the ordinary sense of those words.

Certainly, Bulgakov goes way beyond Augustine when he suggests that Adam was in some sense a pan-hypostasis, a hyposta-sis who included beforehand in himself all our persons, our hypostases, and not simply our human nature. The suggestion is reminiscent of a hint dropped by Origen in his *Commentary on the Letter to the Romans*.

God cast Adam out of paradise and established him in this earth, in contrast with the paradise of delights; and this was the condemna-tion of his sin, which has undoubtedly come down to all men. For all have been set in this place of humiliation and this vale of tears:

either because all who were born of him were in the loins of Adam and were cast out of paradise together with him; or else it means that in some other mysterious way which is known to God alone each individual has been thrust out of paradise and has received condemnation.[18]

Bulgakov has an extra philosophical reason for taking up this cue. He thinks that, unless we can say we were incorporated in Adam in our persons as well as our nature, there would not have been from Adam onwards a single human world. Each hypostasis, if it was just an individual left to itself, would have its own world, its own world-view, without having necessarily any communication with other people. In other words, Bulgakov has a high metaphysical interpretation of what St Paul and such later Fathers as St Irenaeus meant by our solidarity with Adam, our incorporation in Adam as our natural Head. Moreover, without such a high metaphysical interpretation, so Bulgakov thinks, we cannot fully understand what is meant by saying we are all incorporated in the new Adam, the second Adam, Jesus Christ. The Word of God is our heavenly Prototype, just as Adam was our earthly prototype. When the Word takes on our human nature he unites with himself in a certain way not just the nature we all share (that was the conviction of the Fathers at large) but the many hypostases, the many persons, that live in our nature. Of course, such a relative union will not mean salvation for this or that person unless they ratify it by an act of their own freedom through voluntary adherence to Christ in faith. But every human person as soon as he or she comes into existence already enjoys a certain relation with the Word who took our humanity in blessed Mary. This goes beyond what many of the Fathers say, but it has a certain plausibility. If the Word in assuming our human nature united himself to that degree with all who share that nature, then he united himself to them as persons, because in the case of human beings, the bearers of our nature are always persons.

For Bulgakov though, as the Latin theologians also say, while the most obvious consequence of the Fall is the instability which comes over us, and in particular the difficulty we have in governing our passions, the worst consequence of the Fall is failure in our most fundamental vocation. This is not so immediately apparent but it is far more basic than an occasional struggle with gluttony, anger or lust. Our most fundamental vocation is Godmanhood but by yielding to the temptation to seize divinity on the Devil's terms ('You

[18] Origen, *In epistolam ad Romanos,* V. 4.

shall be like God' says Satan) we sought to be divine in the wrong
way. At once we became distanced from God, our love grew cold,
we lost the original harmony of grace and became subject to
deviant desires. In this sense, our struggle with the disordered
passions comes from the collapse of our God-given vocation, not
the other way round (our God-given vocation collapsing because
we lost the struggle with those passions). What sort of freedom
have we left and to what extent can God help us to use it to recover
our position? This will be our next topic.

Freedom and Providence

Bulgakov leads into the topics of freedom and providence by
looking at what happened to our liberty in the Fall. The Fall enfee-
bles us in our liberty and creative energy. It does not destroy the
image of God in us, but it obscures it. Despite some occasional
extreme statements by St Augustine, Catholicism and Orthodoxy,
remarks Bulgakov, are agreed on this, over against magisterial
Protestantism, the doctrine of the sixteenth-century Reformers.
The potential we have in our freedom is impaired but not wholly
ruined. We can avoid using our freedom so as to do evil, but our
capacity to use it for the good is variable, unreliable. This would
not make sense, writes Bulgakov, if freedom meant the power of
self-determination of an autonomous self (that is how, for instance,
the classical German philosopher Johann Gottlieb Fichte
(1762–1814), understood it). For then freedom would either be
absolute and total or it would not exist. The question, 'Are you
free?', on this view, can only be answered 'Yes' or 'No'. But
freedom is not like that. Freedom is, in Bulgakov's word, 'modal'.
It can have different ways (modes) of being, various degrees of
intensity. We can have more or less of it. Freedom does not have to
be all or nothing.

As a result of the Fall, then, we are still free but our freedom is
unstable. This instability is both bad and good. Bad, in that, as hard
experience shows, people stand on the edge of a slippery slope,
down which their abuse of the freedom they retain goes from bad
to worse. Good, in that this very instability provides an opportunity
for divine action, divine grace. It is the way our hypostasis lies open
to transformation which, says Bulgakov, 'allows the possibility of
salvation by redemption': that is, the possibility of God bringing us
to our eternal destiny (salvation) precisely by rescuing us from evil
(redemption). In simple language: God has an opportunity

because we cannot trust ourselves not to make a mess of our lives. Original sin tends to dehumanize man, to drag him down to the animal level. There is nothing to be said in favour of that. But original sin also has the effect of making us aware of a 'tragic contradiction' between what we would like to do and be and what we actually do and are.[19] St Paul analysed that in the Letter to the Romans (7: 18b–19):

> I can will what is right, but I cannot do it.For I do not the good I want, but the evil I do not want is what I do.

That awareness on our part gives Providence its opportunity, and it will take it all the way to the Incarnation of the Son of God.

The nature of Providence

What, then, is Providence? Providence, which we know about, says Bulgakov, only from revelation, concerns two things: the preservation (first) and the direction (secondly) of the created world. Granted that the being of the world is already established in the Wisdom of God, the world's foundations are necessarily beyond the power of anything to destroy. The creative act which brings the world into existence guarantees its being. In this sense, the world would appear not to need a further divine act to sustain it in being, to preserve it. And in fact the lion's share of Bulgakov's doctrine of Providence concerns the second function of a doctrine of Providence: the way God guides the world he wisely made. For Sacred Scripture, divine Providence guides the world and human history within it either directly or through the mediation of the angels (a point particularly clear in the last book of Scripture, St John's Apocalypse, to which Bulgakov had a special devotion).

Bulgakov's initial aim in his theology of Providence is to dissuade us from any form of deism. Deism is the philosophy which holds that though God creates the world, he only does so in the sense of establishing its initial conditions of existence. He sets it going, sets it ticking – quite a good word to use since the usual comparison is with a clock, which needs a clock-maker to start it off but then has a life of its own. That would be, of course, a mechanical life, and in the case of the world, then, the comparison suggests a world closed in on itself, closed off to any further

[19] Ibid., p. 208.

impulses from the side of God. Bulgakov calls deism 'an extreme form of anti-sophianity'.[20] It is so much at the extreme from a vision of the world as founded on and in the Wisdom of God as to amount practically speaking to atheism. For Bulgakov, the creation is not just a momentary exercise of the divine will, when God said 'Let there be a world', and there was one. As we have seen, creation is founded on the abiding relationship of God's uncreated Wisdom to his created wisdom. Both are the Wisdom of God: only their mode of being differs, not their content. God and the world lead a 'common life'.[21] That is not, says Bulgakov, an altogether satisfactory phrase, not when we think of the abyss that separates God and the creature. Yet there is a 'commonality' between them, there is something they have in common: namely, wisdom. Created wisdom turns the world towards God and uncreated Wisdom turns God towards the world. This entails that God is not only Creator, he is also Providence.

Bulgakov considers the objection that such a view relativises God and deprives him of his true transcendence as the Absolute. He denies this is so. Of course God remains the Absolute, the utterly transcendent One of whom we must speak by saying what he is not, and saying how he is beyond our definitions.[22] In the Greek patristic tradition that means two things. First, the Greek Fathers say of God what he is not by using the form of speech called the 'alpha-privative', putting the letter alpha in front of an adjective so as to negate its force rather as we do with the part of speech 'un' in English. (God is unutterable, unknowable, and so forth). Secondly, the Greek Fathers use the modifier 'hyper' to express how God exceeds all our definitions because he is whatever we say of him in a superlative way that exceeds the normal force of words. (God is not just good but super-good, not just beautiful but super-lovely and so on.) Bulgakov is keen that we should continue to adore God with our minds as the transcendent Absolute in these ways. But he insists it is central to the revelation of God in Scripture that the Absolute also determined himself by an outpouring of love to be the world's Creator. The divine life has flowed out into the realm of nothingness. In creaturely wisdom God's Wisdom lives extra-divinely, outside God, in the world.

---

[20] Ibid., p 210: *krainyaya forma sofieborstva*.
[21] Ibid.
[22] Ibid., pp. 211–212.

Providence and the angels

Of course, Bulgakov does not think that everything about the world as it currently exists fully reflects God's wisdom. The seeds of wisdom have been sown, but the conditions of their development are not all equally propitious. The holy angels, for instance, express the sophianic archetypes to perfection. And yet they are certainly part of the creation. They are the 'heavens' which God made in the beginning, or what the Creed calls the 'invisible' things God has made. Earthly reality, on the other hand, the 'visible' things of the Creed, still has something chaotic about it, despite the 'creative energies and vital principles' which reflect its habitation by wisdom. This contrast between the heavens and the earth, the angelic realm and the rest of the cosmos, explains, indeed, why the angels are frequently the intermediaries of divine Providence in our regard. The angels are the guardians of the non-angelic creation's sophianic quality, and they now have their 'time cut out': their task is a vast one. How so?

Even without the Fall we earthlings should have needed God's providential guidance. But since the Fall the need for that providential guiding has become greater still. Not only do we have the evil angels to contend with. Our reason, our rationality, has become clouded, darkened. (Notice here that Bulgakov says nothing about the perversion of our will, which at this juncture in such an account would normally be mentioned in a Catholic theology of sin and grace. This is a point we shall be returning to shortly.) The world has been damaged in its development. Not only is that development incomplete: that was true before the Fall. It is also off-track. And that is something new. Bulgakov cites the Letter to the Romans: the creation suffers and groans 'because of him who submitted it to vanity' (Romans 8: 20).

Bulgakov's chief interest in Providence is in how it relates to ourselves, to human beings. But he wants to make clear its overall context. Providence is the ongoing work of the divine Trinity which creates the world in Wisdom and keeps it by means of Wisdom. It is the work of the Father through his two 'hands', the Son and the Holy Spirit. Though the triune God makes providential use of the holy angels this should not be misunderstood. The angels do not introduce anything alien to our world. They simply help nature to become more fully itself, to realize its sophianity, the form the Creator always intended for it. They assist the world to become a symphony. Through them, Bulgakov writes, divine Providence:

unveils the luminous figure of divine Wisdom in the midst of the hostile 'nothing' which received being through [God's] creative act.[23]

The interplay of Providence and freedom

So what about man? What about the interplay – if that be the right word – between God's Providence and human freedom? It is easy to speak about Providence acting through the angels on non-human nature (easy theologically, at any rate, if not philosophically). That is because non-human nature is either pre-conscious, as with stones or plants, or, if conscious, it is at any rate 'anhypostatic', without hypostasis: animals are not persons and so they have no direct relation with God. But we humans are free spirits, able to engage directly with our Creator for good or for ill.

Now, says Bulgakov, someone might object, But surely, as a result of creating humankind in his own image God gives man the prerogative of making his own way in the world by his own divinely gifted resources. Should man need any other guidance from God – for example, via the holy angels – if he is already the image of God? If he is already a 'created god' with the Godlike gifts we see manifested every day in science and technology, art and literature, as well as in the virtues by which people make a success of living their daily lives? This question expects a similar answer to that given be secularized Protestant theology in the 1960s, for which prayer, especially petitionary prayer – asking God for help – was a waste of time or worse, because, it was said, man once redeemed in Christ was in a sense emancipated from dependence on God. He was man 'come of age' and so, like any adult, should stand on his own two feet. Bulgakov says this too is a misunderstanding. Liberal Christians, without realizing it, are adopting the principle of mangodhood, which is, actually, implicit atheism. Man is the image of God, yes. But, as he puts it:

> By its very nature, the image is in an indissoluble liaison with the Prototype it reflects.[24]

And Bulgakov draws from this the strong conclusion that the image of God in us only is in any full sense this relation with God when we are activating the image, when the image is functioning

[23] Ibid., p. 217.
[24] Ibid., p. 218.

in human activity. Unless we are continually relating ourselves to God, the image of God within us will become more and more distant from its divine Prototype. The fact that our being is sophianic does not mean we are automatically in a positive relation with God. The manner of our creation gives us 'unlimited possibilities of movement, both upwards and downwards'.[25] We need God's help, the help of his Providence, if we are to remain on course for the destiny for which the Wisdom of God has shaped us. In other words, we need the grace of God. We need God's Providence to make available to us fresh influxes of the divine energies, so that we can move towards our 'deification', towards 'Godmanhood', by becoming truly Godlike, truly holy. We need the grace of God not only to become what we were meant to be as creatures. We also need that grace so that what the Father has offered the world through the Incarnation of his Son and the Descent of the Holy Spirit at Pentecost may become a reality for our personal lives.

Grace and freedom

And this of course brings Bulgakov to the heart of the matter which is the inter-relation of God's causality and our creaturely liberty, the inter-relation of grace and freedom. Along with many other modern Orthodox theologians, Bulgakov has a shorthand term for this inter-relation, one borrowed as with so much in Eastern dogmatics from the Greek Fathers. He calls it the divine-human 'synergy', literally 'co-working', the collaboration of God and man. What he has to say is partially coloured by his rejection of the Augustinian-Thomist view of grace (Thomas building on Augustine and later Thomists building on Thomas). As usual when Eastern Christian writers take this line, there is a failure fully to appreciate the deeper way (compared with the common remarks of the Greek Fathers) in which St Augustine understood the human will. But before tackling these negative comments on Latin theology let us see what Bulgakov has to say that is positive, constructive.

Attempting – but not always succeeding – to leave behind the language of God's causal action in the world, not least in human freedom, Bulgakov offers the following picture. By relation to the divine Wisdom, created wisdom is not a secondary cause through which the Wisdom of God is communicated to the world. Rather,

[25] Ibid.

it is a 'reiteration' of the divine Wisdom outside the divine being
– in what is not God, indeed in the 'nothing' where or in which
God created the world. As the foundation of created being such
wisdom has within it the energy of the divine being, and so if we
are to speak in terms of causes at all, created wisdom is not so
much a secondary cause through which God, the primary cause,
acts as it is what Bulgakov calls the 'primary immanent [as distinct
from transcendent, then] cause of the world'.[26] Now the sophianity of the created – God's direct presence to the creation – is
nowhere more apparent than in the hypostatic realm of being:
namely, in persons. And it is persons who in their freedom receive
from God 'divine suggestions', suggestions that reach human
freedom through grace and bond or unite with that freedom
through *synergia* – 'synergistically'. The first and most general
form or degree (Bulgakov's words) of such grace is what he calls
'natural grace', offered man simply as such on the basis of his
nature. This grace is the 'energy of sophianity', an energy – we
could perhaps paraphrase that by the words 'a powerful impulse'
— God gives to human beings. Since this is the energy of sophianity, the wisdom in which we were created, this powerful impulse
does not aim to make us other than we were meant to be from
the beginning, because from the start we were intended for
Godmanhood. Right from the beginning men were meant to
become expressions of the Theanthropy. This is the only meaning
Bulgakov is willing to give to the idea of predestination, and even
then he will not accept the prepositional prefix 'pre-' which, he
says, implies that God took a decision in time, which is ridiculous.
All God's plans are eternal. Natural grace, the energy of sophianity, does not overwhelm us (which is, he thinks, what grace
always does in Augustine and Thomas). Instead, it arouses us and
persuades us by, fundamentally, the force of love. The freedom
of the person, writes Bulgakov:

> remains invincible and impenetrable even for God. By his freely
> accepted kenosis as Creator and as Providence, God suspends his
> almighty power at the threshold of our freedom.[27]

And Bulgakov relates to this the words of the glorified Christ in the
Apocalypse (3: 20):

[26] Ibid., p. 243
[27] Ibid., p. 247.

Behold, I stand at the door and knock; if any one hears my voice and opens the door, I will come in to him and eat with him and he with me.

This 'door', comments Bulgakov, is itself freedom which is the 'foundation of . . . the reality of the creature in its relations with the Creator': a very strong statement.[28] Here freedom is not just an attribute of the human being, and specifically of his or her will. It is described as if it were the very foundation of their creaturely existence – that is, not in itself (for in that sense the foundation of humanity's creaturely existence can only be divine Wisdom) but *in our personal relations with God.*

What Bulgakov envisages is really two freedoms, one divine, the other human, that are fundamentally alike. And his key word for understanding the relation between God's gracious freedom and its human counterpart will be 'conformity'. To give us a taste of what such conformity may mean, he also uses a term from the Trinitarian disputes of the fourth century, by saying that divine and human freedom are 'of a like substance' or 'of a like nature': they have between them, he says, a *homoiousia*, an essential likeness.[29] In terms of his wider theology of wisdom – the single wisdom shared in different ways by God and the world, we might perhaps expect Bulgakov to say something of this kind. But there is more, and this 'more' very specifically concerns the theme of freedom. In the kenosis by which God condescends to 'place' his being beyond himself, in what was nothing, thus becoming the Creator of the world, he voluntarily limits his own freedom out of respect for the creature, above all the spiritual creature endowed with a freedom akin to his own. He gives his creature, especially his free spiritual creature – the angels and human beings – what Bulgakov calls 'a power of resistance' vis-à-vis God.[30] It is these two factors taken together that enable Bulgakov to speak about the interaction of essentially similar divine and human freedoms. These freedoms are 'essentially similar', above all because God conforms his freedom to ours, limiting his power to the 'measure' of the creature's receptivity. God will not act towards us by his grace beyond what we collaborate with him to receive.

[28] Ibid.

[29] In the patristic centuries, some bishops and ecclesiastical writers tried to find in the formula 'of a like substance' a mid-way position between the faith of the First Council of Nicaea (325) that the Father and the Son are 'of the same substance' and the belief of Arius that they are nothing of the kind.

[30] Ibid., pp. 252–253.

That might seem to indicate a rather bleak outlook for the world because so often human beings are not at all well-disposed to receive the grace of God. Bulgakov more or less admits as much. He writes:

> Thus Providence is a dialogue of the Wisdom and the all-powerfulness of God with the life of the free creature, in the course of which the infallible action of God is exercised in the world (with the participation of the angels) in conjunction with the action, hesitant and never infallible, of the free creature.[31]

But fortunately God can, as the English proverb has it, 'write straight with crooked lines'. So Bulgakov adds:

> Providence operates in an absolutely effective and inventive manner to redress and compensate for the work of this liberty ... , to lead the world along the path of salvation; nevertheless, it always respects the identity and autonomy of man.[32]

Somehow, despite resistance to grace, Providence finds a way to secure God's overall goal for humanity.[33]

We cannot know this way – or these ways – of Providence in their entirety but so far as the sacred history of the Bible is concerned divine revelation lifts a corner of the veil for us. Thus we know that in the history of Israel, despite its 'meanderings', its often very indirect course, full of wrong turnings and setbacks, God was preparing human salvation. We know that in the last book of the Bible, the Apocalypse of St John, we are given a symbolic account of the final destiny of the Church and the world. But a total account of the providential action of God in the world is impossible, precisely because the two freedoms – God's and our own – are constantly interacting, and the justification of what happens in the world is therefore not open to us as yet. At present, then, no 'rational theodicy', proving the justice of God to any reasonable person,

---

[31] Ibid., p. 254.

[32] Ibid.

[33] In Thomistic language: Bulgakov accepts that God is the creature's exemplary cause as also its final cause, but he will not hold with God's being its 'efficient' cause. The reason is surely a misunderstanding of the due autonomy conferred on the creature's existence *by virtue of its very dependence on divine agency*. The free action of creatures derives entirely from them, if also entirely from God, albeit in different modes. On this *see* G. Emery, O. P., 'Questions d'aujourd'hui sur Dieu', in S.–Th. Bonino, O. P., et al., *Thomistes, ou l'actualité de saint Thomas d'Aquin* (Paris, 2003), p. 91.

is possible. Only in the fullness of time, at the Last Day, shall the evidence for God's justice appear, when all his ways will be made plain. As St Paul tells the Corinthians (1 Corinthians 13, 9–10):

> Our knowledge is imperfect and our prophecy is imperfect; but when the perfect comes, the imperfect will pass away.

Synergism in Scripture

However, what we can definitely say on the basis of Scripture is that these relations of God and man are synergistic. Thus near the beginning of the Old Testament revelation, in the sagas of the patriarchs, we hear how Jacob wrestled with God in the form of a stranger (Genesis 32: 24–30), in what Bulgakov calls a 'theo-polemic' act of *synergia*, a collaboration with God which takes the paradoxical form of a struggle with him. That certainly implies a distinct liberty for Jacob over against God. Or to take another example of what he has in mind: in biblical prophecy, we see a 'synergy' of one human gift, the gift of historical imagination, and one divine gift, the gift of inspiration. The prophets make use of a normal human gift, the capacity to discern coherence in historical events and to discern their tendencies and probable outcomes. But in their case, this natural gift is strengthened and clarified by divine assistance, so that in the Old Testament, they can grasp the overall direction of God's plan for his people, and in the New Testament actually apply this to particular figures and events. At the summit of Israel's spiritual development we have a very differ-ent and even more exalted example of synergy or collaboration, when the woman who is to be the Mother of the Lord declares her total obedience to God: 'Behold, the servant of the Lord' (Luke 1: 38). And then at the climax of all salvation history, in the life of Jesus Christ, we find One in whom the divine and human natures co-existed in a perfect synergy. That – the Incarnation – is not a 'normal' example of synergism, which is a collaboration between the tri-hypostatic God and a human hypostasis. In Jesus, there was no distinct human hypostasis. Nonetheless the Son of God took on himself a human will as part and parcel of the humanity he assumed in his holy Mother. As the Sixth Ecumenical Council teaches, the two wills of the Word incarnate, the divine and the human, collaborated in him in perfect integrity. That is only conceivable, thinks Bulgakov, if the Word voluntarily limited his divine freedom, so as to initiate a genuine interaction with the human freedom he had assumed. In this sense, the collaboration of divine and human freedom in Christ is the model for our practice of collaboration with God. Jesus teaches synergy in his doctrine of prayer. 'Ask and it will be given you' (Matthew 7: 7); 'whatever you ask in prayer you will receive' (Matthew 21: 22). Accordingly, Bulgakov sets out for us a sort of 'ontology of prayer'.

> Prayer is a form of immediate synergy, a living encounter of God and man. By prayer as glorification, man is penetrated by the life of God and, to this extent, is deified by contemplating God's mysteries and marvels.[34]

Grace as deification

The phrase 'is deified' tells us that Bulgakov does not think the only kind of grace is 'natural grace', the grace of sophianity. It is already indeed a grace, in the sense of a wonderful gift, that God should want us to coincide with the idea he has of us in his divine mind, and by his Providence should so guide our lives that this can come about, if we let our freedom collaborate with his. But the will of God is not just that we should reach the fullness of our sophianic being. It goes beyond that. Or rather God calls us beyond even that. As Bulgakov writes:

> In the true sense of the word, grace is precisely the power of deification by which what is created is surpassed in man, so that the creature is raised beyond the limits of its natural or physico-sophianic being.[35]

This comes about when God communicates to the creature a share in his own personal divine life. He does so *in the manner in which* he realizes the Theanthropy, the divine plan to unite humanity with himself through the sending of the Son and the Holy Spirit.

Considering all we have heard about natural grace, Bulgakov is remarkably brief on this topic, but then he still has the rest of his theology of Christ, the Holy Spirit, Our Lady, the angels and saints to lay before us. But we can note some points here, by way of anticipation. It is by sophianic conformity to God through 'natural

[34] NA, p. 271.
[35] Ibid., p. 270. This means that, despite what he imagines, Bulgakov is *not* an exponent of Baianism, the Latin deviation in the theology of grace condemned by Church authority in 1567.

grace' that the divinization of the human becomes possible – and
a way is opened to a life in God that will know no end, either in this
world or in the world to come (a favoured theme, this, of the Greek
patristic tradition, most classically expressed in St Gregory of
Nyssa's [c. 330 –c. 395] idea of *epektasis*, 'stretching forward'). The
Father sends the Son and the Spirit to adopt men as his children,
uniting us with the Son not in any way to suppress the created
person but on the contrary to transfigure him or her so that they
acquire in Christ their truest hypostatic face. And this is the work
of the Spirit who realizes this union with Christ, rendering man
pneumatic and introducing him into the love of the Most Holy
Trinity. Its figure is the glorified Mary: 'a hypostasis created and
raised up and thus communing with the life of the three divine
persons'.[36] This is the endless, ever developing life in God of the
creation, its *aeviternitas* as distinct from the *aeternitas* proper to God
alone. Bulgakov stresses that the gift of grace is not itself hypostatized. Those Latin divines (like Peter Lombard, c. 1100–1160) who
have tried to identify the gift with the Giver (that is, with the Holy
Spirit) encountered problems. Surprisingly, but consistently,
Bulgakov calls grace an 'impersonal', *bezlichnii*, gift, even if the
gift's actualization is proper to the Holy Spirit, the Dispenser of
gifts, which themselves, however, bear the 'seal' of all three
Trinitarian persons. The effect of grace is always in some way 'the
gradual and unceasing *rapprochement* of the divine and human
essences',[37] Godmanhood in the accomplishing. The various
distinctions, however imperfect, made in the Schools about the
'different aspects of the doctrine of grace, its classes and categories'[38] have a degree of theological and pastoral utility as they try
to identify the many ways of this ongoing divine work. Here is
another surprising judgment, remarkably favourable to Latin
Scholasticism in an area where many would see its methods as
dangerously over-schematic when applied to what is ultimately the
inter-personal reality of God's grace. One reason is that Bulgakov
finds the Latin distinctions cognate with a feature of the Orthodox
theological tradition present – albeit in a low-key way – in his work:
namely, that fourteenth-century Byzantine movement in defence
of our gracious divinization known as 'Palamism'. If, as Bulgakov
thinks, Gregory Palamas (c. 1296 – 1359) does not present the
divine energies as fully hypostatised, leaving the relations of the

[36] Ibid., p. 328.
[37] Ibid., p. 331.
[38] Ibid., p. 332.

Holy Trinity with the energies of God's nature less than fully explored, those energies are in any case 'undetermined' owing to

> their number and many forms, since their reception by man depends on his own diversity and the different degrees of his spiritual development.[39]

A second reason for exploiting an impersonal vocabulary of grace is that for Bulgakov personalistic language in these matters can be overdone. Grace works not only on our consciousness but also on our unconscious life, including that of the body. As the hesychast monks patronized by Palamas would say, the light of Mount Thabor, mountain of the Transfiguration, pierces through awareness from below or from within. That is described nearer to Bulgakov's lifetime by that marvellous nineteenth-century Russian saint Seraphim of Sarov (1759–1833). And yet ultimately this is always in the service of the inter-personal encounter, as Christian prayer testifies. Thinking back to the pre-Revolutionary controversy on Athos, Bulgakov calls prayer in this connection 'the sacrament of the Name of God'.[40]

In conclusion we must return to the theme of the conformity of the two freedoms (which is where his theology of prayer in the Trilogies chiefly belongs). I mentioned that Bulgakov does not really understand St Augustine, and after him St Thomas, on freedom. This is because he does not see that, in the condition of original sin, the drive of our freedom – of our will – towards God is blocked. It needs to be unblocked, to be liberated. At a deep level the will has itself to be freed before we can choose the divine good, the good that is God. When God intervenes to act on our will at its deepest source, he does not – as Bulgakov seems to think – despise our freedom by treating us as though we were machines or marionettes (two of Bulgakov's favourite comparisons when outlining the Augustinian-Thomist theology of grace). On the contrary, he acts so as to release the spontaneity of our wills, to renew our freedom from within. And as our Creator, to whom we owe everything, including our capacity for free choice, this is no invasion of us. He is already, as Augustine wrote in the *Confessions*, 'more intimate to me than I am to myself'.[41]

---

[39] Ibid., p. 335.
[40] Ibid., p. 337: *tainodeistvie Imeni Bozhiya*.
[41] *Tu autem eras interior intimo meo*: Augustine, *Confessiones* III. 6, 11.

5

The Basis of the Incarnation

The advent of paganism

After the expulsion of our first parents from Paradise, the religious situation of humanity was in a bad way. The elements of cosmic nature, the world of plants and animals, retained much of their sophianity as did human nature itself. That meant that these things continued to reflect divinity in some fashion. But fallen man easily misunderstood the reflection of divinity in them. He no longer distinguished readily between the created and the divine, hence the pagan worship of gods identified with the animal world, vegetation and the yearly renewal of nature, or the pagan cultus of divinized heroes and rulers. That does not mean, Bulgakov hastens to add, that all paganism was in every respect evil. In the Letter to the Romans, Paul says that idolaters are without excuse since 'what can be known about God is plain to them, because God has shown it to them' (Romans 1: 19). As Bulgakov points out, the words 'God has shown it to them' suggest a more active engagement on God's part than simply the idea that pagans could look at his works and judge for themselves who made them – the other idea found in this section of Paul's Letter. He thinks the Holy Spirit was here and there active in paganism, which if true would explain St Peter's words to the household of Cornelius in the Acts of the Apostles (10: 34):

> God shows no partiality, but in every nation [including, then, pagan nations] any one who fears him and does what is right is acceptable to him.

However, at best such inspirations of the Holy Spirit made possible a genuine understanding of the Wisdom of God, the divine nature. They did not entail personal communion with God, the disclosure of the divine hypostases. They did not involve *person to person encounter* with the God who is not just divine being, divine nature, divine Wisdom, but a tri-hypostatic Personality. That is another way of saying that these religions – Hinduism, Buddhism, traditional African religion or whatever, are not *revealed religions*.

The religion of Israel

When we do come across genuinely revealed religion it is in Israel, and what we find straight away, on Bulgakov's interpretation of the Old Testament, is that revealed religion is essentially preparation for the Incarnation. How does Bulgakov claim to establish that? Essentially, in three stages. First, the religion of the Old Testament is strongly personal. God speaks to man by his Word and inspires him by his Spirit thus creating a personal communion between himself and Israel by means of signs: the theophanies to the patriarchs and Moses; the giving of the Law and its attendant worship. Secondly, Bulgakov follows the great majority of the Church Fathers in holding that in the Lord's disclosures of himself to Israel, it was already the second person of the Holy Trinity, the Logos, the Son of God, who was communicating. As always, the Father is the hypostasis who does not do the revealing work immediately but rather so acts that he is revealed – revealed in and by the hypostasis of the Son. Many theologians would argue that Lord God of Israel, as named in the Hebrew Bible with the Tetragrammaton, the holy name of YHWH, is the Father of the Son, because that would make better sense of some texts in the Gospels. But following the majority view of his patristic sources, Bulgakov prefers to think that YHWH is the Word. As he puts it:

> The immediate divine subject in the Old Testament is the same as in the New: the second hypostasis, the Logos.[1]

And then thirdly and finally in his attempt to show that the entire sacred history of Israel leads up to the Incarnation, Bulgakov holds that the revelation given in the Old Testament, though 'divine in its origin and content', was also human. It was deliberately fitted to human needs. Which is to say, it was already *theanthropic*, already concerned with the divine-human union that was going to come about in the God-man Jesus Christ.

[1] AB, p. 190.

Now Bulgakov is keen on the idea that the Father never acts in revelation without using simultaneously his two hands, the Son and the Spirit, so we shall expect that in this account of the build-up to the Incarnation he will have a good deal to say about the Holy Spirit. And so it proves. He identifies with the Holy Spirit of the New Covenant the Old Testament Spirit of the Lord who descended upon the prophets as they uttered the Word of God in their oracles, and thus became the Word's interpreters. In the Old Testament the Spirit is given to the prophets so that they can receive the Word. Bulgakov is able to cite here the Book of Ezekiel where the prophet says, 'The Spirit entered into me ... and I heard [the Lord – which means for Bulgakov the Logos] speaking to me' (2: 2). In this way, the joined economies of the Son and the Spirit in the revelation to Israel anticipate what will happen at the Incarnation. At the Annunciation, the Spirit who rests on the Son in the eternal Trinity will make possible the union of our humanity with the Son of God in the womb of Mary. And later the Spirit will descend at the river Jordan to consecrate that humanity for the saving mission at the Baptism of Jesus by the Forerunner, St John.

Finally, Bulgakov links to the Incarnation the Old Testament revelation of the glory of God. The glory of God for Bulgakov, we remember, always follows on the revelation of the heavenly Wisdom in whose image the world of man was created. That Wisdom has at its heart the humanity of God, which means that the glory of God, inseparable as this is from God's Wisdom, must have the humanity of God at its centre likewise. Bulgakov finds that confirmed in the vision of the divine glory in the opening chapter of Ezekiel where the prophet writes:

> Above the firmament ... there was the likeness of a throne, in appearance like sapphire; and seated above the likeness of a throne was a likeness as it were of a human form. (Ezekiel 1: 26)

This is the One like a son of Man who came on the clouds of heaven (a sign of the glory) to the Ancient of Days in Daniel 7, and was presented before him (verse 13). Thus, Bulgakov feels he can rest his case. The Bible of the Jews looks forward to the moment when the divine Son took our human flesh in Blessed Mary.

Ground and rationale of the Incarnation

What, then, is the foundation of the Incarnation: the ground and rationale for it, how it happened and the reason it happened?[2] The ground, the question of how it happened, is easy to deal with. The Incarnation belongs with the eternal counsel or eternal plan of God. Christ is what St Peter calls in his first Letter the

> Lamb without blemish or spot [who] was destined before the foundation of the world but was made manifest at the end of the times for your sake. (I Peter 1: 19b, 20)

In Christ, God chose us, cites Bulgakov from the Letter to the Ephesians, 'before the foundation of the world' (1: 4), having

> destined us in love to be his sons through Jesus Christ, according to the purpose of his will, to the praise of his glorious grace which he freely bestowed on us in the Beloved. (Ephesians 1: 5–6)

By this God

> has made known to us in all wisdom and insight the mystery of his will, according to his purpose which he set forth in Christ, as a plan for the fulness of time, to unite all things in him, things in heaven and things on earth (Ephesians 1: 9–10)

That is

> the plan of the mystery hidden for ages in God who created all things; that through the Church the manifold wisdom of God might now be made known to the principalities and powers in the heavenly places. This was according to the eternal purpose which he has realised in Christ Jesus our Lord (Ephesians 3: 9–11a)

The eternal design of God is to manifest his love for us not only in creation but also in the Incarnation of the Son, following the words of Jesus in St John's Gospel (3: 16–17):

> God so loved the world that he gave his only Son, that whoever believes in him should ... have eternal life.

All of which raises the question for Bulgakov, would the

---

[2] Compare the Christological section of L. A. Zander, *Bog i mir*, op. cit., pp. 72–132.

Incarnation have happened anyway, even if Adam had never fallen?

This is a familiar question in Latin theology since the Middle Ages, so it is interesting to see it raised here explicitly by an Eastern writer. Bulgakov's view is similar to that of John Duns Scotus (*c.* 1265–1308), the mediaeval Scottish Franciscan. The Incarnation, he says, is not the means only of the redemption. It is the means of God's showing his love for his creation. And this is something more. So much more that Bulgakov echoes (probably without being aware of the fact) the theology of the later Franciscan school, when he says that God created the world so as to become incarnate there. He made the world for the sake of the Incarnation.

Bulgakov admits that the Fathers of the Church place the Incarnation overwhelmingly in a soteriological perspective. It was a soteriological act, aimed at getting humanity out of the hole into which it had fallen. Thus in his *Commentary on John*, Origen declares that had man not sinned:

> we may suppose that [the divine Son] would have remained Wisdom and Word and Life; and certainly Truth. But he would not have had all the other attributes which he took upon himself for our sake.[3]

And for St Athanasius

> Our guilt was the cause of the descent of the Word, and our transgression called forth his loving-kindness, so that he came to us, and the Lord was displayed among men.[4]

But Bulgakov argues while indeed it was that, it was also more than that. In a sense the Incarnation was independent of the need for redemption. What is Bulgakov's justification for claiming this? It is no particular text of Scripture. He justifies it by way of analysis of the wording of the Nicene Creed, or the Creed of Nicaea-Constantinople to give it what should probably be its proper name. That Creed declares that we believe in Jesus Christ the Father's Son, our Lord, who became incarnate 'for us men and for our salvation'. In Bulgakov's proposal, the bishops at the Councils that promulgated this Creed were not given to useless repetitions of words. The phrase 'for us men' has a more general significance

---

[3] Origen, *Commentarium in Ioannem*, I. 20.
[4] Athanasius, *De Incarnatione*, 4.

than the following formula 'and for our salvation', so that the
second formula can be regarded as a particular application of the
first. God became incarnate in order to crown his works of love for
the human race: he did so 'for us men'. But additionally or
complementarily or by application of this first rationale for the
Incarnation, he took into account the fact that, at the time –
indeed, throughout all time since the Fall – we human beings
stood in need of redemption and not just consummation, reconciliation with God and not just the completion of his work. In other
words, the Incarnation was not simply 'for us men'. It was also 'for
our salvation'.

Bulgakov puts the two points together in a very careful, nuanced
sentence when he writes:

> As a consequence of the fall, the Incarnation appeared as above all
> the means of salvation and redemption [that is, after all, how the
> Bible and the Fathers predominantly present it]. But it conserved all
> the fulness of its meaning, even beyond that of redemption, because
> the latter in no way exhausted the Incarnation's significance.[5]

And perhaps once one has hold of this idea it is possible to see the
great texts of Ephesians on the divine plan in its light. If the
Incarnation was God's design from 'before the foundation of the
world', it can hardly have been the world's error in falling into sin
that made the Incarnation desirable. Someone may say, but God in
his prescience foreknew the Fall and that is why from the first
moment of the creation he had the Incarnation in view. Bulgakov
does not like this way of arguing which, he says, works better for
human decision-making than for divine. He means that the initiatives of the Holy Trinity are never just responses to dilemmas
people set for God. What he prefers to say is that from everlasting
God knew how one of the possibilities built into the creation was
the possibility of the world segregating itself from him. And this he
did know, and the manner in which he determined the
Incarnation should take place shows as much. In concrete terms
the Incarnation was carried out precisely as an act of redemption.
From all eternity the divine Son was marked out by the Father as
the *immolated* Lamb of God, the Lamb who would be sent to be
sacrificed.

However, this concession does not mean Bulgakov will abandon
the idea of a wider rationale for the Incarnation. It means simply
that he will have plenty to say about the Incarnation as a redemp-

[5] AB, p. 193.

tive work as well. He will offer material to satisfy both kinds of reader: in Latin terms we could call them the Scotists and the Thomists (though in fact St Thomas was more sympathetic to what would later be called the Scotist view than is often realised). Concretely, the Incarnation *does* mean salvation for fallen man. And yet:

the theology of the Incarnation cannot be limited by the categories of soteriology ... It must be understood in all the fulness of its meaning: from viewpoints theological and cosmic, anthropological, christological, soteriological.[6]

The general ontological foundations of the Incarnation

What, then, Bulgakov asks, are the 'general ontological foundations', *obshchii ontologichskii osnovanii*, of an Incarnation which goes beyond a merely redemptive action even though it takes such action's form?[7] The first answer to this question concerns God. And it is that God is love, Love as the Absolute in his own tri-hypostatic life, and, as the Creator, Love for us. Love for man not only as immaculate humanity in the unfallen state but as fallen man as well. And therefore a love willing to take on our human nature despite everything. The second answer concerns the creature, and it is that there exists a created world and in that world man with, Bulgakov says, 'everything that is immortal about him'.[8] The creature with which God unites himself must be, he writes, 'apt to receive God and to be worthy of receiving him, desiring this by its own will'.[9] As we shall see, though Bulgakov does not make it clear at first, this is a reference to two things: his theological anthropology and specifically his doctrine of the image of God in man, but also his Mariology, his theology of the Mother of God, Blessed Mary.

The Incarnation cannot happen from the side of the creature unless there is already in humanity a fundamental receptivity to God, a capacity to be united with God, however latent or dormant as a result of sin. There is no question of God becoming incarnate in a donkey. But in man there *is* the sort of fundamental receptivity required, as the doctrine of the image of God in man tells us.

[6] Ibid., p. 195.
[7] Ibid., p. 194.
[8] Ibid., p. 195.
[9] Ibid.

We have seen Bulgakov's high version of this doctrine. Even as an
animal animated by a human soul, man is already the only full realisation there is of the creaturely wisdom of God. Considered as a
microcosm of the universe, man with his world reflects the
Uncreated Wisdom with its world, the world of God. But man is not
only an animal with a human psyche. He also has a spirit which is
immortal and hypostatic; he is a person, as God the Word, through
whom all things were made, is a person. So the Prototype of man is
the Word in whom all the divine Wisdom coheres as a heavenly
archetype of humanity, the divine humanity. That answers the
question sometimes asked in mediaeval and later theology, Why
was it the Son who became man and not the Spirit or the Father?[10]
But it also informs us about those 'general ontological foundations' of the Incarnation. It tells us that one of the foundations of
the becoming human of the Word was already laid when man was
created as the image of God. Which is not to say of course that man
could ever have evolved into personal union with the Word. The
hypostatic union of God with man goes totally beyond human
powers or possibilities. It has to be a sovereignly free divine action.

Of course any action of one divine hypostasis has implications
for the others. There are not three Gods. There is only one tri-
hypostatic divine personality. So the Father and the Spirit must be
engaged in the Incarnation in ways we can, hopefully, state.
Bulgakov tries to do so. The Father who generated the Son now at
the Annunciation to Mary sends him on his mission into the world.
The Holy Spirit participates in the Incarnation by descending on
the Virgin Mary in order that the Logos may become flesh in her
womb, and subsequently by accompanying the Son made man, so
that the Incarnation may be shown to others and accomplish its
purpose. Bulgakov regards the missions of the Son and the Spirit
as inseparable in the Incarnation. He maintains that that is already
the view of the Councils which drew up the Ecumenical Creed,
when the bishops who produced the Creed settled on the words
'he [the Son] was conceived by the Holy Spirit from the Virgin
Mary'. That shows, says Bulgakov, that two acts were involved in the
Incarnation. There is not only the 'introduction, *vseleniya*, of the

---

[10] Bulgakov's answer is remarkably similar to one, at least, of the rationales for
     Incarnation in the person of the Word given by Thomas Aquinas, in *Summa
     Theologiae* IIIa., q. 3, a. 8. There is, for Thomas as for Bulgakov, a special affin-
     ity (in Aquinas, *convenientia*) between the Word and human nature, derived
     from the fact that 'the Word is the intelligible expression of divine wisdom,
     and as such is the source of human wisdom'. Highly pertinent are two other
     'questions' of this work: Ia., q. 34, a. 3, and Ia., q. 44, a. 3.

divine hypostasis into humanity'; there is also '[the] reception, *prinyatiya*, [of that hypostasis] by humanity'.[11] The first was the proper work of the Son, sent into the world by the Father; the second was the proper work of the Spirit, also sent by the Father but to the Virgin Mary.

The roles of Mary and Joseph

And so we come to the crucial role of Our Lady, the Lady Mary. As Bulgakov writes:

> The Logos could not take flesh that was tainted by the fall, aggravated by original sin; no more than such flesh could find within itself the will or power to receive the Incarnation.[12]

In a Catholic writer, such a statement would generally be a prelude to speaking about Mary's Immaculate Conception, the doctrine defined dogmatically by Pope Pius IX (1792–1878) in 1854. As an Eastern Orthodox Christian, Bulgakov has no such commitment to that doctrine, and indeed in the Mariological volume of his Little Trilogy, *The Burning Bush*, sets out at some length his difficulties with it. However, his own account of Mary's spiritual condition at the moment of the Annunciation comes fairly close to the Catholic position. He feels the need to affirm, as 'Immaculist' theologians did before the 1854 dogma was promulgated, the 'congruence' or fittingness that Mary (of all possible women) should become the Mother of God. For Mary to be suitable for that role it was, he claims, 'indispensable to enfeeble [original] sin to the point of rendering it inactive'. In the one who was to be the Mother of God, original sin 'lost its power'. In her, evil was reduced to a 'mere potentiality, *chistaya potentsiya*, without any influence on her will',[13] a statement so strong as to make one wonder quite what he means when he says that original sin was not without all effect in her. If its malign consequences in no way even influenced her will, what could its effects on her have been? (It would fit in with his theology of the Fall if Bulgakov answered this question by saying, Mary's intellectual outlook – her 'reason' – was shaded, obscured, even in what concerned her own destiny. But we must return to this in the context of the Mariology of the Little Trilogy.)

[11] AB, p. 200.
[12] Ibid.
[13] Ibid., p. 201.

Despite his formal denial of the Immaculate Conception, Bulgakov can hardly be accused of having a low Mariology. He will go into the subject more fully in the Lesser Trilogy but here he tells us that Mary's appearance in the world was the main achievement of Israel, the Church of the Old Testament people of God. Thanks to the grace of the Holy Spirit working among God's chosen people, generations and millennia prepared the Jewish holiness of which she was the finest flower. As he writes:

> The summit of this sanctity was attained in the Holy Virgin whose purity was such that she appeared 'full of grace', aureoled even before the Incarnation with the continuous light of the Holy Spirit.[14]

Though she was united to a humanity still held in the bonds of sin, no sin touched her soul, or the flesh she inherited from her holy parents, Joachim and Anna whom the Byzantine tradition calls 'the ancestors of God'. Already adorned with superabundant gifts of grace, she reached in the moment of the Annunciation a condition where she could bear the 'direct and immediate illumination of the Holy Spirit'.[15] It was then that the Incarnation happened. Unlike Eve, she does not hide from the Face of God among the trees of the garden. Instead, she 'advances with submission to receive the Lord'.[16] In the Mother of God, the creature at last realizes its own freedom, no longer in arbitrary decision-making but in loving obedience. And Bulgakov concludes

> The divine Motherhood is the human side of the Incarnation, the precondition without which it could never have happened. Heaven could not have stooped down to earth unless earth had received heaven.[17]

Mary thus receives the Word by the power of the Holy Spirit. Only the Word becomes incarnate but the Spirit carries out the Incarnation, making the Virgin the 'earthly heaven'. And so the hypostasis of the Logos is adopted by humankind, entering human nature and renovating it – making it new again – without in any way abolishing whatever is essential about it, as the genealogies showing the human descent of Jesus in the Gospels of Matthew and Luke indicate.

[14] Ibid.
[15] Ibid., p. 202.
[16] Ibid.
[17] Ibid.

Of course, Jesus's descent from Joseph, which dominates St Matthew's genealogy, is not a biological reality. Jesus was only the adopted son of Joseph. But that should not be taken to mean, says Bulgakov, that his belonging to Joseph's family is just a legal fiction. As he writes:

> It also had a certain mystical reality: there was a confession of adoptive sonship, for the parents as well as for the son.[18]

But Jesus had no male biological parent because he was virginally conceived. Bulgakov presents the virginal conception chiefly in terms of the avoidance of original sin, for it is by carnal intercourse, where flesh envelops spirit, that the inheritance from Adam is passed on. (Here, in linking the transmission of original sin to the reversal of the proper order of spirit and flesh in sexual arousal, Bulgakov is actually more Augustinian than many Western doctors and divines.) He stresses that the absence of original sin does not undermine Jesus's humanity. Original sin is simply not part of our created nature. It is only a defective modality of its working.

Two titles of the Child born of Mary sum up the actual form taken by the Theanthropy, as God put it into action for our sake in the saving Incarnation which, at the first Christmas, was finally achieved. Jesus is Son of God, and he is Son of Man. The Logos, through whom all things were made, kenotically – by an act of self-humiliation – enters the world, subjecting himself to its laws and to man whom he had himself created. He does so in order to become a human brother to us, going through the human experience we also go through. He is Son of God, truly divine, and Son of Man, truly human. The Theanthropy is fully achieved. It enters our world. In a few centuries' time it will be summed up in the definition of Chalcedon, which Bulgakov takes to be its fundamental dogmatic statement. In the next section of the Great Trilogy he will look into what that implies.

[18] Ibid., p. 203.

6

The Theanthropy and its Implications

Bulgakov is very keen on the Chalcedonian Definition.[1] Jesus
Christ is a single hypostasis, the bearer of two natures which are
united in him in a manner that is inseparable and yet unconfused.
Under the 'rule' of the person of Christ is a 'new and particular
dual unity, which exists neither in divinity nor humanity'.

> In the Godhead, there is natural unity and hypostatic tri-unity, given
> that each hypostasis possesses the nature entirely. And in humanity,
> there is unity of nature and plurality of hypostatic centres, of which
> each has the nature by way of personal possession. But in the
> Theanthropy of Christ, there are two distinct natures, reunited
> without division in a single hypostasis, each conserving its
> autonomous being.[2]

This is the starting point, then, of Bulgakov's Christology.

The Chalcedonian antinomy

The trouble is that at first sight the Chalcedonian doctrine seems
an ontological paradox. A hypostasis only exists in its nature, and
a nature – if it is that of a personal being – only in its hypostasis.
Nature and hypostasis are not independent principles to be
combined and re-combined according to whim. And yet for
Chalcedon the human nature of Christ, though entirely real, lacks
its proper hypostasis. Or rather, as Neo-Chalcedonians later
inferred, reasonably enough, from the Definition of the 451
Council, the human nature of the Lord is hypostatized – rendered

---

[1] For his view of the status of conciliar dogma, see 'Dogmat i dogmatika', in
auctores varii, *Zhivom predanii* (Paris, 1936), pp. 9–24.
[2] AB, pp. 205–206.

personal – precisely in the divine hypostasis of the Word. Is there not something ontologically bizarre here – something that 'blurs the boundaries of being, in a general confusion'?[3] Bulgakov in no way proposes to challenge the Chalcedonian dogma. But he considers that the theological work has not yet been done which will show the appropriateness of the ontological conjunction it identifies, the personal union of divinity and humanity in the Son of God. He rejects the idea that, because in its essence the Incarnation is a mystery, any attempt to elucidate it is impious. Rather, he implies that taking refuge in an 'asylum of ignorance' is the more impious proceeding. As he puts it:

> The illumination of the Chalcedonian dogma, in the measure of the possible, is a pious duty for theology. If we fail in it, the treasure of dogma is buried in the earth, in the name of an illusory security, by the lazy slave.[4]

That is a reference of course to the Gospel parable of the Talents.

Bulgakov's question is, How is the hypostatization of human nature in the Logos possible, and why is it possible? Of course one answer to this twofold question is to refer the questioner quite simply to the almighty power of God. Surely God can do anything! (A Western writer might add 'anything logically non-contradictory'.) Bulgakov finds this appeal to divine omnipotence a quite inadequate response. As he points out, in the act of creation it was God himself who put in place the ontology of the world. The Creator put in place, presumably, a suitable ontology, one which he himself declared to be very good. From that moment on, his relations with the world were not based on omnipotence but on a providential inter-action respectful of the structures of the world God himself had made. While there is a legitimate sense in which the Incarnation can be called a new creation, more marvellous even than the first, it is not a creation out of nothing, as was its predecessor. In the Incarnation of One through whom the world was made, it would be incongruous for God to abolish the natural ontology of the world, and of man within it. Moreover, were he to do so, we could not speak, as the Creed *does* speak, of the divine Son being made man. If the human nature assumed by the Word was in its own proper consistency destroyed by that act rather than simply surmounted, there would be no true Incarnation. There would be

---

[3] Ibid., p. 206.
[4] Ibid., p. 207.

no recognizable humanity into which the Son of God could descend. And in any case this would be to deny what Chalcedon itself affirms, namely the 'perfect' or 'integral' (*teleios*) character of the humanity assumed into personal union with the Word.

Nature and hypostasis in the Incarnation

What is Bulgakov's own answer to this conundrum? It falls into two parts. First, he considers the appropriateness of a human being having the hypostasis of the Son as the personal subject of his humanity. And secondly, he considers the appropriateness of the divine and human natures entering into union by means of the hypostasis of the Word. So the first part of his answer concentrates on the idea of hypostasis, and the second on the idea of nature.

He begins from the assumption that, if the divine hypostasis of the Word indeed became the proper hypostasis of a human nature – if it really could function as a human hypostasis – then that must have been, by the pre-established conditions of God's relations with the world, a genuine ontological possibility from the beginning of time. And Bulgakov's Trinitarian theology and theological anthropology have already thrown light on how this is so. The divine Word is from the beginning the heavenly Humanity of God, the One in whom all the divine ideas arrange themselves around the idea of man, who is to be centre of the created world. From all eternity the Word is the heavenly Adam. Bulgakov now coins a term for this. The hypostasis of the Word was always 'co-human'. That is why the hypostatization of humanity by the divine person of the Word does not overthrow the nature of a human hypostasis. From the first moment of the human creation, there was always what he calls an 'initial correlation' between the divine person of the Word in heaven and human persons on earth.

We can also look at that from the human side, and say that from the beginning human persons were called and destined to be theanthropic, to live out the life of Godmanhood, the Theanthropy. Or as Bulgakov puts it: man was

> apt to receive and contain, in his quality as human hypostasis, a hypostasis that was divine.[5]

---

[5] Ibid., p. 209.

And this is because, from the first, the human hypostasis was summoned to live in communion with the divine Trinity. This is why by the divine power our nature was created in hypostatic form: to be able to enjoy communion with the hypostases of Father, Son and Holy Spirit. The creaturely wisdom of God became hypostatic in man. Man is, in Bulgakov's words, the 'sophianic hypostasis of the world'.[6] What he means by that is, the world is meant to have solidarity with God through the communion our hypostasis can enjoy with the hypostases of the world's Maker, the Holy Trinity.

But the vocation of the human hypostasis does not stop there. It is as natural man, by what Bulgakov, in the third volume of the Great Trilogy, called 'natural grace', that human persons are sophianic, bearers – and the crucial hypostatic bearers – of the Wisdom of God. But they are actually called to go beyond that, to make their own a supernatural vocation. From being natural men, we are meant to become divinized, to go beyond our nature, even in its sophianity, and enter the condition of the glorious sons and daughters of God, the condition of fullest Theanthropy. This is the perspective in which Bulgakov understands two important New Testament texts, one from St John's Gospel (3: 13):

No one has ascended into heaven but he who descended from heaven, the Son of Man, who is in heaven ...

and, even more tellingly, some words of St Paul in First Corinthians (1 Corinthians 15: 47–49):

The first man was from the earth; the second man is from heaven ... Just as we have borne the image of the man of dust, we shall also bear the image of the man of heaven.

These considerations, then suffice to show, in Bulgakov's view, why it was that:

the hypostasis of the Logos, the heavenly Man, could itself become the hypostasis of created man and make of the latter the authentic God-man, by realising his eternal Theanthropy.[7]

---

[6] Ibid., p. 210: *mirovaya sofiinaya ipostas.*
[7] Ibid., p. 211.

The Incarnation is no violation of man's make-up but its perfect fulfilment.[8]

What, then, of the second 'focus' of Bulgakov's argument, his understanding of the suitability of the union of divine and human natures in the person of the Word incarnate? He writes:

> We need to seek for the foundation of the Incarnation not only in the relation between the hypostatic principles in the Logos and man, but also in the relations between the divine and human natures.[9]

The 'co-humanity' of the divine life of the Logos, and the 'aptness' of humanity to receive him, need to be shown at the level of nature and not just of person or spiritual subject if we are to grasp as fully as we can the ontological possibility of the Incarnation. Bulgakov restricts himself here to a consideration of the divine nature as found in the second divine person because, as he rightly says, only the Son – not the Father or the Spirit – became incarnate, even though, as he acknowledges, the entire divine Trinity was engaged in this saving action. The Logos is eternally 'co-human' with us in his divine nature because the 'supernatural image' of humanity has always been imprinted on his divine life. Likewise, human nature is intrinsically related to the Logos since it 'bears his seal' and 'discloses his image'. This for Bulgakov is what is meant when in the Prologue to the fourth Gospel St John declares that the Word 'came to his own and his own received him not' (1: 11).[10]

The sophiological contribution to Chalcedon

Only a sophiological theology, so Bulgakov thinks, can bring out the meaning of these statements, or, to put it another way, can point up what is merely tacit, unspoken, in the terms of the Chalcedonian Definition. How so? Bulgakov begins his bringing to bear the resources of a theology of Wisdom by telling us that

---

[8] Bulgakov's view that the human hypostasis represents the principle of divine-human communion in man is acceptable. But it is curious to find him calling it, on that account, 'supernatural', *sverchprirodnii* (thus *Agnets Bozhii*, p. 211), unless by this is meant the bearer of a vocation to the vision of God.

[9] Ibid., p. 214.

[10] Translation of the Greek slightly changed from the RSV to bring out the sense Bulgakov finds in the passage.

the task before us is inescapable. To suppose that in the Incarnation the divine nature dissolves the human nature was a great temptation for those in the ancient Church he calls the 'militant Monophysites', and even, he says, for some of the Orthodox. (He does not regard St Cyril of Alexandria [d. 444] as always impervious to it.) But the solution is crazy. If in the union of divine and human natures the human nature is abolished so likewise is the union! At the other extreme, some people have held that it was the divine nature that was extinguished in the union. But partisans of this view simply exclude themselves from Christianity altogether. Again, it would clearly be false to regard the union as a compenetration of two independent natures which produced as a result a new personality, never before existing.[11] We must hold to the royal way which is that of Chalcedon itself, avoiding at once both any suggestion of a complete separation of the two natures in the Incarnation and that of their total fusion. As Bulgakov well says, it is the function of the four celebrated negative adverbs in the Chalcedonian Definition to help us in this. Those adverbs tell us that the two natures were united in a single hypostasis: *asynchytôs* (without confusion), *atreptôs* (without change), *adiairetôs* (without division), *achôristôs* (without separation). In a careful balancing act, these adverbs enable the Fathers of Chalcedon to affirm a certain form of continued distinction, but also a certain form of fusion. What kind of form? On the basis of the text of Chalcedon, we can only reply, a kind of form that avoids both confusion and separation. What Bulgakov wants, however, is to know the positive meaning which these negative formulations shield. To wish to work that out cannot in itself be wrong. After all, the Sixth Ecumenical Council went beyond Chalcedon precisely in this direction through its teaching that there are in the Word incarnate two energies, divine and human, and two wills, likewise divine and human. So it seems that we may proceed further in this direction if we find ourselves able. Here Bulgakov is drawing a line between himself and more strongly 'apophatic' Orthodox theologians who would *not* want to attempt a positive statement of what lies behind the negative adverbs of Chalcedon for fear of becoming excessively 'affirmative' and not

---

[11] That is the line taken by a Lutheran theologian briefly popular in German Protestantism, Isaac August Dorner (1809–1884). His *Entwicklungsgeschichte der Lehre von der Person Christi* (I, Berlin 1851, 2nd edition; II, Berlin, 1853) was still cited with respect by Alois Cardinal Grillmeier, S. J., in the 1960s, as in his standard work, *Christ in Christian Tradition. From the Apostolic Age to Chalcedon (451)* (Et London, 1965).

respecting sufficiently the bounds divine revelation sets for human understanding.

Bulgakov's question is, What explains the union of the natures other than the hypostasis they share? Chalcedon has no answer. Bulgakov's answer is sophianity – which is common to the divine nature and the human, to the Uncreated and the created alike. After all:

> The world of the creature is created according to the prototypes of the divine world, as the created image of the Wisdom of God in the realm of becoming. But this divine Wisdom is itself the divine nature of the Logos.[12]

In the creation, the Word 'repeats himself' – repeats, that is, the content of the ideas and archetypal images he contains. But he does so outside himself, in what was nothing. And this explains, then, in a nutshell, *both* the relation of identity *and* the perfect difference between Uncreated Wisdom and created, the divine *ousia* and the world in its sophianic essence. The application of this to the Incarnation is not far to seek. It fits beautifully with the teaching of Chalcedon. It gives the positive sense of those key negative adverbs in the Chalcedonian Definition. Bulgakov explains:

> Having the divine Wisdom as his nature, the Logos enters by means of the Incarnation into the process of his own created becoming, and thereby, even in the plenitude of his being, humbles himself. The Incarnation, considered as the fact that the divine eternity condescends to the level of temporal becoming, is identical with the creation of the world by God – inasmuch as it is the going forth of the divinity from itself into the extra-divine realm of created becoming.[13]

The only difference – but it is an at the same time an enormous difference – is that in the act of creation the world remains outside God, as the object (only) of his saving action. In the Incarnation, by contrast:

> God accepts in the interior of his own life the becoming proper to a creature and becomes himself the *subject* of that becoming, all the while preserving the eternal fulness of his natural and sophianic being.[14]

[12] AB, p. 124.
[13] Ibid., p. 223.
[14] Ibid.

Put in terms of the Wisdom of God – put *sophiologically* – that is what the dogma of the two natures united in a single hypostasis positively means.

That is not to say that Bulgakov considers he has now 'explained' the Incarnation which therefore has ceased to be a mystery of faith, in the full sense of that word 'mystery'. It is still very much a mystery for human understanding that the immutable eternal God should be united to temporal becoming. It is a source of perpetual wonder for us. At the same time, however, this amazing truth is not to be thought of as a strange truth, an alien truth, something far removed from us. Since our own humanity, in its sophianic aspect, is one with the uncreated Wisdom of God, we are not only at home on earth. Bulgakov thinks he has shown how we are at home in heaven too. Some philosophers and many mystics, not necessarily Christians, in all ages have known this. Thanks to the Incarnation, the Church can tell us where our double existence – in time and in eternity – is leading, where it is all going.

Moreover, there are still aspects of the union so far left in the shade. Thus, for example, surely the sophianity of the human nature assumed by the Word was adversely affected by the Fall? Is it a corrupted nature, then, that the Son of God took on when he became the hypostasis of a creature? Bulgakov has an answer to this. The 'second nature' of the Logos is taken from the most pure Mother of God, whose human nature enjoyed the highest degree of sophianity possible thanks to the descent on her of the Holy Spirit at the time of the Annunciation (as well as, adds Bulgakov, Pentecost – something that would eventually become manifest in her Assumption into heaven). If we think of it in reference to Mary, the Incarnation is not only the union of two natures in one hypostasis. It is also the union of two hypostases – those of Mary and the Word – in a single nature, the human nature the Word took from her. Protestantism is blind to the fact that Mary shared in the Incarnation not only by her flesh, in the biological life that was necessary if the Word was to enter the physical human world, but also by her hypostasis – that is, in a 'spiritual, conscious, inspired and sacrificial way'.[15] It was a fully sophianic humanity which gave the Logos his human nature. It was the work of Blessed Mary, the God-bearer, the full of grace. This thought leads Bulgakov into one of the most lyrical passages of all his writing on the Mother of God.

[15] Ibid., p. 227.

Inasmuch as she *received* him in perfect union of life through the self-renouncing love proper to the 'handmaid of the Lord', she is the betrothed of the Logos, or his spouse, who has prepared herself for the marriage feast (Apocalypse 19: 7; 21: 9). Inasmuch as she is the bearer of [our] creaturely human essence in its immaculate state as restored by the Holy Spirit, she is the personification of the Church. She is also the Queen of heaven, who can no longer remain on earth after her Son has returned to heaven, to where he raises her in her turn.[16]

The proper image of the Incarnation is not Jesus only but the Mother and Child. That was a conclusion Bulgakov had come to earlier. But now he supplies an important further inference. In his two natures, Jesus Christ hypostatizes both the uncreated Wisdom of God and the perfect created wisdom. Thus he can be called the 'Wisdom of God' *par excellence*, as the apostle Paul does so call him (1 Corinthians 1: 24). But at the same time, the perfect created wisdom is also hypostatized in a way that is entirely creaturely, in a purely human hypostasis. That is Mary – to whom also then, albeit in a secondary manner, the great Wisdom texts of the Bible can be applied.

Panhypostasis and theandrism

There are two more aspects of the union of natures Bulgakov would like to touch on before leaving this subject – at any rate as a formal tractate of his dogmatics – behind. Each aspect suggests a question. And these are: with the union of natures, was Jesus, according to his humanity, a human individual in exactly the same sense as we are? And finally, to what extent did the life of the each of the two natures affect the other?

On the question of the human individuality of Jesus, Bulgakov proposes that while indeed his empirical personality was quite as particular as any of ours and therefore as limited (thus, for instance, if he were a Jew he could not at the same time be a Slav or a Greek), as the New Adam he nonetheless contained 'all the human conditions'. That is, beyond the empirical, his human individuality knew no ontological limitation. That is why everyone of any time or place can encounter him. 'He is the immediately eloquent image for the reason and for the heart.'[17] For Bulgakov,

[16] Ibid.
[17] Ibid., p. 229.

that constitutes the foundation of the 'ecumenicity' of the Gospel, the fact that the Gospel is destined for the *oikoumenê*, the whole world. Christ took upon himself our human nature without any limitation (except sin) and Bulgakov adds that we should also say he took on the cosmic nature of which man is the microcosm. That too is an aspect of his 'catholicity', his universality, as more recently the Western Catholic theologian Cardinal Avery Dulles (b. 1918) has also argued.[18] Individuality as we know it, with the habitual tendency of persons to affirm themselves as distinct by seeing themselves as separate, closed off one from the other, is not, writes Bulgakov, part and parcel of our humanity in its sophianic condition. We were meant to be transparent to one another, not sealed off. In the 'all-humanity' of Christ, this 'evil individuality' is surmounted and the self-renouncing which enables inter-personal transparency is restored. Humanity in all its shapes and sizes finds its true life in him. This may seem to be a unverifiable claim, but it is being verified, insists Bulgakov, in the experience of the Church which is precisely the Body of Christ where he is all in all.

On the issue of the influence of one of the two natures on the other, Bulgakov leaves us for the time being with a question rather than an answer. By the time the Greek patristic tradition reaches St John Damascene (*c.* 655–*c.* 750), sometimes regarded as the last of the Eastern Fathers, the idea that the action of the Word incarnate was 'theandric' action, at once divine and human, was well-established. But, complains Bulgakov, neither patristic nor Scholastic theology gave much thought to what that term 'theandric' might imply. True, a certain amount was made of the notion of the 'communication of idioms' whereby the properties of one nature in Christ could be ascribed to the other thanks to the unity of his person. Thus, one could say that, for instance 'divinity died' or 'a human being was the Saviour of the world'. In the Alexandrian tradition, more was made of the actual influence exerted by one nature on the other – but always in terms of the divine nature affecting the human essence of Christ, notably by its sanctification of his humanity. And this is certainly a truth. But what of the possibility that in the dynamic inter-relations of the two natures the human might have influenced the divine? We hear nothing of this, perhaps because the natures were affirmed as co-existing rather than inter-active. Here is a case, Bulgakov thinks, where the Christology of the Councils is still awaiting its full theological elucidation.

[18] A. Dulles, *The Catholicity of the Church* (Oxford, 1985), pp. 30–47.

The descent of the Son of God

Bulgakov's Christology is very much a theology of descent. It tells
the story of the divine One who, despite as well as because of his
affinity with us as our heavenly Archetype, descended. He emptied
himself to be with us where we are while not ceasing to be with his
Father where he is, in his unchanging eternal life. St Paul's word
for that self-emptying (see Philippians 2: 7) is *kenôsis*. A Christology
which makes this concept central is called a 'kenotic' Christology.
Some Christologies of this kind, chiefly produced by Lutherans
and Anglicans, are incompatible with orthodoxy because they
speak of the Word as renouncing his divine attributes or at least
suspending completely his exercise of them. If so, it becomes
unclear in what sense the One who became man as Jesus also
remained God. Bulgakov does not fall into this trap. He holds that
though the Word, once incarnate, in one sense did not exercise his
divine prerogatives, in another sense he continued to exercise
them. That saving clause 'in another sense he continued to exercise them' allows us to consider his Christology as one that has a
home in the 'Great Church' of both (Eastern) Orthodox and
Catholic tradition.

How then does Bulgakov's account of the 'descent of the Son
of God' unfold? He begins from the Philippians hymn, which
occupies verses 6 to 8 of the second chapter of St Paul's letter.
(My translation attempts to convey the character of Bulgakov's
own.)

> Although he was in the condition of God, he did not retain avari-
> ciously his equality with God, but emptied himself out, taking a
> slave's condition, becoming like unto man. Recognised as man by
> everything that was manifest of him, he it was who lowered himself,
> making himself obedient unto death, to the death of the Cross.

Unlike some exegetes, Bulgakov insists that the hymn concerns not
only Christ's attitude and experience during his earthly course.
Rather, it conveys the divine 'counsel' or decision whereby the pre-
existent Word – the Word before he entered the world – consented
to the humiliation of becoming one of his own creatures. As
Bulgakov writes, the Son's earthly obedience is founded on his
heavenly obedience. The 'coming down from heaven' is realized in
his humiliation on earth. An event (for want of a better word) takes
place in the Trinitarian life which has its issue in events in history
on the soil of this planet. The Word alters his *morphê*, exchanging

the divine 'condition' ('form' would be the more usual English translation) for that of a slave. Does this mean that the divine nature – the divine *ousia* or being – itself undergoes change? For Bulgakov, and this saves his doctrinal orthodoxy in terms of Church tradition, the answer to that question is, Certainly not! Nothing is said in the hymn about a change to the divine nature which, surely, remains immutably itself. What changes is the condition in which the person of the Word freely lives out that unchanging divine nature of his.

Likewise, on Bulgakov's reading of Paul's text, 'taking a slave's condition' means the Word began to be in a new relation to God, the relation of a creature. Taking on the likeness, *homoiôma,* here translated 'becoming like unto man', refers for Bulgakov to the Word's acceptance of human nature – a new ontological dimension. Complementarily, the phrase 'recognised as man by everything that was manifest of him', by his *schêma,* expresses his day-today condition of life as a human being. We could call the latter his empirical – as distinct from ontological – humanity. Finally, says Bulgakov, the Word:

> crowned his earthly course by the death on the Cross, thus showing his obedience to the Father's will ... So in the Cross of the earthly way there was realised the Cross of the heavenly kenosis.[19]

For Bulgakov, the clearest signal of the kenosis, the Son's 'not retaining avariciously his equality with [the Father]' would seem, however, not to be so much the Cross as the fact that he prayed – a practice which should not be reductively construed as only 'in appearance' or 'by way of setting an example', even though this is how many of the Fathers do in fact understand it.

A quasi-Cyrilline theology of kenosis

The shape of what Bulgakov understands as the kenosis begins to be clear. He further emphasizes its outlines by distinguishing it from the picture found in some other Christologies. Thus he will have little (if not quite nothing) to do with the Antiochene Christology, which, he says, represents the ascent of humanity towards God and the descent of God to man as two parallel paths of equal importance for understanding Jesus Christ. If they are

[19] AB, p. 245.

parallel paths, then of course they cannot converge. No, a proper understanding of the God-man will never be built on a symmetry, or supposed balance, of this kind. All proper Christology is *asymmetrical*. It must put its emphasis not equally on the exaltation of man and the humiliation of God in the Incarnation but more – much more – on the humiliation of God. It must not attempt to be balanced. It must quite deliberately strive to be *un*balanced. So Bulgakov turns away from the Christology of the school of Antioch which was not in any case particularly influential in the Great Church as a whole. Will he turn then to the great competitor of the school of Antioch, the school of Alexandria? In a sense, yes. But not totally or in an uncritical spirit. His fear is that, in its heated debate with the Antiochenes, the Alexandrian school – for instance, in its greatest representative, St Cyril – made too little of the humanity of the Saviour. Sometimes, writes Bulgakov, the Alexandrians sound as though for them the humanity of Christ is little more than a screen on which the Godhead is projected. That is of course a metaphor taken from the cinema, which was just establishing itself as an art-form, or a form of communication, in the years when Bulgakov was writing.

In the opening historical section of *Agnets Bozhii*, omitted in the French translation by Bulgakov's pupil and collaborator Constantin Andronikoff, Bulgakov had traced the development of Christological doctrine. His account begins from the fourth-century teacher Apollinaris of Laodicea, in whom – as Bulgakov sees things – the 'Christological problem' of the unity yet duality of Christ was clearly posed for the first time. It closes on the eve of the Seventh Ecumenical Council, Nicaea II, in 787. For Bulgakov, neither Alexandrianism in Cyrilline form nor the theology of the Antiochene school stated in suitable manner the fundamental 'antinomy' of Christ's 'dual-unity', *dvyedinstvo*. This antinomy Apollinaris's affirmation that, in the Word incarnate, the divine Logos *took the place* of man's spiritual intelligence, his *nous*, was in its own way a botched attempt to serve. With Leo the Great as midwife and Leontius of Byzantium as interpreter, the Council of Chalcedon was more fortunate. But '*the*' problem – that of the bi-unity – surfaced again in the dispute between Monothelites and Dyothelites in the course of the succeeding patristic centuries. What, evidently, Bulgakov hopes is that a sophiological Christology of a moderately kenotic kind will commend the Chalcedonian faith in the twentieth century. It will affirm in coherent – and even cogent – manner both the unity of Christ's divine hypostasis *and also* the way that hypostasis acts as the immediate subject of integrally human powers. This would be, presumably, to combine Apollinaris's dogmatic intention with the judicious avoidance of his errors.

Despite his criticisms of the Alexandrian doctor, Bulgakov admits that some passages of Cyril come very close to the position he – Bulgakov – would like to defend. The fourth of the *Twelve Anathemas* is an example:

> Being equal to God, the Word who draws from him his origin did not retain avariciously his being equal with God, as it is written, but submitted himself to a voluntary emptying, and voluntarily stooped down to our likeness, without ceasing to be what he is, *both remaining God and not despising the measure of humanity*. That is why all is his: both the divine and the human: since *in what would he be humiliated if he was ashamed of the human measure*, and if he had distanced himself from the human, who would have constrained him, as by necessity and coercion, to be like ourselves? Thus all the sayings in the Gospels, whether they designate the human or the divine, are predicated by us of one single person.

But what Bulgakov is hoping to write is a complete Christology of the descent of the Son of God whereas, he thinks, St Cyril only left some fragmentary statements of one.[20]

One thing in particular pushes Bulgakov towards adopting the kind of Christology he does. For once, it is *not* sophiology. Created wisdom, and its special relation with uncreated, is a ground of possibility for the encounter between God and man in the Incarnation. It helps to explain how the Incarnation could take place. But it is not that encounter – that unique union – itself. What presses Bulgakov to his distinctive theological understanding of the God-man is the conviction that Christ in his 'theanthropic I' must enjoy *edinstvo zhizni*, 'unity of life'.[21] He must *feel* like one person inside, and *behave* as one person outside. The divinity must become other than itself (while all the time remaining itself) and humanity must give itself to be the 'place' of divinity (while also preserving its own essence). If the Word incarnate is to possess a single life, these postulates, or demands on our Incarnational thinking, seem unavoidable. But how can they be affirmed? Here despite his limited enthusiasm for St Cyril Bulgakov shows himself to be very much in the Cyrilline

---

[20] Despite its shortcomings, and as he recognizes in some of its practitioners these were enormous, Bulgakov thus hails the Germanophone kenoticist theology as the most important contribution to Christology since the age of the Ecumenical Councils.

[21] AB, p. 249.

tradition. The conviction that, above all, Christ must be shown to be really *one*, and not just a conjunction of divine and human existence, is the main key to St Cyril's Christological thought.

Bulgakov believes he can make progress in showing how the unity of Christ's life, as the life of the single God-man, is feasible. First of all, though, he wants to underline once again his determination not to undermine the doctrine of God's unchangeableness as such. After all, this is founded in the witness of Scripture and the Fathers as well as the demands of a sane philosophy. 'On the one hand', he writes:

> God dwells in the Holy Trinity, in the tri- hypostatic relationships and he lives in a nature. This essential ontological plenitude of divinity cannot be modified or diminished.[22]

Of course the expression 'on the one hand' tells us that there is shortly going to be an 'on the other hand', and what Bulgakov does is to distinguish between God's nature or being and God's life or the 'condition' in which he lives out that nature or being. The form in which he lives out the divine fullness is his affair, a matter for his sovereign independence and freedom. Using the vocabulary of the classical German philosophers, Bulgakov suggests that

> We cannot get away from the fact that the being 'in-itself' of the Holy Trinity is joined with being 'for-itself': namely, with the divine life in its freedom.[23]

What does he mean? He means that the divine being, which is personal in Father, Son and Holy Spirit, may be made manifest in a different form than that in which it is possessed by God in his own eternal life. Bulgakov uses the modern Western Catholic vocabulary of the 'immanent' Trinity (the triune God in himself) and the 'economic' Trinity (the triune God as disposed towards us, as related to the world). He rightly says that the immanent Trinity is always immutably present in the economic Trinity. What is shown to us in the economic Trinity is nothing different from the immanent Trinity, the Trinity in itself. But in the economic Trinity, the Trinity has freely chosen to manifest itself in a different condition from that in which the divine persons possess their essential being or nature in all eternity. And he goes on to explain:

[22] Ibid.
[23] Ibid., p. 251.

The foundation of this possible variation in the divine freedom, in the 'economic' Trinity, is uniquely and exclusively the love of God, which overflows the frontiers of the Trinity itself to spread out in the being that is a kind of non-being, the extra-divine being put in place by God, so that the divine love may discharge itself into creation.[24]

This already happens in the act of creation, as Bulgakov has tried to show in his sophiological account of the making or coming forth of the world from God. In the way he lives his own fullness God is free to limit himself, and has done so in creating. The same kenotic act of divine self-limitation now appears, but in absolutely new form, in the Incarnation, when the Word of God unites himself with creation and becomes human there.

In the Incarnation, for Bulgakov, though the divine nature of the Word remains entirely unaffected, he strips himself of the *glory* which is the intra-divine manifestation of his possession of the Wisdom of God. In this self-humiliation what the Word loses is above all the *joy* flowing from the 'love of the hypostatic God for his divinity'.[25] In an unusual translation of Hebrews 12, Bulgakov finds this notion anticipated in the New Testament writer. '[Jesus] who, instead of the joy he had before him [namely, as the pre-incarnate Word], suffered the Cross' (Hebrews 12: 2): here *anti* is translated 'instead of' rather than the more customary 'because of', and this is a perfectly possible exegetical choice. The Word exchanges the joy of his pre-incarnate existence for suffering in this world, ultimately the suffering of the Cross. The glory of the Word continues to be potentially in his divine nature, but it remains to be re-actualized – as is suggested indeed by one of the Saviour's petitions on the eve of his Passion in St John's Gospel:

And now, Father, glorify thou me in thy own presence with the glory which I had with thee before the world was made. (John 17: 5)

In some sense, then, the Son temporarily surrenders his glory.

More daringly still, Bulgakov draws from the Son's consent to his mission from the Father the inference that his own life now 'ceases to be his own'. From the moment of the Annunciation onwards, his divine life as the Word 'belongs to the hypostasis of the Father'. The Holy Spirit was always so transparent to the Father and the Son, so much simply at the service of their mutual love, that he seemed to have no life of his own. Now, with the moment of the

[24] Ibid.
[25] Ibid. p. 252.

Incarnation, the Son is in that position too, so far as his divine existence is concerned. From this moment on the hypostasis of the Son
is manifest only as a human hypostasis, the personality revealed in
human form, while his divine 'I' is invested wholly with the Father.
This is, Bulgakov tells us, 'a miracle of the divine love'. It is 'metaphysically divine'. Angels desire to see it. It can only make a
creature stupified with sheer amazement, and leave it bowing low
in adoration before God unto the ages of ages.

However, Bulgakov immediately goes on to qualify these strong
statements, explaining that what he has just said has reference to
the existence of the Son not 'in itself', objectively, but only 'for
itself', subjectively, as the subject – the divine Son – experiences it.
So far as objective, 'in itself', reality is concerned, the Son remains
what he always was, the second Trinitarian person enjoying all the
attributes of the divine nature. In this sense, neither the Holy
Trinity in general nor the relation of the Son with the other divine
hypostases is affected by the Incarnation. Nor does the kenosis
alter the Son's share in the divine nature. Nor again does it affect
the fulness of his participation in the glory of uncreated Wisdom
in itself. As Bulgakov writes:

> The fact that he devastates himself subjectively for himself [i.e. in
> his own self-perception] does not at all modify his objective partici-
> pation in glory. The 'immanent' Trinity *does not know* the kenosis of
> the Word, which only exists in the 'economic' Trinity.[26]

This is not, then, a really radical theology of the kenosis on the
model of some nineteenth- and twentieth-century Lutheran and
Anglican theologians. Bulgakov feels the need to restrict his theology of the kenosis so as not to exceed the bounds of orthodoxy (or,
indeed, philosophical good sense). He is able to do this thanks not
only to the distinction between the immanent and the economic
Trinity, which, in his theology, is very much a distinction within a
unity (for him, the immanent Trinity remains at every point the
ground of the economic Trinity). He is also helped by the distinction between the 'in itself' and the 'for itself', which I have
expressed somewhat baldly in the words 'objectively' and 'subjectively'. It is the distinction between what a reality is in its own
inherent character and the manifestation of that reality to itself.

So for instance the Word when incarnate continues to be the
foundation of creation in its unity and multiplicity, and to have his

---

[26] Ibid., p. 255. Italics original.

properly divine share in the providential guidance of the world. Sleeping at the prow of a fishing boat on the Sea of Galilee the Word still contains all things in the universe. Nailed to the Cross and in agony, he is still the Creator and the principle of life.

The kenosis and theanthropic consciousness

But the difference made to the Word in his subjective experience by the Incarnation is that from now on he begins to lead the life of a human personality – a life where the eternal is only accessible through time.

Now on Bulgakov's view, the human 'I', the human hypostasis, has, so we have seen, *something* eternal about it. Not only does the human person have the chance, in the course of his or her life, to become aware of eternity. The spirit of each human person has its origin in eternity. My 'I', the subject of the whole life of my mind and soul and body, is, for Bulgakov, a supra-temporal 'I'. And yet in this world, our 'I', our spiritual personhood, is completely submitted to time, to growth, to becoming. As he writes:

> Being in itself intuitive and immediate, it appears discursive and discontinuous, clothed in temporality, and it has access to eternity only in and through time.[27]

And this is what the Word became – for himself – in his own self-experience. This is the stupefying part of the Incarnation, the measure of his self-abasement. Bulgakov calls it

> The metaphysical Golgotha of the Logos in time of which the historic Golgotha was only the *consequence,* which it had made both possible and real.[28]

And yet our human 'I' *does* know eternity. Though it can only get to know the eternal in the course of a life, eternity is its 'foundation, its spirituality, its inalienable treasure'.[29] We only discover our

---

[27] Ibid., p. 259. This is the sort of passage which would repay attention in the perspective of Bulgakov's debt to Schelling, though the common indebtedness of the two to the Platonist tradition must always be born in mind. For Schelling in Russia, see now V. F. Pustamikov (ed.), *Šellinga v Rossii* (Saint Petersburg, 1998).
[28] AB, p. 260.
[29] Ibid., pp. 260–261.

royal riches bit by bit, and yet we belong to eternity. Now if that is true of my hypostasis, and yours, and the hypostasis of any human being, how much more can it be true of the *theanthropic* hypostasis of Jesus Christ, the Son of man, reckoned the son of a carpenter, who is also the Son of God. And just as over a lifetime we gradually become aware of our relation to the eternal – we wake up to ourselves religiously in relation to God – so in Jesus Christ this 'incessant and irresistible disclosure' came about as *his* realization of being divine in the fullest sense, the Son of God. But, warns Bulgakov:

> This knowledge of the mystery of [his] divine Sonship, this divine awareness, in no way abolishes in Christ his temporal, human aware-ness, *through* which and *in* which ... [these divine forms of awareness] shine through in time, like an inner sun, illuminating the moving clouds of empirical consciousness.[30]

Bulgakov finds this perfectly expressed in two of the Last Words from the Cross. During the Passion, Christ's human consciousness and his awareness of his divine Sonship are clearly united in him as we see from two exclamations.

My God, my God, why have you forsaken me? (Matthew 27: 46b)

expresses the human consciousness.

Father, into thy hands I commit my spirit. (Luke 23, 46b)

expresses the divine Sonship.

Our Lord has, in fact, a theanthropic self-consciousness, *bogoche-lovecheskoe samosoznanie,* which is what we should expect from one who is the God-man. In his human personality, Jesus becomes aware in the course of his life of his hypostatic identity – his hypostasis as the divine Son inseparable from the Father and the Holy Spirit. He now knows himself to be the Logos not only with his eternal knowledge but in a human way. Bulgakov speaks of this 'human way' as through discursive consideration leading to true intuition whereby the eternal Light of the Logos came to illumi-nate Jesus's human intelligence from within. Thus in the Lord's consciousness as the Word incarnate, the Logos now recognizes himself through the lens of his humanity. The union of natures in

---

[30] Ibid., p. 261.

Christ is so complete, says Bulgakov, that it penetrates what is most intimate about Jesus, the inner sanctuary of his consciousness.

Although Jesus came to know himself to be the Son of the Father, existing from all eternity – 'before Abraham was' (John 8: 58), it was essential to the kenotic Incarnation that he should abstain from exercising that knowledge, and the divine power which went with it. During his earthly mission:

> he took it upon himself to be humiliated, and to bury his divinity kenotically in the realm of becoming – possessing it but without turning it into effective reality.[31]

What about the miracles, then, which were, surely, acts of divine power? Bulgakov does not think it right to say that Christ performed his miracles as God. True, the Tome of Leo treats them so, contrasting them as divine with Jesus's human infirmities. That can only be 'a brilliant rhetorical antithesis', not a 'healthy dogmatic idea'.[32] Christ's miracles, though wonderful, are not an expression of omnipotence. Christ did not perform them specifically as God but, as with all the actions of his life, as the God-man. To try to separate out some of his deeds as done by him exclusively as God overthrows the Chalcedonian dogma by forcing us either to segregate his divinity from his humanity in the way Nestorians do or to treat his humanity, in the context of the miracles, as only apparent (since it was as God that he was acting) and this is the mistake made by 'Monophysite docetism'. Christ's divinity showed itself – even to Jesus himself – only in an indissoluble liaison with his humanity. Before his Resurrection, when the kenotic phase of his Incarnation begins to come to an end, Christ could not have said – as he says at the end of St Matthew's Gospel, 'All [divine] authority in heaven and on earth has been given to me' (28: 18). His life on earth was a constant kenosis both exteriorly in what he did and suffered and interiorly, in his own self-awareness. He was aware of his own divinity *to the extent that his human essence could receive and contain that divinity*. It is in that limitation that the incessant kenosis consisted. Of course, all this time Christ was perfect God. But this perfection relates to the authenticity of his divine nature and not to the form of its manifestation in him, itself determined by the kenosis. That will remain so until the limits he voluntarily set himself in his Incarnation are overcome from within by his glorification, in his Resurrection and Ascension.

[31] Ibid., p. 264 .
[32] Ibid., p. 267, note 1.

Bulgakov has another way of putting this which is helpful. The *principle* that determines the content of Christ's unique life as the God-man is his divine nature, but his human essence fixes the *measure* or *extent* to which this principle is disclosed to him. If, as the Chalcedonian Definition proposes, the divine and human natures remain inseparable in the incarnate Word – exist in him in perfect harmony – that cannot be because the human nature is raised into complete co-ordination with the divine. It can only be by the divine nature adjusting itself kenotically to the human. The divine nature remains the principle that governs the life of Christ, but in the divine plan this principle allows itself to be measured by the human nature with which it has been made one. The aim of the fathers of Chalcedon was to prevent our thinking of Christ's two natures as mutually absorbed or even altered, and to make us think of them rather as conjoined 'in a unique life embodying the authenticity and plenitude of each'.[33]

The 'equality' of the natures and wills

It is of course obvious that the divine and human natures are unequal, for the human is colossally inferior to the divine. Yet it was the Father's good pleasure that his beloved Son should be the God-man, and so the humanity has for Bulgakov an 'equality of right' with the divinity in its presence in the Saviour.

Bulgakov allows that Christ made a divine impression on his contemporaries – a divine impression but not an inhuman one, for this was divinity in humanity, perfect God in perfect man. 'Christ is a God-bearing man and a humanised God.'[34] The kenosis of divinity was the apotheosis of humanity. What wisdom and power were given him! He himself said his teaching was not his own but his Father's, transmitted in human words. Contemporaries, despite their monotheism, were moved to confess his divinity: 'You are the Son of the living God' (Matthew 16: 16). But his humanity was not for one moment diminished or obscured by his humanity. Even the Transfiguration, when he revealed his glory to his disciples, was accessible to human comprehension. His miracles were manifestations of the divine power in him as man and precisely *through* his humanity. His divinity did not constrain his humanity, it inspired that humanity. In the voluntary humiliation of his becoming man,

---

[33] Ibid.
[34] Ibid., p. 267: *Christos yest bogonosnii chelovek i vochelovechivshiisya Bog.*

he sought this inspiration and found it in his prayer to the Father.

Bulgakov has been saying that he wants us to have an 'asymmetrical Christology' where the descent and humiliation of one who was God are given greater weight than the ascent and exaltation of one who was man. But it now transpires that this is a matter of emphasis, however crucial. In Jesus Christ, our humanity *did* ascend to God, and it *was* exalted to the divine realm. A strange ascent, a strange exaltation because its centre point will be the Cross. Humanity is being brought into this total union with the Word for the sake of human redemption, of victory over evil and reconciliation with God. Though the God-man is the holy, innocent and just one who took his flesh from the spotless Virgin, the consent of the Word so to be born as man is his agreement to take on a humanity enfeebled by the consequences of Adam's sin: consequences which are 'not abrogated even in the human essence of the New Adam'.[35] The Agony of Christ in the Garden of Gethsemane is the best evidence of this. Obedience to the Father as man is now only 'natural' for the New Adam through distress and anguish, through struggle and anxiety. All the time, the two natures were penetrating each other, and doing so more and more completely. And all the time his way is a way of the Cross, from the manger at Bethlehem till he reaches Golgotha. Two currents of life, corresponding to the two natures, influence each other and enter, not without tension, into harmony. That the Redeemer has two wills is the teaching of one of the successor Councils to Chalcedon, the Third Council of Constantinople, reckoned by the Orthodox and Catholic Churches the sixth ecumenical Council of 681. Because Christ is in two natures he has two wills: in Bulgakov's preferred vocabulary, two currents of life. He would add, however, to Constantinople III that if the divine current of life is not to overwhelm the human then we should be clear we are speaking of the divine will of the Word in its kenotic condition, a condition of self-limitation. As Bulgakov sees matters, the human will of the Lord at all times enters freely – surmounting the difficulties – into obedience to the divine will, thus bringing about in practice a single current of life in the person of Christ: what he calls the Saviour's theanthropic will, which is made up of his divine will in its kenotic state together with his human will – like two cords, writes Bulgakov, woven together to form a rope or two streams flowing together as one river.

The single theanthropic person wills by a single act of will, even

---

[35] Ibid., p. 271.

though this comes from a double source in his divine and human essences.[36]

The Third Council of Constantinople does not say this in so many words. It has no positive teaching on just how the two wills of the Redeemer are inter-related. It contents itself with a negative statement: the wills must never be seen as opposed. But that his view is consonant with the dogmatic tradition Bulgakov considered indirectly proved by what the succeeding Council, Nicaea II, had to say in 787 about the icon of Christ – which that Council declared it lawful to make and to worship. The icon of Christ testifies to the possibility of representing the God-man in the theanthropic unity of his person. And when (we can add) those icons are not simply icons of the face of Christ but narrative icons that tell the story of his actions precisely as the actions of the God-man, what they portray is the conjoined unity of his divine and human wills in act: his single theanthropic willing. Reference to such narrative iconography seems necessary so as to complete Bulgakov's argument at this point. Remembering the Athonite controversy of the Name, he is distracted by the parallel between the icon of the face and the Name of Jesus – which is the Name of God as well as man, triggering the thought that

all the Names of God are in a certain sense theanthropic, in the measure by which God reveals himself to man in human speech.[37]

The communication of idioms and the consciousness of Christ

Before turning to the work of Christ, his saving action for humanity, Bulgakov wants to think more about how the divine and human natures of Christ collaborate and mutually influence one another. His starting-point, we shall not be surprised to discover, is the affirmation of Chalcedon that the natures are united indissolubly. If they are so united, he says, then they must influence each other. They must not only cooperate but interpenetrate.

It is in this context that he wants to place the patristic idea of the 'communication of idioms'. Too often, he thinks, that idea has been used merely to state a convention about the use of words. The

---

[36] Ibid., p. 274. For Bulgakov, St Maximus Confessor's (c. 580 – 662) affirmation that will belongs to nature is too abrupt. There must be *some* relation to the one subject of the two natures of the Word incarnate.

[37] AB, p. 275.

convention he has in mind is the way (for many theologians) we can, if we wish, in our language about Jesus Christ ascribe qualities of the divine nature to the human and qualities of the human nature to the divine while all the time what we mean thereby is simply that one person – the hypostasis of the Word incarnate – was the subject of both natures. That is certainly how the notion started out – as the first ever systematic theology, Origen's *De principiis*, records.[38] We can say 'Divinity suffered' or 'Humanity reigned over the world from the Cross' but what we mean is that 'One who was divine suffered in his humanity', or 'One who was human reigned over the world in his divinity from the Cross'. The principle of the 'communication of idioms' is a convention which enables us to use and understand such statements. It does not literally mean that qualities of the human belonged in Christ to the divine and qualities of the divine in him to the human.

Bulgakov wants to go further. He thinks the 'communication of idioms' *should* be understood metaphysically and not just as permission to use words in a certain way. He is emboldened by a passage in St John Damascene's treatise *On the Orthodox Faith* – a book meant to be – and widely regarded as – a summary of the Greek patristic tradition. Though Damascene is happy with that more restrictive interpretation of the communication of idioms Bulgakov is contesting, he also has more to offer. In book III of *On the Orthodox Faith* John writes:

> We do not say that actions [in Christ] are distinct nor that the natures act independently of each other. But [we affirm that] each of the two carries out what is proper to it with the participation of the other.[39]

In practice, however, St John, like the other Fathers, while, to be sure, willing to speak about the influence of the divine nature on the human, divinizing it, is silent about any possible influence of the human nature on the divine. Perhaps because the Fathers did not work out a consistently kenotic theology, their writings have nothing to say on this. So Bulgakov proposes to pick up the thread where they left off.

His key phrase is 'reciprocal limitation', *vzaimogranichenie*. One nature does not affect the other without being affected in its turn. The 'divinization' of Christ's humanity by his divine nature is not

[38] Origen, *De principiis* II. vi. 3.
[39] John of Damascus, *De fide orthodoxa* III. 19.

like the physical force exerted externally by one substance on
another – even if the Fathers can use similes (such as fire transforming iron) which inevitably, if perhaps inadvertently, suggest as
much. What is involved is a spiritual penetration which, accordingly, must be *accompanied by an interior acceptance* of this effect. The
humanity of Jesus should not be regarded as passive in relation to
his divinity. It is no mere tool of that divinity. The humanity of the
Word had to 'incline' ever more fully towards its own transformation if God were really going to divinize the essence of man: to
regenerate fallen nature by establishing it in divine sonship. In
Christ man's divinisation comes about as

> the constant identification of the divine and the human, without
> division, without confusion or abolition of the natures in their vital
> organic unity.[40]

For this to happen, the divine nature must allow itself to be in a
condition of continuous self-adjustment to what the human nature
can accept. Thus for example the plenitude of the divine glory was
constantly in readiness to illuminate the God-man in the measure
that his humanity was able to receive it. But in fact his humanity
was not able to receive it fully until the Resurrection.

The two principal examples Bulgakov uses to illustrate his thesis
are the ignorance of Christ and his prayer. In a Gospel text which
caused the Church Fathers considerable embarrassment, the
Saviour confessed he did not know the time of his glorious Coming
(Mark 13: 32). For Bulgakov the Fathers worried needlessly. Jesus
did not know the day or hour of his Parousia because, during the
public ministry, the measure of his God-manhood was not yet
complete. The divine nature had not yet attained the fulness of its
revelation in the human. His divine knowledge was only gradually
realized in him just as his human understanding also developed
gradually. And in fact the two grew together.

Again, the prayer of Christ shows how his divine nature, united
to his humanity in the state of humiliation:

> not only was not an obstacle to prayer or rendered prayer superflu-
> ous, but on the contrary inspired his human essence to pray
> ceaselessly, since prayer *is* divine inspiration.[41]

There is in the life of the God-man no manifestation of divine life

---

[40] Ibid., p. 279.
[41] p. 284.

that is not also human, just as in him there is nothing human that is not in principle divinised and full of grace even if it is not yet glorified. This, then, is the sense in which Bulgakov would see the divine nature affected by the human and not just, as in patristic theology, the human nature affected by the divine. His divinity is not realized 'except in indivisible union with the human and thanks to the receptivity, *vospriimchivost'*, of the humanity'.[42]

Implications for Christ's Passion

Finally, on the communication of idioms, Bulgakov turns to an especially knotty question. Do we want to say *ad litteram* that in Christ divinity *suffered?* Or shall we rest content with the interpretation that One who was personally divine suffered – but in his humanity? Bulgakov thinks we must go further than the latter. We must say that, in the Passion and Cross, the human nature brings the divine nature to a communion in its fate, *not excluding its sufferings.* Bulgakov knows that Damascene taught an acceptance by the divine person of the Word of the sufferings of the flesh. Why then does John consider such sufferings altogether alien to the divine nature? How can this be compatible with Chalcedon's teaching that the natures are united *indivisibly?* Can something so vital for one nature leave the other utterly unaffected? Is this not to say the Word incarnate lives a double life, not a single one? Too many questions arise. So, aided by the kenotic idea, this is one of those points where we must go beyond the Fathers. Treating the voluntary humiliation of the Word as the principle of the union of natures, Bulgakov writes:

> By virtue of the interchange, [between the natures], in some mysterious fashion the human nature marks the divine nature with its seal.[43]

Certainly, we cannot say that the divine nature suffered *in the same sense* as the humanity, the 'flesh' (like St Athanasius, and in the spirit of the fourth Gospel, Bulgakov treats those terms as synonymous in this section of *Agnets Bozhii*). But even as ordinary men we know there to be such a thing as spiritual suffering caused by sympathizing with the – perhaps very different – suffering of others. So likewise here. The divine nature whilst remaining wholly

---

[42] Ibid., p. 285.
[43] Ibid., p. 288.

other than the flesh of Christ co-suffered spiritually with it, since it cannot be the case that the nature does not suffer if its hypostasis is suffering. Taking a further step still, Bulgakov would add that there must be *some* sense in which the non-incarnating persons, the Father and the Holy Spirit, share this spiritual co-suffering. We should support the Church's rejection of Patripassianism, the heresy for which, on the Cross, the Father was crucified along with the Son. But, says Bulgakov:

> That in no way suppresses [the] bond of love in the Holy Trinity by virtue of which the mystery of Golgotha in this special sense was accomplished also in heaven in the heart of the Father – that heart which is the Holy Spirit.[44]

Here he can point to the post-mediaeval Russian iconography showing the Father, full of grief and compassion, leaning over the Son on the Cross – a type of icon not known to the Byzantines but familiar in the Western image called the 'Throne of Grace'. (That latter image completes the Trinitarian reference by portraying the dove of the Holy Spirit between the Father's hands or on the Son's breast.) Bulgakov accepts the doctrine of God's unchangeableness but not the theological idea of his 'apathy' or impassibility. Impassibility or imperviousness to suffering, says he, implies non-participation, whereas God is immutably all-participating – citing Deuteronomy 4: 24, 'the Lord your God is a devouring fire'.

Bulgakov has now established, to his own satisfaction at least, that the communication of idioms ought not to be regarded as just a rule about how to use language in connexion with the Word incarnate. More than that, it is a statement about the *reciprocal* limitation of the human and divine natures in the Incarnation and consequently the *perichôrêsis* or 'circumincession' which goes on between these natures in Christ.

Perichoretic theanthropy and the mind of Christ

And this encourages him to revisit the topic of Christ's theanthropic self-awareness one last time before coming on to deal with the saving work of Christ. After all, we want to understand as well as we can the One who saves us in his three offices of prophet, priest and king – though we should, of course, seek to understand him in a *properly theo-*

---

[44] Ibid., p. 289.

logical way, not just by attempted psychological interpretation of him which is, remarks Bulgakov, 'vulgar and doomed to failure'.[45]

Looking at the Gospels with the help of the doctrinal principles he has proposed, we can say that our Lord was conscious of himself under two main titles: Son of God, Son of Man. *Son of God*: even at the age of twelve he asked his parents did they not know he must be about his Father's business (Luke 2: 49). At his Baptism, he heard the Father's voice testifying to this Sonship (Luke 3: 22 and parallels). The Forerunner, St John the Baptist, confirmed that testimony: 'I have seen and have borne witness that this is the Son of God' (John 1: 34). Jesus named his Father, *Abba,* his God and prayed to him in those terms. He was aware, then, not of some general identity with the divine but specifically of himself as Son of the heavenly Father, the unique Son, the only-begotten. The hypostatic 'I' of Jesus is the divine Son. But, as is appropriate in the kenotic state, this divine Sonship is expressed above all in his *obedience* to the Father who sent him on his mission to the world. It is expressed in his renunciation of his own will, his self-abandonment to the Father. Bulgakov goes so far as to say that it comes across from the Gospels as a 'voluntary de-personalisation in the name of filial obedience'. Many sayings of Jesus in the Johannine tradition bear this out, such as John 8: 28. 'I can do nothing on my own authority but speak thus as the Father taught me'; or John 5: 19, 'Truly, truly, I say to you, the Son can do nothing of his own accord but only what he sees the Father doing'; or John 14: 10, 'The words that I say to you, I do not speak on my own authority, but the Father who dwells in me does his works'. The essence of his divine consciousness is this perfect communion with the Father. As the Writer to the Hebrews will say (1: 3), the Son is the image of the hypostasis of the Father. To show Jesus as the divine Son is, writes Bulgakov, integral to the aims of the evangelists, and this is so from the Gospel of Mark's opening words, 'The beginning of the gospel of Jesus Christ, the Son of God' (Mark 1: 1), to John's explanation nearly at the end of his Gospel that his book was written 'that you may believe that Jesus is the Christ, the Son of God, and that believing you may have life in his name ' (John 20: 31).

Bulgakov notes, however, that, while Jesus may *confirm* that his name is the divine Son (as to Peter at Caesarea Philippi), this name is given him by others – whether this be the divine Father at the Baptism and Transfiguration, or the angel of the Annunciation, or again his human contemporaries. The reason for this, Bulgakov

---

[45] Ibid., p. 340.

thinks, is that the Saviour prefers to use the title *Son of Man,* which means, on his lips, a man who is more than a man – not just the messianic king but the One who was to come to inaugurate the new earth and new heavens when the barriers between God and his people will be brought down. Indeed, the title 'Son of Man', in Jesus' intention, indicates not only his humanity but also his divine Sonship. In his dialogue with Nicodemus in John 3, Jesus passes insensibly – almost without our noticing it – from 'Son of Man' to 'Son' where 'Son' evidently means 'Son of God'.

> No one has ascended into heaven but he who descended from heaven ... For God so loved the world that he gave his only Son, that whoever believes in him should not perish but have eternal life. (John 3: 13, 16)

Here we have not only a complete identification of the Son of God and Son of Man but the rooting of that identity in what Bulgakov has called the 'heavenly Theanthropy', since the divine Son is also the archetype of our humanity from the beginning of the world. These references in the Gospels confirm Bulgakov in his view – which is also that of Chalcedon – that Jesus is not Son of God without relation to his humanity nor Son of Man without relation to his divinity. Nor is he God *and* man, as though these could be alternated or separated. He is the God-man, with a unique theanthropic self-awareness. He announces his divine sonship to his brothers but he does so as their fellow man, as 'co-man' with them.

When we read the Gospels – something we should never do without also reading what Bulgakov terms the 'Gospel of the Old Testament', full as this is of Christological prophecies and prefigurations, we need to remember that the Gospels were not written to record the awakening and development of Christ's divine awareness. Rather do they 'flow from this awareness and presuppose it'.[46] The four Gospels approach the figure of the God-man from different sides: in the Synoptics, from the angle of the humanity, in John from the angle of his divine image. Not for nothing do Matthew and Luke begin with Jesus's earthly birth, John with the eternal being of the Logos. But in all the Gospels the theanthropic unity of Christ is preserved: either a Gospel represents the man Jesus as the bearer of divinity, or a Gospel represents God speaking through this man. The common premise of the Gospels is therefore the *continuity of humanity and divinity in the God-man.* Though

---

[46] Ibid., p. 305.

they contain real history, their structure or, as Bulgakov says, 'architecture' is dogmatic. And this is as it should be. They are given to the Church as 'revelation and a witness to faith in Christ, the Son of God'; if we take away their dogmatic and 'artistic' framework (as many Protestant scholars were doing in Bulgakov's lifetime), all we are left with is a lot of little pieces different if not impossible to put together again. In general, the *Synoptic* image of the God-man is

> pre-eminently the image of the Messiah, the Anointed of God, the Man on whom the Father's favour rests by the power of the Holy Spirit.[47]

The Synoptics do not show us *just* a human being, They show us a man who has been raised up to more than human possibilities, and one, furthermore, whose personal consciousness is determined by his sense of divine Sonship – something which is given particularly clear expression at one point in the Gospel according to Matthew.

> All things have been delivered to me by my Father; and no one knows the Son except the Father, and no one knows the Father except the Son and any one to whom the Son chooses to reveal him.
> (Matthew 11: 27)

That saying already takes us into the world of the Gospel according to St John, the Gospel of the Theanthropy in its divine aspect. This is a Gospel where, says Bulgakov, a supernatural breath suffuses the historical element, above all in John's representation of Christ himself. But even in this Gospel, with its many speeches where Jesus testifies to his divine hypostasis, he is not presented (except in the Prologue) as the Logos through whom the world is made but simply as the *Son of the Father*. For – again – he is not *just* God, he is *the God-man on earth*, and in this kenotic condition he comes to a knowledge of his divine Sonship only through the Father – by the Father's gift in the Holy Spirit who rests on Jesus. It is of course the same for us who are Jesus's disciples. We receive our divinization as the Father's gift through the Spirit to those who are sons in and with the Son. But there is this crucial difference: we receive that divinization as the new life of grace which to us is supernatural – more than our nature could even ask for. By contrast, Christ receives it as the restoration of the divine life he enjoyed with the

---

[47] Ibid., p. 307.

Father from the beginning. The prayer of Christ and the works he carried out in loving obedience to the Father restore him to what he was from all eternity, but they bring us something altogether new.

But if the Son needed the Father's help so as to recover the fullness of divine life, can he really be fully divine – be God as the Father is God? Did not Jesus himself say, 'My Father is greater than I' (John 14: 28)? That was a text used a lot by certain Christians in the early centuries, both moderately – as with Subordinationists for whom the Son occupied a lower level of divinity than the Father, and radically – as by Arians for whom he was not divine at all in any proper sense but only a sublime, exalted creature used by the Father as his instrument in the making of the world. Actually, says Bulgakov, if one looks at the Gospels one finds many texts in which the Son declares his utter dependence on the Father and likewise many texts in which he affirms the perfect unity of Father and Son. The Church solved the problem of Arianism (intellectually, that is, not practically) at the First Council of Nicaea when, following the lead of Athanasius the Great, she testified that the Son is not a creature but is of one substance with the Father. There was never a time when he was not, or was not divine. But she has not yet resolved the problem to which, by treating the Son as an inferior divinity to the Father, Subordinationism proferred a false solution. That problem lies in the Gospels themselves, in the two kinds of text Bulgakov has cited – what we can call the 'total dependence' texts and the 'perfect unity' texts. Accepting simultaneously the truth of these two sets of texts may seem to be a paradox – until we have got hold of a kenotic Christology of an orthodox kind which shows their real bearings and their proper limits. How so?

In the unity of his theanthropic consciousness, the God-man relates to his Father at one and the same time as Father and as God. By his freely chosen self-emptying at the Incarnation he has allowed his own hypostatic will, in itself as 'honourable and divine' as those of Father and Spirit, to give way to the Father's will alone. Of course, as the one God, the Tri-unity, Father and Son cannot will anything differently from each other in any case. But the point is that now, in the kenotic condition of the Incarnation, the Son 'hears' the divine will not as his personal will but as coming from above, paternally. As Jesus declares indeed:

> I have come down from heaven, not to do my own will, but the will of him who sent me. (John 6: 38)

Here, says Bulgakov, the idea of the Father's *sending* the Son – the idea of *mission* – emerges as crucial. Mission is why the kenosis happened, why the divine will now comes to the Son from above, from the Father, and is not present in him as his own hypostatic decision. But though he is obedient to the Father for the sake of his mission, the Son knows himself to have everything from the Father – his divine nature, his divine life. He is the Godhead *as received* just as the Father is the Godhead as giving. So in all the manifestations of his human nature, there was

> irradiating the [life of the] Lord, inexpressible but perceptible to spiritual eyes, the light of the divine dignity, like a cloud of glory.[48]

The temptations of Christ

Perhaps the most vigorous challenge to this statement, more difficult to meet than any objection to Christ's divinity based on his ignorance of the totality of the plan of God in all its detail, is the diabolic temptation in the Wilderness. If Jesus could truly be tempted by the Devil, how can we say his humanity was ever covered by the divine glory? For Bulgakov we must consider this question in the context precisely of Christ's mission, which was to vanquish evil divinely and yet as man. As human, Christ was called on to perform a high ascetic work – the key Russian word is *podvig* – by a struggle or combat, in a hard discipline sustained by spiritual ardour, all with the aim of reversing Adam's sin which had made the flesh to rule the spirit rather than – as ought to have been the case – the other way round. His kingdom is not of this world (John 18: 36), and he tells his disciples that 'if the world hates you, know that it had hated me before it hated you' (John 15: 18). But he also tells them, 'Be of good cheer, I have overcome the world' (John 16: 33). It is important, says Bulgakov, not to accept the implicitly Monophysite view whereby God so possessed Christ's humanity that no element of true struggle could be found in Jesus' life. Rather:

> [the Son of God] accomplishes the kenotic work of struggle with all the tension of his human essence, illuminated and inspired by his divinity.[49]

Bulgakov also asks, more specifically, that we should guard

[48] Ibid., p. 316.
[49] Ibid., p. 317.

against an idea associated with a particular Monophysite school, Aphthartodocetism, whose best known theologian was Julian of Halicarnassus (d. after 518). The conviction that gives Aphthartodocetism its name is the belief that the body of Jesus only seemed to be corruptible, as are our bodies. It only appeared to be the kind of body that can crumble into dust. In reality, so Julian and his friends taught, Jesus's flesh was from the first moment of its conception immune to corruption. A different but related Aphthartodocetic commonplace more pertinent to the temptations was the view that each and every act of Jesus's human life was accepted by the Logos in a specific decision corresponding to any given action. It was not enough that the heavenly Word consented to take on human nature. The Word on earth had to agree to every act carried out in that nature, on each and every occasion when action was envisaged. Such a notion, Bulgakov protests, is incompatible with real Incarnation. If we believe in the Incarnation we have to say that when in heaven the Word agreed to assume our humanity he also consented to be involved in the full range of activity human nature entails. If the Logos has to take a specific decision to allow himself to carry out a human act whenever, for example, Jesus eats or drinks, this – whatever it is – is not what we mean by Incarnation.

Bulgakov's response to Julian is highly relevant to the problem of the temptations of Christ. First, if the body of Jesus was in all its properties identical with that of Adam before the Fall (and before the Fall, Adam's flesh did not know corruption, just as it did not know the victory over corruption), then we shall have to say Jesus's body was not as ours is. But in that case he is not, as the Chalcedonian Definition holds him to be, consubstantial with us in our humanity – and so our salvation has not truly been effected. But no. The flesh Jesus took from his holy Mother was *our* flesh. It was

> altered by the consequences of sin, by the weakness which now belongs to the human essence as well as to the universe.[50]

That Bulgakov believed to be proven by the fact that, though the Virgin Mother gave birth to Jesus without the pains of childbirth, the superabundant grace of the Spirit resting on the *Pneumatophora* delivered her neither from natural death nor from the spiritual 'co-crucifixion' with her Son which her standing by his Passion brought. (Here Bulgakov can appeal to Simeon Metaphrastes' [d.

---

[50] Ibid., p. 321.

circa 1000] *Lamentations of the Mother of God* – incidentally, his identification of this Symeon with his near contemporary Symeon the
Logothete is now generally rejected – and the liturgical sequences
called in Greek the *Stavrotheotokion,* which correspond to the
Western *Stabat Mater.*) Of course, sin in all its forms, original as well
as personal, is incompatible with the absolute holiness of the One
who became incarnate as Jesus. But infirmities, weakness, were not
incompatible. On the contrary, their acceptance was an integral
part of the Word's sacrificial abasement in his descent from
heaven. These weaknesses were precisely what had to be
surmounted by him in our human nature itself if we were to be
saved.

This is the background, then, to the temptations of Christ.
Those temptations were:

> a work of the Devil during which, in a vision or in inner contempla-
> tion, there rose up before Christ three forms or possibilities of a
> non-divine way, a way that would not follow the way of the Father but
> an arbitrary way: that is, three forms of the Satanic way.[51]

Could Christ *really* be tempted? The Letter to the Hebrews says as
much: it is 'because [Christ] himself has suffered and been
tempted' that he is 'able to help those who are tempted' (2:
17–18). But surely such temptations can have no force. How can
One who is God be tempted by evil? To Bulgakov, this objection is
fundamentally Docetic. He responds:

> If the God-man could consider the temptation uniquely as God, that
> is, as something that was simply non-existent for him, then that
> would signify that the human essence had no real existence in him
> but was swallowed up by the divinity.[52]

In that case, the temptations would have been play-acting,
perhaps for our benefit, but play-acting all the same. (And why,
asks Bulgakov in passing, should Lucifer who, though malign, is
an intelligent spirit, join in 'playing a ridiculous, stupid role'?)
There is, however, a more searching objection harder to answer.
At a certain spiritual level, it is suggested, temptation by evil
becomes inoperative. Look at the holy angels. They are in a state
of not being able to sin. Similarly, or indeed *a fortiori*, the holi-

[51] Ibid., p. 322.
[52] Ibid., p. 323.

ness and spirituality of the God-man must have been such that no
temptation aimed at unsettling him in goodness could possibly be
crowned with success. Bulgakov points out that this objection
embraces two distinct hypotheses. For one hypothesis, the temptation to evil, impotent to gain its end, was for that very reason,
without effect. But that would once again imply the theatricality
of the temptations, presumes Docetism, and consequently fails.
There is also, however, a second, more subtle, hypothesis which
this objection brings to light. What if the temptation to evil,
though powerless to gain its end, was nonetheless perfectly real
in its effects – effects that were the opposite of those the Devil
intended? The temptation *could* reach the humanity of Christ
because that humanity, though not separated from the divinity in
the .God-man, remained itself. Moreover, the humanity of the
Lord *needed* this test. It was for this that the Holy Spirit led Jesus
into the desert. The temptation represented a question to which
Jesus had to give a free response. Christ took upon himself the
fullness of the human essence not only in his nature but also in
his freedom which was 'not paralysed or abrogated by the divinity but inspired by it'.[53] Since the nature he had taken on was
weak and infirm, he was genuinely tempted and had to overcome
this test in freedom.

> In other words, he really experienced the difficulty of his way and
> made himself the Master of it.[54]

In the first place the difficulty was natural. He had to win a victory
over the flesh in the name of the spirit. But in the second place
it was also a question of a struggle with the enmity of a world
become detached from God, and the creation as detached from
God made its voice heard in Satan who is himself 'the personal
expression of creaturely egoism' in the spiritual world.[55] For
Bulgakov, though the Devil did not know the theanthropic
mystery, did not know that this was the God-man, he knew that
man was always intended to enjoy divine Sonship and that this
One before him was 'some sort of man-God'. The three temptations, then, come down to this:

> To provoke in the New Adam the awakening of this same self-
> centredness which is proper to Satan himself and which he had

[53] Ibid., p. 325.
[54] Ibid., p. 327.
[55] Ibid., p. 328: *lichnoe virazhenie tvarnoi samosti.*

aroused in the Old Adam.[56]

Following the sequence given in the Gospel according to Matthew, the temptations were: the temptation of economic materialism; the temptation of magic or wonderworking inspired by a proud affirmation of self; the temptation of rulership acquired by the worship of the world's diabolic prince. After the rejection of these temptations – that is, 'after the weakness or self-centredness of human nature had been vanquished', the God-man 'knew himself in a commerce of grace with heaven'. Thus Matthew 4: 11, 'behold, angels came and ministered to him'. The temptations were the first true victory won by divinisation over the recalcitrant human essence in its estranged state. And this victory was not, writes Bulgakov, *darovoe, avtomaticheskoe, mekhannicheskoe*, 'gratuitous, automatic, mechanical'. Rather was it *vistradannoe, trudovoe, tvorcheskoe*, 'achieved through suffering, laborious, creative'.[57] That means then that the Writer to the Hebrews was right. Though the Son of Man was in no way imperfect in his divine nature, in his kenosis he had submitted himself to the realm of becoming. And now he followed out in his human essence the way of obedience which would lead to the Cross, and thus was raised up to perfection, manifesting by his work the divine power.

The obedience of Christ

The 'way of obedience', the obedience of a Son. Investigating what *that* means is Bulgakov's final undertaking before getting down to the study of the *work* of Christ – of which, however, the temptations are, even before the public ministry opens, a first instalment. Bulgakov's theology of the obedience of Christ will consider his obedience in the Incarnation, the Passion and the Lying in the Tomb before looking at the glorious transformation of his kenosis in the Resurrection and Ascension.

We have seen how Father and Son are related as the Godhead giving, the Godhead receiving, and how in the Son's kenotic condition as the God-man on earth, that is expressed in the total dependence of Jesus on the Father. We should not be afraid of affirming here an *order* in the persons of the Trinity. It is not in a pejorative sense subordinationist to say that Father, Son and Holy Spirit follow in a certain order so long as we confess their equal

[56] Ibid.
[57] Ibid., p. 332.

divinity. And in fact Scripture reveals just such an order. The Father is first. He is the principle of the entire Trinity because the other persons proceed from him. That order in the immanent Trinity is reflected in the economic Trinity, and already so in the creation of the world where the prime Originator is the Father who creates through the Son by the Spirit, just as he acts likewise in the providential government of the world. We see it again in the Incarnation where the Father sends the Son and the Son consents kenotically to be sent, emptying himself by allowing his own will to be surrendered to that of the Father and, so surrendered, to be accomplished by the Holy Spirit. *Christologically* he *is* subordinate to the Father but that should not mislead us into thinking he is subordinate – a lesser divinity – in the Holy Trinity. This subordination is entirely a result of the kenosis. Similarly, says Bulgakov, there is in the life of Jesus a certain christological subordination not only in relation to the Father, but also to the Holy Spirit. (Did not the Spirit 'lead out' Christ into the wilderness?) During his earthly life, the Spirit does not rest on the God-man as a matter of the Son's eternal nature. Rather is he sent onto him by the Father for the purpose of Jesus's ministry – above all, at the Baptism in the Jordan, just as the Spirit was sent onto the Virgin at the Annunciation and will be sent onto the apostles at Pentecost. Up until the Resurrection, Christ is the recipient of the Holy Spirit, the Spirit-bearer. Only with the Resurrection does he actually give the Spirit to others. If during his ministry Christ is subordinate to the Holy Spirit that is quite natural for him in his kenosis – but it would *not* be natural for the eternal Logos in the immanent Trinity. And yet the Holy Spirit is doing for the God-man what he has been doing for all eternity. The Holy Spirit is the One in whom the Father's hypostatic love for the Son takes place, the One in whom that love is fully achieved.

The obedience of the God-man in bearing or supporting the movement of the Holy Spirit for the purpose of accomplishing the Father's will is a triumphant obedience. For Bulgakov it is also a many-sided one. He uses in this connexion the Latin Scholastic catchphrase *obedientia activa et passiva*. Christ is 'actively obedient' to the Father in executing the divine plan; he is 'passively obedient' to him in accepting suffering right up to the death of the Cross. His had to be a total obedience if it was to achieve its goal. It had to take over the entire human essence of the Son, leaving nothing outside. As the God-man he was not subject to death as to a necessity. So he had all of his life to give as a free possession. Thus John 10: 18:

No one takes [my life] from me, but I lay it down of my own accord.

I have power to lay it down, and I have power to take it up again.

This is why his death can be a sacrifice, pleasing to God.

> For this reason the Father loves me, because I lay down my life, that
> I may take it again. (John 10: 17)

Had Jesus's life just gone on for ever and ever he could never have gathered it up as a total gift to the Father. It would have been an example of what Georg Wilhelm Friedrich Hegel (1770–1831) termed 'bad infinity' where the fact that something is endless deprives it of its positive character. It was fitting that Jesus's life should be interrupted by death precisely so that his obedience could be exhaustive.

The acceptance of the death on the Cross is the high point – or, if one prefers, the low point – of the kenosis. As on the topic of divine suffering, Bulgakov thinks it goes against the grain of the Chalcedonian Definition to separate out the divinity from the humanity and say that the Saviour's divine nature in no way at all participated in his death. The God-man dies in his integral unity though what that means for each of his two natures will differ. In what sense did the divine nature share in the death? Bulgakov will only say:

> In an unknowable way, it experienced death, certainly without itself
> dying, yet also without opposing dying.[58]

This divine participation in Christ's dying extends to the entire Trinity. When the Father allows himself to abandon the Son on the Cross he himself in some sense takes on the death the Son dies. Letting the Son undergo the death of the Cross is for the Father a spiritual 'co-dying' in the sacrifice of love. In Jesus' dying, the Word incarnate becomes *dis*carnate. Body, soul and spirit fall asunder. The Father's task it is to receive the spirit of the Son, now separated from the body, so as to guard it in the three days before the Resurrection. There are implications too for the Holy Spirit. The Spirit had descended on the Son in the Jordan waters, symbolising the death that was to come. For the Bible, *seas and rivers* always have something about them of the chaos waters of the opening of the Book of Genesis. But now, with the Father's abandonment of the Son, the Spirit, comments Bulgakov, 'goes away, so to speak, towards the Father'.[59] What might that mean? It means that the Spirit shares in the kenosis of Christ on the Cross by ceasing to

[58] Ibid., p. 343.
[59] Ibid., p. 345.

manifest himself to the beloved Son. This is, as it were, the worst thing that can befall the Holy Spirit. It is the emptying out of his hypostatic love, and his hypostasis is nothing if not that love, since he is the living bond of love between the Father and the Son. Bulgakov suggests that Our Lady, standing at the foot of the Cross, is here the human counterpart of the Spirit in the latter's humiliation on Calvary. A sword pierces her heart just as at Golgotha the Spirit can no longer act as the Joy of the Son, his Consoler – the Paraclete.

Such is Christ's obedience to the Father in his redemptive plan that he who confessed himself in his divine Sonship the 'resurrection and the life' (John 11: 25) and said of himself 'as the Father has life in himself so he has granted the Son also to have life in himself' (John 5: 26), lies in death in the Tomb. What the Latin church calls the *triduum*, the three day sojourn there, signifies the reality of that death. The descent of the world's Creator towards non-being (Christ's spirit remained linked not only to his soul but also to his body) reveals the love of God. The Son tasted death until the end because unless a wheat-grain dies it produces no fruit. This stay in the heart of the earth, like Jonah's in the belly of the whale, is 'the time of kenotic silence and concealment'. It is the sabbath rest in death of the Son of God. On the Cross Christ put himself back into the hands of the Father and it is in those hands that he rests, passive yet receptive, in the Tomb.

And the word of God as found in Scripture and the preaching of the Church confesses that he was raised by God the Father through the power of the Holy Spirit. The Resurrection could be accomplished owing to the victory the Saviour had won over the world, the flesh and this world's prince. That the resurrection is an act of the Father raising the Son shows – so Bulgakov argues – that the kenotic phase of Christ's life is not yet over. Thus the words of the risen Lord to Mary Magdalen, 'Do not hold me for I have not yet ascended to the Father ... I am ascending to my Father and your Father, to my God and your God' (John 20: 17). The content of this 'returning' is hidden from us except for the brief glimpses we get in the Resurrection appearances, but we see from St Luke's account of the Ascension event in the Book of Acts that the kenosis is still in force even in its conclusion. Luke says of the ascended Lord, '[he was] exalted at the right hand of God' – again as though Christ were relatively passive. The Letter to the Ephesians says, 'God made [Christ] sit at his right hand in the heavenly places' (1: 20), but note the repeated formula, 'he sat down at the right hand of God' (Mark 16: 19; Hebrews 10: 12; Colossians 3: 1) which announces the end of the kenosis when

> the heavens close again, and we adore the Son, like the Father and
> the Holy Spirit, with an equal divine worship.[60]

The kenosis is overcome when the Son is invested with the Father's
glory: namely, when the glory that belongs everlastingly to the Son
in his Godhead is received by him as the God-man. Christ's prayer
to be delivered from the kenosis, 'Now Father, glorify thou me in
thy own presence with the glory which I had with thee before the
world was made' (John 17: 5), is answered. It is because the kenosis
extended to the length of the Cross that

> God has highly exalted him and bestowed on him the name which
> is above every name that at the name of Jesus every knee should
> bow, in heaven and on earth and under the earth, and every tongue
> confess that Jesus Christ is Lord, to the glory of God the Father
> (Philippians 2: 9–11)

The image of the humble Lamb of God is now replaced or, better,
'completed', *vospolnyaetsya*,[61] by the image of the triumphant Lamb
in whom the kenosis is at last surmounted. The Apocalypse of John
is the only New Testament book which presents not a kenotic but
a glorified image of the Lamb. Thus Apocalypse 3: 21, 'I myself
conquered and sat down with my Father on his throne'.

In his glorified state, Christ's theanthropic awareness, as we
glimpsed that during his earthly ministry and Passion, becomes
unknowable for us. It is hidden from our sight by the blinding radiance of the Resurrection. What we know is that we have been called
to follow Christ in that earthly ministry, to follow and learn from
him, and also that he will bring us, if we are faithful, into his
Theanthropy, his glorified consciousness and life.

> Beloved, we are God's children now; it does not yet appear what we
> shall be, but we know that, when he appears we shall be like him, for
> we shall see him as he is. (1 John 3: 2)

---

[60] Ibid., p. 348.
[61] Ibid., p. 349. The alternative verb Bulgakov proposes here, *sminyaetsya*, is unde-
sirable, suggesting as it does the reversal of Good Friday by the mysteries of
Easter, which is clearly not Bulgakov's intention.

7

The Work of Christ

Bulgakov follows a number of modern dogmatic works – but the practice has some early anticipation in the Greek ecclesiastical writers – by dividing up the saving work of Christ into three aspects – his prophetic work, his priestly work, his royal work.

He begins, however, by indicating the unity of Christ's saving activity. He notes the text in John 17: 4 where the Son addresses the Father, 'I glorified thee on earth having accomplished the work, *to ergon*, which thou gavest me to do'. This 'work', in the singular case, embraces his entire ministry. It is *par excellence* a theanthropic work, one which 'while nourishing itself from divine sources' is also a human work, being carried out through his humanity 'in inseparable and unconfused union' with his divinity.[1] In its entirety, this work is the centre of all the life of humanity on earth and gives it its principle. In its unity it cannot be fully comprehended since it is humanity's entry into eternity. But while a threefold-analysis is inevitably not only a division but an abstraction, it has sufficient biblical and theological basis to be useful.

The prophetic work

First, then, Christ's prophetic work. The Jewish people were expecting a great prophet, exceeding all the prophets since Moses and in line with Moses' own prediction in Deuteronomy 18: 15, 'The Lord your God will raise up for you a prophet like me from among you, from among your brethren – him you shall heed'. The people acclaim Jesus as a prophet and venerate him as such, and he does not protest against this title. Indeed, he even refers to himself as such, albeit in the third person. For example, 'a prophet

[1] AB, p. 351.

is not without honour except in his own country and in his own house' (Matthew 13: 57). When in the Gospel of John (18: 37), he tells Pilate, 'For this I have come into the world, to bear witness to the truth', he shows he has taken on the work of a prophetic ministry – the ministry of a true not false prophet. Announcing truth is the prophetic task 'whether that truth concerns the present, past or future, the destiny of each man or a whole people, or all humanity, the human soul or the natural world'.[2] Prophecy is the highest form of personal inspiration – namely *divine* inspiration. In the prophetic experience, the spirit of the prophets becomes, in its depths, 'permeable to the Spirit of God', and in this moment the prophet 'attains to the knowledge of something that goes beyond him, goes beyond humanity'.[3] And this is what he then has to clothe with expression, using his own means, his own style. Bulgakov stresses the creative role of the prophet – seen most clearly for the Hebrew Bible in the spiritual struggles of Jeremiah. The prophets exert their powers of mind and heart to the utmost. They have a love that is sacrifice and a faith that is fire. Before the divine revelation can be received there must be intense labour on the part of the human spirit – much of it at a sub-conscious level – until a new thought, word, vision arises in the prophet's awareness. Which is as much as to say that, when God uses a prophet, he uses and does not bypass the humanity of the chosen person.

But unlike the prophets of old, when Christ utters prophetically it is Truth himself who is talking. This does not prevent his prophecy from being a human word. In fact, his word is more accessible to us than any other – and this because it deals with fulfilment, not promise. As with all the prophets, Jesus received a word from the Logos (all the prophets received the 'word of the Lord') and was moved by the Holy Spirit (the 'Spirit of the Lord' descended on all the prophets: as the Creed confesses, the Holy Spirit 'has spoken through the prophets'). In St Luke's Gospel, Jesus opens his preaching by applying to himself the words of the prophet Isaiah, 'the Spirit of the Lord God is upon me' (Isaiah 61: 1). And St Matthew reports another oracle from the same source concerning the prophetic Servant of the Lord (Matthew 12: 18, cf Isaiah 42: 1). For Bulgakov, we need to see the Spirit's action on Jesus in the context of the Lord's kenotic humiliation.

---

[2] Ibid., p. 352.
[3] Ibid., p. 353.

> In the same way that the Holy Spirit discloses to a [merely] human
> prophet the depths of his own spirit, and makes him prophesy from
> there, so in Jesus, the God-man, the Holy Spirit enlightens and
> divinises his humanity to make more complete its co-penetration
> with the Logos's divine essence, thus unveiling to Jesus his own
> divinity, and bringing about in him the theanthropic unity.[4]

After all, according to the Creed, Our Lord was conceived 'by the
Holy Spirit' as well as 'of the Virgin Mary'. In general, his whole
life, in the circumstances of the kenotic Incarnation, is carried
forward by the Holy Spirit, and, in particular, the Holy Spirit is the
active principle of his prophetic ministry insofar as this is a theanthropic work. Moved by the Holy Spirit, Jesus reveals the divine
Word that, in the last analysis, is himself. Just as in the immanent
Trinity the Holy Spirit reveals the Son to the Father and the Father
to the Son, so in the God-man he manifests to the Father his
beloved Child and the loving Father to the Only-begotten. The
Holy Spirit is the power of the Son's identification with the Father
– which explains how Bulgakov can write of Jesus's declaration, 'I
and the Father are one' (John 10: 30) that the 'are one' here
means the 'living unity' that *is* the Holy Spirit.

The content of Jesus's preaching

So much for the *means* whereby Jesus's prophetic ministry was
performed. But how does Bulgakov see its *content*? First and foremost, the object of Christ's preaching was himself – and all the
other themes of his preaching radiate out from this burning
centre. In other words, Bulgakov is against the idea that the focus
of Christ's preaching was the motif of the Kingdom of God,
conceived anonymously and, often, moralistically. It is of course
undeniable that Jesus's preaching opens with the announcement
that the Kingdom of God is drawing near. But so did that of the
Forerunner, John the Baptist. And there is nothing impersonal or
merely moral about the Kingdom of God as Jesus spoke of it –
not, at any rate, in Bulgakov's interpretation. The Kingdom, he
wrote:

> is the Holy Spirit, reuniting the divine and the human in the God-
> man. He, Christ, is its divine Incarnation and its power in the

---

[4] Ibid., p. 355.

personal lives of human beings in the world, in history, in the Age
to Come: 'now and for ever and to the ages of ages'.[5]

From such a centre, at once Christological and pneumatological,
there issues a religious morality, a direction for the spiritual life of
man in God and for God. God has come so close to man in his presence and power that the highest commandment can now be given
them, 'Be perfect as your heavenly Father is perfect' (Matthew 5:
48). This is why in the Sermon on the Mount all earthly values are
(not abolished but) relativized. The Master is now here, the God
who is love is revealing himself.

Bulgakov thinks we can look from two points of view at Christ's
preaching on the subject of himself. We can approach it as a theological teaching about the divine Logos, or as an eschatological
teaching about the Last Things. Jesus's teaching about himself is
chiefly found in the great christological discourses of St John's
Gospel, but implicitly it is contained in the Synoptic tradition as
well. Here the personal self-awareness of the Logos reveals itself in
the form of a prophetic illumination in the God-man.

Bulgakov gives more time to the eschatological aspect of Christ's
prophetic work. Though not all the prophets were future-oriented
(Elijah and Elisha, for instance, had nothing to say on the topic so
far as we know, and Moses and John the Baptist very little), the
great majority of the company of the prophets announced the
future by the Spirit of God and their greatest single subject was the
coming Messiah. So much indeed was implied by the risen Lord on
the road to Emmaus when 'beginning with Moses and all the
prophets he interpreted to them in all the Scriptures the things
concerning himself' (Luke 24: 27). At the same time, the prophets
also announced the destiny of peoples and kingdoms, presenting
that either in an apocalyptic scheme of history or (at least) in
eschatological images, images of the End. In the case of the
prophetic work of the Word incarnate, the Messianic coming had
of course ceased to be future, but Jesus had much to say on the End
both in the Gospel, in the so-called Little Apocalypse (Matthew
24–25 and parallels) and in the Apocalypse of St John, for that is
described in its opening verses as 'the revelation of Jesus Christ,
which God gave him to show to his servants what must soon take
place' (Apocalypse 1: 1). In eschatology too the prophesying of
Jesus remains theanthropic. It is a very human thing, reflecting the
concepts of its epoch, the images current in the prophetic and

[5] Ibid., pp. 356–357.

apocalyptic literature. That is one reason why we have to take these
texts in their general sense rather than quite literally. The other
reason is that these prophetic discourses harbour an 'unsoundable
and absolute meaning which will appear in the fullness of time'.[6]

Unusually, Bulgakov regards the miracles of Christ, more
normally considered part of his kingly work, as an integral feature
of his prophetic ministry. Though miracle-working was never
essential to prophecy (John the Baptist worked no miracles), it
frequently accompanies it, beginning with Moses and Elijah. Their
preaching was not just in words but by the works they did through
the divine power. In the Book of Acts, St Stephen calls Moses
'mighty in his words and deeds' (Acts 7: 22), and the same is said
of Jesus in St Luke's Gospel by the two unnamed disciples on the
Emmaus road: 'Jesus of Nazareth who was a prophet mighty in
word and deed' (Luke 24: 19). In the days of the public ministry it
could not have been, strictly speaking, a royal power the God-man
exercised in his miracles since he had laid aside that power in
descending into the world and would not receive it again until
after his Resurrection and Glorification. Of course, in the case of
this 'thaumaturge', the person is divine – which was not the case
with the other prophets. Yet Christ's miracles are not so much God
acting on the world as the God-man acting in it. It is by the Spirit
that Jesus claims to act as exorcist and worker of signs as it is by the
same Spirit that he speaks his words of power.

The priestly office

What, then, does Bulgakov have to say about the second of Christ's
offices as our Saviour, his priestly work? For most theologians, the
high priesthood of Christ concerns his work as redeemer of the
human race, through the sacrifice of his life – of himself – which
he made to the Father. That is certainly not incorrect. But it is
partial. It is to look at the high priestly office of Christ exclusively
from the angle of salvation from sin, whereas in fact the high
priestly work goes beyond that and concerns the divinization of
the created human being and the foundations of realized
Godmanhood. Between redemption and divinisation or sanctification there is, though, a crucial relationship. The redemption is the
way toward divinization. That is why theology at large is right at
least to begin with it.

[6] Ibid., p. 362.

While our most direct witness to the priesthood of Christ in the New Testament is the Letter to the Hebrews, Jesus himself bears testimony to it as well. His foundation of the divine Eucharist 'gives the Incarnation a sacrificial character and gives it to the entire work of Christ on earth'.[7] Thus the words of institution,'This is my body, broken for you'; 'this is my blood, the blood of the New Covenant poured out for the multitude, for the remission of sins', are in line with the promise that the bread 'I will give for the life of the world is my flesh' (John 6: 51). For the Writer to the Hebrews, Christ's priesthood is not Aaronic: that is, subject to the Law. Rather is it a priesthood 'according to the order of Melchizedek': that is, of immediate divine institution – by virtue, comments Bulgakov, of the humiliation of God in his Incarnation. On Bulgakov's interpretation of the Letter, Christ as high priest offers himself to the Father by the Holy Spirit. He acts, then, with the participation of the entire divine Trinity, each person operating according to the character of its own hypostasis. 'This oblation', writes Bulgakov:

> is expressed in obedience, by the proof of weakness and temptations and finally by the shedding of his blood in the moment of his death on the Cross. He is not only the Victim, the sacrificed Lamb; he is also the sacrificer, in the sense that his sacrifice is his voluntary work. It is he who brings himself in sacrifice to the Father. And yet he does not present this oblation by his own will, but by that of the Father to which until the end he has inclined his own filial thean-thropic will.[8]

So what is 'victimal' about Christ is not just his first state on the Cross, it is his will from the beginning of his incarnate work. The Flesh-taking is 'already the Lamb's sacrifice of love'. His entry into the world 'is already the beginning of his priesthood'.[9]

The place of the Transfiguration

The whole life of Jesus could be regarded as sacrificial. To be the One without sin in a world of sin, to 'breathe the pestilential air of

[7] Ibid., p.364. Bulgakov's emphasis the oblationary nature of the Eucharist by using two mutually supporting adjectives for 'sacrificial': *zhertvoprinosyashchii i zhertvennii.*

[8] Ibid., p. 366.

[9] Ibid.

this fallen world',[10] to be constantly outraged and wounded (though not as yet physically) until the moment came when the breach with the world and the 'Church of the Old Covenant' was declared: was not all this a continuous Passion? In a sense it was, and yet in Our Lord's life as in our own there were times and seasons. As is generally agreed, the Baptism of Christ marks one important turning-point. Not only can it be considered Jesus's personal Pentecost when the Holy Spirit came to rest hypostatically on his humanity. More than this, it equipped him for his whole earthly ministry, and specifically it was Christ's anointing for his work as prophet. To the Baptism in the context of the priestly office there corresponds the Transfiguration, where the Spirit, symbolised in the cloud of divine glory, descends on him again, this time to anoint him for his coming sacrifice. Not by chance, the Transfiguration is bound together with Jesus's adjuring the disciples to take up their cross and with the first prediction of his own Passion. Beginning in the divine realm with the Incarnation, Jesus's 'will to sacrifice' came only gradually to expression in his human mind as the implications of the negative reactions of so many people were brought home to him. So the inner disposition to found a prophetic ministry which took him to John the Baptizer becomes now an inner disposition toward the Cross and it takes him to Thabor. Since the Transfiguration is one of the twelve (by general reckoning) great feasts of the Byzantine tradition, for Bulgakov, as for all Orthodox theologians, it is an episode of enormous significance. Jesus Christ is transfigured with the glory to come, and not only he but with him some of the things in this world – clothes, ambient air, mountain. And this shows as already achieved what in time was still to come. It shows what was as yet hidden in the Lord's decision to go up to Jerusalem for the sake of his saving Passion. The paschal sacrifice had not yet happened, but it was 'pre-accomplished' in his will, as in the divine counsel, and he already possessed its virtue. (Just so at the Last Supper, Christ lets his disciples communicate in his body broken for them, his blood poured out for them, before the nails had touched the first or the spear set flowing the second.) And this bond, then, between the Transfiguration and the mysteries of Good Friday and Easter, the death and Resurrection, gives the Transfiguration its special meaning for Christ's high priestly work. At the Transfiguration the Son is once again, as at his Baptism, covered with the grace of the Holy Spirit, because this is the beginning of the sacrifice of

[10] Ibid.

Golgotha, and it was, as the Writer to the Hebrews tells us, 'through the eternal Spirit that Christ offered himself without blemish to the Father (9: 14).

The nature of redemption

How, then, does Bulgakov see the redemption won on the Cross of which the Transfiguration, to his mind, is the anticipation? He says we cannot avoid those New Testament texts which tell us that Christ offered a propitiatory sacrifice in his blood, taking upon himself the sins of the world. Nor should we want to avoid them, for this is what 'our immediate religious consciousness' as Christians in any case tells us.[11] The theological doctrine of redemption asks such questions as, For whom was this sacrifice put forward? How, why, and from where comes its power? The various 'theories' of redemption found in the history of Christian doctrine tend to focus on one or another aspect of the possible answers, 'stylising' accordingly.

Bulgakov thinks one should begin from first principles. In creating the world, God takes on himself the responsibility for its salvation, willing himself to supplement the inadequacies of the creature and to give a share in eternity to the world of becoming. Thus the idea of redemption is linked to that of creation. By the saving Incarnation God, 'crowns his creation and *justifies* the creative act'.[12] The Incarnation saves the world not only from its 'convertibility' – the fact that, if it chooses, it can be converted to evil. It saves the world too from its actual sin, the fatal consequences of choices already made. This is a necessary pre-condition if man is really to enter into communion with God and be divinized, made holy. During his ministry, the God-man suffered from the creature's capacity to sin and from actual sinfulness, come to that – not in himself, of course, but in the general run of the people he encountered. But then in his Passion and Cross he did something more positive, infinitely more positive. He 'took upon himself the sin of the world and made it pass into his own life'.[13] In the depths of the Son's identification with all mankind, by assuming the human essence he also accepted human sin – and therefore sins – as his own. That was possible because the divine

[11] Ibid., p. 373.
[12] Ibid., p. 375.
[13] Ibid., p. 377.

Lamb knew what sin was with all its possibilities. His humanity could thus become redeeming for us.

This Christic humanity in which he carried out the redemptive work in place of all human beings and in regard to all their action, does not abolish the old Adamic humanity. Rather, in humanity after the Incarnation there are two centres or poles, one deriving from the old Adam, the other from the new. Each human being is now called upon to relate the old Adam in him or her to the new: that is, to receive the work of the new Adam by faith and make it his or her own in ever-renewed acts of personal freedom. In his spotless humanity Christ 'took over again' – *recapitulated*, the term is Irenaeus's and behind him Paul's – the fallen humanity of Adam. The beloved Son in whom the Father was well pleased was burdened with all the divine anger at sin which he bore. 'It was the will of the Lord to bruise him' (Isaiah 53: 10). Bulgakov writes, 'The heart remains stupefied before this sacrifice of saving love and reason is thunderstruck by this mystery'.[14] Here the kenosis of the Incarnation reaches its nadir. It was for this hour that the Word came. Since divinity is incompatible with sin, for the God-man to take upon himself the sin of the world is for the Godhead to empty itself utterly. Though the Logos still possesses the divine nature, he has it stripped of the kingdom, the power and the glory.

> The divine 'I' of the Logos, which has become a theanthropic 'I' in Christ, manifests itself in him as the human 'I' of the new Adam; and by his identification with the old Adam he takes on himself the sins of the world while remaining unchangeable in his divinity.[15]

The Trinity and the Cross

And as Bulgakov has already indicated, in the human crucifixion of the Son there takes place a divine 'co-crucifixion' for the Father, and in this Love itself is 'co-crucified' – the hypostatic love of Father and Son who is the Holy Spirit, the Joy of love. The entire divine Trinity is involved: the Son as the Lamb of sacrifice, the Father accepting the sacrifice, the Holy Spirit accomplishing it. In the 'night of Gethsemane', sensing the approach of spiritual death brought on by this sin which estranges from God, Jesus cries out, his human nature exhausted, 'with loud cries and tears' to the 'One

[14] Ibid., p. 381.
[15] Ibid., p. 382.

who was able to save him from death'. (Bulgakov interprets this as the death of sin.) And he was 'heard for his godly fear' (Hebrews 5: 7). Help came from heaven, as Luke's account of the Agony in the Garden testifies – 'there appeared to him an angel from heaven strengthening him' (Luke 22: 43), and, as the next verse tells us, 'being in an agony, he prayed the more earnestly', and won through. The agony ended in victory, victory over the tempter who had wanted him to refuse the chalice. For Bulgakov, the night of Gethsemane 'constitutes an indivisible whole with the day of Golgotha'.[16] The darkness of the night conceals: *the love of the Son*, weighed down by the burden of sin and the wrath of the Father which overwhelms him through this sin; *the love of the Father*, who presents the deadly cup to the beloved Son; *the love of the Holy Spirit* accomplishing the sacrifice of the love of the God-man for humankind.

Spiritual and physical dying

In the soul of the God-man this is a trial which is not in any quantitative sense equal to the evil human beings have committed, but it has a qualitative intensity which makes it, says Bulgakov, the real equivalent of that ocean of guilt.[17]

> The assumption of sin would have been Docetic, had it not been followed by all its consequences, the weighing down by the divine anger and abandonment by God.[18]

Eternity too is quality not quantity. Only One who was the God-man could take this on and yet it was achieved by his human essence, itself in accord in all things with the divine. The intensity of this substituting of himself for us, carried out by compassion, goes beyond our thought, beyond our imagination. But, says Bulgakov:

> whoever approaches him with faith, love and penitence learns and knows in this sadness his own sin, lived out by the sufferings of the God-man.[19]

---

[16] Ibid., p. 386.
[17] Ibid., pp. 390–391.
[18] Ibid., p. 388.
[19] Ibid., p. 391.

This can be, because Christ is not just another individual being. The new Adam includes in himself every human being.

> He is integrally man, naturally in his essence and compassionately in his love.[20]

But the spiritual death of Gethsemane must be complemented by the physical death on Golgotha. Bulgakov sees two reasons for this. The first is based on the insights of the monk-archbishop Anselm of Canterbury (*c.* 1033–1109). Since sin is committed against God who is infinite good, it takes on from that very fact a kind of infinite malice. How can that infinity be reflected in the offering Jesus makes as man? Only by the gift of his very life, after which in death remains nothing more that *could* be offered. Secondly, since man is not only made of spirit and soul but also of flesh, the redemptive oblation had to be made in the psychosomatic realm as well as in an offering of mind and heart. The sufferings caused by sin are often enough physical as well as spiritual, so in taking on the sin of the world the Saviour could not restrict himself to spiritual trials, like the temptations and Gethsemane. He had to take on also the sufferings of the body and taste death. Again, there is here a unique qualitative intensity, by which the new Adam accepted all possible bodily sufferings and the death each human being undergoes. He took on, says Bulgakov, not only death but mortality; not only physical pains but the very condition of suffering. From Gethsemane, Bulgakov concludes, 'the way leads of necessity to Golgotha'.[21]

This death crowns the entire redemptive work and is the beginning of the new life. Thus St Paul in the Letter to the Romans: 'Do you not know that all of us who have been baptised into Christ Jesus were baptised into his death?' (6: 3). Since this is the redemption's climax, Bulgakov returns yet again to the question of the co-involvement of the entire Trinity, repeating his earlier affirmations with fresh vigour

> It is in general impossible to believe that in the Holy Trinity only the Son suffers on account of the sin of the world, while the other hypostases remain indifferent or only participate in an external, 'non-compassional', fashion. That would contradict the essential trinitarian dogma of God as tri-hypostatic love, the consubstantial and inseparable divinity, having a unique life in the threeness of the

[20] Ibid., p. 298.
[21] Ibid., p. 397.

hypostases. In extracting one single hypostasis, the second, from the single life of the entire Trinity and the inter-hypostatic love, one goes against this unity and ruptures the Trinity in its indivisibility.[22]

And yet just as in creation and Providence, the work of the Trinity while common is carried out by each hypostasis according to its own particular character, so here too with the redemption. The 'effective redemption belongs to the incarnate Son, while the crowning – its beginning and its end – belong to the Father and the Holy Spirit'.[23] Through the spiritual compassion of Father and Spirit

> The Cross of Christ, the Tree of life, contains mystically the image of the Trinity, *qua* that of divine tri-hypostatic love.[24]

There is involved here a kenosis of the whole Trinity, something supported, Bulgakov claims, by the Byzantine Liturgy in which the prayers that accompany the Eucharistic action are directed either to the Father or to the triune God, thus showing the Trinitarian character of the redemptive action of which the Eucharist is the sacramental sign. What the Church condemned as 'theopaschism' was not this but an anti-Trinitarian modalism which saw Father and Son on the Cross as fused.

The death and descent into Hell as priestly work

In an extreme act of divine kenosis, One who is God dies and enters the sabbath rest: for the Liturgy, the day following Good Friday is 'the day of rest when the only Son of God rested from all his works'. Christ unites himself with all his human fellows in death, so as to vanquish death. In the death are consummated all the works of Christ's high priestly office – this for Bulgakov is the sense of the cry from the Cross reported by John, 'It is finished' (John 19: 30). He can take his repose. The God who in letting himself become incarnate submitted to natural necessity did not refuse to die as man. But more than this, he had the power to give his life by a 'voluntary *podvig* [ascetic deed] of love and obedience'.[25] And this is what made it redemptive sacrifice. Though in an obvious sense his death was coercive for his humanity (while his

[22] Ibid., p. 400.
[23] Ibid.
[24] Ibid.
[25] Ibid., p. 403.

natural – sophianic – humanity was not mortal, he had accepted the mortality that derives from sin), that death was free for his divinity. And just as in his Passion was dynamically condensed all human suffering, so in this death there was present universal human death. Conquering his own death, therefore, Christ could conquer death itself.

In death the structure of the human being falls apart. The human spirit finds itself in a state unnatural to it, that of the immaterial. But with the spirit remains the soul, and thus the power of created bodily life. In Bulgakov's anthropology, the soul as animating principle of the body does not possess immortality in itself. It merely acquires immortality by its bond with the spirit which is what for a human being determines hypostatic identity. But after death the soul, being separated from its proper element which is natural life, only exists in a condition of potentiality until the Resurrection. Though this can weigh the spirit down it can also leave it free in its own being – in which case death becomes not only a divine punishment for sin but also a divine blessing on fallen humanity in a moment of initiatory purification. In this latter sense, Bulgakov calls death 'the mysterious night where life matures towards the immortal day'.[26] Now in the death of the incarnate Word, the divine essence is not separated from the human for the divine spirit continues to be uninterruptedly united with the human soul of Jesus. Thus in the realm beyond the tomb, Christ 'appears' to those who had not been able to see him or know him on earth. That 'limbo', says Bulgakov, should not be regarded simply as the 'place' of the 'fathers', the just men of the Old Covenant, the saints of Israel. It should be taken as the dwelling of all those in every age who had or have no experiential access to him. The redemptive sacrifice manifests its power in this post-mortem activity of his which for Bulgakov is a continuation of his priestly ministry on earth. The great high priest continued to offer his sacrifice for the salvation of the world – albeit as One who was already dead, That Christ's body did not corrupt during the three day sojourn does not imply that his death was unreal, but simply that his dead body was not definitively separated from his divine spirit though it no longer had the benefit of the mediating role of his human soul. And in this condition, the Lord's body represents the 'principle' of all the sacred relics venerated by the Church. It is the 'absolute Relic', *absolyutniya Moshchi*.[27] This points to a

26 Ibid., pp. 404–405.
27 Ibid., p. 407.

boundary in the action of death. It is from the Tomb that Christ will rise.

The Resurrection as a work of the priestly office

In his high priestly prayer, Jesus prays that the Father may give the Son the glory the Son had with him before the creation (John 12: 5). He prays, in other words, that the kenosis may be concluded once it has brought forth the fruits of salvation. Since the God-man has continued his kenotic task to the end, the Father will give him through the Spirit the glory of the eternal Son.

> The Son does not glorify himself in his humanity by virtue of his omnipotence but he receives glorification from the Father.[28]

This glorification will thus be in harmony with his humanity and the whole ethos of his life. It will include the Resurrection, the Ascension, the Session at the Father's right hand and the Sending of the Spirit at Pentecost. This should not be misunderstood as the abandonment of the kenosis in its conclusion, but rather as its confirmation or crowning.

> The sinless humanity of Christ, which had preserved the original purity of the image of God ('natural grace') was sanctified by its union with his divinity, in the free accord of the two wills, divine and human, in the unity of the hypostatic life of the two natures, without separation and without confusion. This accord of the two wills in the God-man, to accomplish the will of the Father to the end, unto the death of the Cross, had as its natural consequence his glorification in the two essences, being granted the perfect divinisation of his humanity.[29]

Even in the glorification, Chalcedon retains all its force. The glorification does not absorb the Lord's humanity into his divinity. That humanity abides at the Father's right but it is so divinised that it can enter integrally into the life of the Trinity. But why does Bulgakov say the glorification forms part of the priestly work? When the Father receives as acceptable the sacrifice the Son has offered in humanity's name, Christ enters as high priest with this sacrificial blood into the holy of holies, the heart of heaven. The

---

[28] Ibid., p. 409.
[29] Ibid., p. 410.

glorification belongs both to the kenosis and to the priestly office. It is 'glory in humiliation'.[30]

Christ rose – or was raised. In his sacerdotal ministry:

> The God-man accomplishes all that can and must be done from the side of the human essence to become worthy and capable of resurrection, and so death becomes powerless to retain him.[31]

Yet in his humiliated condition, the Son of God does not raise himself. His Father raises him by the Holy Spirit.[32] Strictly speaking, the Resurrection is a new creative act by which the Father gives the soul of Christ the power to be united with its body, to awaken from the sleep of death – an act in which the Son, still in his kenotic condition, participates by his obedience to the Father and the Holy Spirit participates as the Lifegiver, the One by whom all the Father's creative activity is brought to completion. But the human nature of the Lord would not have been able to bear this new creative act unless it had first been sanctified and acquired the potential for sharing in God's deathless life. The immortality the God-man had potentially acquired by his life and death was now actually given him in the Resurrection. By his priestly ministry, by the sacrificial quality of his entire life, Christ merited immortality – merited a share in God's immortal life. Thus the gift of immortality – not just as continued existence after death but as life in God – a gift which Adam had failed to confirm by his own freedom and thus had lost for himself and his descendants, this Christ triumphantly confirmed for himself and for all those who are in him. Hence the words of St Paul in First Corinthians:

> Christ has been raised from the dead, the firstfruits of those who have fallen asleep. For as by a man came death, by a man has come also the resurrection of the dead. For as in Adam all die, so also in Christ shall all be made alive. (1 Corinthians 15: 21–22)

So in the Resurrection both divinity and humanity are active together. In one sense, the Resurrection is a gift to the Son from the Father. In another sense it is his achievement. Bulgakov sees it as the supreme example of 'synergy', God and man co-working, and applies to it Augustine's dictum (which originally belonged in

[30] Ibid., p. 411: *slava v voskresenie.*
[31] Cf. Acts 2: 24.
[32] Cf. Romans 4: 24.

another context), that God who created man without man's help
will not save him without his participation.

Of course the Resurrection of Christ is not just his bringing back
to life as Lazarus of Bethany was brought back to life or likewise
with the son of the widow of Nain. It is the raising of his humanity
to a 'new, deathless life in the spiritual and glorified body'.[33] As the
forty days between the Resurrection and Ascension will show,
Christ's body, though it keeps a bond with its earthly nature, is now
supra-earthly, no longer bound by earth's laws. His bodiliness
retains its relations with this world yet outside the Resurrection
appearances it is not accessible to the disciples' perception. It has
its own spatiality which, however, meets our space at points of
intersection. Until the Ascension, Christ remained in our world
but in a new fashion. The 'coming down from heaven' had not yet
ceased. So for Bulgakov the Lord's glorification is not definitive at
Easter. Christ had not yet completed his theanthropic journey, not
yet ascended to his Father and his God. And this is so even if the
'forty' of the forty days implies how Eastertide is the time of full
and final preparation for the ascent – just as Moses had spent forty
days on Mount Sinai before the vision of the glory of God and the
receiving of the Law. For Bulgakov, the glorification due to Christ
from his Passion and Cross has been *given* him ('Now the Son of
Man has been glorified', John 13: 31) but it has not yet been
accepted by him, because he still has the task on earth of 'supporting the lack of faith and ardour of his disciples' by word and
signs.[34] In this sense, the forty days constitute the last act of Jesus's
prophetic ministry. The sojourn on earth of the Risen One and his
appearance to a very un-risen humanity in a non-glorified world
demonstrated the natural unity of the man Jesus – the 'humiliated'
creature – with the risen corporeality of the Lord – the 'glorified'
creature. Earth and heaven are in him united. The lack of an
Ascension narrative in Matthew and John points to the way Christ
is both 'there' and 'here', beyond the world and in it, at the
Father's right and still on earth. It is to this that the Eucharist
gestures, that 'mysterious bridge … between earth and heaven',
the 'bond between the incarnate Christ who has come down from
heaven and the Christ who has gone up to heaven'.[35] Bulgakov
cites the Byzantine Liturgy's kontakion for the Ascension:

---

[33] AB, p. 413.
[34] Ibid., p. 416. Cf. Matthew 28: 17; Mark 16: 13; Luke 24: 11.
[35] Ibid., p. 418.

Having united us on earth with the heavens, you rose into glory,
Christ our God, and in no way distanced yourself, but you remain
now and proclaim to those who love you, 'I am with you'.

The Ascension and the priestly work

So what *does* the Ascension add to the forty days? In the Ascension
Jesus was taken up by the Father through the Holy Spirit in an act
which the Letter to the Hebrews describes as an ushering into the
heavenly places as high priest – thus showing Bulgakov is right to
bring all this within the category of the priestly office of the
Redeemer. But just as the Resurrection was not only the Father's
act by the Holy Spirit but was also Christ's own, so here too the Son
on earth can speak of his forthcoming Ascension as his own deed:
('I am going to the Father', John 16: 28; 'Now I am coming to you',
John 17: 13). By the Ascension the Saviour's prayer that the kenosis
might cease and he return to the Father in glory is accomplished
in the God-man. Christ's human nature has reached such a pitch
of divinisation that in it he can will what otherwise he could only
actively will in his divine nature: co-existence on the Father's right
in a state of indescribable majesty and honour. The heaven into
which Christ ascends is 'the Holy Trinity in all its glory, the divine
Wisdom'.[36] His divine nature had never left the Father's side but
now his glorified humanity enters into the depths of the divine
Trinity where Christ sits by power not only of the nature he shares
with Father and Spirit but in the power of his human nature in its
glorified condition. The body in which the Ascended One now
lives is at once totally transparent to his spirit and an indication
that he remains fully connected to our world to which he will
return in his Parousia.

Bulgakov is convinced that a distinction must be made between
the condition of the glorified body of the Mother of God, when she
is assumed into heaven, and that of her Son when he ascends and
takes his place there. We would not say of the glorified body of the
Virgin that it is taken 'into the depths of the Trinity'. Mary keeps
the flesh in which she lived on earth. Even though in her glorification her immaculate body is *as such* inaccessible to us, in the
measure that, by God's providence, it *becomes* accessible, we can
speak – as many Greek and Russian legends do – of her subsequent
'descent onto earth'. There is an apparent analogy here with the

---

[36] Ibid., p. 421.

Christ of the Resurrection appearances – which, in at least one
case, that of the appearance to Paul on the Damascus Road – can
be timed to after the Ascension and not just to before it. But for
Bulgakov we should not think of the Saviour's post-Ascension body
on this Marian model. For firstly, we need to speak of its continuous presence to the Church, not least in the Holy Eucharist, and to
the humanity with which Christ is solidary at all times and in all
places. And then secondly, there is the unspeakable intimacy with
which *this* body has entered the life of the Trinity itself. The body
of the ascended Jesus has, as it were, too many tasks to fulfil in the
creation in its relation with God for us helpfully to think of it as
simply the Son's human flesh next to his Mother's in heaven. So
Bulgakov turns to sophiology for assistance. In Christ's humanity a
creature has undergone 'complete sophianization' and in this – for
the first time – fully sophianic creature there is – again, for the first
time – full identity of content between the uncreated Wisdom and
its creaturely counterpart. The 'spiritual body' of the ascended
Christ is the created image of the eternal Primal Image, the
Godmanhood of the Heavenly Man. And this 'spiritual image', in
the ascended Lord's continuing bodiliness, is to be realized, until
his second Coming, in the 'flesh of the world' – that is, in the
world's history. That continuing bodiliness is best thought of, for
Bulgakov, not as the flesh that once belonged to this world, simply,
but as the 'entire energy of the Incarnation', now channelled into
making the God-man's presence in heaven a presence on earth
that is not merely, as with blessed Mary, occasional but rather
continuous.

Though this account may seem to be in some danger of volatiliz-
ing the human reality of the Lord's body, it will become clear from
Bulgakov's theology of the kingly office of Christ that, for him, the
real humanity of Jesus is undiminished with the Ascension and
Session. For it is only with these events that, in Bulgakov's
Christology, the royal office is properly begun.

In the Ascension when, to our stupefaction, the human essence
appears in the very heart of the Trinity, is the Trinity itself
changed? The answer must be for Bulgakov both 'Yes' and 'No'.
And first of all, 'No'. The being of God cannot change: 'for him'
and 'in him' there can be no alteration. But also 'Yes' inasmuch as
when the humanity of Christ comes to abide in God's eternity
(*aeternitas*) as 'another eternity' (*aeviternitas*) albeit one with a
created principle, then the world is in God. Bulgakov says we
should be able to live with this antinomy. It is, after all, only the
strongest version of something which has held good ever since the

Absolute, while remaining the Absolute, beyond all relations, became the God who is Creator and thus essentially relation with what is outside him. The 'shock' of the arrival of the most human Jesus in the bosom of the Trinity may, however, be diminished by the following consideration. Just as, owing to the uncreated Wisdom of God, God in his eternity already contained the ideas of created things in their plenitude, so the eternal Godmanhood of the Son already comprised that fullness of his theanthropic being which was to be expressed in all the ways of his incarnate life. In this sense, the locus of the Session at the right hand is eternally prepared by the Son, eternally possessed by him.

> That is why neither the Ascension nor the Session at the Father's right introduce any change into the divine eternity, and [yet] together they are achievements, realised by the theanthropic process of God's relation with the world.[37]

The Session, Pentecost and the priestly office

Scripture discloses, says Bulgakov, that Christ's ministry and therefore his kenosis continue in heaven for what – in earthly terms – we can only call the ten days that separate the Ascension from Pentecost. He had said, 'I will pray the Father and he will give you another Counsellor to be with you for ever' (John 14: 16). His intercession is effective. The great high priest, offering the sacrifice of his humanity, prays the Father for the consummation of his earthly work through the activity of the Spirit whom the Father sends from the Son. The sending of the Spirit is the last work of Christ's priestly ministry and, significantly, it follows on the Ascension. When in St John's Gospel, the risen Christ breathes on the disciples and says to them, 'Receive the Holy Spirit' (John 20: 22), this is not yet Pentecost, for the Ascension has not happened. Rather is it a testimony to the presence of the Spirit resting on the Son in his Resurrection and the glorification that is taking place in Christ as Pentecost beckons. By the Pentecostal descent, heaven is thrown open to earth and earth to heaven. The priestly ministry comes to its final fulfilment as God is reconciled with fallen man and man has communion with the divine life in the God-man at the Father's right.

Let us be clear, though, what this means. Christ is a 'high priest

---

[37] Ibid., p. 429.

for ever according to the order of Melchizedek' (Hebrews 5: 10), ever ready to save those who come to God through him. The final act of the priestly office is itself an act without end, for he is the Mediator not only between God and sinners – who can be forgiven and then there's an end of it – but between God and creatures. As pontifex, the bridge-builder, he surmounts the ontological abyss separating Creator and creature. He will continue for all eternity to offer his Eucharist to the Father no longer – after the resurrection of the just – as a propitiatory sacrifice but as an oblation of love and praise. This is a priestly office exercised no longer in humiliation but in power.

So now the kenosis really does end. The glorification of Christ is complete, that of the Virgin and subsequently of the entire Church begins. The Logos is now no longer simply the 'demiurgic' Logos, the One with responsibility for creation in its becoming. He is also the 'Logos of history', the One with responsibility for history in its unfolding, who leads it to fulfilment by the Holy Spirit. The Word incarnate and glorified does not leave us orphans. He renews what he did on earth in the Holy Eucharist and is found on earth in his real if sacramental presence there. In assessing his continuing impact, we must also bear in mind the abiding power of the historic events in which the Theanthropy was enacted, a power with effects in future time. Witness is given that in the Church's wider liturgical life, in the feasts of our Lord and his Mother where we do not simply commemorate the original events but penetrate and relive them.

For the Church, then, the events of Christ's earthly life, his kenotic existence, enjoy lasting reality.

> For himself, the kenosis is finished in his glorification and has become so to say the past. Nevertheless, by relation to the life of the world, it can still keep its virtue. Christ is in agony and he is crucified in the world, since the sacrifice of Golgotha is brought there 'until he comes'.
>
> (1 Corinthians 2: 26)[38]

In his glorified humanity, the Saviour sits at the Father's right, but in his body as the new Adam, his Church-body, he is not only in glory but in humiliation too. That humiliation, however, concerns no longer his divinity but only his humanity and not his personal humanity but its ecclesial counterpart – which is still, though, truly *his.* 'In the Church, Christ's already consummated earthly life, with

---

[38] Ibid., p. 436.

its prophetic and priestly ministry, is mystically accomplished in post-Pentecostal time.'[39] Moreover, to judge by St Matthew's parable of the Grand Assize, he lives not just in his baptized, ecclesial members but in every human being. His humanity is enlarged to embrace all mankind. As the Apocalypse of John suggests, he participates in the destiny of all human society until the End – especially, thinks Bulgakov, in his compassion with those who suffer – as well as alongside the Church militant in ceaseless combat with the powers of Hell.

On the Cross Christ cried out, 'It is accomplished', and 'this accomplished work can contain as its consequence further accomplishments'.[40] It can be – and it is – the foundation of new tasks. For Bulgakov, as the prophetic and priestly ministries end, a new ministry opens up – the royal office of Christ.

The royal office

It is a topic on which Bulgakov found the work of his Russian predecessors – the great manualists of the nineteenth century – rather disappointing. They link it to the miracles which for him are an aspect of the prophetic office or to Christ's glorification which for him belongs to his priestly ministry. In Bulgakov's eyes, the royal office begins only when Christ's work as teacher and high priest is completed, for that work is this third office's foundation. Of course, Christ's kingship goes back beyond the Ascension and Session. At the Annunciation, the archangel tells the Virgin, 'The Lord God will give to him the throne of his father David ... and of his kingdom there will be no end' (Luke 1: 32–33). The Magi bring him royal gifts and a kingly title is appended to his Cross. He had told Pilate, after all, 'I am a king' (John 18: 37), even if he also added that his kingdom was not of this world. This is all very well. But only once during his earthly ministry did Christ manifest his royal magnificence – at the Entry to Jerusalem. This the Byzantine tradition keeps as one of the twelve great feasts of the Church even though, sandwiched as it is between the Sunday of the Raising of Lazarus and the celebration of the Passion, it can receive insufficient attention. But the triumphant entry of the very gentle king into the holy City prefigures his glorification. The crowd cries, 'Blessed is he who comes, the king, in the name of the Lord' (Luke

[39] Ibid., p. 437.
[40] Ibid., p. 438.

19: 38), and Jesus accepts this messianic salutation. But for Bulgakov he accepts it as a *sign* of his real entry on kingly power which will only come about eschatologically. That is confirmed in St Matthew's Gospel where Jesus in effect tells the inhabitants of Jerusalem they will not see him again until his *glorious* coming (Matthew 23: 38–39). The entry into Jerusalem is a sign of future achievements, beyond and as a result of Christ's sufferings and resurrection. In Jerusalem the people acclaim Jesus as king of the Jews but the kingdom he is interested in is the kingdom of God. That kingdom is life in God: peace and joy in the Holy Spirit. It will arrive through the action of God himself – at once in history (the reign of the saints over the world) and beyond history (the coming of Christ in glory). Christ's victory over the world, by which he will found the kingdom, is not to be achieved by political means but only by obedience to the Father. It is through this he conquers and becomes as man worthy to hold the power of which as God he emptied himself at the Incarnation. The Father gives him this power not just as his only-begotten Son but as the God-man who accepted the condition of a slave. In the Resurrection the Father gives all power to the Son as Jesus attests in Matthew 28: 18: 'All power in heaven and on earth has been given to me'. And, writes Bulgakov:

> The communication of this power is identical with the Resurrection – indeed, it *is* the Resurrection itself.[41]

It is in the Resurrection that, as the Letter to the Colossians has it, the Father 'delivered us from the dominion of darkness and transferred us to the kingdom of his beloved Son' (1: 13). The Son has his kingdom, his power over creation, as an effect of his priestly self-offering.

That the royal office only begins with the Resurrection, Ascension and Session gives it – so far as we on earth are concerned – a mystical character. Though real it is hidden to the world until unveiled at the end. It does, however, possess a preamble we can be directly aware of, and this is the struggle for the kingdom between the power of Christ and what Bulgakov calls the 'anti-Christic powers'.[42] If Christ's kingly office is a hidden reality with a non-hidden side to it, then it meets the conditions for what contemporary biblical scholarship calls 'apocalyptic'. But the

---

[41] Ibid., p. 446.
[42] Ibid., p. 447.

overall outcome of this process, though known from revelation, is
not manifest at all. The outcome will be when the Son hands over
the kingdom to the Father, thus crowning the apocalyptic process.
And that is not apocalyptic, it is eschatology.

Living as he had in what contemporary secular parlance would
term apocalyptic times (Bolshevism, Fascism, the world wars),
Bulgakov was not unnaturally interested in the Johannine
Apocalypse, the Book of Revelation. When in chapter five of that
text, the sacrificed Lamb – already proclaimed by an elder the Lion
of Judah who alone has power to open the seven seals – takes the
divine book to the tumultuous applause not only of saints in
heaven but of all creatures on earth, in the seas and under the
earth, this is for Bulgakov the moment of the Lamb's advent on
earth to begin his reign, his royal ministry. Bulgakov's copious cita-
tions from the Apocalypse of John leave little doubt of the work's
theocratic quality, even if this is divine rule in a history that is
passing over into eschatology via the final judgment and the
general resurrection. He stresses that, for St John, this is a new
action by the Lamb – and not just the demonstration of the inner
force of his already accomplished redemption. He also emphasizes
the way Christ will not be alone in his new descent from heaven to
earth as king. Taking part with him will be those who serve, and,
Bulgakov adds quietly so as to eliminate any jarring note of human
triumphalism, 'do his work'.[43] In the meantime, the life of the
Church will be no idyll, no peaceful interlude. Tragedy, war, division, are the themes for the interim not only of the Johannine
Apocalypse but also of the so-called Little Apocalypse too. Here the
themes are orchestrated in the typical language of Old Testament
prophecy. For Bulgakov, the Parousia of the Little Apocalypse (cf.
Matthew 24: 30) corresponds to what the Johannine Apocalypse
calls the 'first resurrection'. In each case, history continues in some
sense. The Little Apocalypse does not address the issue of the End
as entry into meta-historical time, doubtless because, in a celebrated saying of Jesus, neither the angels nor the Son but the
Father alone knew this.

By his royal ministry, then, Christ submits the world and his
enemies to himself so as to give his Kingdom to the Father, He
does this in an initial, partial way through other human beings and
then through his personal return which will be followed by the
world's end. First, then, he will be reigning in us – meaning not
only the royal priesthood of the Church (what Bulgakov calls

[43] Ibid., p. 451.

'Christian humanity') but also a wider 'Christic humanity' who, unbeknownst to themselves, serve the King by actions congruent with his revelation, being joined to him, unwittingly, as the new Adam. All human history after Christ is, despite appearances, a Christian history which has the Church of Christ as its entelechy, its hidden inner goal. As Bulgakov puts it, 'The Resurrection extends to all human beings independently of the personal relation of each of them to Christ'.[44] (It is standard doctrine that *all* will rise physically, by the simple fact of their humanity which has become 'Christic' – Bulgakov's term – in the new Adam, at the resurrection of the righteous.) Despite his awareness of the danger of a sectarian ecclesiasticism, Bulgakov tries at the same time to do justice to the confessing 'Christian' humanity of the Church. That is where Christ carries out his royal office openly and explicitly, through the Church's teaching, through the presence in the Eucharist of his Body and Blood on her altars, and through the effect of his holy image on her members' hearts.

Apocalyptic in history becomes eschatology at the end of history. The world has to mature towards the end, through the work of Christ in the history of humanity, and yet the end will be a new beginning, a new birth. Apocalyptic must not abolish eschatology nor must eschatology swallow up apocalyptic. Each conditions the other, and the point of transit is the Parousia and the 'first resurrection'. History

> is not an empty corridor which we must cross in whatever way we can so as to escape from this world into the beyond. It comes from the work of Christ in the Incarnation. It is apocalyptic leading to eschatological consummation, it is the theanthropic work on earth.[45]

All culture then – shades of the early essay 'Tserkov i kul´tura' to which reference was made in the opening chapter of this book – is called to be transfigured in the kingdom of God, to be the revelation of the true humanity, even if this means its immediate form needs purging as if by fire. It is this process which the final intervention of God will bring to wondrous term. Like Irenaeus in the ancient Church, Bulgakov accepts that the first resurrection will be followed by a reign of the saints, an immediate preparation for history's end. Then comes the judgment in which Christ's royal

[44] Ibid., p. 460.
[45] Ibid., p. 464.

ministry closes, the final overthrow of the anti-Christic powers. The creation is consummated in the Father's kingdom. When we pray 'Come, Lord Jesus!' we are also saying to the Father, 'Thy kingdom come'.

8

The Place of the Holy Spirit in the Trinity

What is the 'place' of the Holy Spirit in the Trinity?[1] Of course Bulgakov's theology of the triune Lord (and his nature as Wisdom) gave us an entry into this. But now Bulgakov wants us to look at the Spirit again through considering – in the first place – the different controversies about his being, person and work in the history of Christian thought – and notably the great crisis over the origin of the Holy Spirit which pushed apart the Eastern and Western Chalcedonian churches, Eastern Orthodoxy and Roman Catholicism.

The Spirit is God

Bulgakov opens his *The Comforter* by a ringing affirmation. The divine personhood of the Spirit was 'written in the Gospel in letters of fire'. This is the 'other Paraclete' the Son will send from the Father and whose name, 'Holy Spirit', he reveals in disclosing the Trinitarian Name in that 'baptismal formula' which forms part of the 'great commission' at the end of Matthew's Gospel. The Spirit's Godhead is an 'unshakeable dogma', writes Bulgakov, which the Church has 'always received' because the moment of Pentecost, the Church's manifestation to the world, was its 'living revelation'.[2] So abundant were his gifts to the primitive Church (consult the Acts of the Apostles) that his action was incontrovertible, transparent in its self-evidence. It was the sheer overwhelmingness of this fact that made dogmatic commentary superfluous.

---

[1] For Bulgakov's pneumatology, *see* L. A. Zander, *Bog i mir*, op. cit., II., pp. 133–183.
[2] U, p. 7.

That is Bulgakov's explanation of the tardy development of an adequate theology of the Holy Spirit in the patristic Church. In any case, the Apologists have to concentrate on Christology (especially the doctrine of the Logos); Irenaeus, despite important comments on the Spirit's role in creation and salvation, is himself a theologian of the Incarnation. And when the need to think through what is involved in the Trinitarian life and activity begins to impose itself in the third century, it presented Christianity with a task of exceptional difficulty. Just as Judaism was incapable of resolving theologically the 'concrete doctrine of God' even as contained in its own sacred books, certainly ancient philosophy could furnish no scheme in which monotheism might be combined with a trinity of persons equally honourable and divine – persons consubstantial with each other in the single divine nature and defining each other by their mutual relations in the Trinitarian life.[3] At the best – and not all was for the best – such philosophy could offer some conceptual instruments, some means. The false tracks of Subordinationism and Modalism were hard to avoid. Fortunately, the great doctors of the fourth and fifth centuries illuminated the Church's doctrinal mind on the Trinity in general and pneumatology in particular. Afterwards, we have only the contribution, in sadly negative circumstances, of the polemical writers of the ninth, tenth and eleventh centuries – the authors who commented for or or against the *Filioque* (the putative origin of the Holy Spirit from the Son as well as the Father), that dividing issue between Constantinople and Rome.

Strength and weakness in the theology of the Fathers

But Bulgakov is dissatisfied with the efforts of even the greatest of the Fathers, as well as impressed by them. He praises Athanasius for seeing how Son and Spirit work 'dyadically' – distinctly yet in perfect unity – for our salvation, and yet Athanasius's doctrine of the Spirit in the famous *Letters to Serapion* is too Christocentric to be satisfactory: he has nothing on the Spirit's relation to the Father. And the great Alexandrian bishop treats the Spirit, complains Bulgakov, in a fashion almost exclusively economic. Even then it is only the Spirit's role in the economy of grace he considers, not the economy of creation. Again, the Cappadocians – Basil (*c.* 330– 379), his brother Gregory of Nyssa (329–389) and Gregory

---

[3] Ibid., p. 13.

Nazianzen (330–390) – can be congratulated on establishing a doctrine of the Holy Trinity that is classic. Bulgakov calls it the 'royal road' in guarding orthodoxy against deviations whether Subordinationist or Monarchian: they are 'ecumenical masters' whose merits 'cannot be exaggerated'.[4] But neither their general theological explanation of that doctrine nor their particular account of the Holy Spirit will fully do. He says this partly because these Fathers did not entirely anticipate Bulgakovian dogmatics! Thus, first, they showed how the divine Three enjoy a common *ousia* and to that extent are one, but not how they constitute a single tri-hypostatic subject, crucial as that is to Bulgakov's own theology of the triune Lord. Secondly, the Cappadocians make no attempt to show why the divine life is tri-hypostatic – that the persons are neither more than three nor less than three, leaving this simply to the witness of revelation. Rather harshly, Bulgakov says that the Cappadocians leave the hypostases 'juxtaposed' rather than united. This they do by defining them in terms of their specific distinguishing marks or characteristics (ungeneratedness for the Father, generability for the Son, procession for the Spirit) instead of by the persons' relations of communion. Third, these Fathers find a supplementary way of establishing the tri-unity of the persons by appeal to the idea of the monarchy of the Father, who is the Principle without a beginning. But while this is on the right lines inasmuch as the unity of the triune God cannot lie in the unity of his nature alone, it is left by them too vague and undeveloped. Fourthly, though they correctly stress the importance of the Trinitarian *taxis* – the order in which the persons are named – they cannot do much with this theologically, owing – once again – to the lack of a fuller understanding of the bonds between the persons. Fundamental perhaps to all these criticisms is Bulgakov's observation that the Aristotelean concept of hypostasis as concrete substance, on which the Cappadocians leaned, was insufficiently personal to help them build the edifice they wanted. (It was, he says, too 'thing-y', *veshchnii*.[5])

So far as their doctrine of the Spirit is concerned, all three men were valiant defenders of his Godhead – even if St Basil was reticent (so indeed was the Creed of the Third Ecumenical Council over which assembly his friend St Gregory presided for a period) in calling the Holy Spirit, quite simply, 'God'. To Basil, however, goes the honour of filling in two major gaps left by Athanasius. He

[4] Ibid., p. 43.
[5] Ibid., p. 42.

defines the Holy Spirit by his procession from the Father, following the principle of the monarchy (Athanasius, as already mentioned, had dealt only with the Spirit's relation to the Son.) And Basil, unlike Athanasius, makes it clear that the Spirit's dyadic working with the Son includes the work of creation, where he completes or perfects the Son's creative action, and not simply the work of salvation or grace. Moreover, he has a rich theology of the Spirit's gifts (Bulgakov calls Basil's teaching in this regard a 'treasure-house of pneumatological doctrine'[6]). But his writings are far poorer when it comes to a theology of the Spirit himself. What for Bulgakov is important about Gregory Nazianzen in these questions is his intuition that pneumatology is an area of doctrine where developments are providentially intended to occur – even though Nazianzen does not himself have them to hand. Now that the Son's divinity has been vindicated in the Church, Gregory expected a further illumination from the Trinity to light up the New Testament account of the Spirit: thus the great twenty-first Oration. And finally Bulgakov praises Gregory of Nyssa for his more far-reaching story of how the persons are bonded together: the Son drawing his origin immediately from the Father, the Spirit taking his from the Father mediated by the Son with whom he is united. Bulgakov notes in passing that Constantinople I itself, fruit of the efforts of the Cappadocians among others, does not even pose the problem of a formula for the Spirit's origin. The confession 'He proceeds from the Father' merely affirms his true divinity and that is all.

What then of Augustine? His *De Trinitate* includes the most systematic – and to that extent remarkable – theology of the Holy Spirit to be found in patristic times. Here Bulgakov can certainly not complain of a lack of a sense of the inner-Trinitarian relationships. Augustine defines the hypostases in terms of their relations, relations both of origin and of communion. Where the Cappadocians leave juxtaposition, Augustine bequeaths coherence. But Bulgakov is unhappy that Augustine begins his Trinitarian exposition from the unity of the divine nature – and the weight he gives this can be seen in, for example, his theology of the Old Testament theophanies. These Augustine is inclined to interpret not as theophanies of the persons but of the sole God who is 'in' the Trinity. Bulgakov's here is a common Orthodox criticism of Augustine and indeed of much later Latin theology as well. But Bulgakov is even-handed in noting that the Cappadocians, beginning from the opposite angle of the three-ness of the

[6] Ibid., p. 46.

persons, have just as much difficulty as Augustine in showing how God is the divine 'I'. But much can be forgiven Augustine for his 'veritable discovery' of the triune God as love, with the Spirit in particular as mutual love of Father and Son. This is an idea 'utterly unknown to Oriental theology' and Bulgakov finds it wonderful.[7]

His last port of call among the great Fathers is St John of Damascus, since he is the figure most generally regarded as summing up the entire preceding Greek patristic tradition. His *On the Orthodox Faith*, already used by Bulgakov in the opening Christological volume of the Great Trilogy, is, after all, the *Summa theologiae* of the Byzantine Church. Bulgakov praises Damascene for the way that, though his theology of the persons is Cappadocian, he tries to think through more fully their inter-personal relatedness. Thus for instance John is rightly keen to relate the Spirit to both Father and Son rather than to have in effect two dyads, Father-Son, and Son-Spirit, as happens in much earlier theology. This John does by speaking of the Spirit as the Spirit of both the Father and the Son since it is through the Son that he proceeds from the Father.[8] And where the economy of the Spirit is concerned, Bulgakov will take from Damascene's pneu-matology the idea – expressed by John in various similes or symbolic images – that the Holy Spirit is that trinitarian person who accomplishes, achieves and completes in reality what the Father has willed and the Son put into action. Here John makes more amply a point already indicated in Athanasius and the Cappadocians. But, as we shall now see, Bulgakov is not so happy about the general context in which these particular truths appear.

Damascene finds the starting-point for his fundamental doctrine of God in the sixth-century Syrian monk, much influenced by Neoplatonism, who wrote under the pseudonym of Dionysius the Areopagite. Accordingly, he takes 'divinity' – conceived not as the 'I am' of the Sinai revelation but as the divine *ousia* – to be what Bulgakov calls the 'ontological and logical prius' of his account of the existence of the persons.[9] What has happened to God as the 'absolute personality, the absolute I' to which the Hebrew Bible bears such eloquent witness? This decision imparts what is to Bulgakov's mind a false direction to John Damascene's Trinitarian thought. When John thinks of the hypostases he thinks first of all of their relations of origin from the divine being – not, as he should, of the divine Personality's tri-hypostatic life. True, Damascene tempers this imper-

[7] Ibid., p. 54.
[8] *De fide orthodoxa* I. 13.
[9] U, p. 56.

sonalism (as did the Cappadocians) by a tendency to identify the primordial 'divinity' with the Father. But this is also, for Bulgakov, a misleading move. The absolute Personality is the triune Subject, not the Father. To fail to see this is to open a door for the return of Origenist Subordinationism. To be fully orthodox we need to affirm the equal selfhood of the hypostases as mutually constitutive centres within the divine I, a tri-hypostatic I which is, then, both singular and plural, like the Old Testament *Elohim* – the one God who says 'we'. (Bulgakov calls *Elohim* the divine 'I-we'.)

But perhaps the most vehement objection of Bulgakov to what Damascene has to say about the monarchy of the Father concerns the way that, for John, the Father is the *cause* of the Son and the Spirit. As we shall see, Bulgakov has an extraordinary animus against the idea of causal relations between the persons. It leads inevitably, he thinks, to a view of Son and Spirit as quasi-created by the Father – notwithstanding, apparently, all the protestations of later writers in the tradition that 'cause' here means 'origination as in a principle', not creative making by God. His sweeping decision to do away with all talk of causal relations between the persons will have the effect – possibly desirable in the eyes of ecumenists! – of dismissing the entire Byzantine-Latin controversy over the procession of the Spirit as a waste of energy, a waste of words.

The Filioquist catastrophe

One can sympathize with Bulgakov when he complains that this issue – Filioquism and its Byzantine opposite, Monopatrism, has dominated pneumatology unwarrantably for a thousand years (at least so far as Catholic and Orthodox dogmatics are concerned).[10] What is less persuasive is his solution. The Conciliar affirmation of the Spirit's procession, *izkhozhdenie*, from the Father was only ever intended as a way of asserting his Godhead. Considering our lack of information about the circumstances of the Second Ecumenical Council that might be thought an over-ambitious statement but it is one in which the majority of historians of doctrine would probably concur. Bulgakov is inclined to say that, so far as verbal formulae are concerned, there is more in the Greek Fathers to support the Latin position than modern Orthodox will allow (notably in Epiphanius of Salamis [*c.* 315–403] and Cyril of Alexandria). Is the Latin teaching, then, so terrible? Many would say so, at any rate as a unilateral

---

[10] Ibid., p. 93.

addition to the Creed. But Bulgakov finds it striking that at the Seventh Ecumenical Council, Nicaea II, in 787, the solemn confirmation of faith sent to the eastern patriarchs include the words, 'I believe in the Holy Spirit, the life-giving Lord, who proceeds from the Father through the Son'. On that occasion the bishops evidently did not cavil. They quite naturally saw the words 'through the Son' as an explication of the existing symbol of faith. At the very least, this implies that the formula of the Nicene-Constantinopolitan Creed was not seen by the ancient Church as meant to be exhaustive. In the West, Augustine's theology of the Holy Spirit as the hypostatic love of Father and Son and thus proceeding from both, their common Gift, aroused no contemporary protest in the East, and it was subsequently confirmed by numerous Latin authors, including popes, venerated as saints by the Orthodox Church. The effort of St Maximus the Confessor to interpret the Western doctrine in an Eastern spirit is well-known.

For Bulgakov, this tolerance arose from a widespread awareness in the Church that the teaching on the Spirit of Constantinople I was incomplete. But in the deterioration of relations between Latin West and Greek East at the end of the patristic period and in the early Middle Ages, the inclusion of the *Filioque* in the Creed, first in Spain, then in the Frankish empire, and finally in Rome, drove such tolerance out. By briskly brushing away the ambiguity surrounding the issue of the Spirit's procession in the East and asserting so vigorously the procession from the Father alone, the Byzantine patriarch Photius (*c.* 810–*c.* 895) in his treatise of (roughly) 885, *The Discourse on the Mystagogy of the Holy Spirit*, 'founded the Latinising polemic against the Latin theology'.[11] Bulgakov finds it amazing that with all his erudition Photius did not see that the 'through the Spirit' of Damascene and others constituted a different theology from his own, just as it is almost incomprehensible to find him trying to range the Western Fathers and popes on his Monopatrist side. But for Bulgakov Photius' main error is to treat the whole thing in terms of *causality*. Photius' complaint is that the *Filioque* detracts from the unique causative power of the divine Father (though to be fair that is objectionable to Photius because seeming to distance the Spirit from the Father's intimate closeness). And so the polemics started and never stopped in a process Bulgakov describes as 'ever more able, ever more sterile'.[12] And always it is causal origin, causal origin, that is

[11] Ibid., p. 123.
[12] Ibid., p. 137.

the drum being beaten. For Bulgakov, this is simply the wrong
music. It was also playing from a hopeless score, since the attempt
to bring coherence – and indeed unanimity – into the patristic
literature on the point when many of the Fathers had never
consciously confronted the issue at all, could lead to no worthwhile
outcome. There *is* no homogeneous patristic doctrine on the
procession of the Spirit. After Lyons II and Florence, the *Filioque*
would be for Catholics dogma. Yet in practice for the Orthodox too
there is an 'anti-dogma' defined over against the Western teaching.

For his part, Bulgakov is equally opposed to the Florentine and
the Photian solutions. He thinks the Florentine theology brings
back a Subordinationism whereby the persons are unequally divine
– for only the Father is the fulness of the divine nature, *Deitas*; the
Son is *Deitas* minus the power to generate, the Spirit *Deitas* minus
the powers both to generate and to spirate. The Florentine teaching, moreover, divides the Holy Trinity into two sets of pairings:
Father to Son and Father and Son to Spirit, leaving the fashion in
which these sets may be reintegrated altogether obscure. Likewise
the Photian doctrine reduces the Trinity to two dyads, Father to
Son and Father to Spirit, thus producing not a triangle where all
points are joined to each other but an angle where from one point
lines descend to two further points that themselves never connect.
But above all Bulgakov complains that the entire theology of
processions as productions of persons, whether Filioquist or
Monopatrist is radically mistaken. Within the tri-hypostatic Subject
that is God, the persons are not 'produced'. They eternally *are*.
Both the Latin and the Byzantine theologies must be set aside as a
'millennium and a half of logomachy whose result is nil'.[13] 'Nil' not
least in the sense that Bulgakov has been unable to detect any fruit,
whether sweet or bitter, either of the Latin dogma or the Photian
doctrine. The Latin tendency to see the Church more in
Christological terms than pneumatic ones – sometimes cited by
modern Orthodox in this connexion – is for Bulgakov more likely
to be the background of Filioquism than its consequence.

Of course if the entire polemic can be set aside as misplaced, an
ecumenical advantage will follow. The *Filioque* ceases at once to be
an obstacle to Christian reunion. If anyone is to blame for the
impasse it is neither Augustine nor Photius but (says Bulgakov)
Basil, who first applied the language of cause, *aitia*, to the
Trinitarian relations – though even there it was, we can piously
hope, more a maladroit choice of metaphor for the Father's

13 Ibid., p. 161.

monarchy than a philosophical-theological commitment. Anyhow, let it be enough, says Bulgakov, to speak of the correlation of the hypostases, their mutual definition, and leave aside all talk of causal origins as unbiblical and, as events have shown, ecclesially unhelpful to boot.

Bulgakov's proposal

What Bulgakov proposes is in effect to limit an account of the Trinitarian relationships to a theology of the inner-Trinitarian revelation. On this view, it is not so much that the Father (for Bulgakov, the test case of his theory) gives rise to the other hypostases as that he reveals himself in them. Such self-revelation is not just a matter of the subjective consciousness of the divine persons. It is, so Bulgakov insists, a matter of their objective reality, since each person hypostatises the divine nature in himself. Each of the divine Three poses himself eternally as his own self-definition, a self-definition which supposes an act not only distinct in each person but also tri-hypostatic – 'in other words, personal and Trinitarian'.[14] Or again:

> The Holy Trinity is the Trinitarian act of self-determination of the hypostases, and each of the moments of this 'trinitarity', *troisvennost,* despite the autonomy and equidivinity of the three hypostases, is correlative to the two others and thus finds itself conditioned by them. The fulness of the natural being, *qua* that of the self-revelation, is only given in the trinitarity of the hypostatic self-definition.[15]

But the very fact that Bulgakov continues to use the language of generation and spiration, unavoidable unless the authority of Scripture be denied, forces him to describe the self-definition of the Father in terms of his arousal of the other persons, while his statement that the Father is Father as much by spiration as generation surely contradicts the plain sense of the Father's name. Be that as it may, Bulgakov's conclusion is that the Father spirates the Holy Spirit on the condition of the presence and participation of the Son, and generates the Son on the condition of the presence and participation of the Spirit. Thus both the Byzantines and the Latins are bypassed – at a price. What Bulgakov has done is to make affirmations that are indubitably true of the relations of communion of

14 Ibid., p. 172.
15 Ibid., p. 174.

the divine persons (where each relation conditions the others) and to let these stand in place of any account worth the name of the originating relations of those persons. Where this substitution is accepted, reconciliation between divided Christians in East and West can follow. The Orthodox East can now receive the *Filioque* which henceforth will signify: the third hypostasis must be understood not only by relation to the first, conformably to the principle of the monarchy of the Father, but also by reference to the second. The Catholic West (and Oriental Catholics) can accept Photian Monopatrism which will now mean simply: the Father alone expresses the idea of the monarchy, initial principle of the Holy Trinity. After all, it is the first hypostasis who is the centre of revelation, the One who is to be revealed. The others are his dy-hypostatic disclosure, but in such a way that each of these two hypostases depends not only on the Father but also on its co-revealing counterpart.[16] Though Bulgakov is too modest to say so, this is the theological thesis he would have liked to see dogmatized at a future ecumenical Council on the person of the Holy Spirit.

Bulgakov's survey of the Fathers left him with the distinct impression that they

> felt a certain perplexity before the very fact of the third hypostasis as that is given us in revelation and consequently proposed to rational study in theology.[17]

Quite apart from the – to his mind – insoluble *Filioque* problem, that is why he feels the need to offer his own theological picture of 'the place of the third hypostasis in the Holy Trinity'.[18] What he has to say on this in *The Comforter* naturally bears some relation to the general theology of the triune God offered in the opening volume of the Great Trilogy, *The Lamb of God*. Let us extract what is relatively new.

Bulgakov stresses more than before that the Holy Trinity is not a series of persons which just happens to stop at three. Rather, the Trinity is what he calls a 'closed whole', *zakliuchenno tselo*,[19] and this is crucial to locating the place of the Spirit, the Third. In 'Trinitarity', the 'I' of each person is not simply one of three or else there would be a society or alliance and this is tritheism. No, each 'I' posits itself in the others, for this alone is the divine triune Subject

---

[16] Ibid., p. 185.
[17] Ibid., p. 63.
[18] Ibid., p. 65.
[19] Ibid., p. 66.

to whom we pray as 'Thou'. Now Bulgakov can find no other explanation for the life of the triune Subject than love. In that perspective it is plain that to consider any divine hypostasis in its pure subjectivity is to admit an abstraction. Concretely, the Three are reciprocally defined by an unchanging correlation, even if they always retain their specifying properties which render them non-interchangeable. For Bulgakov, the total correlation is such that it is inappropriate to say of them, 'The Father *and* the Son *and* the Holy Spirit' – as, for instance, the Cappadocians do. Such a conjunctive 'and' is out of place in their perfect Trinitarian correlation. Bulgakov considers abstraction far too common a vice in Trinitarian theology. It is the root of the *Filioque* problem. We speak of the 'birth' of the Word and the 'procession' of the Holy Spirit and these are, he admits, good biblical words. But only by abstraction can they be interpreted, he suggests, as two aspects of origin – just as only by abstraction 'Fatherhood' is interpreted, in regard to both that birth and that procession, in terms of causality. Why, he asks, may not birth and procession be *sui generis* relations that differ so much in kind that they cannot be brought together under the common heading of aspects of origin? And is not the language of cause singularly inappropriate for the relation to Son and Spirit of the Father if we bear in mind its empiricist sense (a temporal sequence) or its Kantian sense (a category for co-ordinating empirical phenomena) or its scholastic sense (a foundation)? The first two senses of cause are obviously inapplicable to the Godhead. The third may look more hopeful but just watch! Soon we shall be conceiving the origin of the Trinity after the manner of the Stoics and Neo-Platonists: a primordial principle determining itself by posing other principles that are second and third in its regard. We shall end up with 'the most pernicious of Subordinationisms or finally Monarchianism'.[20] Despite the best intentions of the Cappadocians, what is it but Monarchianism to make Son and Spirit self-definitions of the Father outside himself? Let us by all means keep the monarchy of the Father, but let us also deprive it of all that smacks of cause. This, in one sentence, is Bulgakov's programme.

Person as revelation, not cause

Forget origin since in revelation the three hypostases are *givens*, a priori realities, and be more faithful to divine revelation by think-

[20] U, p. 72.

ing through the Holy Trinity as the divine Spirit whose life is love. The life of spirit, remarks Bulgakov, in one of the most strikingly Idealist sections of the Great Trilogy, consists in living out the reve-lation of personality in nature.[21] In the Holy Trinity, of course, the nature or *ousia* is in its transparency to the divine Spirit. It is the Wisdom of God which leaves no place for anything hypostatically unenlightened, no *Urgrund* or 'God behind the Trinity'. Nor is there, in the triune Lord, any place for a mono-hypostatic limita-tion such as self-love always entails. As triune, the divine Spirit abolishes in itself the frontiers of self-dilection. It is not self-love, it is *love*. The self-revelation of the Trinity is achieved first in that the Father, the initial hypostasis, who contains in himself the fullness of the divine nature, 'refuses' that fulness in his self-disclosure since he comes out from himself *by means of the generation of the Son* – which is not the Son's causal origin (perish the thought!) but simply the fact that the Father reveals, the Son is revealed. For Bulgakov, the Son is not so much *from* the Father's being as he is *in* that being. To Bulgakov's mind, that is the proper meaning of the Nicene *homoousion*. Father and Son are mutually defined by these relations in the *ousia* of God.

But then secondly, self-revelation is proper to the absolute Spirit as being in beauty by the living out of his own content. And this will bring Bulgakov back once more to the chief topic of *The Comforter*.

> The Father, the initial hypostasis, not only reveals himself in his *ousia*-Wisdom through the Son but he lives in it by the Holy Spirit. And the Son does not only reveal the Father through himself, in his *ousia*-Wisdom but again he lives in it by the Holy Spirit.[22]

As the divine actuality of truth and beauty that life realizes in itself the mutual existence of Father for Son and Son for Father not only in the 'statics' of ideal self-definition but also in the 'dynamics' of the life of one hypostasis through the other. Such a dynamics, says Bulgakov, cannot be simply a condition or state. There can be no such 'datum of external definition' in the absolute Subject. It can only be a person, a person who is (as the copula between the subject and the

---

[21] For Bulgakov's thesis that the general scheme of reality, as of language, is that of a subject revealing itself in an ideal element (a 'logos'), which is predicative, the disclosure of its nature, and a real element (the copula), joining the subject to the predicate, and this in such a way that Trinitarian belief is presup-posed by both ontology and grammar, see his *Die Tragödie der Philosophie* for a brief description of which *vide supra*, p.9..

[22] U, p. 77.

predicate, presupposing both Fatherhood and Sonship) the life of Father in Son, Son in Father. In this way, the 'procession' of the Spirit completes the self-revelation of that divine Subject in such a way that we can now put forward a compendious pronouncement. It runs:

All the being of God is personal and at the same time natural; there is no extra-hypostatic nature and no extra-natural hypostasis. The subject is defined by the predicate in a perfectly exhaustive form and the bond between them is also wholly exhaustive. In all its phases, natural being is rendered personal[23]

– and that in a way which shows how the persons can neither be less than three nor more.

This can also be called a tri-hypostatic revelation of divine love, which Bulgakov interprets, along lines we have seen, as a threefold 'sacrificiality' in the Trinitarian life issuing in joy, beatitude, triumph. Really, this is what gives the central volume of the Great Trilogy its title – 'The Comforter'. The first axiom of love, that there is no love without sacrifice, is always accompanied by a second, that there is none without joy and blessedness either. This 'blessedness of love' in the Holy Trinity, this 'consolation', *is* the Holy Spirit. As the inner-Trinitarian consummation of the sacrificial love of Father and Son, the Holy Spirit is triumphant love. This is the meaning of his person not only for God but for the world. He is the common love of Father and Son. To this degree Filioquism is justified though not in any sense which would obscure hypostatic distinction – and distinctiveness. He is love itself, realizing hypostatically the fullness of the love that is the essence of the Trinity in unity.[24] He is the 'Third'.

Number and the Trinity

Why such ordered number in God? Cognizant as he is of the problem the Cappadocians faced in showing how the enumeration of the Trinitarian persons according to a fixed order had to be squared with their equality of dignity, Bulgakov is interested to find Basil insisting that, in itself, the category of number is inapplicable

---

[23] Ibid., p. 78.
[24] These ideas are far more common in the Christian West, as is recognized by M. A. Meerson, *The Trinity of Love in Modern Russian Theology. The Love Paradigm and the Retrieval of Western Mediaeval Love Mysticism in Modern Russian Trinitarian Thought [from Soloviev to Bulgakov]* (Quincy, Ill., 1998).

to divinity. One does not add persons nor, by the same token, in calling one the sole God of Christians, is the oneness professed number rather than essence. A pity, Bulgakov thinks, that Basil and other like-minded ancient theologians such as Ambrose (*c.* 339–397), did not take their principles further. Basil's idea that what we are dealing with is 'supernumeration', *hyparithmesis,* can be extended.[25] The notion of number as the counting of units in their abstract equality or likeness does not exhaust the nature of number which can also have a qualitative sense in expressing a 'special type or structure', 'an internal correlation proper to the structure as a whole', its 'specific qualification'.[26] What Bulgakov would like to say is that the divine triunity is a *sui generis* number that is absent from our numeration. A rationalistic theology fails to notice the fact that triunity penetrates both nature (tri-*unity*) and person (*tri*-unity).

So much for the cardinal numbers – 1, 2, 3 – but what of the ordinals, 1st, 2nd, 3rd? Bulgakov points out that in principle, for given purposes, to grasp this or that inter-relation, one could count ordinally among the Trinitarian persons in any of six ways. But the baptismal formula in the Gospel of Matthew (28: 19) gives primacy to a particular *taxis* which has become in practice an 'exclusive usage in the Church'.[27] This *taxis* must neither be over- nor under-estimated. If each hypostasis has a trinitarian definition, it is the first, second and third *together* and this primordial ontological fact ought never to be obscured. To over-interpret the *taxis* ontologi-cally as the order of origination from a cause or common source leads inevitably to a defective appreciation of the Paraclete who then appears as the sole 'infertile' hypostasis compared with the second and first. We are not surprised to find that, in place of an understanding of the *taxis* as concerning origin, Bulgakov wishes to see it in terms of the trinitarian self-revelation, where generation and procession are *forms of co-revelation.* On such a view, the *taxis* states the ontological *prius* and *posterius,* in no way threatening the equal dignity of the Three. The *taxis* includes the revelation of the Father in the Word realized in the Holy Spirit, or, put in terms of the tri-hypostatic love: Loving-Loved-Love itself. On any such view, the Father must be numbered ordinally first but – says Bulgakov – we cannot speak apodeictically about the place of the Son and Spirit. The order of relation of Son and Spirit 'is not stable; it can

---

[25] Basil, *De Spiritu sancto,* 18, 44.
[26] U, p. 84.
[27] Ibid., p. 86.

be reversed'.[28] To be sure, there is an obvious *prius* of the Son over against the Spirit: he is the condition of the Spirit's procession. But there is also a sense in which the Spirit is *prius* for the Son, resting on him and uniting him with the Father.

This should strike us in the economy – for which Bulgakov *is* happy to use the language of the Father's causally originating activity in the missions. The Father *sends* the Son and Spirit. Yet precisely in the economy – as indicated in the Christological chapters of this book – the roles of the second and third hypostases in the *taxis* appear to be reversible: the Spirit begins the Incarnation by descending on the Virgin and accomplishes the work of salvation by descending from heaven at Pentecost. In this sense there is something to be said for speaking not of the first, second and third, but of the first and the two 'not-firsts'. But the crucial point is given in the patristic master-idea from which Bulgakov set forth: what we are dealing with here is not so much number as correlation.[29]

[28] Ibid., p. 91.
[29] Ibid., p. 92.

9

The Spirit in Creation, Inspiration, Incarnation

The divine triunity reveals itself conclusively in the hypostasis of the Holy Spirit.

> In the fullness and perfection of his self-revelation God is the third hypostasis, last and concluding, who is also so to say the first.[1]

Not for nothing is the name of the divine Spirit – the Spirit of God, the triune Lord – so closely allied to that of the third hypostasis, the Holy Spirit. As we saw when looking at the distinctive roles of the Trinitarian persons in regard to creation, the immediate revelation of the hypostasis to creatures is the action of the Holy Spirit whose revealed content is the Word who himself shows forth the Father. The issue is raised in Holy Scripture by the way it speaks 'promiscuously' of the Holy Spirit and the Spirit of God. Bulgakov proposes as a rule of thumb that wherever in Scripture we hear of God as Holy Trinity but without distinction of hypostases we should discern a reference to the third person – or, more precisely, to his action or manifestation. It is a matter of the 'spirituality of the divine Spirit in the fullness of his revelation'.[2] The paradox is: the Old Testament 'is completely ignorant of the Holy Spirit yet knows perfectly the action of the Spirit of God'.[3]

The Holy Spirit and the Old Testament

Bulgakov finds in the first Genesis account, and more especially at Genesis 1: 2 in the Spirit's 'moving over the waters', the most

[1] U, p. 188.
[2] Ibid., p. 189, note 1.
[3] Ibid., p. 190.

important Old Testament witness to the Spirit of God. What is described is a primal Pentecost. It is not yet of course effective for humankind which still has to make its appearance in the cosmos. But it takes place by way of anticipation of man's coming into the world. Yet neither the first nor the second Pentecost, the Pentecost of the infant Church, know the Spirit himself in his hypostatic being. In each case, the creation can only receive his power, in what concerns the 'fecundation of the world [the first Pentecost] as well as [in the second] the souls embraced by the tongues of fire'.[4] Bulgakov has already suggested how the Old Testament texts that speak of prophesying by the Lord's Spirit witness indirectly to the third person though not as yet in his distinct hypostaseity. Now he adds that we also hear a good deal in the Elder Covenant about his gifts. Such gifts as art and creativity, governance and warrior-ship, kingship and priesthood can also be considered, along with prophecy, types of the Pentecostal outpouring that follows on the Session of Christ. In Old Testament terms, this is the Spirit of God and not the Holy Spirit even if there is a degree of legitimacy in finding here a pre-application of Paul's words in First Corinthians:

> Now there are varieties of gifts but the same Spirit ... To each is given the manifestation of the Spirit for the common good. (12: 4, 7)

The Holy Spirit in the Gospels and Acts

To pass to the New Testament, however, is to move into a world where at last:

> particular manifestations and revelations of the Spirit of God are actually related to the Holy Spirit and receive, so to say, his hypo-static coefficient.[5]

The Synoptic accounts of the conception of Jesus, Simeon's meeting with the Lord, the Baptism of Christ, his entry into the wilderness, his first preaching, exorcistic activity and (especially significant for Bulgakov's Triadology) his joy: all these are given as their explanation the particular action of the Holy Spirit. To the Spirit's role in Christ's activity John the Baptist bears witness, just as had the angel Gabriel to the Forerunner's filling with the Spirit 'from his mother's womb' (Luke 1: 15). But it is John's Gospel

---

[4] Ibid., p. 191.
[5] Ibid., p. 195: *upostasni koeffitsient.*

which is 'pneumatological *par excellence*'. Bulgakov would expect this. As the

> work of the beloved disciple who had welcomed into his home the Mother of God, the *Pneumatophora*, and had been adopted by her, this Gospel is filled with knowledge of the Holy Spirit and a very special revelation about him.[6]

Directly, it provides a teaching on the Holy Spirit that is spread throughout this text; on the Spirit specifically as Comforter that teaching can be found in the Farewell Discourse. Indirectly, the Gospel according to John allows us to perceive the dyadic relation of the second and third persons, such that in this Gospel 'logology', the doctrine of the Word, becomes pneumatology, the doctrine of the Spirit.

Bulgakov's exegesis of the Johannine Prologue is rather ingenious than persuasive. He finds the Holy Spirit in the 'with' of 'The Word was with God' (1: 1), and in the 'were made' of 'All things were made through him' (1: 3) – the tense of the verb suggesting the perfective quality of the third hypostasis. The 'glory' which the Evangelist and his fellows have seen in the only Son (1: 14), like the life of 'in him was life' (1: 4) will surely – again – be the Spirit who, resting on the Son, makes up with him the dyad of the Father's co-revealers.

It is when Bulgakov turns to the body of the Gospel, and notably to the Farewell Discourse, that his exegesis comes into its own. In John 4 the Evangelist himself identifies the 'living water' Christ will give (4: 4) with the Holy Spirit (cf. 7: 37–39). Nor does it seem far from John's mind to make of the 'worship in spirit and truth' of the same Encounter with the Samaritan Woman (4: 24) worship 'in the Spirit and the Son'. Bulgakov finds the Spirit in the 'life the Father has given the Son to have in himself ' (5: 26), as well as in the 'other' who 'bears witness to [the Son]' in the same Discourse at the Pool of Bethzatha (5: 32). In a similar forensic context in chapter eight, when Jesus is teaching in the Temple precincts, Bulgakov finds in the two 'witnesses' to whom Jesus appeals (cf. 8: 17) the Spirit and the Father (and not, as would be more usual, the Father and the Son). In the Discourse on the Bread of Life, the 'spirit that vivifies' (6: 63) must surely be he. And in the dialogue which accompanies the Raising of Lazarus, Martha's words, 'I believe that you are the Christ, the Son of God' (11: 27) constitute

---

[6] Ibid., p. 196.

a covert reference to the Spirit if 'the Christ' means, as it must, the Spirit-anointed One. But it is in the Farewell Discourse (chapters 13 to 17) that Bulgakov finds:

> not only an exceptional and abundant source of revelation on the Holy Spirit, the hypostatic Consoler, but ... the very clear doctrine of [the Spirit and the Son's] dyadic unity, their twofold identity, their twofold quality of Consoler, *dvu-Uteshitelstvo* ... It is in their twofold unity that the Father is unveiled.[7]

This is the 'marvel of marvels, Gospel of Gospels'.[8] Christ is leaving the world while not abandoning it. He is sending the Holy Spirit whose revelation carries the disclosure to the Church of the Trinitarian love as glory, union and perfect joy – a complex of elements which it is impossible not to connect as closely as possible with the central promise of the Spirit. The Farewell Discourse is 'the promise of Pentecost'.[9] Here the Passion, glorification and sending of the Spirit are one single complex act. 'Now is the Son of man glorified.' (John 13: 31).

And as to that name, 'the Comforter', for Bulgakov the work of the *first* Paraclete, Christ the Intercessor, is above all to obtain the sending of that *other* Paraclete, the Holy Spirit. Sent dyadically by Father and Son, his mission must be interpreted by reference to the sending of the other dyad: Son and Spirit. The Paraclete it is who brings consolation to the apostles and the entire world by his descent from heaven. Through him is bestowed the presence of Christ, 'always, to the close of the age' (Matthew 28: 26). Bulgakov shows great dialectical skill in suggesting how in the Farewell Discourse 'the intra-Trinitarian determination of the place of the third hypostasis is furnished in a complete and exhaustive way: both triadically and dyadically'.[10]

The divine love-command was already known in the Hebrew Bible. The 'new' commandment of love (John 13: 35) speaks rather of ecclesial love, love among the disciples, here traced back to its highest source in the Holy Spirit. In the 'we' who will come to the disciple who keeps Jesus' words, Bulgakov finds 'mystically hidden the hypostasis of love, the One who bonds, the Third'.[11] The 'day' on which the disciples will know the Son to be in the

---

[7] Ibid., pp. 199–200.
[8] Ibid., p. 200.
[9] Ibid., p. 201.
[10] Ibid., pp. 202–203.
[11] Ibid., p. 203.

Father, they in the Son and he in them (cf. John 14: 20), is at once
Pentecost and the Parousia.

Bulgakov does not want to leave the fourth Gospel without refer-
ring to the post-Resurrection 'breathing' whereby the Son gives the
disciples the Holy Spirit (John 20: 21–23). Splendidly, Bulgakov
calls this the:

> enthronement of the apostles in the rank of hierarchs, effected by
> Christ the High Priest while still on earth, in anticipation of the
> Pentecost which will extend to the whole Church.[12]

Moving on from the fourth Gospel, the Book of Acts has been
called the 'Gospel of the Holy Spirit' so Bulgakov can hardly pass
it by altogether. And yet like Pentecost itself, the Acts speak of the
gifts and operations of the Holy Spirit: not his hypostatic being but
his charactistic action. The same is true, by and large, of the New
Testament letters even though (against Unitarians and Binitarians
of all ages) there are sufficient texts that make his distinct divine
personhood clear.

So Bulgakov calls the Holy Spirit the 'secret hypostasis'. Even
Pentecost is only the beginning of the fulfilment of the promise to
send the Consoler, not its fullness. The abundance of the Spirit's
gifts in the Church, so Bulgakov is inclined to argue, differs only
quantitatively from its Old Testament predecessor. As he explains:

> The qualitative difference concerns not so much the revelation of
> the Holy Spirit as the Incarnation of Christ which is completed in
> the Church. The context of Pentecost is in this sense more
> Christological than pneumatological, and it finds its immediate
> expression not in preaching about the Holy Spirit but preaching
> about Christ and his Resurrection.[13]

The Spirit reveals himself by his operative grace, not his personal
presence. Only in one New Testament text does the Holy Spirit
speak in his own name (Acts 13: 2). Always he is referred to by
others. It seems 'the Face of the Holy Spirit remains veiled in
mystery'. It is unknowable, in itself unrevealed.[14] Bulgakov puts the
question, Is the hypostatic revelation of the Spirit a mystery of the
Age to Come in the kingdom of glory? Or does the silence come
from the proper character of the Holy Spirit as third hypostasis?

---

[12] Ibid., p. 204.
[13] Ibid., p. 206.
[14] Ibid., p. 207.

The lack of biblical enlightenment on the topic encourages Bulgakov to seek illumination from what sophiological theology might be able to say on the dyad of the Spirit with the Son.

A sophiological approach to the Holy Spirit

The two hypostases are united in the gracious revelation of the Father in the divine Wisdom 'without separation and without confusion', each carrying out its irreplaceable task in union with the other. In the correlation of the hypostases 'there is and can be no mutability which would have signified the abolition of their personal characters', thereby introducing a hypostatic indifference.[15] Divine Wisdom, as the 'all-reality containing all the creative ideas and "words"' can be realized in the creation by neither alone. In the dyad of Son and Spirit in the Godhead, the kenosis of the Son and the triumph of the Spirit's procession are, by a single eternal Trinitarian act, at one. The presence of the Son is the condition of the Spirit's procession yet the Spirit proceeds so as to rest on the Son as the triumphant love which crowns the sacrificial revelation accomplished in the Father's engendering of the Word. In his existence as a Go-between, the Holy Spirit possesses himself hypostatically as the Love of the Others: their consolation which thus becomes his *own* consolation and he himself *Uteshitel'*, 'The Comforter'. His transparency to the Others makes him seem anhypostatic, such is his humility. But it is precisely by this – his 'impersonal' personality – that he has the perfection of the divine life we call 'glory'. In the dyadic revelation of the Father, while the Word reveals the Father as content, the Spirit reveals him as beauty. The inseparability of Son and Spirit is founded not only on their common 'principle' in the Father but also in the way they reveal him together in the Wisdom of God by a concrete act itself determined by their mutual relations.

This everlasting correlation in the immanent Trinity becomes accessible to us in the economy – which is as much as to say, christologically. The Spirit is the Spirit of the truth of Christ. Resuming the conclusions of his study of the Trinitarian presuppositions of being and language, the early *Die Tragödie der Philosophie*, Bulgakov writes:

[15] Ibid., p. 211.

The hypostasis of the Word is expressed in itself by the fact that it is born of the Father. The Father is the Subject of the Word-Predicate. He has in himself his Predicate, the Word, and by that his hyposta-sis is, at it were, self-evident. We can say the same of the third hypostasis in the measure that he is the Spirit of the second (the 'Spirit of truth'). By his content, he is correlative to the Word. He becomes transparent to the Word and is now only as it were the form of the being of the Word, or the Copula uniting Subject and Predicate. In this transparence to the Word, the hypostasis of the Spirit discloses itself and, one can say, identifies itself with him.[16]

Characteristically, Bulgakov moves from this austere analysis to a lyrical paean. The Spirit's hypostasis, having no face of its own, is but the face of the Son *in his glory*. Yet in the 'sunburst of this glory', the Spirit declares himself as personally the glory of the Trinity, even though that glory is, for him personally, only allu-sively seen.

We see the sun in light as the source of light, but we do not see the light itself in which and by which alone the sun can become visible to us.[17]

A sophiological theology of the Holy Spirit's work will apply these themes of wisdom and glory – reworked, the key biblical themes of Bulgakov's theology of the divine nature – to the topics of creation, Old Testament inspiration, and inspiration in the incarnate Word, centre of the New Testament revelation.

The Spirit and creation

What, sophiologically investigated, is the Spirit's part in the Father's creative work? The investigation *should* be sophiological because, as the 'objective' principle of the divine being, it is in and by means of his Wisdom that the Father both creates and reveals. And in fact for Bulgakov, the Spirit, who like the Word is not mani-fested in creation according to his own hypostasis, is appropriately said to co-work there by disclosing the Father's Wisdom. The creation displays the sophianic, not the hypostatic, in God (until, that is, there is question of creating human personhood 'in his image and likeness'). Specifically, the Spirit by his action invests

[16] Ibid., p. 220.
[17] Ibid.

the creation with beauty – which, for Bulgakov, is what lies behind the reiterated statement of the Hebrew text of Genesis that God saw that each created realm was 'good'. To this he would link that initial but non-lasting transfiguration of matter that was the garden of Eden. The spiritualization of matter is a tell-tale sign that the Spirit has been at work. And this is important, because when the Spirit, like the Son, acts sophianically rather than hypostatically (a distinction, that, and not a division), he 'in some way effaces himself kenotically in the person of the Father' – of whom, after all, we proclaim in the Creed that *he* is the Creator of all things, visible and invisible.[18] Like the creation, the Old Testament will be the Spirit's sophianic revelation *anhypostatically* – not in his person but in his gifts. Not of course that any gift of the Spirit can by 'extra-hypostatic', unrelated to his person. That is why:

> all the little particular pentecosts which will be united in the single hypostatic Pentecost of the Holy Spirit cannot be understood separately from him.[19]

On creation, Bulgakov stresses in the pneumatological context that the divine command, 'Let it be!', should not be thought of as a word pronounced once for all but as 'ever being pronounced, since it is the universe's foundation'.[20] Integral to the creative act is an aspect of plenitude signalled mythopoeically by the way the Lord 'rested' on the seventh day after his labours. The initial creation contains embryonically all the 'logical seeds' of everything made in the Logos, the Word. But equally there is an aspect of incompleteness. It is only by the Spirit resting on the Word that what is non-manifested in created wisdom becomes manifest through coming to its proper term. 'This dynamic of universal life corresponds to the domain of the Holy Spirit in creaturely wisdom.'[21] Not for nothing does the Creed call the Spirit the 'Giver of life'. Daringly, Bulgakov speaks of earth – on its own level also life-giving – as the power of the Holy Spirit. 'Earth' here cannot be the planet Earth as geophysically surveyed. Rather is it earth metaphysically conceived as

---

[18] Ibid., p. 228. So Bulgakov can add that when, with the great majority of the Church Fathers, he says of the Old Testament theophanies it was the Logos who appeared as YHWH, he means the 'divine Logos who effaces himself kenotically and renders his Face invisible in the light of the Fatherly hypostasis, speaking as the latter's voice', ibid.

[19] U, p. 229.

[20] Ibid., p. 230.

[21] Ibid., p. 231.

the *natura naturans* which brings to birth, by means of the Word
lodged in it, the *natura naturata* – or which becomes this last ..., the
natural energy of life which can never be extinguished or interrupted in this world but bears always within it creative activity's
principle of growth.[22]

Silently, the Spirit acts in created wisdom by rendering earth fruitful for the Word – and was honoured by pagans, without their
knowing it, under the names of Pan, or Isis, or Gaia. (Little did
Bulgakov himself know what would be, long after his death, the
resonance of that last name to the practitioners of 'New Age'!)
Bulgakov accepts the term 'panentheism' for his point of view.
But he builds in safeguards. The creative power in nature is not
God; it is only the energy of God. God is personal, the cosmos
impersonal. The divine basis to the world consists not in hypostatic
presence leading to an identification with the world but in the
sophianity of the world's foundation. Moreover, the world has its own
creaturely *aseitas*, its 'being by itself', which is God-given. For this
very reason, its being must not be understood as 'outside' or
'without' God. But though Bulgakov has conceded that the divine
presence in the cosmos is not, as such, hypostatic, he wants to say
nonetheless that the power of God in creation corresponds to the
action of the third divine person. The Holy Spirit's living power is
the 'grace of creation' in that distinctive term of Bulgakov's theology of the nature-grace relation. And by rendering the structure of
created things transparently, beautifully *formal*, filled with intelligi-
bility and meaning, the Holy Spirit shows himself to be the 'Artist
of the world, the Principle of form, and the Form of forms'.[23] But
this is no idyll, for there is perpetual struggle in nature with the
negative aspect of the 'relative nothingness of the world: chaos is
not yet fully mastered as cosmos. Nature is awaiting its humaniza-
tion – for Bulgakov a pre-requisite for full coherence with the
Logos. And yet, insofar as it bears the Holy Spirit nature is already
'God-carrying' and proclaims his glory. That explains how life in
conscious enjoyment of nature can yield a touch of the Holy Spirit
(Bulgakov was thinking, perhaps, of his own converting experience
of the beauty of the Caucasus).

Nature exists through the sophianic action of the Holy Spirit and
it is normal that the hypostasis of Beauty invests it with beauty –

---

[22] Ibid.
[23] Ibid., p. 233: *mirovoi Khudozhnik, Nachalo formi, Forma form'*.

which is already the *preliminary* image of God's advent by the Holy Spirit.[24]

From a moral standpoint, beauty is now, after the Fall, highly ambivalent. In an ontological perspective, however, it remains the 'flowering of the creature': *tsvetenie tvari*, the flower of creation.[25]

Beauty is form realized: the 'exteriorised sophianity of the creature, reflection of the eternal mysterious light of the divine Wisdom'.[26] Where that meta-empirical foundation goes unrecognised, aesthetics is reduced to psychology, beauty confined to the subjective. And yet the beauty of nature is *pre*-human and to that extent amoral. It is the freedom of the rational creature that gives natural beauty a moral co-efficient, which consists in the way such natural beauty is *applied*. The tragedy of a beauty which expresses the Spirit and yet, given the right – which means the wrong – subjective conditions can corrupt man is a supreme symptom of the tragedy of the Fall itself. Beauty perdures not just in Eden but in Sodom as well. Bulgakov finds here an illustration of the kenosis of the Holy Spirit on which the Great Trilogy has already touched in its theology of the Trinity and to which we must return. The Spirit freely accepts the limited, laborious receptivity which is all that is offered him by a creation become to a degree deaf to his 'interior calls', an arena in which fallen angelic powers are active. It is a creation vulnerable to intrusion by 'vanity', the term of the author of Ecclesiastes for what Bulgakov analyzes as the threatening chaos of non-being. In this context, the Holy Spirit's characteristic kenosis is God's patience with the world.

That world is a developing world – the very word *natura* says as much. For a 'blind and incredulous science' evolution means transformation 'denuded of all plan', whereas only a goal-directed evolutionism actually makes sense.[27] By the 'grace of creation', bestowed on each level of natural reality according to its capacity, the Spirit inspires the life of nature to contribute to its own unfolding.

---

[24] Ibid., p. 234.
[25] Ibid., p. 238.
[26] Ibid., p. 235.
[27] Ibid., p. 240. Bulgakov points out that few evolutionists are nihilists or complete relativists, or they would not use the language of 'higher' species: tacit ordering is always sub-intruded somewhere.

The Spirit and inspiration

In the human being, the power of inspiration that comes from the Spirit by way of the sophianic foundation of the human mind is a creative illumination that expresses itself in natural prophecy, cosmic consciousness and what the ancients called the 'muses'. Though disturbed and even deformed, the outlook of paganism, sophiologically speaking, is for this reason far from null and void. Bulgakov is particularly interested in the muses. While we need to distinguish different intensities or qualities of inspiration (biblical prophecy is of a higher order than the inspiration accorded Fathers and liturgists, and *a fortiori* than the inspiration behind human creativity at large), it would be impossibly narrowing of the Spirit's sophianic – rather than hypostatic – action to exclude from its purview natural religion, philosophy, art. It remains the case, however, that sharing the lot of the fallen creation, the manner in which such 'natural' inspiration is received and exercised can require rectification. Bulgakov uses a stronger term: 'exorcism'.[28]

All in all, one can say that the Word supplies the 'what' of creation, the Holy Spirit the 'how'. Bulgakov's description of the 'modal' nature of the Spirit's role in bringing about the world made through the Word comes to its climax in an account of *novelty*. The human creature cannot 'enrich' God by supplying what is utterly original (all is found aboriginally in the Word). Yet the manner in which the Spirit throws open creation's potential to human creativity enables man to realize the world's plenitude in ever new ways.

In his kenosis the Spirit is the power of being, the Life-giver, for that which is merely in becoming – so unlike the utter fullness which, in the eternal Godhead, is his native home. 'Plenitude accepts the unfulfilled, eternity becoming.'[29] The extent of this kenosis is quite beyond creaturely appreciation. And yet it is what renders the Spirit the Creator. The natural 'grace' of the Creator Spirit, present in the 'flesh' of the world, is the condition for the sanctification of worldly being by the Spirit's fresh dispensations – most obviously, for the supernatural sanctification of matter by sacramental blessing. For Bulgakov it is inconceivable that matter could receive spirit unless there were met beforehand the prior condition of the Spirit's kenosis in creation. This is his Orthodox response to his own earlier position as a Marxian materialist as well

---

[28] Ibid., pp. 246–247.
[29] Ibid., p. 254.

as his rebuttal of those who consider the Church's sacramentalism a superstition. It is not only in Eucharistic transubstantiation but in every sacramental act that matter communicates with divinity in a union without separation if also without confusion. Matter is being taken forward, for man's sake, into that future when God will be all in all.

As that last formulation suggests, there is a theanthropic principle at work here which can only be seen fully in the communion of humanity with God. Short of the unique Incarnation, that is glimpsed in the divine inspiration of human beings so key to the story line of Scripture, in both Old Testament and New. The human hypostasis remains what it is – human, but it is called to yield up space in itself for a 'diphysite' life. Bulgakov will have nothing to do with a 'pneumatological docetism' which would suppress natural human integrity in the name of divine inspiration: what is this but Monophysitism applied no longer, as with its historic original, to Jesus but this time to prophets and apostles? Nor on the other hand will he countenance a separationist style of Nestorianism – not, as in the patristic period, dividing the Saviour in two persons, but, equally divisively, treating the human spirit of the prophetic disciple as a *tabula rasa* on which the divine Spirit engraves any words he pleases.

And yet the historic Nestorian notion of a conjunction, *sunapheia*, of two heterogeneous persons in a 'union according to *prosôpon*', however inadequate in Christology, *does* fit the bill here. Whereas in the Incarnation, the single divine hypostasis governs the life of two harmonized natures, here by contrast it is the case that, thanks to the accord of the divine and the human, the human hypostasis discovers a person not his own and in the process finds his own spirit 'glowing' as a result.

> The Spirit of God gives to the man who sounds his own depth to know in and through that depth the depths of God and to live by those depths, thus becoming transparent to the Spirit of God.[30]

And so the inspired man or woman, while retaining to the full their natural being, becomes 'pneumatophoric' not only in that natural being but in their personal being and hypostatic consciousness as well. The Blessed Virgin Mary and the other saints are the expression of that. But, helpfully for human understanding, it has its lower analogues in sages and poets of many kinds. (Like all

[30] Ibid., p. 257.

students of Russian literature of the nineteenth and twentieth centuries Bulgakov would have been aware of the marked tendency to present creative writers as prophets.) The latter are useful to doctrinal theology: they can persuade people that the human spirit is not closed off from the divine. The permeability of the human spirit to other spirits is one of its most salient characteristics. Such influences compose a web in which we are not so much caught as sustained, our personalities functioning as mosaics of influence both given and received. (This may sound Post-modern, but Bulgakov is keen to insist that hypostatic awareness itself remains, within this complexity, both unique and also simple.) Bulgakov extends the scope of this web to the influence on us of the companionate animals as of the angels, both holy and otherwise. The 'communional' nature of the human spirit makes it easier to find credible the immediate influence on us of the Holy Spirit.

To the reality of this influence, the Old and New Testaments bear their witness. The 'Church' of the Old Covenant is theanthropy in process of realization but not as yet realized. The communication of all the Lord's 'words' in the Hebrew Bible presupposes the ready-making action of the Spirit. There is already in ancient Israel a 'Pentecost' of the Spirit. The descent of the Spirit for inspiration is as necessary to the divine plan as is the descent of the Logos in Incarnation.

> All Old Testament 'ecclesiality', tserkovnost', in the Temple and outside the Temple, was moved by the Holy Spirit.[31]

And if the inspirational graces to Israel reach their apogee in Mary, the spiritual heiress to her ancestors, who are thus made to point to the Word taking flesh at Nazareth, that christological trajectory is not the whole story. The way the people of the Old Testament Church receive so many of the gifts the New Testament describes as proper to the action of the Spirit as Spirit of the Messianic Lord, suggests that Israel anticipates not only the Annunciation and the beginnings of divine gestation but also Pentecost and the appearance of the tongues of fire.

Israel was the 'protected vine of God'.[32] The Gentile nations cannot be compared with her. But does it follow that those other nations were completely bereft of the inspiration of the Holy Spirit? Bulgakov makes much of the case of the pagan centurion

---

[31] Ibid., p. 265.
[32] Ibid., p. 269.

Cornelius in the Book of the Acts: it was by his pagan piety and prayers that Cornelius was found worthy to enjoy the angelic vision that preceded his conversion and that of his household (10: 1–48). And this makes us think about that shadowy figure the priest-king of Salem, Melchizedek who in Genesis (14: 18–20) blesses Abraham. Rather as with the Jesuit patrologist Jean Daniélou (1905–1974), who was thinking through these same issues at Paris in more or less the same period, Bulgakov sees Abraham and Melchizedek as (equally[?]) representatives of the Old Testament, one for the elect people, the other for the contemporary 'holy pagans'.[33] The inspired author, after all, does not hesitate to say of Melchizedek that he served 'God the Most High'. Indeed, without this addendum, could he have played his – major – part in the dogmatic structure of the Letter to the Hebrews where, without genealogy, he appears as the type of the great high priest Jesus Christ? A cognate significance attaches to the pagan prophet Balaam in the Book of Numbers of whom it was explicitly written, 'And the Spirit of God came upon him' (24: 2). Of Balaam's four oracles, one is direct messianic prophecy of considerable importance for later Judaism and the New Testament. Bulgakov can only conclude:

> Clearly, the night of paganism was not opposed to penetration by rays issuing from an authentic priesthood and prophecy – that is, from direct gifts of the Holy Spirit.[34]

The Holy Spirit was breathing in these non-revealed (and in this sense, natural) religions. *That* is the proper conclusion to draw and not the homogenizing reductionism practiced by a 'science' of comparative religion which, Bulgakov scornfully but not unfairly remarks, 'does not know what to do with the documents it accumulates nor how to give them a religious meaning'.[35] What are these gifts to the pagans if not verification of Peter's expostulation to Cornelius, 'Truly I perceive that . . . in every nation any one who fears [God] and does what is right is acceptable to him' (Acts 10: 341b–5). The Church, moreover, continued to accept the gifts transmitted via pagan philosophy and art: 'the presents of its mages and the wisdom of its teachers'.[36] When the Church places the images of the pagan philosophers at the entrance to her own

---

[33] J. Daniélou, *Les 'saints païens' de l'Ancien Testament* (Paris, 1956).
[34] U, p. 275.
[35] Ibid.
[36] Ibid., p. 276.

temples, as in the Annunciation Cathedral in Moscow, is not this in testimony to their possession of the Spirit of God?

But refracted as they are through the prism of sinful humanity, the inspirations of the Holy Ghost in paganism do not generate religion pure and undefiled. Rather, in a fatal complexity truth is mingled with error, moral good with evil. In the light of revelation we can see this complexity for what it is – but, *by the very same token* we can acknowledge the valid elements in the pagan religiosities of various times and places. Bulgakov emphasizes the partial quality of the teachings of the different world religions. Only dialectically, by negative as well as positive relation, can they achieve between themselves some simulacrum of the truth contained as a single vital synthesis in the actual historic revelation: Christianity as borne by the Church, mandated by the Word incarnate, himself prepared in Israel. Indeed, only by reference to that revelation can we identify the points in the other religions that, suitably inter-related, approximate to truth. In any other approach, these religions, taken singly, are dangerous to us. Not for nothing did the prophets of Israel so jealously guard the people against spiritual contamination by them. Only a 'positive philosophy of the history of religions'[37] – Bulgakov means one that starts with the epistemological advantage of recognising the truth of the Gospel – can deal equitably with the world religions, sorting out grain from chaff.

When Bulgakov thinks of the 'new atheistic paganism' of the nineteenth and twentieth centuries, he sees the merits in elements of the old which, within limits, served as a *praeparatio evangelica* to the Church of the Gentiles. Even then the 'will of [the] heart' can be 'clearer than the reason', as self-sacrificing works of love in 'post-Christian' humanity show.

The Spirit's inspiration in Jesus Christ

There remains to consider the power of the Spirit's inspiration in the central figure of the New Testament, Jesus Christ. By an inversion of the Trinitarian *taxis*, the action of the Holy Spirit *precedes* that of the Son, for the very good reason that the hypostatic manifestation of the second divine Person is 'sole and entire' whereas the third, by his – very different – multiple non-hypostatic epiphany in his gifts, is, by contrast, well-placed to *prepare the way for* the redemptive Incarnation.

[37] Ibid., pp. 278–279.

In the climactic event of this process, the Annunciation is the Pentecost of the Virgin before it is the Incarnation of the Son in the flesh – though in this case, to be sure, we are speaking of the descent of the hypostasis of the Spirit, and not simply of a gift of grace. Unknown to the world, the Virgin becomes the sealed fountain, the sacred ark, and this because she is the 'hypostatic receptacle of the Holy Spirit'.[38] Mary's divine Motherhood did not cease when she bore the Child. She remained to her life's end 'in the power of the Annunciation' – which is to say in the power of the *presence of the Holy Spirit*.[39] The Baptism of Christ is *his* Pentecost. Christological doublet of the Annunciation, it tells us that the Spirit who rests eternally on the divine person of the Logos now comes to rest likewise on his humanity as well. In a series of miniatures, Bulgakov shows us the principal tableaux of the ministry, Passion, death and glorification of Christ in the perspective of the Spirit's indwelling and empowerment, thus summing up in a pneumatological way the material laid out at greater length in *The Lamb of God*. At the Transfiguration, the Son of Man is 'glorified' – that is, covered with the cloud of glory of the Spirit. But this is to indicate that fullness of the Spirit which will belong to him in his human nature with the events of the coming Passion. Awaiting the advent of that fullness is for the Spirit another mode of kenosis, another kind of restraint on his action and presence.

> Christ's death is thus not only the extreme limit of the Son's kenosis: it is also the extreme limit of the kenosis of the Spirit who rests on him. One could put it in a paradox: in this common exhaustion of Son and Spirit, the hypostatic Love, while in the act of loving and for its sake, restrains his love and its manifestation.[40]

The Spirit's continuing resting on the man Jesus even in the internal dissolution of his body-soul unity is shown for Bulgakov in Christ's preaching in the 'limbo of the fathers' (cf. 1 Peter 4: 6): that preaching can only be, as with the proclamation of his earthly ministry, in the power of the Spirit. This carries an important corollary for human salvation: the post-mortem condition does not mean being beyond the power of the Holy Spirit's action. Bulgakov has already spoken of Christ's Resurrection (and Ascension) as in different senses the work of the Father and the Son. Now he wants to add that in each case it is through the Holy Spirit that they do

[38] Ibid., pp. 285–286: *upostasno vmestilishche Dukha Sviatogo.*
[39] Ibid., p. 285.
[40] Ibid., p. 289.

these works, albeit in appropriately different respects: the Father
through the creative act of the Spirit in his full divinity, the incarnate Son through a common kenosis with the Spirit who inspires
him by a new manifestation of his power. The 'Glory' with which
the Son asks the Father to glorify him in his Last Supper discourse
(John 17: 5) *is* – once again – that Holy Spirit. Even though the
glorification is not complete till the mysteries of the Ascension and
Session are put in place, we can tell from the first moment of the
Resurrection that it is underway since the Son, breathing on his
apostles, at once sends them the Spirit by way of prelude to the
Pentecost of the Church. We can tell that the kenosis of the Son is
coming to an end when we find him not merely praying the Father
for the sending of the Spirit but sending him in his own Name.

In the last chapter we saw the basic lines on which Bulgakov
would 'solve' the *Filioque* 'problem' of which this moment in the
Gospels is the genesis. Here it suffices to note how for him the
Son's sending of the Spirit does indeed have a foundation in the
eternal Trinity even if it is also true that in the Economy, the divine
persons establish a 'a new domain of correlations'.[41] The immanent eternal relations remain in place, but they are 'complicated'
by the saving plan as it unfolds in time. In particular, the Dyad of
Son and Spirit changes its pattern of operation. Previously, the
Spirit was sent into the world by the Father to rest on the Son for
the work of Incarnation. But now the Son himself sends him by
virtue of the Incarnation which has been effected. The Son's intercession with the Father for the Spirit only survives now in the form
of the abiding power of his redemptive sacrifice to which those
who are saved through faith in him have access. What remains
constant is the ultimacy of the Father as the missioning person *par
excellence,* and the centrality of the Theanthropy for whose better
realisation the roles of Son and Spirit are, in these two great
phases, deployed.

[41] Ibid., p. 295.

10

Pentecost and its Gifts

Hypostatic descent – in the form of gifts

At Pentecost, so it would seem, the Spirit descends not just in his gifts but hypostatically, in himself – and no longer within the 'narrow' constraints of his descent on Christ and Mary but on the entire apostolic company. And yet in fact, in the Book of the Acts, the Gospel of the Holy Spirit *par excellence*, we find no direct witness to his hypostatic revelation but only to a revelation of his gifts, albeit gifts in superabundance. It is the Gospel of John that gives us to understand how the promise of Jesus at the Last Supper is of the Spirit's personal coming. In the light of Luke-Acts, this can only mean: his personal coming Pentecostally. The Spirit *does* come hypostatically – but in his gifts. Bulgakov cites the English Anglican Henry Barclay Swete (1835–1917) on the point: if the Spirit, as Paraclete, fulfils all of Christ's personal functions towards the Church, then he surely possesses all the essential attributes of what we understand by personality.[1] And this is so even though he finds no hypostatic expression comparable to the Son's. But precisely this corresponds to what we have seen of the dyad in the eternal Trinitarian foundation of their economy. That union of the divine and the created wisdom which in the single hypostasis of the Logos *is* Incarnation, is effected by the Holy Spirit. 'He is himself this union',[2] making the Incarnation real. When Christ 'leaves' this world by the Ascension, that does not signify any rupture in the bond between humanity and the incarnate Word.

> This liaison must be rendered real and so to say confirmed as the life of Christ in humanity and that of humanity in Christ. And the

---

[1] H. B. Swete, *The Holy Spirit in the New Testament* (London, 1909), p. 292, cited U, p. 307, note 9.
[2] U, p. 308.

actualisation of this liaison – in some sense a new manifestation or renewal of Christ's Incarnation, is the descent of the Holy Spirit who is united without separation or confusion to the Son, to Christ, the God-man and rests on him.[3]

In his Pentecost descent from heaven, the Spirit brings with him the incarnate Christ who is never separated from him in the dyadic union. From this, Bulgakov derives dogmatic conclusions of the highest importance.

First, this simply cannot be a descent only in gifts. Only a hypostatic descent can suffice to bring the world the life and strength of Christ and his spiritual presence. Only the Grace-giver in person can continue and finish Christ's theanthropic work. This implies, of course, the integral fulness of his gifts, exceeding the previous dispensation of the Spirit.

Secondly, there is not here a different revelation. There is a bi-unique revelation, where the Spirit manifests the truth of the Son. Why else, on the day of Pentecost, is the subject of Peter's discourse the Christ himself, to whom the apostles witness *by the power of the Holy Spirit* (Acts 5: 32). Since the Spirit, by contrast, remains unknown to the world, what we are dealing with is a non-hypostatic manifestation of a hypostatic descent. But Bulgakov notes that Pentecost is not yet finished. Indeed, whereas it had a beginning it will have no end: the Consoler is sent to be with the disciples forever (John 14: 16). There are no limits, no frontiers to his action, he is as the wind blowing as it will.

> He has no human face, though every human face is adorned with the Spirit's grace – and pre-eminently hers who is the Full of grace makes him manifest.[4]

Bulgakov testifies to this 'caressing diaphanous finger [which] touches the hardened heart and the heart melts and takes fire'.[5]

> He comes, and one becomes different from oneself, one senses the plenitude in the partial, the richness in indigence, eternal joy in the sadness where one is only half living, catharsis in tragedy, the triumph of eternal life in the journeying towards one's passing, resurrection in death.[6]

[3] Ibid., p. 309.
[4] Ibid., p. 313.
[5] Ibid., p. 314.
[6] Ibid., p. 314.

This is a definitive presence. He comes to all humanity, and to all nature (hence the 'cosmos'-figure in the icons of Pentecost). Here is extensive universality, and not just the intensive universality of the work of the Son.

Pentecost is thus oriented towards eschatological fulfilment, just as is the Ascension whose promise was that he who ascended to heaven will redescend in the same manner (Acts 1: 11). The Joel prophecy applied to Pentecost by St Peter (Acts 2: 14–21) says as much. Shall we see the Spirit's Face at the End? Our longing is comparable to that of Old Testament people for the Redeemer, but, unlike them, we have no presentiments. We know, however, from the image of the Mother of God in her glory that the beauty of holiness is invincible. *Pace* Dostoevsky, who once famously (if, perhaps, ironically) declared that beauty would save the world, the *beauty of holiness shown us by the Spirit* will save the world – save it not least from the false beauty that is alien to holiness and even antagonistic to it.

This is a new relation of the Spirit to the world: 'new', that is, in comparison with the relation established at creation and throughout the Old Testament where the Spirit is sent exteriorly, so to speak, by the Father's act. After the Incarnation, he abides in the world by virtue of that Incarnation – precisely as the work of Christ accomplished through the Spirit himself. The power of this abiding, however, is limited by the degree of receptivity humanity or the world shows. Although these are the Last Times, they are times of the growth – merely – of Christ's body, not its full measure. The Spirit must show himself as patience and humility, his kenosis consisting in his voluntary self-restraint before the creature's liberty and even inertia. This endures for the whole of our aeon – which means that, while Christ is king, he does not yet reign. Having received from his Father as fruit of his ministry all power in heaven and on earth, he does not exercise that power in fulness until the Spirit has taken possession of the world and transfigured it. It is the power of Pentecost that prepares the final achievement of the royal office of Christ. 'Christ becomes king in the world by the Holy Spirit.'[7] So Pentecost continues in the communion of the Spirit's different gifts in the creative activity of man.

---

[7] Ibid., p. 321.

The gift of prophecy

Bulgakov has a rich theology of the *gifts of Pentecost*. This is where
we can find, among other things, his *spirituality*. The descent of the
Holy Spirit gave the apostles and, through them, the whole Church
knowledge of the Theanthropy, not only as life in Christ by the
Spirit but as unity in ecclesial charity – something manifested in
the common life of the Jerusalem church in Acts 2 and, above all,
in the Eucharist which itself is 'only possible by virtue of
Pentecost'.[8] The filling of the people with the Holy Spirit and the
often overwhelming sense of his personal direction are the sign of
an exceptional springtime, and should not give the impression that
in other phases the Holy Spirit does not expect human effort and
search. Bulgakov is particularly struck, however, by the new
prophecy of the apostolic Church which, surprisingly (given his
fear of an excessive supernaturalism) he treats not as some special-
ized gift or one more or less confined to the post-apostolic
generation but as a

> general gift of Pentecost, namely that henceforth Christian man will
> make history under inspiration, prophetically, and that he is respon-
> sible for it. Pentecost ... is the universal consecration of prophecy.[9]

But Bulgakov would hardly have come to this conclusion were he
not predisposed to see in prophecy a supremely active and creative
state of the human spirit, well-suited to godly purpose. Put
humanly, prophecy is 'the eros of the spirit', already known as to
its natural component by the Plato of the *Symposium*. In its supernatural form, it is the universal Spirit-bearing of Christianised
humanity after Pentecost, a divinisation of the human spirit from
within. Prophecy is the 'qualification of all the gifts possible'.[10]
And since all gifts are set to work in history, prophecy's true subject
is history in its inner content, apocalypse, and what is beyond
history at the end of the aeon, eschatology.

However, the Church of Pentecost also has her eternal aspect,
and this at least shows how the gift of prophecy, historically
oriented as it is, does not exhaust God's Pentecostal bounty.
Corresponding to the two natures in Christ, the Holy Spirit gives
the Church a twofold being, both temporal and eternal. For
Bulgakov, it is to the ministerial priesthood that care for the latter

[8] Ibid., p. 324.
[9] Ibid., pp. 333–334.
[10] Ibid., p. 334.

is committed: they are the stewards of the Church's 'immutable dispositions' in sacramental life and grace. After all, the aeon where we live now has its limits. Hence the circumscribed importance Paul ascribes to prophecy compared with the 'royal gift of love'.[11] The candle of the prophetic gift is extinguished in the flooding daylight of the eternal love.

Spirituality

Which brings Bulgakov to his spirituality of the Pentecostal gifts – an immensely rewarding section of his dogmatics. The spiritual life springing from Pentecost is the new birth spoken of by Jesus (John 3: 6), a new life in Christ by the Holy Spirit. The apostolic letters report almost indifferently on life in Christ and life in the Spirit. Understandably so, because divine adoption means putting on Christ by the Holy Spirit. In his human nature the God-man had been adopted by the Father at the moment of the Spirit's descent in the Jordan. We too by the Spirit of adoption through whom we cry, 'Abba, Father!' (Romans 8: 15) have access to the divine life. As well as the natural grace whereby in virtue of our sophianity we live a spiritual and not just a natural life there is another level of supernatural gift. Our fundamental capacity to receive the Spirit of God, while at the same time preserving our natural hypostatic life, requires for its realization a 'certain condition of the human spirit'.[12] Paralysed by original sin, and its 'secularisation' of our spirit, that condition is received as a possibility thanks to the new Adam, but it only becomes a reality when the Holy Spirit gives man communion with the life of Christ in the waters of baptism.

But when assimilating the divine life, man with his liberty keeps his natural essence, itself pock-marked by the old Adam. That is why the spiritual life is a battlefield between spirit and flesh, the righteous life and sin. And this in turn means that the spiritual life has to be an *ascetic* life, and one that may even be 'tragic in its gravity'.[13] Fortunately:

> the more man advances in the spiritual life, the more his own spirit and spiritual life become concrete realities for him, and the less possible it is to doubt the gifts of grace, the fruits of the Spirit.[14]

[11] Ibid., p. 337.
[12] Ibid., p. 342.
[13] Ibid., p. 343.
[14] Ibid.

In the words of St Seraphim of Sarov, the aim of the spiritual life
is to 'acquire the Holy Spirit'. But efforts towards that end have
a principally negative character. Incessant repentance, the desire
to transform ourselves and become new persons by renunciation,
acceptance of the Cross, patience, spiritual poverty, humility. 'The
illumination of grace descends on the bowed heads of peni-
tents.'[15] Die and become: only dying grain fruits. We need what
Bulgakov calls 'active passivity'. (The consonances here with the
thought of the Swiss Catholic dogmatician Hans Urs von Balthasar
are, once again, striking.) The gift of the Spirit is always received
as gift – or not at all. Thus the continuing descent of the tongues
of fire.

Too often we consider the ascetic life only as the concern of
individuals. But Christian asceticism should not be the 'religious
egoism' of a salvation separated from the rest of the body of
Christ. The personal consciousness of the Christian is 'catholic',
universal, because the Spirit's gift of love makes the Church a
reality as 'multiple unity' and those who receive this gift not
isolated individuals but essentially ecclesial beings. The inseparability of the Gospel love-commands – love God, love your
neighbour – proves as much. Christian asceticism is not like its
Buddhist counterpart, the suppression of self but the 'affirmation
of life in love'.[16] It cannot be 'a-cosmic', for the cure of man is
the cure of all creation. Christian asceticism means configuration
to the Cross of Christ, love for which is a gift of the Holy Spirit.
The Cross must be not only carried but chosen – which may mean
more than simply accepting difficult circumstances. The choice of
the Cross means both renunciation of the world and the acceptance of responsibility for it. It is a vocation not to be expressed
only in withdrawal to the desert, though that too can be a creative
election.

> Christ was himself the author of his life by a determined resolve,
> conformably to the will of the Father that he uncovered by a creative
> act, we can say, in the depths of his own theanthropic awareness. He
> walked to meet the Cross, rather than accepting it as a necessary
> destiny.[17]

Or better: accepting the Cross in obedience to the Fatherly will was
allied in him with awareness of liberty.

[15] Ibid.
[16] Ibid., p. 346: *utverzhdenie zhizni v liubvi.*
[17] Ibid., pp. 348–349.

Under the impulse of the Spirit natural aptitudes enter into Christian ministries, conformably to the Spirit's special gifts.

> All the human work which is accomplished in history and in the different manifestations of culture can become capable of the Spirit and the inspirations of Pentecost.[18]

The Church canonizes princes, iconographers, teachers, medical doctors, and Bulgakov expects her life in the future to bring forth new forms of holy living.

Both ascetic humility and creative audacity are needed in the Christian life. When one is absent, the other is enfeebled. To choose between a formalist ecclesiasticism and the secularizing demolition of ecclesiality is to submit to a false set of alternatives. Fallen man can only appear before God in humble contrition; yet man is also a king, a priest and a prophet in the world where the Kingdom of God is under construction. A just relation between humility and assurance is necessary for the Church if she is to teach all nations to fulfil the precepts of Christ. Bulgakov recommends assurance in humility and humility in assurance. There must be faith *and* work. While, it is true, we are still in our nature as the old Adam (hence, humility and contrition), we are also reconciled with God by our new birth in Christ by the Spirit, living in the new Adam (hence the loving assurance of the children of God).

Bulgakov fears that the creative boldness of the monastic founders has degenerated into the dutiful keeping of laws – whereas true monasticism is full of assurance. In the spiritual life, obedience should be considered a means, and valuable only where it is a function of freedom. Not that Bulgakov is against all notion of obedience to spiritual directors. He thinks there can be a spiritual science whose subject-matter is 'the depths of the soul and the pathology of the passions'. Those who are wise in it can legitimately intervene in the lives of others. Alas that the complementary virtues of creative assurance have no *Philokalia*, no spiritual textbook.

The gift of love

Subjacent to all Bulgakov has said so far on the topic of spirituality has been the Pentecost gift of love, a consideration of which will

---

[18] Ibid., p. 349.

take him to his final description of the Theanthropy in *The Comforter*. The love of God has been 'spread abroad in our hearts by the Holy Spirit who has been given us' (Romans 5: 5). Since the Spirit is hypostatic love in the Trinity it is not surprising that he manifests himself as supernatural love in the world.

Bulgakov distinguishes between the natural, human version of this love, and the grace-love which cannot be acquired by our efforts for it can only be bestowed in God's response to our quest or search. At the level of the first creation, the most basic capacity to love is the 'seal' of the divine image in us. Were we simply mono-hypostatic, we would be egoists incapable of loving. But in fact we are pluri-hypostatic, just as the holy angels, likewise, are a 'concert'. And in each case, angels and men, such social love is in the image of the tri-hypostatic God. Even the animals, however, have *a* version of this, in the gregarious love of their own species and maternal – and in some cases, paternal – love for offspring, though it is only with the intervention of man, in whom love becomes *psycho*-somatic, that 'fundamental spiritual love' comes into view. Humanity, which can draw the animal world close to the divine love by humanizing it, has access to 'higher forms of love, of spirit for spirit': the love of God and the love of neighbour.[19]

'Love in the Holy Spirit' is something else again. It is charismatic love for which we have a 'new commandment' not so much (in the first instance) to practise as to beseech. Bulgakov describes the modalities of this distinctively Pentecostal love. They will take us almost to the close of this chapter.

The first of them is '*ecclesial love*', foundational as this is for the being of the Church. The first gift of Pentecost is that *koinônia* which is the foundation of the Church. The 'new love' unites people spiritually by introducing them into the sophianic reality of a Church which has existed for all time hidden in the mystery of God (cf. Ephesians 3: 9). The 'communion' of the Holy Spirit is at once the universal assembly of the Church and our transport from out of the old Adam into the new, the Lord Jesus Christ. The Church has her own ontology thanks to this 'communion of grace in love'.[20] One important feature of ecclesial ontology is that it enables us to surmount the opposition of the person and everyone else, the 'all'. Every worthy bonding, whether inter-personal or group, can be and is included – and exalted – in ecclesial love. There is a remarkable anticipation here of the ideas of the Greek

---

[19] Ibid., p. 358.
[20] Ibid., p. 362.

dogmatician, and historian of patristic thought, Metropolitan John Zizioulas (b. 1931).[21]

Bulgakov took the idea of including Christian *friendship* within a doctrine of the Church – and so, in the present context, within a theology of Pentecost – from Father Paul Florensky's (1882–1943) idiosyncratic masterpiece, *Stolp i utverzhdenie istiny*, 'The Pillar and Foundation of Truth'.[22] Whenever a network of friendship covenants is established among a selection of people, some kind of natural hierarchy emerges among these sets of bonds. Why, then, should not the total network have its own sacred principle or *archê*? That it can do so is plain from Christ's words to his disciples, 'I have called you friends' (John 15: 15). In the spiritual pairing ('syzygy') which friendship – including Christian friendship – entails there is always an 'erotic' element which Bulgakov defines in such a way as to remove from it the now customary sexual connotation of that word. There must always be a component of 'eros' which, in this context, means, in effect, mutual inspiration. In its various fashions, ecclesial love is always composed of agape and eros *together*. As Bulgakov explains:

> In agapeistic love, man dies to his egoism in order to live in the whole and by the whole. In 'erotic' love, experiencing the inspiration which impels him to go beyond himself, he rises to the creative revelation of himself.[23]

Here the self-affirmation which is otherwise so poisoned and poisoning has all its venom sucked out. This is friendship ordered by the love of Christ.

Not, however, that Bulgakov can – or even wants to – escape all discussion of how sexuality itself relates to ecclesial love. Supremely, the realm of eros is the 'correlation of the masculine and feminine principles in man' – whether interiorly, in each human spirit, or between representatives of the sexes.[24] Genesis 1: 27, in speaking of the divine image as set in man as male and female together, points to a particular form of love which Bulgakov calls 'syzygic' or 'pairing' love. This term, with its high metaphysical overtones, he borrows via Florensky from Soloviev – who himself took it from the ancient Gnostics. In question is an inspi-

[21] J. Zizioulas, *L'Être ecclésial* (Geneva, 1981).
[22] P. Florensky, *Stolp i utverzhdenie istiny* (Moscow, 1914); Et *The Pillar and the Ground of the Truth* (Princeton, NJ, 1997).
[23] NA, p. 366.
[24] Ibid.

rational friendship-love founded on the complementarity of masculine and feminine gifts, but as the Gnostic-derived term indicates, loving reciprocity here is complicated (and not necessarily enhanced) by the introduction of sexuality and reproduction. In the animal creation, physical intercourse as the means to biological multiplication is God's 'immediate will'. The animals know no shame in sexuality. In them the fire burns but does not consume. But man is differently placed. In the creation of Adam, there is at first no partner, sexual or otherwise. With the creation of Eve, a bond with the animal realm is kept at the psycho-somatic level (hence the command, shared with the beasts, to go forth and multiply). But the overall context is different. It is the granting to Adam of an 'other' to be his complement. For Bulgakov, this shows how the sexual element in syzygic love is subordinate for Scripture to a more primary principle which requires its spiritualization. Such primacy is largely ineffective in fallen man, who knows sexuality as attraction and passion rebellious to spirit and subjecting it to themselves. Eros is so enslaved by sexuality that many no longer understand the distinction between them. Equally tragic in Bulgakov's eyes is the false ascetic response which, by wholesale 'desexualization', would render the divine image that of a neuter androgyne, suppressing the significance of the masculine and feminine principles and tending to kill off eros by an act of spiritual suicide. For the erotic imperative 'seek and you will find' retains its 'value in relation to the gifts of the Paraclete'.[25] This is, surely, the *desiderium*, 'passionate desire' for God, so often mentioned in the preaching of St Augustine and the writings of the monastic theologians of the western Middle Ages. We cannot tear out of the Bible those pages that speak not just of charity-love or the love of friendship but ecstatic love, the love of eros. In making this caveat, Bulgakov refers above all to the Song of Songs. For Bulgakov, that Old Testament book is not just an epithalamium, a piece of marriage poetry. Its subject is Love itself, the flame of YHWH, the Holy Spirit. Or rather, the Song *is* marriage poetry inasmuch as, in the Holy Spirit, Christ and his Church-Bride are celebrating their wedding-feast. And insofar as, thanks to the Spirit's economy, this ecstatic, erotic image of love belongs to the Church's being quite as much as does the image of agape, such supernaturalized eros must be counted an essential aspect of ecclesial love, the primary Pentecostal gift. As with all gifts of supernatural grace, its foundation in the gifts of nature should be

[25] Ibid., p. 370.

respected, not spurned. The spiritual union of masculine and feminine is a hallmark of sophianity in the Theanthropy, a fruit of natural grace seeking its own sanctification in the Church. So often degraded since the Fall, such eros can be ascetically sublimated in a way respectful of itself. It can also be consecrated in its psychosomatic expression in Christian marriage whose sacramental grace can 'immunize' concupiscence. Sexual love is admitted ascetically into Christian marriage – that is, blessed yet restrained. That for Bulgakov is the justification of the Church's insistence on exclusive monogamy.

Ecclesial virginity and sacramental marriage are complementary vocations along the way of Pentecostal love. The monastic way emulates the condition of the angels who are not a race, a biological unity, but a choir or 'concert'. The angels, however asexual, preserve the concrete qualification of finite spirit. So in their different realm, monastics must remain firmly men and women, and not attempt to seek gender neutrality which would be 'a criminal attack on the ontological substance of man'.[26] To exalt marriage at the expense of virginity, lauded by the Saviour as a higher call, is culpable. But condemned by the Church is the disprizing of marriage through revulsion from its sexual component. The taking of the habit, and the making of the marriage vow, must be understood in terms of each other, by antinomic conjunction. For Orthodoxy, all must practise asceticism in some manner, not excluding the married. Bulgakov contrasts this with the sharp Roman distinction between precepts (for all Christians) and counsels (for Religious). In fact, late twentieth-century Catholicism came increasingly to emphasize that ordinary Christians, bound to the precepts, must live with the spirit of the counsels. That spirit is really no different from the ethos of the Sermon on the Mount.

The monastic way remains a way of love of neighbour and not of God alone. One senses Bulgakov's preference for its coenobitic form, though his devotion to St Seraphim, hermit saint of the closing decades of the Tsardom, prevents him from treating eremitism merely 'dialectically', as a 'moment' within the experience of communitarian monasticism. The hermit life, this 'ministry of the desert', may be lifelong. If so its quality should be 'catholic' through an 'agapeistic union of ecclesial love realised through prayer'.[27] For Bulgakov, the negative asceticism of cold 'eunuchs by nature' never suffices. There must be positive, ecstatic

[26] Ibid., pp. 377–378.
[27] Ibid., p. 381.

exaltation in loving union with the mystical Christ that spills over
into love for others. There must always be some loving material for
the Spirit of Pentecost to transform. Needless to say, Bulgakov was
hostile to the opposition of agape and eros found in the influential
twentieth-century Swedish Lutheran theologian of this subject,
Anders Nygren (1890–1977).[28] The 'loving material' in question,
though, must be nicely adjusted if the higher grace is to make use
of it for the mission of Pentecost. It must avoid a Luciferian individualism which would deny the bonds of love with (the human)
race, people, ancestors, family. At the same time, it should
renounce a 'generic conservatism' that stifles individuals and
conscience. When it succeeds in this twofold task, it can receive the
gift of love that comes personally from the Holy Spirit.

For Bulgakov, the power of Pentecost has and can have no limit.
The Spirit descends to unite heaven with earth. It is only owing to
the kenotic character of this descent that its operation is both
hidden and, seemingly, slow. In reality, the destiny of the world is
won by this event: the world's ontology, history, eschatology, are in
principle achieved. Visibly come down as fire dancing on the heads
of the apostles, invisibly he descends on all the world. The walls of
the Cenacle do not hold him. That, once again, is the meaning of
the 'Cosmos' figure in the Pentecost icon, and the Russian custom
on this feast of decorating churches with plants and flowers. It is all
a matter of 'pre-accomplishment', just as man's divinization was
pre-accomplished in the Annunciation, and the victory over death
at Easter.

> In the same way that Christ has no more need to be glorified and
> raised so as to come again into the world, so likewise the Spirit has
> no need to come down again from heaven to transfigure the world
> for the hour of the Lord's second Coming.[29]

The sacramentalism whereby the Church invokes the Spirit over
the world-substance shows how spirit and matter must be juxtaposed or coordinated. The first Pentecost was the Spirit's hovering
descent over chaos to draw out primal order from the energy of the
world-stuff. This was essential, comments Bulgakov, if finite spirit
were to have a 'non-I' by which to support itself and through which

---

[28] Ibid., p. 384, note 1. The reference is to A. Nygren, *Den kristna kärlekstanken
genom tiderna. Eros och agape*, I (Stockholm, 1929). Bulgakov used the English
translation: *Agape and Eros. A Study of the Christian Idea of Love*, I (London,
1932).
[29] U, p. 389.

to find its manifestation. (The 'I' of spirit, we recall from Bulgakov's Trinitarian theology and theology of creation, must have its nature in and by which it has its world.) With the second Pentecost, the supreme descent of the Spirit at the Pentecost of Zion, that first sketch of the divine plan becomes definitive. In creation, matter has been introduced into the life of spirit where it gains limpidity and consciousness just as in turn spirit gains determination from corporal embodiment. It is easy to see how spiritualized matter can become the 'substrate' of the Spirit's work in the sacraments – even before we add that in any case the matter of this world 'underwent modification when it became the flesh of Christ'.[30] Spread abroad in the world at Pentecost, the Holy Spirit gives to matter the power of the Transfiguration and Resurrection. St Paul asserts as much of the matter of human bodies.

> If the Spirit of him who raised Jesus from the dead dwells in us, he who raised Christ Jesus from the dead will give life to your mortal bodies also through his Spirit who dwells in you. (Romans 8: 11)

Evidently, such a risen humanity can hardly live in a non-transfigured world. So it is fair, thinks Bulgakov, to include the cosmic within the scope of the apostle's argument. The power of Pentecost, though recognized only in the 'Kingdom of grace' (the Church and her sacraments) and treated as non-existent elsewhere, can carry this world through to the future aeon, the Age to Come. Kenotically – accepting the slow, patient labour of it – the Holy Spirit is preparing the world for that *dénouement*, the glorious Parousia of Christ. Thus his aboriginal eternal kenosis, whereby in his own hypostasis he is content with pointing to Father and Son, is prolonged and deepened in the post-Pentecost economy. The voluntary self-limiting in which all kenosis, in one form or another, consists, becomes here the accommodation to human fragility of divine love and condescension. It is that accommodation which makes claims for the scope of divine action seem tenuous in the eyes of the world. Precisely so, Bulgakov implies, can we detect his measureless might. The Spirit too and not just the Son shows us God as the 'mystery of humiliated love':[31] the words are the apt sub-title chosen by Andronikoff for his French version of this section of *Uteshitel'*. So to return to Bulgakov's question about the limits of Pentecost in the world: we should answer that it has none *save the Spirit's own kenotic limitation of himself.*

[30] Ibid., p. 393.
[31] *Le Paraclet* (Paris, 1944), p. 336.

Theanthropy perfected

Pentecost, then, is perfectly realized Theanthropy – not just in this world but in the realm of the redeemed dead beyond the tomb. There is no other way than via the Pentecostal Spirit for man to identify with the God-man, the Primal Image, and creaturely wisdom to be one with the uncreated Wisdom from which it came. For the eternal Theanthropy, as for divine Wisdom, Son and Spirit are equally necessary to the revelation of the Father. The descent of the Spirit into the world is, accordingly, as necessary to its divinization as is the Incarnation of the Son. Bulgakov wants to end like this to rub in the point that Pentecost concerns not only soteriology and the doctrine of grace but the foundations in Trinitarian ontology of human divinization and the complete sophianization of the world as the Spirit unites creation through the Incarnation and his Paschal descent to his person, his own hypostasis.

11

The Church

The Church as divine mystery

Bulgakov has an extraordinarily high doctrine of the Church.[1] In *The Bride of the Lamb* he introduces the Church via the topic of synergy. That might lead the reader to suppose that the Church belongs entirely on the side of human co-operation with the divine. But this is not at all what Bulgakov has in mind. The Church is the fulfilment of God's eternal plan for the creation – human salvation included. This means sophianization for the world and deification for man. In these two related senses, the Church can be called the foundation of the created order and its internal finality or goal.[2] In a note, Bulgakov draws his readers' attention to that early Roman Christian document *The Shepherd of Hermas* (treated in some circles as so authoritative that it now forms part of the canon of Scripture in the Ethiopian Orthodox Church). While pre-Revolutionary Russian patristic scholarship treated *The Shepherd*'s ecclesiology as a sad reflection of Gnostic influence, Bulgakov is happy to stand by its author's claim that it was for the Church that the world was made. *The Shepherd*'s portrayal of the Church as both a very old woman and a tower that is still in the building corresponds well to Bulgakov's own notion of her as not only foundation but also goal of the world. The topic of synergy leads into ecclesiology for Bulgakov not because the Church is a human work but

---

[1] For an overview of his ecclesiology, *see* L. A. Zander, *Bog i mir*, op. cit., II., pp. 275–318. Another account is included in A. Nichols, O. P., *Theology in the Russian Diaspora. Church, Fathers, Eucharist in Nikolai Afanas'ev, 1893–1966*, op. cit., pp. 145–153. For a more substantial study, comparing and contrasting Bulgakov's ecclesiology with that of another theologian of the Russian diaspora, George Florovsky, see now M. De Salis Amaral, *Dos visiones ortodoxas de la Iglesia: Bulgakov y Florovsky* (Pamplona, 2003).

[2] NA, pp. 274–275.

because she shows both the eternal and the temporal dimensions of God's work: Uncreated Wisdom and created wisdom in their collaborative interaction.

The Church was not so much founded – 'instituted' – in time as 'born' or 'made her appearance' in that dimension. She is not only, as Augustine would have it, *Ecclesia ab Abel*, 'the Church since Abel', the first just man. She is also *Ecclesia ab Adam*, 'the Church from Adam', the Church from Paradise on. She will continue to exist not only till the close of the age, but in the Age to Come. Bulgakov's ecclesiology takes its departure-point quite explicitly from the opening chapter of the Letter to the Ephesians. Before the creation of the world we were chosen in the Christ through whom the Father has now revealed the mystery of his will, to recapitulate in Christ all things in heaven and on earth in view of the 'economy of the fullness of time' (Ephesians 1: 10). Human beings are to see the 'plan of the mystery hidden for ages in God', so that through the Church the 'many-faceted Wisdom of God' can be made known (Ephesians 3: 10). Bulgakov comments:

> One could hardly indicate more clearly that sophianic foundation of the world which is the Church. And the sophianisation of the world is accomplished thanks to the redemption brought about by Jesus Christ, according to his Incarnation through the Holy Spirit.[3]

As the gift of grace – bestowed and received synergetically – brings about our salvation and with it the sophianization of the world, so the Church is the organization of the life of grace. Indeed she *is* this grace itself.

Universal and local

Like all ecclesiologists, Bulgakov is aware that in the New Testament, as in later tradition, the word 'Church' has two senses. It refers to local communities of the faithful bonded together by the unity of their life. And it identifies the single Church which is that same life considered as 'a mystical and unique essence'.[4] Only the latter as found – to be sure – in the former can bear the great ecclesial titles: the Body of Christ, animated by the Holy Spirit, and so the Temple of the Holy Spirit and the Bride of Christ. The one Church unites her many members thanks to the Holy Spirit and the Word

[3] Ibid., p. 275.
[4] Ibid., p. 278: *edinaya mysticheskaya syshchnost'*.

Incarnate – and these twin pneumatological and christological aspects, closely juxtaposed in two crucial sections of Paul's correspondence with his difficult daughter church in Corinth (1 Corinthians 6: 15, 19 and 12: 4–13 and 28–30), must not be sundered from each other. Noting in this connection the significance of the Eucharist for the Church's unity (1 Corinthians 10: 16–17), Bulgakov returns to the Letter to the Church at Ephesus: perhaps the most favoured New Testament writing in his entire *oeuvre*. In that letter the multiple unity of the Church is presented as the fulness of Christ owing, once again, to the conjoined economies of Son and Spirit (cf. Ephesians 2: 18 and 22). Finally, in the Letter to the Colossians, it is from the Head of the Church, Christ, that 'the whole body, nourished and knit together through its joints and ligaments, grows with a growth that is from God' (Colossians 2: 19).

From this brief survey of texts Bulgakov takes first and foremost the key concept of all distinctively Russian ecclesiology, that of *sobornost'*: 'gathering' or, in the widest sense, conciliarity. 'The Church', he writes, 'is an organism or a body, a living, multiple unity' endowed with different gifts whose 'pluri-unity', *mnogoedinstvo*, is 'recapitulated' by Christ and 'animated' by the Holy Spirit.[5]

More distinctively, however, Bulgakov appeals to the notion of divine Wisdom as a way of explaining how the Church can both be characterized by fullness and yet at the same time be a pilgrim people. The Church *can* be both if she in some sense embodies not only the eternal divine Wisdom but also the creaturely wisdom that is still in process of becoming. The Church's unity is not empirical but ontological (she is a body, not a conglomerate) though certainly it is empirically that she *grows*. As the body of Christ, and through her unity in the Holy Spirit, the Church is the revelation of the divine life by means of the deification of the creature even in its becoming.

The Church as Body of Christ

The affirmation that the Church is the Body of Christ means first for Bulgakov that it is appropriate for the God-man to have a body and that, secondly, this body is the Church *qua* divinised humanity, the theanthropic life.

The doctrine of the Church-body of Christ contains a teaching on

[5] Ibid., p. 280.

man, in his relation with the eternal Theanthropy which is his foundation.[6]

Not only is humankind in its natural essence one but there is in Christ as Word incarnate, anointed by the Spirit who rests on him, a multiple unity of human hypostases. The divine hypostasis of Christ multiplies itself into the diversity of human persons who, while preserving their personal identity, identify with him and immerse themselves individually in his personal being. These are strong and even alarming words, but how else (asks Bulgakov) are we to take Paul's cry in Galatians: 'It is no longer I who live, but Christ lives in me' (Galatians 2: 20).

Such 'pan-Christism' tries to affirm two things at once. Each member of the body belongs to the body in its unified togetherness, which belonging is manifested in each such member (compare Paul's words: 'Just as a body is one and has many members, all the members of the body, though many, are one body', 1 Corinthians 12: 12). But each member is distinct, with its own relation to that unity (compare Paul again: 'you are the body of Christ and individually members of it', 1 Corinthians 12: 27). That 'pan-Christism' is inseparable from a 'pan-Pneumatism'. It is 'by one Spirit we were all baptized into one body ... and all were made to drink of one Spirit' (1 Corinthians 12: 13). Not only Christ, through his Incarnation, but also the Holy Spirit, with the gifts of his Pentecostal mission, lives in all. As everything in Bulgakov's theology so far would lead us to expect, the Church is the *dyadic* revelation of the Logos and the Holy Spirit.

Bulgakov comments how it is typical of Paul to turn straightaway to practical implications. Supremely, these concern mutual love. To this extent, Bulgakov sees Paul's ecclesiology as pointing the way to that of his own nineteenth-century Russian precedessor, Alexei Khomiakov (1804–1860).[7] Even though the latter's name is not given, his theological accent is unmistakable as Bulgakov writes of Paul's doctrine of the Church:

[6] Ibid., p. 284.

[7] See P. P. O'Leary, *The Triune Church. A Study in the Ecclesiology of A. S. Khomjakov* (Dublin, 1982). For how Bulgakov viewed his predecessor, see his 'The Problem of the Church in Modern Russian Theology', *Theology* XXIII (1931), pp. 9–14; 63–67. He accepts two key Khomiakovian positions. First, 'Protestant individualism and papal absolutism ... being contradictory [doctrines] are both cut in the same mould', ibid., p. 10; secondly, while the Church has a visible hierarchical aspect, she is essentially 'a mystical organism in which many live in the unity of charity', ibid., p. 11. Otherwise, the essay functions as a summary of Bulgakov's own, sophiological, ecclesiology.

It witnesses to the mystical unity of humanity which is the mystery of the Church, at the same time as it calls us to order our lives by reference to this mystery so that all of us may abide in the union of love. In modern language, one could say that this ecclesiology is the doctrine of the Church's *sobornost'*, understood as much ontologically as practically, as *the principle of ingathering and assembly in love*, in corporate communion.[8]

In the Church we see synergism in practice: divine gifts accorded and received. Given in plenitude, they are appropriated by personal reception and so in their diversity they represent the different ministries found in her. Bulgakov thinks that in the apostolic generation we are dealing with an 'organic and creative life' preceding not only ontologically but also chronologically the 'hierarchical principle'. Though there is no contradiction between institutional hierarchy and ecclesial ontology their ordering must not be reversed. That would be for the institution to attempt – vainly – to suppress ontology which here is for Bulgakov, in effect, the sophiological perspective on the Church.[9] Bulgakov fears that, in reaction to the claims of Rome, many Orthodox theologians treat the episcopate as a collective Papacy, seeing in it the true foundation of the Church. But her foundation lies elsewhere, in the interpenetration, without separation and without confusion, of the divine and human principles.

The Church as Bride of the Lamb

Even more obviously sophiological than the New Testament teaching on the Church as body of Christ is that implied in the image which gives the final volume of the Great Trilogy its title, *The Bride of the Lamb*. The imagistic formula is taken from the Book of the Apocalypse where, in chapter 21, the Bride descends as the new Jerusalem from heaven to earth. And yet, as the cognate uses in the Letter to the Ephesians show, she is also on earth awaiting the coming of Christ in the fullness of divine revelation. Put sophiologically:

---

[8] NA, p. 284: *printsip sobiraniya i sobranosti v lyubvi* are the original of the words italicized.

[9] For Bulgakov's approach to the Church as sacramental institution, see S. Świerkosz, *L'Eglise visible selon Serge Bulgakov. Structure hiérarchique et sacramentelle* (Rome, 1980).

> As Wisdom, the Church dwells in him; she is the heavenly Jerusalem
> ... , the holy city which must descend to earth. But as the Bride await-
> ing her Bridegroom she is the created, earthly Church, herself
> calling out by theSpirit for the descent.[10]

That is a reference to the cry 'Come!' with which the Johannine
Apocalypse ends at 22: 17. The Church is heavenly not just in her
foundation but also in her 'entelechy', her inbuilt goal. And yet
she remains part of the world-process until the world's end. The
relation of these two aspects of her life is achieved by divine
Providence in its salvific form: namely, as redemption.

And yet Bulgakov finds the summit of the 'mystical' doctrine of
the Church as love in what he terms, with great originality, the
'Apocalypse of the Old Testament' – not any of the books or
sustained passages which critical scholarship would place in that
genre but the Song of Songs. There the relation of Christ and the
Church is unveiled by depiction of the love of bridegroom and
bride – the love that, hypostatically, is the Holy Spirit. Christ the
Word and the Holy Spirit witness to the Father who dwells in
heaven as this marvellous book:

> sings the relation between God and the world, the Creator and the
> created, the divine Wisdom and the creaturely, the Son incarnate by
> the Holy Spirit and the Bride unwedded, his Mother.[11]

The mention there of Mary is hardly fortuitous. The 'most pure
Mother of Christ', the *Pneumatophora*, is the hypostasis who
happens to enjoy first place in the Church. Indeed, she is its
personal 'centre', *sredotochie*.[12] Elsewhere he writes that

> in the person of Our Lady we have a personal revelation of the
> Church, not as a society, visible or invisible, but as eternal being, the
> real principle of all creation, of humanity, of the Wisdom of God.[13]

Bulgakov, however, does not wish to give occasion for his readers
to spiral off into the heavens in an excess of symbolist fervour for

---

[10] NA, pp. 287–288.
[11] Ibid., p. 288. It may be worth noting that Origen of Alexandria's teaching that
the Church as bride of Christ, existing not just 'after the coming of the Saviour
in the flesh but rather from the beginning of the human race, from the very
foundation of the world', is found in his *Commentarium in Canticum Canticorum*,
ii.
[12] NA, p. 289.
[13] 'The Problem of the Church in Modern Russian Theology', art. cit., p. 65.

the 'eternal Feminine' (Goethe's celebrated and perhaps disastrous phrase). The divine Wisdom, which abides at the Church's origin and goal, is hypostatized, after all, as Father, Son and Holy Spirit; the creaturely wisdom is hypostatized in created persons gathered together in the hypostasis of the God-man. The Church on earth finds *her* hypostasis as 'Woman' – Bride of the Lamb – *in* Jesus Christ.

Bulgakov is very much among those theologians who say we know from divine revelation where the Church is, but not perhaps where she is not. For him:

> the limits of the Church coincide mystically and ontologically with those of the power of Incarnation and Pentecost.[14]

Which is as much as to say, she has *no* limits humanly delimitable. Bulgakov neglects a distinction that has been found useful in Catholic theology when he writes that since the Inhumation of the Word 'all humanity belongs to the Church'. Since Pentecost, the Spirit has descended on all flesh: *potentially*, by a real potency, yes, but *in act*, in full actuality? Hardly. Still, we must be careful here. Bulgakov has so defined the Church that she is coincident with the economy of God's grace, the entire 'field of force of the theanthropy'.[15] One for whom the universe is itself the 'cosmic face' of the Church is not thinking in terms of any definition of 'mere' Church membership. Not that Bulgakov is wholly unaware that so generous an account of catholicity could sink the Church in a night where all cats are black. By giving in one sense too much, it may in another sense not give enough. The need for a complementary precision leads him to consider the Church as 'sacramental and hierarchical organism'.

The Church as sacramental organization

After the fashion of much Protestant scholarship (and some Liberal Catholic – but not, typically, High Anglican), Bulgakov feels confident that in the pages of the New Testament lies an 'absence of hierarchical forms'.[16] Only in the second century does the three-fold ministry appear and we should not fill in the blank

[14] NA, p. 290.
[15] Ibid., p. 292: *oblast' sili Bogochelovechestva*.
[16] Ibid.

spaces on the writing paper of history by dogmatic hypotheses – an exhortation to virtue somewhat weakened when Bulgakov adds we must indeed understand the historical facts 'in the light of the dogmas [of the Church]'. True, he sometimes speaks as if the lacunae in the biblical evidence are what prevent our seeing the embryonic three-fold ministry as clearly as we might like. But his predominant view appears to be that the hierarchical Church of the sub-apostolic period succeeds to that of the apostolic genera-tion from which it must be clearly distinguished: we should not telescope the two by treating the episcopal order as the successor of the apostleship in the 'Roman sense' of continuing bearers of the apostolic charism in its fulness. Here difference is as important as identity, even if the first is denied by Catholic theologians and their epigones in Orthodoxy, and the second by Protestantism (High Anglicans apart). There is one Church, from the origins on; but there is also fairly radical disjunction in the phases of her serial being. As he wrote in his contribution to the (1937) 'Report of the Theological Commission appointed by the Continuing Committee of the Faith and Order Movement':

> We observe, as it were, two epochs: the apostolic and post-apostolic age, when the gifts of Grace associated later with the grace of ordi-nation were poured out freely, so to speak, over and above the hierarchical privileges, and various charismatics acted side by side with the apostles (I Corinthians 12); and, beginning with the second century, the age when the gifts of Grace were regulated through hierarchy of the type of the Old Testament priesthood. There is no need to exaggerate ... the contrast between the two epochs, but the *difference* is obvious [even if it] eludes observation.[17]

How does Bulgakov deal with this problem? At the most funda-mental level of basic ecclesiological presuppositions he does so by exploring the ontology of the Church for which 'mystical realism' is the key. The mystery of the Church escapes comprehensive description. Precisely because there is in her an 'indivisible conjunction of the eternal and the temporal', the Church has a divine ground which calls for an apophatic ecclesiology, proceed-ing by way of suitable negations, as well as an historical manifestation that justifies the cataphatic approach of what he terms 'ecclesial phenomenology', *tserkovnaya fenomenologiya*.[18] The

---

[17] 'The Hierarchy and the Sacraments', in R. Dunkerley (ed.), *The Ministry and the Sacraments* (London, 1937), pp. 95–96. Emphasis original.
[18] NA, p. 295.

upshot is that the Church as visible society – or the churches, the communities where that society can most readily be seen – does not coincide completely with the Church as theanthropic, even though the latter penetrates the former by its power.

That can also be expressed by saying that the Church has a *symbolic* being in this world for which the best term is 'sacramental'. Just as Catholic ecclesiologists in the 1940s and 1950s were redis-covering the idea of the Church as the primordial sacrament (unless indeed they applied that term to Christ as the God-man), Bulgakov argues that:

> at the foundation of the all the sacraments and sacramentals there is a sacrament of sacraments, a 'pan-sacrament', which is the Church herself, considered as the Theanthropy, the Incarnation and the Spirit's Pentecost, with their salutary power.[19]

A sacrament for Bulgakov is the *manifested* action of the Church in humanity. But the significance of the sacramentals – what he calls 'sacraments of the second zone' – lies in their ability to suggest that the boundaries of the Church's action cannot be restricted to the celebration of the seven classic sacraments – *nor indeed to what is 'manifested' ecclesial action at all.* True, when considered in terms of the 'unique and supreme reality of the Theanthropy', the Church was eminently revealed by Christ at his Last Supper: she offers a 'sacramental testimony to the Incarnation of which the Eucharistic sacrament is the manifestation'.[20] But unlike the seven sacraments, she cannot be described as a 'particular institution'. Rather is she the achievement of the work of Providence since the beginning, the plan of the mystery hidden for ages in God. The mystical or noume-nal Church is not precisely the phenomenal institution. The 'ecclesial Pentecost' can be expressed in non-sacramental ways.

On the one hand, Bulgakov regards a 'healthy hierarchism' as a sign of an appropriate docility to the Church as Christ's Spirit-animated body. The canonical institution of episcopate, priesthood, diaconate as we now know it embodies the 'organic and hierarchical principle proper to [the Church]'.[21] But on the other he finds inimical an 'unhealthy clericalism' which in his eyes – and here some personal experience of the functionings of Orthodox hierarchs is evidently in play – issues from a dispropor-tionate inflation of the office of the bishop. Concentrating

---

[19] Ibid., pp. 296–297.
[20] Ibid., p. 297.
[21] Ibid., p. 302.

churches around their bishops was a useful defensive reaction to schisms and heresies in the early centuries. But it also had unfortunate side effects. By contrast to the overwhelming majority, surely, of Orthodox theologians, Bulgakov is not happy with the symbolic associations of the bishop (and to a degree other ordained ministers) with God, Christ and the apostles in the Letters of Ignatius of Antioch (*c.* 35–*c.* 107), nor with the assertion of an episcopal apostolic succession in Tertullian (*c.* 160–*c.* 225), Irenaeus, Polycarp (*c.* 69–*c.* 155), nor again with Cyprian's (d. 258) ringing proclamation of the coinherence of church and bishop. A hypertrophy of sacramental hierarchicalism can upset the ecclesial balance. Bulgakov's fear is that ecclesiology is degenerating into hierarchology – exactly the same anxiety expressed in the Catholic context by the Dominican historian of ecclesiology Yves Congar (1904–1995) at more or less the same time.[22] Christ, writes Bulgakov, is the Church's great high priest. He is not so as the first in a series but rather as one who transcends that series while also founding it. So care should be taken to avoid the notion of the bishops as his vicars – though this has entered in fact Orthodox formulae and manuals, possibly under Latin influence. Bulgakov is even wary of treating the bishops as entering by ordination on the office of the apostles.

> The tongues of flame of the Holy Spirit that descended on the Apostles at Pentecost were infinitely more than the grace of episcopal orders, and included all their prophetic and charismatic gifts ... It cannot therefore be said that bishops alone have *apostolic* grace.[23]

The New Testament priesthood – the royal and universal priesthood of the faithful is what Bulgakov means – flows from the virtue of the Church's Theanthropy. It was in order to *organize* this universal priesthood that the Church of the New Testament established at some historical juncture a structure 'under the form of different hierarchical degrees', with the episcopate at its summit. Somewhat airily, from an historical standpoint, Bulgakov opines:

---

[22] Y. M-J.Congar, *Jalons pour une théologie du laïcat* (Paris, 1953), pp. 68–74.
[23] 'The Hierarchy and the Sacraments', art. cit., pp. 97–98. Emphasis original. Bulgakov adds that, from the viewpoint of *sobornost'*, 'all gifts, including the Grace of Ordination, were given to the *whole* Church as a body, and consequently the Church was able to differentiate various organs for the fulfilment of specific functions and to *establish* hierarchy', p. 103.

According to God's will and by unsoundable ways of Church history, it appeared one day, it exists, and is maintained in the form [of bishops, priests, deacons] ... [24]

For Bulgakov, far from undermining the value of the Church's canonical hierarchy, this sudden eruption exalts it, since, quite dramatically, it points to the real ground of the ministerial hierarchy in the Church's theanthropic life. The ordained ministry is the organized activation of the organically ordered sacred character attaching to the very being of the Church. Hierarchy arose in the Church on the basis of an 'abiding Pentecost' in her.[25] It did so in accordance with the 'spirit' of the apostolic tradition and on the foundation of the Church's divine-human nature which demands human creativity as well as confirming divine guidance.[26] But let us keep a sense of proportion here. Bulgakov's exaltation (in the steps of Soloviev) of a Johannine primacy in contemplation, love, and prophetic inspiration, to complement – and qualify – the Petrine primacy of office and authority exercised by the bishops is intended to keep the ordained ministry to its proper role – subsidiary to the mystery of the Church.[27]

For Bulgakov, apostolic succession means, in effect, Tradition: the transmission of the teaching of Christ and the wider life of the Church since Pentecost. Apostolic succession is the self-identity of ecclesial life shown externally in ecclesial institutions themselves of merely relative and secondary importance. The laying on of hands, which, at various points in the New Testament sources, is normally understood as Ordination, is for Bulgakov to be explained as Confirmation (Chrismation): full entry into the universal priesthood of the baptized. Even Eucharistic presiding Bulgakov is content to leave vague in the early sources. Its reservation by Ignatius to the bishop – or, when impeded, a presbyter – Bulgakov deems an innovation. Why otherwise would be it be the object of the Syrian bishop's 'particularly insistent preaching'?[28] For his own part, he is equally insistent that 'like every determination of the Church', the entrusting of Eucharistic celebration to the hierarchy is 'due to the action of the Spirit guiding her'.[29] The desire (by

---

[24] NA, p. 304.

[25] 'The Hierarchy and the Sacraments', art. cit., p. 102.

[26] Ibid., p. 100.

[27] This is the burden of *Sviatye Petr i Ioann: dva pervoapostola* (Sts Peter and John: Two Apostles with Primacy, Paris, 1926).

[28] NA, p. 308.

[29] Ibid., p. 309.

radicals) to return the Church to her primitive state is 'arbitrary', a fruit (paradoxically) of reactionary Utopianism.

Bulgakov may not agree that the *proestôs*, 'president', of the Eucharist in the earliest churches was expressly ordained to this end in a permanent manner. And yet his account of the Eucharist itself – the Church's central sacrament carried out by the power of the Incarnation and Pentecost in the realized Theanthropy – presumes that this actualization of the Body of Christ was always organized in a liturgical rite celebrated by a minister (be it, as in the *Didache*, prophet or evangelist, specially set apart). As he puts it, somewhat riddlingly:

> In so far as our Lord Himself instituted the sacrament of the Eucharist, hierarchy is included in that institution as one of the conditions of it.[30]

The Eucharist needed an ecclesial guarantee of its authenticity above all when such wild forms of devotion as Montanism entered the picture at the end of the second century. Bulgakov notes how, in the comparable case of Baptism, also a 'Gospel sacrament', whereas the hierarchy regulated its celebration, laypeople have kept till now the faculty of ministering it in certain circumstances. And this is no bagatelle but the first of the sacraments which gives catechumens entry to the body of Christ. So that practice is 'living testimony to the universal priesthood of the people of God as initially preceding the hierarchy'.[31]

The Church's sacraments

Like the Church, the sacraments illustrate synergy: the gracious divine freedom that offers, the human freedom that receives. This removes from them all connotation of magic. Yet Bulgakov's skimpy account of them (and especially of the Eucharist – despite the abstractly high praise he gives it) prepares us for his section in *Nevesta Agntsa* on 'the limits of sacramentalism'. It would be a mistake to suppose, however, that Bulgakov wished to minimise the sacraments.

Elsewhere he shows he has thought a good deal about the Mystic

---

[30] 'The Hierarchy and the Sacraments', art. cit., p. 106.
[31] NA, p. 312.

Supper.[32] In his essay 'The Eucharistic Dogma', he offers a theology of the Eucharistic conversion as the 'transmuting' union of
Eucharistic matter with the glorified Body and Blood of Christ.[33]
Criticising the Thomistic (and Tridentine) doctrine of transubstantiation for 'cosmic immanentalism', he holds that the Latin
theology – adopted by many Orthodox theologians and hierarchs,
not least in the Russia of the nineteenth century – far from enlightening us on the nature of the Eucharistic conversion makes an
adequate understanding more difficult. Bulgakov wanted to see
more stress on the unique spatiality (he uses the term 'supraspa-
tiality') of the Saviour's humanity and (connected with this) the
way his corporeality is now 'energetic': dynamic rather than
'thingy'. To this emphasis there should correspond an underlining
of the way the Eucharistic Body and Blood of the Lord are given to
the Church for the consumption of the faithful, and thus for their
– equally 'dynamic' – transformation in godly existence, body and
soul. It was Bulgakov's conviction that the term 'transmutation',
prelozhenie, insinuated in an appropriate way the *meta*-physical character of the Eucharistic union between the ascended Lord and the
worldly stuff of bread and wine. (As is pointed out, however, by the
Byzantine Catholic priest who introduces the American translation
of Bulgakov's essay, the term 'transmutation' – and presumably its
Russian original – has offputting overtones of alchemy, whereas
'transubstantiation' employs the same foundational ontology as
patristic theology – indeed, we might add, as the early Ecumenical
Councils in their Trinitarian and Christological endeavours.[34])
More helpful – and in line with what is most distinctive in his
thought – is Bulgakov's proposal that the Eucharistic conversion
entails the perfect sophianisation of the matter of the elements,
through their unification with the Lord's glorious body. The vocation of matter to reflect the uncreated Wisdom which is its own

---

[32] Bulgakov's *Nachlass* includes a still unpublished treatise on the Eucharistic
Sacrifice, showing not only the various intrinsic dimensions of the Holy
Eucharist but its wider connexion with the central dogmatic tenets of
Christianity. Some indication of its contents is given in L. A. Zander, *Bog i Mir*,
op. cit., I., pp. 149–150.

[33] 'Evkharisticheskii dogmat', *Put'* (1930), 20, pp. 3–46; 21, pp. 3–33. This text,
along with an essay from the same journal offering an original interpretation
of the legend of the Grail, can be found in an English translation by Boris
Jakim with a valuable introduction, by Father Robert Slesinski, and afterwords,
by Constantin Andronikov and Caitlin Matthews, as: *The Holy Grail and the
Eucharist* (Hudson, NY, 1997), pp. 63–138.

[34] R. Slesinski, 'Introduction', in ibid., p. 20.

ultimate archetype has in the Blessed Sacrament of the Altar a unique realization and radiation.

Bulgakov's ruthless rationing of sacramental theology in *The Bride of the Lamb* is not, then, a 'put-down' of the liturgical mystery. Far from it. Rather is his aim to emphasize that the Church's riches extend beyond the sacraments since those riches also include the *charisms*. These are the many gifts, not as such ordered to the sacramental organization of the Church, that attest the diversity of ministerial activities caused by the 'one and the same' Holy Spirit (cf. 1 Corinthians 12: 11) who blows where he will. After all, it is 'not by measure' that God gives the Spirit (John 3: 8). Such charismatic ministries should be attached, Bulgakov thinks, rather to the inspiration of Christ the Messiah-king than to Christ the high priest. Certainly they are not originated by the priesthood of the hierarchy. Bulgakov looks for them in *askêsis*, teaching and spiritual creativity, and especially in that appropriation of the Holy Spirit by which through inspired illuminations Spirit-bearing people open the Christian life to the skies. Bulgakov finds the Spirit blowing where he will in the twentieth-century Ecumenical Movement which invited the churches to go beyond that confessionalism which would 'supplant catholic unity by an ecclesiastical provincialism'.[35] The Church gazes at an horizon where heaven and earth join. It was by a theanthropic way, at once heavenly and earthly, that the Spirit descended. And we are told it is by the same way that Christ will come in his glory.

One disadvantage of Bulgakov's account is the acerbity he shows toward the classical theologies of the dominical institution of the sacraments (a 'Tridentine myth', he terms it, careless of its presence in, for example, the writings of Leo the Great and its ubiquity in the Orthodox manuals not to mention two major doctrinal instruments of early modern Orthodoxy, the *Confession* of Dositheus of Jerusalem and Peter of Moghila's *Orthodox Confession* which, however, do make use, in anti-Protestant contexts, of Latin models). One compensating advantage is the generous fashion in which he is able to find genuine sacramental life beyond the limits of the Orthodox Church. Cyprian of Carthage, with more influence in East than in West, could not believe sacraments were valid where the visible Church in her unity is not to be found. Bulgakov is strongly anti-Cyprianic. He does not ask, 'Are the sacraments of schismatics valid?'. He asks, 'What is their value?' His answer is,

[35] NA, p. 317.

The sacraments celebrated in the non-Orthodox churches and ecclesial communities are windows onto the same heaven, though they may be windows of clouded glass. We do not possess the means to say just what degree of diminution this entails compared with the fulness given to the Church. But we can affirm that they remain real conductors of the gifts of grace, salutary in joining those who receive them to the body of the Church. (Here we are leaving aside a point equally pertinent to reception by the Orthodox: namely, the question of the individual's own disposition, which belongs to the mystery of Providence.) Bulgakov will not accept, in other words, that other anti-Cyprianic position, St Augustine's, for whom the sacraments of schismatics are valid but fruitless until they return to unity – whereupon all their frozen graciousness melts and warms. So radical a contradiction between ecclesiology and soteriology is not to be endured.

12

The Christian in History

The inclusion of a section on 'History' in a modern dogmatics is a novelty.[1] At least, it is new if what is in question is not just the salvation history of the Bible and its continuation in the sacramental Church. And that is the case here: Bulgakov is a theologian of the historical process *as a whole*. We might look for the explanation to his admiration for the Augustine of *The City of God*. Or to the fact that he began his intellectual life as a Marxist, convinced of the importance of gaining an overall view of the development of history. Or again to his shared interest with Soloviev in the philosophy of history of the founder of social Positivism, Auguste Comte (1798–1857).[2] But probably Soloviev's example suffices to explain his decision, for Soloviev himself had tried to practice both a philosophy and a theology of history joined by the 'bridge' of sophiology.[3] In this novel proceeding, for a dogmatician, Bulgakov's touch is impressively sure.

The frame of history

Within the general framework of the sophianic development of the world, Bulgakov places history between two 'abysses': the entry of man into the world at his creation and the 'new time' of the Age to

[1] Notably, Zander extracts it and places it in the philosophical section of his work: thus *Bog i mir*, I., pp. 415–434.

[2] Both the Marxian and the Comtian interests of Bulgakov, and their afterlife in his use of Soloviev, are extremely well laid out in P. Valliere, *Modern Russian Theology: Bukharev, Soloviev, Bulgakov. Orthodox Theology in a New Key* (Edinburgh, 2000), pp. 227–244.

[3] See M. de Courten, *History, Sophia and the Russian Nation. A Reassessment of Vladimir Solov'ëv's Views on History and Social Commitment* (Berne, 2004), who speaks in a musical metaphor of the three 'registers' on which Soloviev's thinking about history is played.

Come: the 'meta-history' of 'Behold, I make all things new' (Apocalypse 21: 5). History is, then, a specific condition of being in its becoming. History is the story of the human race, and yet each person shares in history. Bulgakov succeeds in integrating the two sides of that equation when he writes:

> It is in the different hypostases that this humanity manifests itself in an individual and multiform manner – but it is a humanity with a certain unity of life, a commonality one can define as simultaneously the transcendental subject and the object of history.[4]

We have already learned from Bulgakov's theology of the Fall that (in his opinion) unless there were a pan-human 'I', shared human understanding would be impossible. He now refines that statement seeing the 'transcendental subject of humanity, gathering all its history into the unity of Adam' as 'the basis of its transcendental functions'. In a sense, this is what the Idealist philosophers would recognize as the universal subject of knowledge, the gnoseological 'I'. But Bulgakov stresses the 'hereditary accumulation of thought and knowledge' which follows from the Adamic starting-point. This unity is realized, moreover, not only in knowledge but also in action. There is a single acting as well as knowing subject. And this is the transcendental subject of *economics*: the husbanding of the resources of nature available to man as agent in the world. (Here Bulgakov returns to his earliest extended sophiological essay, *The Philosophy of Economic Activity*.) As a final element, Bulgakov adds the notion that there is also a transcendental aesthetic subject for humanity. How else, given the 'particularity and diversity of arts and artists could there be general access to the beautiful', rather than an 'atomised polymorphousness', *atomisticheskia mnogobrazie*, resistant to any common language or response.[5]

Historical creativity

All these aspects of humanity's life so inter-relate as to form the ensemble of history in its sequential expression in culture. Considered as the creative self-expression of the transcendental subject of history, the work of historical genesis, however restricted and disfigured by sin, both original and personal, is a disclosure of a humanity endowed with 'natural grace'. The foundational

[4] NA, p. 343.
[5] Ibid., p. 344.

sophianic vocation continues even if *insofar as sin reigns* it is *de facto* suspended. Such a vocation is man's call to bring humanity to its fullest coherence. Involved here is a positive not a negative infinity because the tasks of the sophianic vocation, though staggering, are also determinate – and they can be brought to maturity, to full term. Thus in St Matthew's Gospel (24: 32), Jesus takes the example of the fig tree: when its branches become tender and put out leaves, one knows that summer has come. In biblical eschatology (including apocalyptic) the end of the world and its transfiguration are 'represented as being at once God's action in the world's regard and the fruit of its life'. Bulgakov finds no contradiction in that.

> The actions of God correspond to the age attained by the world, to the times and moments of its organic being. However, history and its maturing to the end are not determined solely by its organic development. The liberty and creative work of man play their part. The humanisation of the world and of man himself, access to fullness, the powers which human nature conceals: all this represents man's creative action vis-à-vis himself as well as the world.[6]

The 'organic' and the 'creative', the 'datum' of human life and its 'agendum', are indissolubly bound together because the human spirit is inseparable from the cosmos. And while the ways in which the world ripens towards its end are multiply different, for the forms and degrees of historical creation are individual and diverse, they are never *just* individual creations but in addition a 'general and pananthropic work'.[7] Otherwise we could not speak of 'universal history' at all.

So the world enjoys either retrospectively or prospectively a twofold fullness: that which is given it sophianically at its genesis and that which it actualizes in and as history. The latter is the Creator's task for man, and the 'universe realized in man is the substratum of the transfiguration of the world'.[8] Here Bulgakov approaches the issue of the transcendental object of human creative work in all its forms, and this is, we are told, 'an integral synthesis of the work of all human beings with a view to humanizing the world and transforming it into an "anthropo-cosmos"'.[9] We recall how, for fundamental sophiology, the world is to be under-

[6] Ibid., p. 347.
[7] Ibid., p. 348.
[8] Ibid., p. 349.
[9] Ibid.

stood *in relation to its human centre,* in so doing replicating the pattern of Wisdom in the Logos of God.

We can neither know nor even define what counts as the accomplishment of this task. That is why the End will inevitably convey some sense of the sudden and catastrophic. But we should not for all that confuse God's almightiness with arbitrary *Diktat* – some sort of integral plenitude is needed for the End.

What is the scope of creative history-making action as Bulgakov understands it? It is everything involved in culture and civilization.[10] Before issuing a Christian-humanist manifesto on the topic, Bulgakov reminds his readers of the likely contribution to human development, for good and ill, of the co-human angels. That pushes back the frontiers of the human world and leaves them less definable. It also assures other Orthodox that he is not offering them naturalistic pottage. He asserts that Christians should not fear the sobriquet 'humanist' from their more a-cosmically inclined brethren but make the latter realize how much of an unconsciously Buddhistic withdrawal there is in a 'No' to the cultural project of humanity. Of course, much human culture is sick. Sophiologically, the doctrine of the Fall tells us that, whereas the essence of natural humanity is sophianic, its condition *is* sick. So it is hardly surprising if the same can be said of human creativity in history. It proposes a common path for all to follow, pagan or Christian. But it also needs Christ to heal its pathology. It needs in fact the tonic of Christian humanism – a phrase to be associated, in the France of the late 1930s with the Thomist philosopher Jacques Maritain (1881–1973).[11]

The making of Christic humanity

For Bulgakov, the real question is, 'Can human activity be exercised in the name of Christ? Can it be the labour of a Christic humanity?'[12] Does man's work, investing his natural talents, belong to the Kingdom of God? Is it destined to future glorification, or is it only the domain of the prince of this world? There can only be

---

[10] Bulgakov belongs with a trio of writers who, with little obvious background in the preceding Orthodox theological tradition, tried to give ecclesial creativity, in the realm of faith and culture, its due. That is how, with good reason, he is presented in P. Valliere, *Modern Russian Theology,* op. cit.

[11] See J. V. Schall, *Maritain the Philosopher in Society* (New York, 1998).

[12] NA, p. 353.

one answer. Christ is king of this world not only as God but also as man, since in becoming incarnate he

> has hallowed all the world's forces and possibilities (sin alone excepted) and there is nothing human that has not become theanthropic – that is, not redeemed and blessed by him.[13]

As Bulgakov's investigation of the work of Christ in *The Lamb of God* has shown, his royal office will continue until the end of the age. In the Book of the Apocalypse the new Jerusalem has inscribed on its walls the names of angels and men – a sign for Bulgakov that the new city is not 'drawn out of nothingness but is the transfiguration of history'.[14] Certainly, it issues from a catastrophic rupture, yet nothing rightly achieved will be abolished.

If anyone thinks this projection of the future too rosy, Bulgakov adds that the 'building of the tower' (shades of Hermas!) is not going to be all peace and light. Rather is it 'struggle and tragedy'. Should not a survivor of the Bolshevik Revolution and the Civil War know? Human nature and activity are 'spiritually qualified' – like the angels – for good or evil. The Satanic spirit is active, pressing mankind towards false self-divinization, impressing on culture the principle of mangodhood, standing contradiction of Godmanhood and so of Christ's work and reign. Bulgakov takes with utter seriousness the Apocalypse's portrayal of clashing armies.

In that book, the beast coming out of the sea stands for the animal principle affirming itself grotesquely as superior or unique. This is 'apocalyptic mangodhood', *apokalypticheskoe chelovekobozhie*, blood exalted above spirit.[15] For Bulgakov we have here the bestial power of the absolute State which recognizes nothing higher than itself, the ideology of force crushing moral conscience. When the false prophet introduces 'spirit' into the beast, we are faced with not merely the bestialization of man but his satanization and fighting against the Holy Spirit. These powers – the beast, the false prophet – are embodied in the many antichrists. For Bulgakov, antichristhood is more a principle capable of multiple embodiment than it is an individual. If a nameable individual is in question at the End, it will be, rather, the 'man of sin' of Second Thessalonians (2: 3–10), a personal leader of 'theomachy' (fight-

---

[13] Ibid.
[14] Ibid., p. 354.
[15] Ibid., p. 356.

ing against God), not least in his parodying of God. He will be, speculates Bulgakov, a 'visible exterior index of the advent of the End'.[16] But the main point to grasp is that, right from the beginning of its story, Christianity has been accompanied by its shadow: anti-Christianity. And the upshot is 'a schism in the soul of the world as in history'.[17] The Woman clothed in the Sun is one epicentre of world history, but the other is Babylon the Great, drunk on the blood of the saints (Apocalypse 17: 1–6).

How, 'historiosophically' speaking, are these related? The heart of man is a battleground. Human nature serves for constructing both the city of God *and* the counter-city, Babylon. Christianity's task is not (*pace* the ultra-ascetics) to mortify humanity but to 'manifest it in the force and fullness of Christian inspiration'. Here passivity would be capitulation to the enemy – and so would reducing the Church to the sphere of the inner world (after Bulgakov's lifetime to be dubbed 'privatisation') or confining its expression to the 'exterior reactions of ecclesiastical organization, in a kind of clericalisation of history'.[18] Yet Bulgakov believes that 'organized ecclesiality' can influence directly the history of culture sufficiently strongly to 'transmute the elements of the world'. It is just that, like all creative energy, this has to pass through the crucible of the personal – the personal as a contribution to universal history.

Our own epoch, writes Bulgakov at the end of the 1930s, is one in which creativity is lauded *per se*. This should alert us to the peculiar dangers – if also the interesting possibilities – of the approach to 'the Christian in history' he advocates. A 'Luciferian intoxication of creativity', itself plunged into an 'obtuse and sensual paganism', has about it the distinctive odour of idolatry of the human. Hence the need to expound an authentically Christian teaching on the world and the creative task of man.

How is to be done? By developing, says Bulgakov, the Chalcedonian dogma and its corollary, defined at the Sixth Ecumenical Council, Dyothelitism: the two wills of the Redeemer. What was accomplished in Christ when the fullness of his human nature, will and thus creative energy was divinized by union with the divine, was 'pre-accomplished' then for humanity at large. In the light of the dogmas, the cosmos is not 'the kingdom of this world'. It is the 'luminous creation of God which rises up through man toward divinisation'.[19] *This* is the perspective in which our

---

[16] Ibid., p. 358.
[17] Ibid.
[18] Ibid., p. 359.
[19] Ibid., p. 360.

contemporary celebration of creativity needs to be seen. It reflects
Bulgakov's background in economics and politics that he numbers
first among these tasks social and political organization: the
common ordering of human life.

Towards the End

At the End, however much there may seem externally to be a
break, we can be sure that a sufficient fullness of human creativity will have been realized for the world to be transfigured. The
old will have passed (compare 2 Corinthians 5:17) but not disap-
peared. It will live in the future, just as the Old Covenant lives in
the New. History will be eternalized in all that is valuable in its
content, and this 'element of eternity in time' belongs by right to
the Church which is not only the ark of Noah saving survivors
from a flood but a leaven working through the whole paste.
Bulgakov is able to call human history 'Church history' precisely
because for him the Church is not only external, institutional,
sacramental, but is the inner spiritual power that takes
Theanthropy forward.
    This 'historiosophy' – which, basically, is that of the Johannine
Apocalypse – is neither pessimist (it seeks to arouse human energies not damp them down) nor optimist (it knows no outcome to
the conflict within history proper). And yet the scriptural theme of
royalty, with its many prophecies and psalms, cannot be so attenu-
ated as to deny genuine Christophany on earth. Despite the
darkness around, the universal preaching of the Gospel and the
conversion of Israel 'solemnly prophesied as a mystery by the
apostle of the Gentiles' (cf. Romans 9–11)[20] precede what the
Apocalypse calls the 'first resurrection' and the thousand-year
reign. On the millennium, Bulgakov is inclined to say that, despite
certain perhaps over-emphasized Judaic traits (he probably has in
mind such notions as an increase in the earth's fertility), the 'first
doctors' were close to the truth. He means Papias (c. 60–130),
Justin (c. 100–c. 165), and Irenaeus, all of whom included an
historical 'reign of the saints' in the scenario of the End. That is
closer, at any rate, to the biblical witness than were supporters of
the allegorical interpretation of the last times which gained
ground with Origen in the East, Tychonius (d. c. 400) in the West.
Bulgakov sees the 'first' resurrection and succeeding 'reign' as a

[20] Ibid., p. 364.

spiritual event with repercussions for human history. Its chief trait will be, he thinks, a

> temporary paralysis which strikes the malign power, whence comes a change in spiritual atmosphere, a sensible manifestation of the victorious power of the good.[21]

The 'resurrection' concerned can only be at a spiritual level. This is not yet the general resurrection, what the Apostles' Creed calls the 'resurrection of the flesh'. It will be, Bulgakov surmises, a communication to the souls of the redeemed of a fresh energy enabling them to 'share from the beyond in the life of the world and the history of human beings'.[22]

The veneration of the saints and our communion with them throws light on this. It is the belief of Orthodoxy, as of Catholicism, that the saints share our life by their prayers and actively help us, in a fashion comparable to that of the holy angels yet also distinct from it. For Bulgakov, the angels are cosmic agents within the world, whereas the souls of the faithful departed, even when glorified and mighty in intercession, are in a condition of ontological weakness, separated as they are from their own bodies. In terms of the Apocalypse, what we can look forward to is such a re-potentialization of the saints and their prayer that it will be as though they were living among us on earth. Such a 'first resurrection' can in a way already be experienced now. Souls saturated in sanctifying grace can know something of that intimacy with the saints. It is, says Bulgakov, proper to the Church at all times to know it. Still, it will take place with peculiar power in the time of the End. And this will be the final anticipation within history of the divine kingdom on earth: *within* history, and as prefigured by the Triumphal Entry on Palm Sunday. Paradoxically, it triggers the last combat, and with it the verification of the Creed's article, 'He shall come again to judge the living and the dead'. Given its crucial position on the boundary of history and meta-history, Bulgakov calls the millennium the 'guiding star of history', *vedushchaya zvedzda istorii*.[23] It expresses a Christian notion of progress, freed from naturalistic reductionisms. It is key to the distinction between Christian humanism and its neo-pagan surrogates. It transcends Manichaean 'anti-cosmos-ism' for which history remains essentially vain and empty. It ought to become the inspiration for all creative activity.

[21] Ibid., p. 366.
[22] Ibid.
[23] Ibid., p. 369.

Here, says Bulgakov, 'historiosophy intervenes ... in sophiology as a necessary element'.[24] In the providential development of sophianity towards the End, a place belongs to free creative human action – as the message to the angels of the seven churches in the opening chapters of John's Apocalypse makes clear. That book is not only an exhortation to martyrdom. It is also a sermon on synergism.

Bulgakov is willing to allow that the millennium keeps on repeating itself in Christian history. But, he insists, it will also have a final, definitive form. In this light, then, sophianization is clearly not evolutionism, which would negate the End. Rather, what we have is eschatological progress as the condition of the End. Bulgakov's commitment to the classic eschatology of the tradition is firm. Only universal resurrection

> synthesises and really re-establishes one single humanity as the subject of its own historical realizations.[25]

The ideology of progress forgets death. The nineteenth-century Russian thinker N. N. Fedorov's (1828–1903) extraordinary (yet deeply Christian) notion that the highest work of man is the resurrection of fathers by sons becomes, once deprived of divine context, the idea of a technical immortality to secure the triumph of immanentism by conquering death on earth. Bulgakov evaluates it caustically: 'the advent of the kingdom of the void and boredom unsurmountable'.[26] It was one of Dostoevsky's nightmares.

The Holy Grail: a world set on course for the new Paradise

Bulgakov's counter-image for the *real* transfiguration of the world by divine agency through Jesus Christ and his Spirit is the unusual one – even more so when it is an Eastern Christian who is writing – of the Holy Grail. From the riven side of the Saviour flowed streams of blood and water, so the beloved disciple, standing at the Cross, could not help observing (John 19: 34). While accepting that patristic exegesis traced here a reference to the sacramental life of the Church (founded above all in the 'blood' of the Eucharist and the 'water' of baptism), Bulgakov claimed that some-

---

24 Ibid., p. 370.
25 Ibid., p. 372.
26 Ibid., p. 373.

thing more was at stake. The blood and water which falls to the
earth from the Cross is not recaptured for the biosystem of the
risen Jesus. Rather:

> The blood and water that flowed into the world abide in the world.
> They sanctify this world as the pledge of its future transfiguration.
> Through the precious streams of Christ's blood and water that
> flowed out of his side, all creation was sanctified – heaven and earth,
> our earthly world, and all the stellar worlds.[27]

The Holy Grail, for Bulgakov, is not a sacramental chalice, even if,
in legendary material whose historicity he leaves an open question,[28] the Grail is the cup of the Last Supper as well as the vessel
that caught the bloodflow from the Cross. Unlike the Holy
Eucharist, it is not given for the communion of the faithful but – as
the passage just cited makes clear – for the transfiguration of the
world.[29] The Holy Grail abides as the mysterious holiness of the
world itself – a holiness indebted to the Incarnation of the Logos
and his redeeming work. To this extent we can speak of a presence
of Christ in his *non*-Eucharistic blood, the blood of Golgotha, and
not in the Eucharistic blood alone. So far, 'the world's treasure'
has only been alluded to in legend and poem. Bulgakov would like
to see the Grail (as he understands it) move to a more central place
in Christian consciousness because it proclaims the Christ-
achieved sacrality of the world itself. Here 'the world' is
understood as nature and humanity taken together. Christ abides
on earth in the midst of humankind, and not only in the festivities
of the Church.

---

[27] Idem., 'Svyatii Graal', *Put'* 32 (1932), pp. 3–42, and here at p. 13 I use the translation given in B. Jakim (ed.), *Father Sergius Bulgakov. The Holy Grail and the
Eucharist* (Hudson, NY, 1997), p. 33.

[28] At one point Bulgakov refers to the Grail as 'the holy treasure of Montserrat'.
The Grail is generally associated with the high mediaeval Romances which can
only be scanned for historical references by some considerable confusion of
literary genre. But a recently discovered sixth-century MS speaks of the Grail's
sending for safekeeping by St Laurence to Roman Spain during the Valerian
persecution (*c.* 258). Monks of the monastery of San Juan de la Peña claim
guardianship of an equivalent relic. *See* J. Bennett, *St Laurence and the Holy
Grail. The Story of the Holy Chalice of Valencia* (San Francisco, 2004). How Church
historians will receive this study remains to be seen.

[29] There is, however, a connection between the sacrament and the world-sacring:
'The matter of the world that turned out to be worthy of receiving Christ's
blood and water is also worthy of the mysterious transmutation of its elements
in the Eucharist': S. Bulgakov, 'Svyatii Graal', art. cit., p. 26; English translation
in B. Jakim, *Fr. Sergius Bulgakov and the Holy Eucharist*, op. cit., p. 46.

This blood and water made the world a place of the presence of Christ's power, prepared the world for its future transfiguration, for the meeting with Christ come in glory ... The world has become indestructible and incorruptible, for in Christ's blood and water it has received the power of incorruption, which will be manifested in its transfiguration.[30]

The world is eschatologically set on course. Sophianity can come to term.

---

[30] S. Bulgakov, 'Svyatii Graal', art. cit., p. 25; English translation in B. Jakim, *Fr. Sergius Bulgakov and the Holy Eucharist*, op. cit., p. 44.

13

Eschatology

Death and beyond

Death is the transition to another life, itself largely unknown, but for which the Word of God gives some directive concepts.[1] Bulgakov begins, though, philosophically. The least comprehensible of all assertions about death, he truculently remarks, is the positivist statement that it consists in the outright suppression of life. For Positivism, the world comes from nothing and in death being becomes nothing again: *nothing*, not just as the destruction of visible corporeal form but the snuffing out of the spirit's creative energy, the vaporization of the heart. Such Positivism is not courageous 'free-thinking' but unbelieving thought taking refuge in an 'ontology of death', *ontologie smerti*, or 'ontology of nihilism', *ontologie nigilizma*, a twofold non-being, before life and after it.[2]

Bulgakov takes *ad litteram* the assertion of the author of Wisdom, 'God did not make death' (1: 14). God made man for incorruptibility: the state of being dead is, accordingly, a parasitic one, a sickness to which life falls victim. Essential to human sophianity – to the 'grace of nature' – is Adam's enjoying the possibility of not dying, albeit as a possibility he had to affirm by his own free act of correspondence with grace. But quite the opposite happened. 'The dust returns to the earth as it was, and the spirit returns to God who gave it' (Ecclesiastes 12: 7). Bulgakov calls that text the 'anthropological monogram of death'. God 'separates what he had originally united'.[3] True, sin could not encompass the dissolution of the immortal spirit as issuing from God. It could only exploit a possibility of disjunction in the complex ontology of the human

[1] See L. A. Zander, *Bog i mir*, op. cit., II., pp. 319–346.
[2] NA, p. 373.
[3] Ibid. p. 378, p. 379.

creature. In the weakening of personal spirit's power over psycho-somatic nature the beautiful unity of the hypostatized earth was lost. Of course the human being did not itself cease to exist. The soul continued to be in certain respects the mediating principle between flesh and personal spirit. Yet considered as the abiding unity it should have been, the artwork was shattered and its components fell apart. Only in conquering death by death will Christ restore the original vessel, establishing life in its 'integral and absolute character'.[4]

For Bulgakov, we must not take comfort too quickly in the thought of Easter. Death is the opening up of the maw of non-being. It is looking into the abyss. It is implacably tragic, inescapably horrible, the 'suffering of sufferings'. Only in doing this full justice, as the Saviour himself did when he agonized, can we appreciate the salutary antinomy which comes to us from the Resurrection of the Crucified. The road of death has been trav-elled by Christ and, after him, the Mother of God, and now it is lit with the tongues of fire of the Holy Spirit. The death of the right-eous who are pure in heart is now the joy of joys, the reversal of all expectation. It was for a sufficient reason that God permitted death.

Despite his emphasis on the horror of death, Bulgakov's initial stand against a positivistic nihilism leads him to hold that death is sleeping, *dormition*, not annihilation. The soul does not so much die as enter into relative depotentialization. Its power to synthesize flesh and spirit is suspended, not annulled.

The sleep in the tomb of the Word incarnate is a death where no rupture supervenes – not between personal spirit, soul and flesh any more than between the divine and human natures in Christ. Corruption did not touch God's holy One (cf. Acts 2: 31). Moreover, the Ascension is the eternalization of this state of affairs. But the Lord's descent in the soul into the realm of the departed originates or at any rate confirms the theological doctrine that in our own death, soul remains enduringly attached to person. How does Bulgakov think of this 'life after death'?

Confrontation with the spiritual world of the angels and sepa-rated souls is accompanied by a sense of triumph for all those who longed for their communion, but anguish for those who rejected any such notions, preferring to experience themselves as entirely carnal. Bulgakov dignifies with theological existence the commonly found belief (possibly based on near-death experi-

---

[4] Ibid., p. 381.

ences) that in the moment of dying one's life passes before the
inner eye, at any rate in its overall shape. A preliminary judgement on that life is carried out by the individual's own conscience,
in the presence of God. This cannot be a definitive judgement,
for it is neither *God's* judgement nor is it a judgement which takes
into account all the ramifications of moral choices in the historical process as a whole. Bulgakov is inclined to think, however, that
such a judgement, limited in scope, is the real gateway to the
inter-mediate state – the Latin 'Purgatory' – which is not, then, a
gage of assured redemption, for the final decision for heaven or
hell, on his view, is still unmade. He regrets that, through Catholic
influence on Orthodox eschatology, the Orthodox too now
consider the souls for whom prayer is sought on earth as essentially passive vis-à-vis their own salvation in the sense that they
cannot 'merit'. He agrees that passivity (incidentally, the word
plays no role in Catholic dogma) is an appropriate term insofar
as departed souls are reduced to contemplators (if that) of the
drama of human life on earth. But, he insists, they retain their
freedom, which now has fresh materials to work on, precisely in
the spiritual panorama of the angelic realm and the communion
of saints and sinners beyond the grave. With so endless a source
of new life and understanding there can be no stasis in Purgatory.
He presents the inter-mediate state as a 'spiritual school', enrich-
ing and reconfiguring the individuals who – so to speak – attend
it. Altering the sense of the Lucan parable, he thinks that Dives,
the Rich Man who, after death, changed his view of Lazarus, the
Poor Man, and wanted his brothers to learn the demands of
charity and justice, exemplifies not only a post-mortem learning
process but also repentance. And this, he feels, can hardly be
disassociated from ultimate pardon. This reading of Luke 16:
19–31 points ahead to Bulgakov's adoption of a soteriological
universalism modelled on that of the fourth-century Cappadocian
doctor, Gregory of Nyssa.

Following the principles of synergism, Bulgakov stresses that the
'gift of ecclesial prayer', expressed in the Church's practice of
interceding for the departed and offering for them the
Eucharistic Oblation, cannot be received without some appropriate action on the part of the holy souls.[5] He acknowledges that
the language of retribution – wages, or their deprivation – is
found in Scripture. But such language should be understood
ontologically, not juridically – and so as a statement of the

[5] Ibid., p. 395.

outcome for someone's being of the tendency certain actions show. Furthermore, retribution discourse seems inappropriate for those who in life lacked a revealed understanding of moral and spiritual demand: and here Bulgakov has in mind not only pagans but, above all, infants. In the case of the latter who, by dying soon after birth, are like 'birds touching with a wing the surface of water',[6] the only view of the after-life which makes sense at all is that it is a continuation of this life, not recompense for it. Those severely mentally handicapped, too, must first experience, beyond death, something of the ethical dimensions of human life before they can be judged on their response to them. How needed is the Lord's saying, 'in my Father's house are many mansions' (John 14: 2)! As to the pagans, surely they will have to learn about Christ after dying if their judgement is to be in any sense of their reaction to him? The Saviour's preaching to the souls in prison, and numerous patristic texts on the illumination of Hell by his victory, betray the conviction, in the Church's deep consciousness, that this is so. The power of Pentecost is not limited by those iron gates. Nor is human freedom defeated by them. Bulgakov does not hesitate to call the life after death an 'unfinished aspect of human creative activity'.[7]

> Beyond the grave conditions consist essentially in living right to the end one's fullness of existence as preparation for the universal resurrection and as contribution to the integral sophianity of the created.[8]

It is possible to agree with this affirmation while leaving open the question just what degree of *roundedness* existential 'fullness' might attain in a discarnate soul. It is, though, by way of being a valuable corrective to the classical Christian view of the essential unsatisfactoriness of the life of the separated soul when Bulgakov points out that *all* life, inasmuch as it *is* life, is sophianic.

Bulgakov's thanatology – his theology of death and dying – has already anticipated a good deal of his eschatology. When we take it in conjunction with his theology of history – itself strongly apocalyptic and eschatological, it might seem problematic quite how much left there could be to say.

---

6 Ibid., p. 400.
7 Ibid., p. 402.
8 Ibid., p. 405.

Kinds of eschatology

But eschatology is for Bulgakov too important to be left as an appendage. 'Crowning the totality of the theological system, it concerns all the dogmas, [being as it is] the last word in Christian ontology... '[9] And since it deals with what is as yet unaccomplished, it necessarily relies, more than any other aspect of doctrinal theology, on the sheer revealed word of God. Though the doctrine of the 'Last Things' is often considered dogmatically self-evident, in reality, at least in Eastern theology, it is, theologically speaking, a woefully neglected field. Bulgakov finds three sub-traditions worth considering: the Origenist, embodied in its more orthodox form in Gregory of Nyssa; the non-Origenist eschatology of the remaining Eastern and the great majority of theWestern Fathers, and that of St Augustine. Eschatology is, at any rate for an Orthodox, a legitimate area of theological research, little restricted – or, to speak less journalistically – little *defined* by the rule of faith. Bulgakov hopes that a sophiological eschatology can make a useful contribution in an area of theological thought too often dominated by rationalism and anthropomorphism. Rationalism, he adds, is precisely the anthropomorphism of thought. For the riches of divine Wisdom much of the traditional treatise on eschatology has substituted a handbook for organizing a detention centre. These harsh – and surely grotesquely unfair – words are another signal that he will, in fact, unveil to us a universalism of Nyssa's kind.

Relying on Scripture, then: the 'end of the age' will see no new creation but the regeneration of the created world at that point of 'maturity' he has already laid out in his theology of history. Its context can be summed up in three words: return, manifestation, glory.

The Parousia of the Lord

The Saviour's return is a manifestation with 'all the signs of earthly concreteness'.[10] It has little if anything in common with those visionary experiences of Christ with which certain of the saints have been blessed as a testimony to the 'spiritual co-existence of Christ and the Church'.[11] The Eucharistic presence is a closer

[9] Ibid., p. 407.
[10] Ibid., p. 416.
[11] Ibid., p. 418.

comparison. Indeed, it contains an element of the Parousia, but, so far from rendering the latter unnecessary, calls out for it. The Parousia is not going to be a hidden sacramental presence, but an unveiled and self-evident one. 'Every eye will see him, every one who pierced him' (Apocalypse 1: 7). The post-Ascension distancing, it will turn out, was not definitive. It was simply providential. It indicated the end of the kenosis and the glorification of the Lord's human essence, not what was to be for the future his final relation with the world. Naturally, the biblical imagery for the Parousia cannot be adequate to its object. We are speaking of a change in the God-world relation, which Bulgakov describes as

> A new drawing near to the world by God, and a new approximation to God by the created.[12]

In the Parousia, the Son does not only come in the glory that is now his. He gives that glory to the world where the Spirit already dwells kenotically. For this moment is the tangible appearance of the Spirit who rests on the Son. The Second Advent, like the Son's entire economy, can only be dyadic.

> The Parousia manifests not only the power of the Incarnation but that of Pentecost as well – of Christ in glory and glory in Christ because the appearance with him, in him and through him of the Holy Spirit.[13]

Not that there is a new coming of the Spirit. But the Parousia draws forth the plenitude of the Spirit's action, bringing his kenosis in the world to an end. It must be remembered that the cosmos is not in a deistic state, closed to divine agency, impermeable to spiritual causality. Metaphysical transformation from the side of God is entirely possible to it. But for the transformation to happen *through glory* is to say that the world will be manifested in an hitherto unknown beauty, as its internal 'ideas', the *logoi*, light up from within in a new transparency to God and harmony amongst themselves. For Bulgakov it is difficult to understand this change except with the aid of sophiology. The power of the Theanthropy lies behind this, in the dyadic action of the New Adam and the Holy Spirit. In the final act of the divine drama, the sophianization of the world is complete. The glory is now the same on earth as it is in heaven. The Trinity is fully revealed.

[12] Ibid., p. 423.
[13] Ibid., p. 427.

And if Christ is in that moment fully King because he communicates the Kingdom that is the Holy Spirit, the Church too, as the body of Christ where his Spirit dwells, has some part in his triumph. Though no man will escape judgement, some members of the Church-body will be so resplendent in holiness, thinks Bulgakov, as to be counted worthy to participate in the Parousia, illumined by Christ's glory. (Compare the role of Moses and Elijah at the anticipation of the Parousia that is the Transfiguration on Thabor.) The biblical accounts speak of the Lord's advent *with his angels*. For Bulgakov, they come as constituting the heavenly Church – as well as in their capacity as God's 'created glory'.[14]

Where, then, if anywhere in this scenario, is the Mother of the Word, the Spirit-bearer? How can she *not* be there who is the living portal through which the Holy Spirit passed to bring the Son to the world? That monument of Tradition we call iconography indicates as much when it sets the Mother by the side of the Son in judgement. (This is a rare passage in Bulgakov's work where the icons constitute the sole basis for a presumed development of dogmatic thought.) The Mother of God shares in the Parousia as hearth and heart of the Church. Gloriously awakened from death in her Assumption, she anticipates all the Parousia means. She is in perfect spiritual conformity with the Spirit of glory. Somewhat more tentatively, Bulgakov suggests she will come before her Son does. Her numerous appearances to the faithful seem to give her a role in *preparing* his triumphal way. In any case, her attitude to the Parousia cannot be ours.

On the basis of the icons, and notably the icon of the *Deesis*, the Intercession, Bulgakov associates St John the Baptist with these Marian privileges – both in accompanying the Lord in his glorious Coming and in exemption from judgement. The Mother and the Baptist: these are the two preeminent intercessors for the whole world.

Transfiguration and general resurrection

The world now enters a condition of *transfiguration*: the Parousia's cosmic aspect. The world will change to the extent that Bulgakov can write of the world that sees the Son of Man that it is not the present world. (Would he have approved the English artist Stanley Spencer's (1891–1959) naïve evocations of the general

[14] Ibid., p. 436.

resurrection in a more or less recognizable Berkshire village? The 'more or less' is key here. Spencer certainly shows landscape changed.) All that is unfit to be 'eternalized', all that is 'illusion' – essentially, the non-sophianic features or contents, will be consumed in the Spirit's flame. The world will become more fully configured to humanity, which is the bearer of its soul. What in nature is psychic, ensouled, will become, so Bulgakov suggests, open to spirit. The prospect has to be large enough to correspond to the Pauline promise:

> The creation itself will be set free from its bondage to decay and obtain the glorious liberty of the children of God. (Romans 8: 21)

The historic achievements of human kind will be fulfilled in a new Jerusalem – not least because they will be filtered out from the distortions for which man in the old Babylon is responsible. But the setting of the city is a nature where the invocations of the Three Young Men in the Furnace – the *Benedicite* of the Book of Daniel, so often sung in the Church's Liturgy – become real. All creatures will praise God, and not just through the vicarious agency of man.

The Parousia also means the *general resurrection*. Since the God-man is the *pan-anthrôpos* his personal resurrection was always in principle the resurrection of humanity at large. But only at the Parousia is this entailment rendered effective. The general resurrection is not a *deus ex machina*. It is inextricably linked with the work of redemption of which it is the manifestation. It is also no new beginning, but the restoration of the initial situation of man under grace – though now exalted in dignity. The resurrection is a Trinitarian task: the Father is its principle, the Son its accomplisher, the Spirit the power of its achievement. The angels share in its prosecution inasmuch as it belongs to their role of overseeing the good of humankind. It is universal and simultaneous. In the former aspect it corresponds to the scope of the Incarnation. In the latter it echoes the revelation given in Scripture: at the sound of a trumpet (1 Thessalonians 4: 15–16). Thinking synergistically, Bulgakov envisages that the resurrection of some is active, others by submission to necessity. Can we suppose that the Baptist, the prophets and apostles, are no differently placed in this regard than worldlings, blasphemers, atheists, persecutors of the Church? The tenor of the pertinent New Testament texts, which speak of an order in being raised (1 Thessalonians 4: 16), and emphasize the 'elect' (Matthew 24: 31) and 'those who are in Christ' (1 Corinthians 15: 23), makes this hardly likely.

As 'apocatastasis', or perfective restoration of the beginning, the resurrection is of course bodily. Bulgakov rejects Origen's speculations about a possible series of reincarnations (or those ascribed to him by Jerome [*c.* 345–420], Justinian [*c.* 483–565], and others[15]) as tending to obliterate the distinction of body and soul, and subverting the concrete unity of man. Bulgakov eschews biological speculation, preferring the simplicity of the saying in St John's Gospel (5: 25) 'The dead will hear the voice of the Son of God and those who hear shall live'. But he does *not* eschew theological linkage – first and foremost to communion in the life eternal. At the Paschal Vigil we experience the spiritual joy which will have its fullness and its bodily complement when the Theanthropy is accomplished in the general resurrection. What unites human beings in a common stock – the 'soul of the world' – is revivified by the Holy Trinity, who thereby re-establish human individuals in all their vitality. Bulgakov thinks of an 'energetic centre', mediating between the personal soul and the molecular composition of the universe, as the instrument for the re-creation of the physical form of this woman, that man. Transparent to the redeemed person, it will make him or her a 'living icon'.[16] Personality will be integrally manifested – so much so that we may add 'for the first time'. This will be a 'spiritual body' in the Pauline term. That does not mean, Bulgakov is at pains to say, something less than a body. It means a body that is wonderfully responsive to the spirit and expressive of it: the 'adequation' of man to his prototypical idea. The spiritual body will be, again in St Paul's word, 'glorious' – an epiphany of the divine Wisdom in the sophianity of the world redeemed by Son and Spirit. This brings Bulgakov to what he considers the hardest problem in all theology. How can we reconcile the 'sophianity of the created in its being with its non-sophianic condition in its freedom'?[17] It is on the issue of judgement, and the separation of sheep from goats, that, leaning on his predecessor Gregory of Nyssa, he will depart most obviously from the ecclesial consensus, or what the Greek theologians call the ecclesiastical *phronêma* or 'mind' of the Church.

---

[15] For an impressive marshalling of the evidence that Origen did not hold the views for which he was condemned, *see* M. J. Edwards, *Origen against Plato* (Aldershot, 2002).

[16] NA, p. 470.

[17] Ibid., p. 480.

Final judgement

The issue preoccupies him for some fifty pages of text. The first thing to be said is that, for Bulgakov, the Parousia – the coming of Christ in the glorious epiphany of the Holy Spirit – *is* the Last Judgement. For human beings, the Parousia means entry into the realm of the divine 'fire', which can not only light up but consume. Here we have the baptism 'with the Holy Spirit and with fire' of which John the Precursor spoke (Matthew 3: 11 and parallels). In this moment Christ judges by the Holy Spirit who confronts each one interiorly with his or her own truth: the truth of what they have made of themselves. More specifically:

> Judgement and separation consist in each being placed before his own eternal image in Christ – which means, in front of Christ. In the light of this image each one will see their personal reality.[18]

In the words of the Apocalypse, the books are opened: the Holy Spirit gives the power to 'read' this 'text' properly for the first time. Considered epistemically, the judgement is both transcendent and immanent: enabled from above the world, its criterion is also within the world, insofar as the Primal Image, the Word in his Godmanhood, is found in us as that image in which we were made. The burning philanthropy of the Holy Spirit in which judgement is made allows the person to see himself as riven by internal conflict. Insofar as he is 'outside and far from Christ' he is alienated from the image that is his own foundation.[19] Judgement by hypostatic Love enables one to measure one's own distance from God. That may sound calculating. But the same judgement is meant to break hearts, and set flowing a never-ending love for Christ through whom alone the Spirit of glory enters the world.

This is, then, judgement by the Spirit through the Parousia of the Son who is the God-man. Since he is Emmanuel, born of a virgin, the judgement takes place in the 'silent presence' of Mary, the glorified Mother of the Lord. Bulgakov considers she has her own role in the judgement, which is to arouse in the human beings who see her 'a knowledge of their own perversion and sinful self-affirmation'. She provokes repentance. She is the 'living conscience in man', *zhivaya sovest v cheloveke*.[20] For the interior quality of judgement does not deprive it of an inter-personal and

[18] Ibid., p. 484.
[19] Ibid., p. 486.
[20] Ibid., p. 487.

therefore social, historical and indeed world-historical reference. It possesses the greatest possible public objectivity. We shall see – and we shall *be* – wheat and tares separated, which brings Bulgakov most directly to his great problem.

The judgement – which, it will be recalled, is universal – comprises either incorruptible glory or expulsion into outer darkness. This is the 'fundamental antinomy of the Kingdom of glory'.[21] Bulgakov will have nothing to do with theories of conditional immortality, whereby the rejected 'chaff' simply ceases to exist. But the general shape of his theology, as well as a temperamental disinclination to believe in eternal perdition, makes him dissatisfied with the orthodox alternative. If it be granted that evil is only known in its contradiction of good (ontological good, presumably), then Hell is 'a function of Paradise'. It is the shadow of goodness. That already suggests it cannot be seen as equally primordial. Bulgakov would go on, however, to add that, since no one save the Mother of the Lord is personally sinless, the line of division between sheep and goat runs more fundamentally *within* each of us than it does among us. That line is, in fact, the ontological norm of our sophianity which no man, living or deceased, has respected altogether. And is there, or has there been, a human being who never to the slightest degree honoured it in any of its aspects? These considerations indicate that in judgement every soul is both glorified and burned (albeit in differing degrees). Bulgakov proposes, accordingly, universal fissure in which all souls, in one way or another, exult in Paradise and suffer in Hell.

Can there be, then, beatitude that is only partial, or must such bliss, if it be what its name implies, a total and exclusive state? Here Bulgakov appeals to the Latin divines who considered Christ on the Cross to be both beatified at the apex of his soul and yet suffering torment in mind and body – or continuing to suffer, despite his Ascension and Session, until the number of the redeemed is complete. He can point also to the Orthodox devotional tradition whereby the Mother of the Lord is at once in the perfect joy of her Assumption and Coronation and yet weeps with the sorrowful on earth. Though we are neither Christ nor Mary, these comparisons make the general anthropological point. Bliss and pain are not unconditionally exclusive one of the other. The 'many mansions' of Jesus's own eschatological teaching (John 14: 2), earlier linked by Bulgakov to the destiny of infants and the handicapped, is now referred to the endless combinations of paradisal and hellish expe-

[21] Ibid., p. 488.

rience which human moral complexity seems to him to entail in
any 'final' judgement. In this it is not so much St Gregory of Nyssa
who inspires him as the Syriac writer Isaac of Nineveh whose homi-
lies are perhaps the only text from a Nestorian source to be widely
read in the Greek and Russian Orthodox traditions. The same love
– from the side of the human subject – tortures in the pains of hell
and exults in the joy of heaven. The suffering of the damned aspect
of the self is awareness of past resistance to the Love now poured
out in judgement. And this opens the possibility that Hell will eventually transform itself into Heaven.

Is the distinction between the consuming fire and the gladden-
ing light one that lasts for ever? Bulgakov's etymological
investigations lead him to think that the likely meaning of the
aiônios of the eschatology texts of the Gospel is 'spiritual' rather
than 'eternal' in the sense of enjoying – or enduring – infinite
future existence in time. However, he is conscious that, if this be
the whole truth, then the teaching of Jesus carries no message at
all about endless life in God. Hence his attempt to argue by analysis of St Matthew's parable of the Grand Assize (Matthew 25:
31–46) that there can be no parity of infinitude between an
'eternal' fire described as 'prepared for the devil and his angels'
and an 'eternal' life in the Kingdom 'prepared [for the blessed]
from the foundation of the world'. From the latter's primordial
quality Bulgakov would infer its real endurance in all future time.
From the former's occasional quality (as a response to the angelic
fall) he would argue its functional continuation, merely, as a state
for as long as it is needed. So as a lexical item (this would appear
to be the implication), *aiônios* has two senses, one temporal, the
other not. If so, that is only to be determined by a systematic theological enquiry, and not by humbler philological tools. What
confers eternity (in the sense of endless duration) is that
'unloseable gift of God to creation' which is face-to-face communion with him, as made possible by the Incarnation, Pentecost and
the ultimate outcome of both in the Parousia. In that face-to-face
vision, the 'secularization' by which man knows God only as hidden
'among the trees [of the Garden]' (cf. Genesis 3: 8) is stripped
away and with it, in a sense, the *aseitas,* or being-by-itself of
autonomous creaturehood.

The way Bulgakov has established his theology of divine judgement affords some help in his great 'problem' over the
compatibility of assured being in the Age to come and the contin-
uance of human freedom there. For the judgement made by the
norm of sophianity is simultaneously God's and the creature's. By

encounter with one's own sophianic Prototype, one incriminates oneself. So synergism persists, even in the eschaton. Essentially, where judgement separates from God rather than joins to him is when the image and likeness are not 'in harmonic accord but ... antinomic conjunction'. And this is wherever the project or *agendum* of sophianization – for which the created hypostasis was commissioned at its entry into the world – is so botched, neglected, or simply refused, that it bears no positive relation to the image of God in man, that image which cannot be lost on pain of a creature ceasing to be itself, for it is, after all, the primordial *datum* and gift of human personhood. That is the antinomy which the goats on the Son of Man's left-hand experience as ruin and spiritual death, as the fires of Hell.

But for Bulgakov that is, in fact, only one side of the schizophrenia of judgement, the curse that, to a lesser or greater extent, a blessing must always accompany. How seriously Bulgakov takes this internal schism in the judged becomes plain when he describes their bodies as glorified with beauty – and yet to themselves *insofar as they are the condemned,* degraded. In coming to terms with this inherent ambivalence, more profound than any internal contrariety we can know on earth, the liberty and dynamism of the finite spirit are engaged as never before. In this supreme expression of man's creative labour, Bulgakov finds resolved his 'great problem': how the divine disposition of the End can be compatible with the freedom of man. After all, what are the saints but those who, in their synergy with grace, have worked hardest to be repentant sinners?

There is then 'no absolute Paradise or absolute Hell'.[22] But that is not to say that the conditions of moral and spiritual striving beyond the grave are, *au fond,* as we know them now. In particular, Bulgakov excludes any question of new falls, fresh lapses, backslidings in growth towards God. For the aspect of the human being that is turned towards God, through beatification by judgement, that sight is such that no subsequent turning away is conceivable. Bulgakov is extremely concerned, moreover, that his highly original eschatological speculations should not be taken to license the moral laxity which is a general feature of secularised cultures (if not only there). Every sin must be expiated, and all its consequences accounted for even – or especially – when one is pardoned. But the salutary fear of the divine curse must not be made into a form of spiritual terrorism which 'sterilises filial love

---

[22] Ibid., p. 511.

and childlike confidence towards the heavenly Father' in Christians, assimilating the faith to 'a kind of Islam where fear supplants love'.[23] Everyone, thinks Bulgakov, will experience the pains of Hell (however, in the case of great saints, passingly and slightly). But the fear those pains will inspire is loving fear, the fear of sons.

As Bulgakov admits, he has revived the eschatology of Gregory of Nyssa in a new sophiological form. For Nyssa, evil does not have the creative power to extend to infinity, while the goal of creation must harmonize with the divine nature. Expressed sophiologically, to recognize in judgment one's sophianic form *is* to know the horror of one's own deformity and to accept the scourge of love. At the Parousia, such is the triumphant love of God, such his salutary beauty, that he convinces every man of his desirability. The question of a continuing rejection of God simply fails to arise. A sophiological anthropology, it would seem, severely limits the possibilities of perversity, though the more it does so the less intelligible becomes its own theology of the (angelic, especially, but also human) fall. Eventually, all evil will be expiated, every tear wiped away, every soul converted in its inmost nooks and crannies to God.

> In our eyes, an eternalisation of Hell would signify that the Wisdom of God, foundation of the created order, is impotent to surmount the inertia, feebleness and opposition [to God], in the latter.[24]

But when all ills shall cease, what will there remain for creative work to do? Bulgakov's answer is that the assimilation of the grace-gifts of God will absorb all the creativity we can muster.

The passing of human evil in its totality inevitably implies a change in the condition of the fallen angels. The 'expulsion' of the prince of this world and his servants means for Bulgakov the separation of the fallen angels from the (rest of) creation. As a consequence, while they retain their own malign life they will lose the capacity to express it. It would cohere with his general metaphysical scheme if, like isolated voices in the Syriac and Byzantine traditions, Bulgakov looked kindly on the prospect of an eventual re-admission of the evil angels to the household of God. But in fact he is cautious, if less so than in his formal treatise on angelology, *Jacob's Ladder*, written some years previously. His first reason would

---

[23] Ibid., p. 365.
[24] Ibid., p. 532.

be that of Aquinas: the sheer lucidity and comprehensiveness of the angelic intellect leaves no room for ambiguity in the fallen angels' decision against God.[25] The second reason concerns, as it were, their ecology. So long as Satan remains the 'prince of this world', the fallen angels have an environment in which they can operate, and on whose materials they can set to work: what Bulgakov calls an *ontologichesko khizhenie*, 'ontological prey'.[26] When, with the Parousia, the Holy Trinity takes fullest possession of this world as its Redeemer, this possibility will cease to exist. The life of the evil angels will become a 'giration begun over and over again'. How could freedom ever manifest itself in such a total void? Still, Bulgakov does not want to exclude completely the possibility that, for the ever-patient God, some opportunity of repentance might arise, even in the case of Lucifer, that would fissure this dreadful in-turned, self-devouring autonomy. He sees such an opportunity in the metaphysical absurdity of a Satanic 'I' that has no 'not-I' to look at, a subject without predicate or copula – in the vocabulary of *Die Tragödie der Philosophie*, which here recurs. Perhaps Satanism will 'exhaust itself', and thus come to its term. *For now* such speculations merit in practice no place in the Church's life or preaching. There is a war on, and Christians must not let down their guard. But that is not to say that some boundary has been fixed everlastingly for the divine mercy. The compassion of a figure like Isaac of Nineveh for the demons may be expressed in few words but they were 'words of gold'.[27] They are not sentimental words. They are the voice of ecclesial love. Meanwhile, if the Parousia renders the world inaccessible to the demons (for the glorified cosmos leaves no place for them), it also enhances the communion between human beings and the angels that were confirmed in goodness, enabling them to enter into more direct relation with a humanity now as glorious in grace as they are themselves.

These reflections lead Bulgakov to ponder the question whether tragedy will remain forever in the divine plan for humans too. Does the Christ who suffers for all human beings without exception before the Last Judgement cease to suffer afterwards for the lost sheep? The command that the cursed should go into the fire is a command of the Saviour, and can only be, therefore, an imperative of disciplining love. Only an individualist eschatology could ignore the fact that the righteous do not forget their brethren, that Moses

[25] J. Maritain, 'Le péché de l'Ange', *Revue thomiste* 56 (1956), pp. 197–239; Et *The Sin of the Angel* (Westminster, MD, 1959).
[26] NA, p. 542.
[27] Ibid., p. 547.

and St Paul were willing to be rejected for their people's sins if only to remain with them. What limit should be placed on the 'love' of the Church and its warming hearth, the love of the Mother of God? Above all, the '*universality* of the sacrifice that the eternal High Priest offers to the Father by the Holy Spirit signifies precisely the "apocatastasis" of everything'.[28] In these words, Bulgakov hoists his colours to the mast of the good ship Nyssa, to whose eschatological doctrine – so far as it deals with the redemption of fallen spirits – a substantial appendix to *The Bride of the Lamb* is devoted.

And so back, finally, to the evil angels. Bulgakov proposes that the power of Pentecost affects them, that it includes what he terms *bogoangelstvo*, a 'new deification of the angels by the mediation of man'.[29] The city of God will not be complete without their number.

The city of God

Nowhere else can a treatise on eschatology be ended. The heavenly city, claims Bulgakov, will not be honourable retirement, but a continuation of human creative activity into meta-history. How can this be compatible with the beatific vision? Bulgakov would rather ask, How can it *not* be? How can the divine Trinity be loved apart from the God-man and the humanity divinized through his theanthropic existence and work? The new creation demands a new love, in Christ and the Holy Spirit, in the divine Wisdom. The image of the bridal City in the Apocalypse of John cannot be made the basis of a systematic exposition. But it can tell us that there will be no place there for anything impure. It signifies 'the world transfigured and glorified' where 'principles of existence' that can find no structural expression in the present order shape a new world.[30] The relation with Paradise is re-established, the duality of good and evil surmounted not in a *tertium quid* but in the reign of ontological goodness without end. It will be the world as Temple of God. And, in the title of *Nevesta Agntsa* itself, the new Jerusalem will be the Bride of the Lamb, the Kingdom of love englobing humanity and nature alike.

Bulgakov's finale is a surprise, not a *reprise*. And yet all that has been said above, on the basis of the imagistic revelation found supremely in the Book of the Apocalypse, points to the *Marian*

---

[28] Ibid., p. 551.
[29] Ibid., 552.
[30] Ibid., p. 557.

character of humanity's corporate 'conclusion' (in inverted commas, because it is as much a beginning as an end).

> Is not the Mother of God in her glory the heavenly Jerusalem return-ing to earth from her heavenly dwelling, in the Parousia of the *Theotokos*, to become the spiritual house of God with men? Is she not Wisdom itself, created, certainly, but entirely deified, the summit of all creation, 'more venerable than the Cherubim and incomparably more glorious than the Seraphim'? Is she not the glory and joy of the redeemed peoples at the wedding-banquet of the Lamb, the perfect union of divine and human 'rejoicing every creature, the angelic choirs and the race of man'?[31]

These rhetorical questions, expecting the answer 'Yes', form the perfect transition to a consideration of Bulgakov's Mariological work.

[31] Ibid., pp. 559–560.

14

Our Lady

The All-pure Mother

Kupina neopalimaya, 'The Burning Bush', opens, and to a fair
degree continues, as an exposition of the all-purity of the Mother
of God – Mary's personal sinlessness and the exiguous sense in
which original sin may be said to have touched her, body and soul.[1]
After all, she is in the words of the Byzantine Liturgy 'more
honourable than the Cherubim and incomparably more glorious
than the Seraphim'. More particularly, Bulgakov laments the way
some theologians in the Orthodox world reacted to the 1854
Catholic dogmatization of Mary's 'Immaculate Conception' by
going so far in the other direction as to betray the witness of the
Church's worship and piety to Mary's all-holiness.[2] Although some
early ecclesiastical writers and Fathers such as Origen, Basil, John
Chrysostom (*c.* 347–407), wondered, others equally authoritative,
as Epiphanius, Gregory Nazianzen, Ambrose, Augustine and above
all (for Bulgakov) Ephrem (*c.* 306–373) had no doubts. The latter
group confessed the personal impeccability of the woman who was
filled with the Holy Spirit from her mother's womb. The negative
sayings of the Gospels in Mary's regard have to do, for Bulgakov,
with 'trials, *ispitanie,* on the human way Mary followed in her divine
motherhood during her earthly life'.[3] She had ceaselessly to sacrifice her natural sentiments in regard to her Son. That was *her*
kenosis. He brings forward texts in abundance to show how the
Marian feasts of the Byzantine church all touch on her sinlessness
not only at and after the Annunciation but during her adoles-
cence, childhood and, indeed, birth. Thus on 8 September, in East

[1] For a précis of Bulgakov's Mariology, *see* L. A. Zander, *Bog i mir*, op. cit., II., pp.
187–224.
[2] KN, p. 5.
[3] Ibid., p. 12.

and West Our Lady's birthday, the Byzantine Liturgy sings at the Office of the Lucernarium:

> Today, God who rests on intelligible altars has prepared a holy throne on earth, he who unshakeably founded the heavens by his Wisdom has formed an ensouled heaven by his love for man.[4]

And indeed on the feast of Mary's Conception, we hear:

> The new heaven is built in the womb of Anne, from which heaven, by the will of God who does all, that Sun rises that will never set, who illumines the universe with the rays of his divinity.[5]

The rhetoric of the Liturgy is simply incompatible with the ascription to the Virgin of collusion in evil.

Does not this inference assimilate Mary excessively to her unique Son? No, says Bulgakov, for he was untouched by original sin and only by his own will accepted death, its outcome. In Mary (says Bulgakov, writing in 1924 – as we have seen, the Mariology of the Great Trilogy, from the 1930s, softens this) original sin was present with all its force, with its fatal consequences. But can there be original sin where is utter absence of personal sin? Is not this a contradiction? For Bulgakov, the primary effect of the Fall on Mary is infirmity of nature as shown in her mortality. The proof is that the very same condition – being subject to death – accepted voluntarily by the Word in his Incarnation, was willy-nilly hers. We may note in passing that by no means all the texts of the Byzantine Liturgy, for Bulgakov a favoured theological authority in Mariology, support this brutal contrast.

Nonetheless, Mary achieves the highest level of grace possible for fallen humanity, gathering up from her holy ancestors all the holiness and grace of the Old Covenant, the 'preamble' of the Spirit. Bulgakov calls the Old Testament dispensation 'prodromic' – meaning, after the manner of the Forerunner, John the Baptist, to whom he is dedicating a work in this Little Trilogy. The Old Testament Church had the firstfruits of the good things to come with the Resurrection and Pentecost. In Israel:

> this *podvig* of human sanctity, the raising of open hands towards heaven does not remain without response, and this *donum* indeed *superadditum* [additional, supernatural gift] re-establishes the fallen

[4] Cited ibid., p. 14.
[5] Cited ibid., p. 17.

being in a certain measure – a measure, to be sure, quite beyond our capacity to grasp.[6]

The weakness of human nature, notably in its mortality, remains a constant, only to be overcome by the power of Christ's Incarnation and Resurrection. Such apparent exceptions to the inevitability of human dying as Elijah and Enoch, by being removed in their lifetime from the world, confirm this point. And yet the extraordinary grace of God, granted to members of Jewry in view of the coming of the Word in human flesh, is by contrast a variable. It can reach the point where, except for the *poena* – the penalty – of original sin, it approximates to the condition of original righteousness in which the protoparents came into being. This, Bulgakov implies rather than states, was the case with Mary. In her – as this time he explicitly affirms – the power of original sin could have been reduced to mere potentiality, leaving her *de facto* personally impeccable.

> It is only by virtue of her impeccability that she could say, 'Behold the handmaid of the Lord' with all her will, with her entire undivided being, say it in such a way that in response to this total gift of God there came the descent of the Holy Spirit and the virginal Conception of the Lord. The least sin past or present would have impaired the integrity of the gift of self and the power of her word. The latter, decisive for the whole human species and for the world, was not only the expression of a given moment: it came *from the depths of Mary's immaculate being*. It was the work and the conclusion of her whole life.[7]

Calling Our Lady the 'New Eve', as Bulgakov does, is, among other things, to institute a comparison with Eve before the Fall. Though the Catholic doctrine is 'inexact', it is right in thinking divine grace acted in Mary's case in an utterly extraordinary manner, unsurpassable for man. Temptation could only reach her as trial, according to the weakness of human nature, 'not as seduction which penetrates to the interior of one's being, poisoning and staining it'.[8] Congruent with the notion that in some indescribable manner, on the threshold between eternity and time, souls consent to the manner of their embodiment, Bulgakov is inclined to think that Mary accepted sacrificially her part in the burden of original

---

[6] Ibid., p. 66.

[7] Ibid., p. 69: *iz glubini neporochnago sushchestva Marii* corresponds to the italicized phrase and suggests, despite everything, Bulgakov's nearness to the Roman dogma.

[8] Ibid., p. 72.

sin in order to contribute to saving the human race. Do not zealous doctors inoculate themselves with dangerous viruses or go to live among lepers? In any case, not the slightest tempting thought or involuntary movement of an inappropriate emotion touched her. A near-inevitable explanatory comment on that would be: so depotentiated was the power in her of Adam's fall.

Problems with the Catholic dogma

Before tackling head on his difficulties with the Catholic dogma of the Immaculate Conception, Bulgakov makes it clear that, looking at the West in its two principal Christian forms, Protestant and Catholic, there is no question of an even-handed 'plague on both your houses'. A Christianity without the Mother of God, and the 'thought, sentiments, conception of the universe which depend on [her]' is 'a different religion from Orthodoxy'.

> Protestantism separates itself from the Church less by its particular errors and arbitrary ruptures. It does so more, and more radically, by its insensibility in regard to the Mother of God.[9]

As to Rome: a pontifical intervention in defence of the unique all-holiness of Mary might have been useful at the time of the Protestant revolt. But none was forthcoming then. No vital need motivated the act of dogmatization of 1854. It flows from 'doctrinal authoritarianism', the desire to make felt in every domain the power of the Pope. Unfortunately, the 1854 teaching is the inaccurate expression of an accurate idea. The Catholic dogma proposes in effect a 'baptism' of Mary before her birth. Writing at a time when, misled by Latin theologians concerned to exalt grace at the expense of nature, he mistook the sense in which, for the Catholic tradition, the image of God in man remains fundamentally intact despite the Fall, Bulgakov laments the soteriological implications of the terms in which Mary's all-purity was defined. He draws the inference that what she needed so as to be immaculate was simply the restoration of the grace of original righteousness sundered from any context in the development of Jewish sanctity. This Bulgakov sees as a merely 'mechanical' requirement, anti-historical in force, tending to suppress the whole meaning of the Old Testament preparation of human liberty by divine Providence. For could not such an interventionist divine act follow at

---

[9] Ibid., p. 78.

any time? Moreover, does not this theology imply in Manichaean fashion a human nature inherently alien to grace, and in semi-Pelagian style find no essential difference between natural man and fallen man? In terms of the history of the doctrine of grace in the Western church, Bulgakov finds his sympathies lie with the sixteenth-century Louvain theologian Michael Baius (1513–1589) or the nineteenth-century Georg Hermes (1775–1831) and Anton Günther (1783–1863), respectively German and Austrian.

Nor does Bulgakov like the notion, derived by Pius IX from John Duns Scotus, of a freeing of Mary from the burden of original sin through anticipation of the merits of Christ. Could not the entire world have been thus guaranteed against the consequences of Adam's sin? Such a 'prejudicial amnesty' subverts the ontology of original sin, which requires for its reversal humanity's transformation by the act of Incarnation. How can baptism be offered before its institution? How can ontology yield to a 'privilege'?

Finally, in Bulgakov's severe indictment, he is unhappy about another premise of the dogma. And this is the common view of Catholic theologians since the time of Pope Benedict XII (d. 1342) that the soul is created at the moment of its infusion into the human body, through which, as inheriting the Adamic nature, original sin reaches us. Though distinguished Russian Orthodox theologians share the Latin view of the soul's origin, Bulgakov demurs. He will have no part in *either* of the principal theories Catholic and Orthodox tradition have espoused – creationism (just described) or generationism (also called 'traducianism') whereby parents themselves originate the soul. And this is because he has his own proposal, already outlined in the chapter of this study on 'The world as God's created wisdom'. The *element* of truth in creationism is that man contains within his make-up a more-than-worldly element – his hypostasis, which 'carries in itself the seal and the knowledge of his eternity and divine source'.[10] At each human birth (conception?) the everlasting plan of God is realized for each human being actualising in time each created hypostasis in human nature. To this *complex* of ideas creationism gives sadly simplified expression. Again, the *element* of truth in generationism is that the hypostasis only has reality in a human essence taken from the world, from Adam's family tree. But note – it is for Bulgakov the 'animal soul', moving the body, which appears thus to be brought into existence by the parents' procreative effort, and not the rational soul which alone permits the body to share in the

[10] Ibid., p. 103.

spiritual capacities of knowing and loving that inhere in the hypostasis. Bulgakov is clear that in the origination of each human being a cosmic principle and a divine principle are, unconfused, inseparably conjoined.

Bulgakov's main gravamen against the *modus operandi* of the Pian dogma of Mary's all-purity is, however, that (as already implied) it cuts her off *spiritually* from the genealogical tree of the old Adam and thus sets her inappropriately far apart from humanity. Does it not devalue the contribution to her inital holiness of her holy ancestors and (on Bulgakov's peculiar view of a 'pre-temporal and supra-worldly self-determination') her own contribution thereto?[11] What Bulgakov likes to call Mary's 'baptism' is not her Immaculate Conception on the threshold of the Old Covenant and the New, but the work of the Spirit at Pentecost which she co-receives with the apostles.

The mysteries of the Virgin

Bulgakov draws from the 1854 dogma the false conclusion that Mary's post-Conception existence had no further decisive thresholds to cross. But the Roman Liturgy, as the Byzantine, celebrates in its festal cycles the events which mark the stages of Mary's spiritual growth – and this is true of the western rite after the dogma (for instance, in the 'Pauline Missal' of 1969) as before it. That being so, Catholic students of Marian theology can draw profit almost as much as Orthodox from the lengthy chapter which – aside from Bulgakov's trio of appendices, themselves trial runs of key notions in the sophiology of the Great Trilogy – takes up the rest of his Mariological study.

In celebrating Mary's nativity, the Church shows how her 'pre-elect' holiness made possible the Virgin's road towards divine motherhood. In effect, Bulgakov presents Mary's childhood and youth as a transition from what, describing the case of Eve (and Adam), he would term in the Great Trilogy 'passive holiness', with its ignorance of evil, to what he would call there 'active holiness', with its conquest of sin. Bulgakov does not query the historical basis of Mary's entry into the Temple (her 'Presentation') and her life there fed by angels. But he concentrates, rightly, on the symbolic theology behind the Jewish-Christian tradition of the Presentation of the Virgin. The value of the Old Testament

[11] Ibid., p. 109.

Temple, as the sole place of encounter between God and man, begins, with Mary's initial sanctification, to disappear. Mary 'becomes the Temple and receives the power of its consecration'.[12] At the Annunciation, the Spirit descends into this new Temple that Christ may dwell there. So far as Mary's personal holiness is concerned, Bulgakov wants to treat the Annunciation not as the Pentecost of the Virgin but as the preparation for that Pentecost. Congruently with his dismissal of the Immaculate Conception, he comments on the Holy Spirit's indwelling, sign of the deification of human nature in the person of the Mother of God: 'It is not yet, for all that, salvation' [meaning: from original sin].[13] His ground for saying so is that otherwise there was no reason for her being present in the Upper Room at Pentecost. 'No reason', we might think, save to receive with the apostles the Spirit who founds the mission of the Church!

In becoming Mother of God, Mary does so for ever. This is not a condition which passes with childbirth. The Church venerates her as perpetually this Mother, as the icons of the Mother and Child declare. At the Visitation, it is this Mother that Elizabeth salutes 'in the name of the entire Old Testament Church'.[14] And despite accepting with enthusiasm the principle of gradualism indicated in the festal cycle, Bulgakov cites approvingly the Annunciation hymn of the Byzantine Liturgy, for which that festival contains in germ

> the principle of our salvation and the manifestation of mysteries from before the ages.[15]

During Jesus's public ministry, Mary remains in the shadow. But as is attested in the Byzantine prayers called the *Stavrotheotokia* ('The Mother of God at the Cross'), Mary shares in the Passion of her Son. Bulgakov refers approvingly here to the Latin devotion to Mary's 'Seven Dolours'. That was her sacrificial ministry, to be followed by her crowning. Bulgakov devotes much space to Mary's Dormition. He follows accurately the thrust of the Orthodox Liturgy when he says of her not that she was *not withdrawn from* the law of death but that she *did not refuse to follow* the human way of death. Appropriately so, the liturgical texts add, because it was the way of her Son. No 'History of Early Christianity' remarks on the fact but her presence in the earliest Church, when, on the eve of

[12] Ibid., p. 112.
[13] Ibid.
[14] Ibid., p. 114.
[15] Cited ibid., p. 116.

her Dormition, 'the Holy Spirit shone out in her most holy figure', was the single most important feature of apostolic Christianity, constituting the true mystery of 'its power and its joy'.[16]

Bulgakov was already aware – in 1924 – of the Catholic preparations for the dogmatization of a second Marian doctrine, the Assumption, which actually followed in 1950, some six years after his death. The Orthodox, he reports, have nothing against the content. But, he asks, does its manner of proclamation reflect the discretion of the Virgin? Let no one question the historicity of Mary's glorification – her Ascension and Coronation. Bulgakov defends that historicity to the hilt. It has been objected that the language of the accounts we have is not naturalistic. Of course it is not, and in this it coincides with the symbolism of the relevant icons. To rationality in a certain style, the silence of the earliest sources condemns the belief. *Tant pis.* Bulgakov, for his part, finds in them:

> a mysterious decree of Providence which has confided the veneration of the most holy Virgin to free inspiration, to faith and love, without making it turn on 'history' ...[17]

– meaning there by 'history' claims about the documented past to be verified by 'scientific' method.

For Bulgakov, it is when the heart and mind of a Christian are at their most ecclesial that a person is most likely to turn to this cultus. (In a certain sense the Church *is* the Mother of God, as such Western theologians as Joseph Ratzinger [b. 1927] and Balthasar have affirmed in their concept of Mary as 'primal Church'.[18]) Expressed in the Liturgy and the icons, the Church's tradition is that the dying Virgin gave over her spirit to Christ come with the angels to receive her into glory by way of anticipation of his second, glorious Coming – though the Mother has no need to stand before her Judge. Bulgakov follows the particular tradition of a three-day repose in the tomb between Dormition and Ascension, itself an obvious Christological doublet.[19] Echoing the lyrical terms of the Liturgy:

---

[16] Ibid., p. 118.

[17] Ibid., p. 123.

[18] J. Kardinal Ratzinger – H. U. von Balthasar, *Maria-Kirche im Ursprung* (Freiburg, Basle, Vienna, 1980).

[19] For the patristic texts, see now S. J. Shoemaker, *Ancient Traditions of the Virgin Mary's Dormition and Assumption* (Oxford, 2002).

In her and with her the world has already as it were a foretaste of the perfection of the resurrection by which it is no longer 'this world', in a situation of lapse and hostility toward God but becomes the cosmos that is 'good', a 'new heaven and new earth where righteousness dwells'. By her risen and glorified body the Mother of God represents already the resurrection and glory of the world.[20]

In her Assumption, the world's goal is attained. She is the world now transparent to divinity, the perfectly deified creation. Her 'queenship' gives rhetorical expression to her primacy among all intercessors with her Son on the basis of her uniquely maximal degree of deification through grace. She is 'above' the angels: Bulgakov is inclined to marry the quality of her glorification with the fact that only humanity and not the immaterial angels can be microcosm and thus 'the centre and king of the world, *tsentr mira i tsar mira*'.[21] And this is pertinent if the Mother of God is the world glorified in God and with God – and in this sense the manifestation of God's Wisdom in sheerly creaturely form, yet as the personal receptacle of the Holy Spirit. 'Even if there is no pneumatic Incarnation [no Incarnation of the Holy Spirit rather than the Son] there can still be a hypostatic *bearing* of the Spirit, *dukhonosnost'*,[22] a 'carrying of God' in a created personality given over entirely to the Spirit who has filled her with himself. As Bulgakov has explained in the Great Trilogy, the Word only manifests the *full* image of himself, both masculine and feminine, in union with his Mother.

The Mother of God

Speaking of Mary's Motherhood, Bulgakov affirms that, paradoxical as it may sound, the relation of spiritual parenting is often more tangible than its physical counterpart. The human father's act of engendering is only experienced, after all, as a possibility, comprised within the sexual act. The eternal Father's generation of the Son is more realistic. Mary's divine motherhood offers likewise an exact image of true motherhood: she bears what is already 'born' before the ages, for only the Father generates, really, and yet she nonetheless 'bears in her womb, she manifests, she gives life'.[23]

[20] KN, pp. 127–128.
[21] Ibid., p. 136.
[22] Ibid., p. 141.
[23] Ibid., p. 150.

Though Mary is not the God-man, she is bound to him by the 'necessary, subtle and undivided bond of motherhood', a relation which is 'precisely a function of the correlation of the second and third hypostases'.[24] How so? It is proper to the Spirit to proceed from the Father through the Son, which Bulgakov explains as 'because of, on, and for the Son'.[25] The Spirit 'has' the Son for the Father 'not by engendering him but by vivifying him'.[26]

> That is why in receiving the Holy Spirit and not only his gifts or his power but the Spirit himself, Mary becomes the Mother of God ... By virtue of the descent of the Holy Spirit, the sacred fruit will be nothing other than the Son of God whom the Holy Spirit has hypostatically.[27]

If there had not been a birth from the Father without a mother in eternity there would not have been a birth from this Mother without a father in time. And the link between the two births is the Holy Spirit. The preliminary, incomplete revelation of the Trinity by Son and Spirit becomes perfect in the God-man in whom the fullness of Godhead dwells bodily, and in the Mother of God, the personal receptacle of the Holy Spirit. As the bestowal of the Spirit's gifts Pentecost is in a sense the continuation of the Incarnation of the second divine hypostasis. The 'Pentecost of Zion', which, beginning from the Upper Room, is to become cosmic, must be preceded by a personal 'Pentecost of Nazareth'.

Like certain of the Greek Fathers, Bulgakov holds that the virginal conception cannot be called – other than statistically – abnormal. Sexual feeling, and the concupiscence that is inseparable from it, like the pains of birth itself, are not a norm for humanity as such. The Virgin frees herself from the empire of sexuality without for all that losing in any sense her feminine nature. Mary thus becomes the ever-virgin one. Virginity becomes her inalienable property, not a state to be confirmed by testing, as with Eve. Here once again Bulgakov rejoins the controverted 1854 dogma in a way Catholics would not usually recognize. Mary, he says, *was* in a quite particular – 'privileged' – position in regard to original sin. She showed her restoration to original righteousness by conceiving in a way that is not the manner of post-lapsarian women. Bulgakov does not deny that a fatherly role of some kind would have been

[24] Ibid., p. 156.
[25] Ibid.
[26] Ibid., p. 157: *ne rozhdaya, no zhivotvorya.*
[27] Ibid.

necessary to procreation before the Fall. But, he holds, no biological exploration now can deduce how it would have worked.

Jesus is born without father. That is because he already has a
father – the Father in heaven. Moreover, a sexual conception
would here have obscured the true character of spiritual motherhood which is love of the one being born by a voluntary gift of self
as life in another. Motherhood is 'the will to incarnate the fruit
conceived though not yet born'.[28] But the wondrous action of the
Spirit is no mere physiological miracle. By his act Mary 'felt in her
mind that she was the Mother of the only-begotten Son of God'.
Compare her response to Elizabeth at the Visitation (Luke 1:
48–49). She conceived spiritually before she did so physically. To
that her Annunciation *fiat* testifies: this was no passive acceptance
but an ardent loving one.

This Mother is pre-established in the divine eternity: in that
sense, Bulgakov can compare her state with the Theanthropy of
the Saviour. In heaven, Mary is the 'pneumatic *Anthrôpos* [human
being] who sits at the right of the God-man'.[29] That is why – *pace*
the recurring Western deviation of thought originally associated
with the Calabrian abbot Joachim of Fiore (*c.* 1135–1202) – there
can be no question of awaiting a new third age of the Holy Spirit.
His personal revelation has already happened, to the degree
necessary on earth, in the *Theotokos*. The Spirit's fuller manifestation will inevitably be hers also. Bulgakov finds it congruent with
Scripture and Tradition that Mary will have a role to play in the
glorious Parousia.

How can the baptism by the Spirit and fire at Pentecost be
compatible with Mary's *Pneumatophoria*? How could she need a new
descent of the Spirit, she who is already his personal receptacle?
Bulgakov replies to this problem of his own making: it is no more
contradictory than for the Spirit who reposes eternally on the Son
to descend on him at his Baptism so as to sanctify his humanity.
More and more, Mary had to let the Spirit penetrate her humanity.
And the fullness of this 'maturation' would be achieved in the
moment of the Assumption when her human nature entered glory.
Pentecost, then:

> was for the Virgin Mary a conclusive sanctification of her human
> essence which delivered her from all the residue of original sin and
> applied to her the redemptive power of Christ. Her personal

[28] Ibid., p. 171.
[29] Ibid., p. 175.

Pentecost, the Annunciation, was completed or, more precisely, manifested as the Pentecost of the world – the foundation of the earthly Church by the descent of the Holy Spirit.[30]

In the assembly of the apostles Mary is the invisible centre. She represents the 'personal embodiment of the Church'.[31]

Mary as Bride, Church, Wisdom

Under the influence of the Song of Songs, Mary is sometimes called '[sister and] spouse': for instance, in Ambrose and Damascene. Icons of the Virgin without the Child, such as the icon of the Compunction before which St Seraphim prayed so fervently, express the notion of the Bride rather than the Mother. The Byzantine Liturgy often strikes this note, and Bulgakov finds the explanation for it in Mary's identification with the Church.

> The Virgin Mary, Mother and Spouse of God is the image of the soul in relation to the Logos, of the soul which in her becomes Church, *votserkovlenii*.[32]

Is this Mary/Church better described as bride or as fully achieved spouse? Both of the terms represent the same reality under different but related aspects: seeking and finding, tending and attaining, thirsting and being satisfied. What these aspects – bridal, spousal – have in common is the disclosure and blessedness of love. Bulgakov finds the Song of Songs the most New Testament-like part of the Old Testament canon. In the Byzantine tradition it is never read liturgically because – so Bulgakov suggests – the Liturgy, like the Church's whole life, *is* the Song of Songs being accomplished. Every 'ecclesial' soul shares in the motherhood of Mary/Church who 'represents all the properties of the Church ... reunited in her person'.[33]

Sophiology helps us to see how the *Theotokos* is the personal image of the Church. The world becomes ecclesial to the extent that Wisdom penetrates it on the basis of the Incarnation. In the service of the Incarnation, the Holy Spirit, inhabiting Mary, unites in her the heavenly Wisdom and the earthly. Like the Church,

[30] Ibid., pp. 179
[31] Ibid.
[32] Ibid., p. 185.
[33] Ibid., p. 188.

Mary belongs essentially to both realms, to earth and to heaven. The properly sophianic veneration of the Mother of God was established by the mediaeval Russian Church when it linked liturgically the celebration of Wisdom with the commemoration of the Virgin – unlike its Greek equivalent which ties Wisdom firmly to Christ even if on occasion, as on the feast of the Encounter of the Lord with Simeon, both themes are sounded together.[34] The text 'Wisdom has built herself a house and she founded seven columns' (Proverbs 9: 1), read at Vespers on Marian feasts has as its corresponding icon at Kiev, chief city and see of the ancient *Rus*. It shows the Mother of God as the centre of a heptastyle temple. Bulgakov calls this Kievan icon, which meant a lot to him, a dogmatic gift of ageing Byzantium to the young Russia. It portrays the Mother of God as the embodiment of the Church endowed with all the Spirit's gifts. At Novgorod too there were pertinent customs. There the Office of the Wisdom of God was in fact the Office of the Dormition. The Wisdom ascribed also to Christ is identified with Mary in the striking troparion (or in Western liturgical terms, major antiphon):

> Great and ineffable power of the Wisdom of God, very celebrated Wisdom, most honourable temple, fiery throne of Christ our God, for in you the Word of God, become flesh, has come beyond all telling to dwell and the Invisible has shown itself to us. Merciful Queen, who love your children, look toward your people.[35]

This prayer, and others like it, was included, Bulgakov notes, in a collection of prayers for services of thanksgiving and vigil approved by the Holy Synod of the pre-Revolutionary Russian Church in 1909.

In particular, Mary personifies the *prayer* of the Church: necessary because while our redemption is a *datum* (it has been accomplished once and for all in its objective foundation), it is also an *agendum* (it is proposed as a task to be accomplished, with the Spirit's aid, in the Church as ark of salvation). Bulgakov calls the Church:

> The Holy Spirit and those who are saved in her thanks to him.[36]

---

[34] Oleg Tarasov suggests a *seventeenth*-century development, but agrees as to its significance: *Icon and Devotion. Sacred Spaces in Imperial Russia* (Et London, 2002), pp. 94–95.

[35] Cited ibid., pp. 197–198.

[36] Ibid., p. 202.

And once again, as the hypostatic manifestation of the Spirit, Mary is the heart of the Church, perfectly containing the Church's substance and power. For Bulgakov, all creation raises in Mary a prayer provoked by the Holy Spirit who 'intercedes for us with sighs too deep for words' (Romans 8: 26). Thus the prayer of sinful humanity acquires wings to rise to the throne of God. As prayer in the Church, it is the necessary prayer of the Mother of God who, so the Liturgy testifies, prays ceaselessly to her Son for all. The Church's prayer is integrated because Mary, the Church's soul, glorifies the Lord. The Virgin's own proper prayer is *Magnificat* – the triumphant prayer of perfect joy. But she sends up to God the imploratory prayer of all creation which she covers with her 'veil' (a reference to the beautiful Constantinopolitan legend of the 'Protecting Veil', associated with the life of the St Andrew the Holy Fool [dates unknown but probably sixth century]). She is 'pity personified towards the world',[37] as she leads the world to her Son, its Saviour.

The pouring out of the Spirit on all flesh is not accomplished without her. (The Latin Church speaks here of the Mother of God as 'Mediatrix of graces'.) Since she is the Spirit's receptacle, the works of the Spirit are not without her collaboration. In *The Burning Bush* this is how Bulgakov understands the large number of miraculous icons that depict the Blessed Virgin Mary, as well as the numerous manifestations of her in the lives of the saints. Bulgakov calls her veneration the 'measure of the ecclesial condition, *mera tserkovnosti*'.[38]

---

[37] Ibid., p. 204.
[38] Ibid., p. 206.

15

John the Baptist

Greatest born of women

One of the few aspects of Christian origins where contemporary New Testament exegetes, however sceptical their mind-set, can be expected to agree with the liturgical tradition of the Church concerns the importance of John the Baptist. According to strict liturgical propriety, he is, after the Mother of God, the most theologically significant saint in the Church, helping to constitute what the Catholic dogmatician most akin to Bulgakov, Hans Urs von Balthasar, would call the 'constellation' of figures who co-define Jesus and his mission.[1] Bulgakov makes some rather acidulous comments about the early modern Western cultus of St Joseph, reaching its apogee in the Catholic Church about the time of his writing. He failed to note that in the classical Roman Liturgy, sometimes called the 'Tridentine' rite, overwhelmingly in use as this was in the Catholicism of his lifetime, the confession which dominates the preparatory prayers mentions in due order the Mother of the Lord, the Archangel Michael, *St John the Baptist* and the apostles Peter and Paul. In this it corresponds almost exactly to the iconographic sequence in the *Deesis* scene of the Byzantine-Slav iconostasis. (The only differences being that two archangels are depicted on the latter, rather than one, and the reversal of the positions, relative to Christ, of St Michael and St John.)

As so often, Bulgakov takes his theological marching orders from the Church's Liturgy and iconography, seen as a prism through which to view the Scriptures and their supreme commentators, the Fathers of the early centuries. In its prayer, the Byzantine Church acclaims St John the Precursor as, after the Mother of God, the

---

[1] See H. U. von Balthasar, *The Office of Peter and the Structure of the Church* (Et San Francisco, 1986), pp. 136–145.

greatest of all human beings in the Lord's sight.[2] Indeed, the prayer texts bracket Mary and John as united by 'natural congeniality and communion of prayer'.[3] In his introduction to *The Friend of the Bridegroom*, Bulgakov suggests there is a profound significance to this liturgical linkage between two figures who, though joined by kinship, are not brought together in the Gospels (save in the Visitation episode when John is still unborn). What binds them together is their *podvig* or spiritual achievement. And this he unhesitatingly identifies as their *humility*, seen as the:

> supreme fruit of the sacrificial love of which it was at once the principle and the resource.[4]

John's 'I must decrease' (John 3: 30), like Mary's 'Behold the handmaid of the Lord' (Luke 1: 38) bring them close to the Word made flesh who 'emptied himself, taking the form of a servant' (Philippians 2: 6). This linkage allows Bulgakov to produce his definition of a 'precursor' (in Russian usage, as primary a title for John as 'Baptist' itself). A precursor is:

> someone who, renouncing his own 'I', dedicates his whole life, his entire being, to *another* who comes after him.[5]

How total a gift of self this was is shown by John's joy, underlined in the fourth Gospel, at hearing the voice of the 'bridegroom'. This 'complete' joy (John 3: 29) is the triumphant apotheosis of renunciation. Already, by her willing obedience, the Mother of God had inverted the reaction of Eve, and become the *novaya Eva*, the 'New Eve'. Likewise, John the Baptist, as Christ's herald, lays a foundation for the obedient way the Son will walk as the *novii Adam*, the 'New Adam', set to reverse the entire history of the Fall.

John's crucial role

We realize how high a doctrine of 'Baptistology' Bulgakov is proposing when we read that 'without John the Saviour *would not have been able to come into the world*'.[6] That, he thinks, is the burden

[2] Compare L. A. Zander, *Bog i mir*, op. cit., II., pp. 225–246.
[3] Cited in DZh, p. 8.
[4] Ibid., p. 9.
[5] Ibid., p. 10.
[6] Ibid., p. 12.

of those texts of the Hebrew Bible, notably in Isaiah, chapter 40, and Malachi, chapter 3, which the Church has seen as prophecies of the role of John, encouraged by the example of Jesus himself (John 1: 23; Luke 7: 27; Matthew 11: 10). For Mark's Gospel, the 'beginning of the Gospel of Jesus Christ, the Son of God' simply *is* the pericope about the Baptist (Mark 1: 1–8), from which Bulgakov infers that this evangelist deliberately inserts the Precursor 'into the very heart of the Gospel, as its necessary condition or integral aspect'.[7] In the Johannine Prologue, St John the Theologian speaks of his namesake twice: once inbetween his proclamation of the divine eternal Word and its Incarnation (John 1: 6), as if to anticipate the latter, and the second time to underline the Precursor's testimony to the Fleshtaking (John 1: 15). The Gospels of Matthew and Luke point to John's role more allusively, but for those who appreciate their literary techniques, no less powerfully. Matthew has John define the message of the Reign of God (3: 2) in exactly the same words as those used by Jesus in Mark, insinuating that the Kingdom of God has already come near in the Precursor. Luke in his 'Infancy Gospel' makes the conception and birth of Jesus a doublet (with differences, of course) of John's. All the evangelists are pointing to the 'necessary and indestructible relation' which binds John to the Incarnation.[8] Bulgakov takes this to mean that John was as necessary to Christ's coming as was Christ's own mother.

How can Bulgakov justify this audacious claim? Just as the divine Incarnation presupposes the divine Motherhood, so that without Mary Jesus could not have been born physically, so likewise without John the Baptist Jesus could not have been born spiritually and received the Holy Spirit for the mission he was to carry out as man. Saying as much is perhaps only to repeat the original claim. From *Agnets Bozhii* we realize how large the Baptism of Christ figures in Bulgakov's Christology, and clearly there could not have been an act of baptism for Jesus to undergo unless there had been a minister of baptism to perform it. This is not, however, where Bulgakov's accent lies. His emphasis falls on the theme which gives *Drug Zhenika* its title: *friendship.*

Born of and nurtured by Mary though he was, the Incarnate could not fully enter human society without being received into that most basic form of human sociality that is friendship. The family may provide the foundational unity of society in the sense of

---

[7] Ibid., p. 15: *v serdtsevinu Evangeliya, kak evo neobkhodimoe uslovie ili chast.*
[8] Ibid.

its single most crucial building-block. But friendship is more fundamental still in that its form of love, indefinitely flexible, furnishes a model for a whole variety of social and religious relations – not excluding, so Thomas Aquinas would say, the charity which makes man a sharer, through divine friendship, with the Trinity themselves.[9] Bulgakov does not appear to have known of, and certainly did not use, the rich Thomist theology of friendship. But something like it is subjacent to his account. To become fully human, the Word had to be received by the human race. He could not remain alone. His mother, like any mother, was too much one reality with him (think only of the umbilical cord!) to serve this turn. There had to be a human being who was worthy to encounter the Word *precisely as friend.* Now since by the Fall man had ceased to live in friendship with God , his return to that friendship, in the person of John, had to be a matter of the saving Economy (and not merely a human sidelight of merely social-psychological interest). Indeed,

> In the same way that it took the long history of the Old Testament Church for the trunk of the tree of Jesse to put forth the paradisal lily that is the Mother of God, so it took the whole of biblical sanctity for there to flourish by her side, 'such a sweet-smelling ear of corn, balmy cypress tree' as the Precursor.[10]

Later on, as St John's Gospel reports, Jesus will declare he calls all his disciples 'friends' (15: 15). But to begin his mission he needed someone who was already equipped in that capacity.

This, basically, is why, for Bulgakov, Jesus could call John the greatest, *ho meizôn,* among those born of women (Matthew 2: 2; Luke 7: 28).

It is difficult, if not impossible, to extract from Bulgakov's various writings a wholly consistent theology of grace. In *The Friend of the Bridegroom,* he havers between the view that John's holiness – a holiness of repentance or preparation for the advent of the new life Christ brings – was itself a work of grace, a fruit of the Lord's sacrifice, and the opinion that it was, rather, the supreme example of natural ascetical effort. We might say that for Bulgakov John is humanity in the moment when conversion can begin and pre-Kingdom existence tip over into the life of the Kingdom. He is 'the appeal to heaven, the opening mouth, the dried out earth thirsty

[9] Thomas Aquinas, *Summa theologiae* Ia. IIae., q. 23, a. 1.
[10] KN, p. 18. The internal citation is from the Byzantine Liturgy's 'Canon of the Precursor'.

to receive rain from the skies'.[11] That liminal situation is brought
home by the paradox that while John declares himself the
Bridegroom's friend, and lives utterly for his mission as Precursor,
he will not in fact live to hear from Jesus's lips the reciprocating
words, 'I call you friend' (cf. John 15: 15). This combination of
circumstances indicates his limits – and at the same time the
breathtaking extent of his self-abnegation. The least in the
Kingdom, *ho mikroteros*, is greater than the greatest outside it. But
as Bulgakov points out, that leaves out of the count the question
what will be John's ranking when (in death) he *does* enter the
Kingdom. The Church's response will be, After the Mother of God,
there is no one great as he.

His universal significance

No Christian who wants to understand who Jesus was can forego
consideration of Mary, and the unique events of her Child-bearing.
That will bring home to him or her the desirability, nay the necessity, of a relation with the most pure Mother of God. But, writes
Bulgakov:

> The Christian must know not only the birth of God, *Bogozhdenie*, but also
> his welcoming reception, *Bogopriyatie*: not only the spiritual achieve-
> ment, *podvig*, of the Virgin Mary but that of the Precursor, John.[12]

Every Christian must have John in his or her life, because he is the
living personification of evangelical repentance. Only by following
the 'Johannine way', *put' Ioannovii*, can one encounter Jesus Christ.
We are freed from ourselves 'in' John: by identification with his
humble, loving, self-renouncing. Every soul must relate to Christ
not only bridally, in the manner the Church does, symbolically
feminine, but also by the virile love – symbolically masculine, then
– of John. Here we find Bulgakov putting to use in pastoral theology the notions on the complementarity of masculine and
feminine, and the need of both for wholeness, worked out in
Uteshitel'. But this is not just a question of taking both
Mary/Church and John as role-model – or perhaps one should say
'soul-model' – *qua* figures from the past. As with the Mother of
God, John 'remains a foundation of the life of the Church'.[13]

[11] Ibid., p. 19.
[12] Ibid., p. 25.
[13] Ibid., p. 28.

Bulgakov has surely said enough to show that John, then, is not just another saint. The liturgical calendar backs him up. In the Byzantine East, his feast is dated, significantly, to 7 January, the day after that of the Baptism of Christ, in parallel with the way the feast of Mary as Mother of God is dated to 26 December, following on that of the Birth of Christ. In the Latin West, one could add, John's two feasts, his Nativity and his Passion, call attention to his difference of standing. Apart from the Blessed Virgin, no other saint has a celebration of his natural birth as well as his or her 'heavenly' birth, their death-day. (That too is reflected in Byzantine practice.) The 'mystical dyad' of the Mother and the Precursor sum up humanity in its highest sanctity and God-centred devotion. That is the basis, Bulgakov thinks, on which their medallia are inscribed on the chalice used for the Divine Liturgy.

A narrative 'Baptistology'

In *The Burning Bush*, once the knotty issue of Mary's predestining election to righteousness was surmounted, Bulgakov produced the rest of his Mariology by exploration of the mysteries of Mary's life in their unfolding. He will follow much the same pattern in *The Friend of the Bridegroom*, moving from John's conception and birth to his preaching and administration of baptism (not least to the person of the Redeemer), and thence to his imprisonment and death. In the midst of this – standard, indeed inescapable – story, however, Bulgakov offers an account of the inner struggle which, he believes, beset John as he mulled over from prison his knowledge of Jesus, a psychodrama inferred from some riddling comments in the Gospels. In the course of his Baptistology, Bulgakov will lay out one of the most extraordinary aspects of his dogmatics, by treating the iconography of John as *angel* as rather more than an artistic trope. So far as the present book is concerned, that will also be a pointer to the next and penultimate chapter, which deals with Bulgakov's wider theology of the angelic essence and mission.

Conception and birth

The *Leitmotiv* of Bulgakov's re-telling of the story of John's conception and birth is Luke 1: 15, where the unnamed angel tells Zechariah of his future son 'He will be filled with the Holy Spirit even from his mother's womb'. John was sanctified even before he was born. Though Bulgakov could hardly ascribe freedom from original sin to John having denied it to the Mother of the Lord, he treats John, in effect, as born in original righteousness. Not only was original sin never actualized in him by any personal sin. Satan never had any empire over him – unthinkable given this aboriginal inhabitation by the Spirit. As in his theology of Mary the Jewess, the Daughter of Zion, Bulgakov treats John's holiness personally but not individualistically. It reflects the spiritual patrimony of his ancestors, and above all the real piety that could be found in the sacerdotal class to which his parents belonged. (Was Bulgakov thinking there of his own 'Levitical descent'?) Doffing his hat as devout student of the Scriptures, Bulgakov then dons the cap of religious metaphysician, applying to John his curious thesis of a pre-birth but non-temporal self-determination of the hypostasis whereby each and every human person receives a 'share in their own origin'.[14]

The Gospels witness to John's holiness at three main points: first, when still being carried by Elizabeth, the baby John leaps for joy at Jesus' approach – something Bulgakov ascribes to a 'charism of immediate knowledge' on the part of the infant in the womb;[15] secondly, his worthiness to baptize Jesus which made him the accredited witness to the Theophany at the Jordan, the hypostatic self-disclosure of the Trinity; thirdly, the laudatory words of Jesus in Matthew 11 and Luke 7 which find their issue in his martyr's death. Without this, the lengthy Lucan conception and birth narrative, which dominates the opening of the third Gospel, would be out of all proportion. Perhaps owing to his feeling of solidarity with sacerdotal parenting, Bulgakov gives a good deal of space himself to the figure of Zachary (and to a lesser degree Elizabeth). Accepting as he does the historicity of the episode of Mary's Presentation and dwelling in the Jerusalem Temple, he also accepts – on the same authority, that of liturgical texts and the New Testament apocrypha – the tradition whereby it was the father of John who as high priest accepted Mary for this unlikely accommodation, and was later murdered for his pains between the sanctuary and the altar. But no exegete could quarrel with his assertion that the Visitation episode brings about for Luke a 'new and mysterious interdependence' of the two annunciations, John's and Jesus's.[16]

---

[14] Ibid., p. 36: *uchastie v svoem sobstvennom.*
[15] Ibid., p. 37.
[16] Ibid., p. 50.

That throws a retrospective light on the *Benedictus*, the Canticle of Zechariah (Luke 1: 68–79). It explains why Zechariah witnesses prophetically to the birth of the Messiah while what he is ostensibly doing is commenting on the imminent birth of his own son. The interweaving of text fragments from the Hebrew Bible into the Canticle constitutes, in Bulgakov's beautiful phrase, the 'reception of the Precursor by the Church of the Old Testament, in the person of its priesthood'.[17]

Preparation and preaching

Bulgakov interprets John's desert sojourn (Luke 1: 80) in terms of the experience of Christian desert monasticism. This is only returning a compliment since there is no doubt of the Baptist's importance in inspiring the desert movement in Palestine and Egypt at the end of the third century. John's ascetic withdrawal into a desert place that by its human emptiness symbolizes purity if also spiritual combat, corresponds to Mary's stay in the Jerusalem temple. John was in the 'temple of nature'.[18] John's 'eremitism' meant a fullness of life in God and for God that left no place for human attachments. Here he accumulated spiritual power. Wisdom, remarks Bulgakov, is virginity *par excellence* because it is 'the power of *tselmudrie*', spiritual integrity or wholeness.[19] He emphasizes the Baptist's virginity: part of the reason the Church's hymnography calls him an angel, and her icons portray him with wings.

Meanwhile, Horace (65 BC–8 BC) had written his odes, Virgil (70–19 BC) his *Aeneid*, Tacitus (*c.* AD 55–*c.* 120) was about to start his histories. Seneca (4 BC–AD65) had started to philosophize and would shortly be joined by Epictetus (*c.*55–*c.*135). None of the latter figures knew that the greatest among women had reached adulthood among them.[20]

John's preaching centred on expectation: that waiting for the coming Kingdom, and its King, which *was* his life. Bulgakov gives a thoughtful explanation of John's extension of proselyte water-baptism to the Jews of the Holy Land. To discern the true character of the Kingdom of God when so many partial, unilateral or down-

---

[17] Ibid., p. 54.
[18] Ibid., p. 57: *khram prirodi.*
[19] Ibid., p. 60.
[20] Tenses modified as Bulgakov's sense of chronology in Roman literature seems remarkably approximate!

right misleading representations of it were on offer was simply impossible without a new and deepened conversion to the plan of God for Israel. Was humanity going to reject the Child now grown to manhood at Nazareth? To ensure humanity did no such thing required John's perfect fulfilment of his task. As Baptist he comported himself, in effect, as a new legislator. He establishing what was for circumcised Jews a new public ritual, which served both to complete the cultus of the Old Testament and to transcend it. Following a patristic interpretation (it is found in Basil the Great and John Chrysostom), John's baptism was preparation for an an introduction to the sacramental baptism instituted by Christ. Not for nothing in the most 'ecclesiastical' of the Gospels, Matthew, does a Gospel-story which, so far as public history is concerned, opens with the baptism of John, end with the dominical command to baptise all nations. Bulgakov is inclined to say John's baptism was nature readying itself to receive the grace of sacramental baptism by a concentrated effort of prayer, repentance, faith. (He assumes the same is true of the 'baptizing' activity of the disciples of Jesus according to John 4: 2.) Not that Bulgakov's account of the baptism of John is naturalistic in atmosphere. Far from it. He speaks of John as revealing the mystical Jordan, choosing the waters in which the Saviour's most pure body would be immersed, 'pre-accomplishing' for all time the mystery of the baptismal sacrament.[21]

The Baptism of Christ

What the Baptism of Christ had in common with that of other Jews and Jewesses at John's hands was humility. It differed from them in that John performed a ministerial act in which the Son received the Holy Spirit according to his humanity and became the Anointed One, the Christ. The Baptism is the spiritual birth of Christ for the Father's mission. This day the Father begot him *in that sense* (which is far from the defective sense of classical Adoptionism). In a marvellous catena of texts from the Byzantine Liturgy Bulgakov brings out the underlying feeling in John's hesitation, as reported by St Matthew, 'I need to be baptized by you, and do you come to me?' (3: 14). That feeling was 'trembling', *trepet*.[22] But it had to be gone through. The Lord's Baptism could not be a hole-in-the-corner affair. As the initiation of his ministry it

---

[21] DZh, p. 73.
[22] Ibid., p. 78.

needed to be carried out with and among the people. But though an act of humility, this was no humiliation. The Baptist was himself free of all personal sin, and prepared for this from all eternity. It was in his purity of heart that he was permitted to see the Holy Trinity at their Theophany.

The crisis in witnessing

After the Baptism, the Precursor's role becomes exclusively the one picked out by the fourth evangelist: that of *witness*. John does not witness to himself, is not tempted by a sense of his own glory to take the place of the Coming One. Neither is he, by metempsychosis, Elijah of old, though an inner link with the spirit and power of that prophet is not ruled out. To the envoys of the Pharisees he will only identify himself by relation to the Christ. In all this John the Theologian shows us, unlike the Synoptic writers, the secret of the Baptist's soul. The Baptist's identification of Jesus as the Lamb of God, taking away the sins of the world (John 1: 29) – a confession of the Gospel in miniature – shows he 'knew the crucial mystery of the redemption, and proclaimed it'.[23] There could be no more succinct evangelist than the man who said these words, which is why the Liturgy acclaims him as 'herald of Christ' and 'apostle'. John the Precursor's use of prophetic texts shows for Bulgakov that he had an Old Testament foreknowledge of the mysteries of Incarnation and the Trinity. At the Theophany he saw by spiritual illumination what the prophetic charism had led him to surmise. Bulgakov can find no other explanation of the way he anticipates the confession of Peter at Caesarea Philippi, and the rest of the apostolic kerygma (not to speak of the development of doctrine in the later Church) when he says 'I have seen and I have borne witness that this is the Son of God' (John 1: 34). This is a key preliminary to the future apostles' own growth in understanding, and we see the chain of testimony when John uses the title 'the Lamb of God' to pick out Jesus for the benefit of Andrew the First-called and the one who will be 'the Theologian', John the Divine.[24] If Andrew is in the Eastern tradition the 'First-called', *Pervozvannoi*, the Baptist, thinks Bulgakov, should be called *Pervo-apostol*, the Proto-Apostle.[25]

John does not become a disciple of Jesus. He does not need to.

[23] Ibid., p. 96.
[24] Ibid., p. 101.
[25] Ibid., pp. 101–102.

He has revealed him, and now he can retire into the shade. The
Latin doctors Ambrose and Augustine point out how his nativity
coincides with the summer solstice, after which the days shorten. If
he continued to practice his water-baptism that was comparable,
Bulgakov suggests, to the rites of the Church's catechumenate,
which are all the more needed when sacramental baptism is close
at hand. John's declaration that now he must decrease is elicited,
however, by the misapprehensions of his own disciples who see
themselves, falsely, as competing with Jesus's. This is also the
context for his self-naming as the Friend, which gives *Drug Zhenika*
its title and Bulgakov his distinctive starting-point. The nuptial
symbolism is plain. John is present in advance at the wedding feast
of the Lamb. The imagery of the Song of Songs, and Psalm 44, the
Epithalamium psalm, as well as Ephesians and the Apocalypse, is
here concentrated in a single, golden phrase. Reverting to his
theme of the universal need for relationship with the Precursor by
every Christian, Bulgakov speaks of the fashion in which every soul
on its way to the great banquet in which the world's *Commedia* ends
must necessarily follow John's footsteps.

The rule of the Christian life is *Stirb und werde*, die and become:
in other words, death and resurrection. In Bulgakov's terms,
without the *podvig* of strenuous moral and ascetical effort there can
be no illumination by grace. And yet as his account makes clear,
this by no means implies a simple two-stage dualism for one's biog-
raphy. Falls and resurrections may be many within the limits of a
single life. And in fact, his presentation of John's spiritual biogra-
phy moves from a high point of divine grace to a real crisis of faith
and hope. Taking John 3: 31–36 to be words ascribed by the evangelist to the Baptist – a profound meditation on the 'measureless'
way the Father gives the Spirit, while simultaneously giving 'all
things' into the hands of the Son – Bulgakov finds in them a translation of the 'whole plenitude of knowledge [John] had of
Christ'.[26] How could he have thought them, spoken them? Simple.
He was the witness of the Theophany, and *this* is its theology, the
'theology of the Theophany', *bogoslovie bogoyavleniya*.[27] But almost
immediately there follows darkness. All the evangelists mention
John's imprisonment by Herod (4 BC–AD 39). Two of them refer,
with discretion, to an utterly unexpected development when the
curtain of silence on that imprisonment is lifted. In the incompe-
tently marshalled quarters of a prison in the ancient Near East,

---

[26] Ibid., p. 116.
[27] Ibid.

John sends disciples to ask Jesus whether he is in truth the One who is to come, or are they to expect another? (Matthew 11: 3; Luke 7: 18–20). How could the witness of the Manifestation at the Jordan ever frame such a question?

Bulgakov rejects both the modern 'solution' of critical scholarship which would deny the fourth Gospel's ascription of high doctrine to John any historical value, and the embarrassed 'explanations' of the Fathers who found here only a pedagogical exercise whereby the Baptist sought to communicate his own understanding of Jesus to his pupils. No. 'This question is the most tragic ever sounded in a human soul.'[28] Jesus's response, as recorded by the first evangelist, consists in rehearsing the list of his wondrous deeds which is not at all a convincing answer (John already had reports of these, and other prophets wrought signs and wonders). In fact, Bulgakov considers this a deliberate side-stepping of the question, But then the Lord adds, 'And blessed is he who does not take offence at me' (Matthew 11: 6). And these words – which are a macarism or 'beatitude', a recognized form of benediction, Bulgakov takes to be Christ's *blessing* of one whom, he knew, had undergone a dreadful trial and tempting of his faith, but had not yielded. This would certainly make good sense of the eulogy of John which Jesus then proceeds to offer the crowds (Matthew 11: 7–15).

We should be clear that Bulgakov does not understand John's inner crisis in a psychologistic sense. It is not as though John was about to chuck everything up and offer to enter Herod's civil service. There are 'spiritual summits that exclude the possibility of a backwards movement, of lapsation'.[29] What John experienced must be understood soteriologically, not psychologically. It is divine trial, 'his personal Gethesemane before the Golgotha to come'.[30] As with Job, there can be such a thing as 'providential dereliction, *promisitelnoe ostavlenie*', or 'divine abandonment, *bogoostavlennost'*', all with a view to scouring the soul and deepening in it the channels of faith, hope and love.[31] *Toutes proportions gardées* as the French say, is not this what befell the humanized Son from the Father on the Cross? Is it not the sacred darkness of Good Friday? If so, how could the Precursor avoid experiencing it in some fashion and yet remain true to his title, his name? 'To the

---

[28] Ibid., p. 123.
[29] Ibid., p. 130.
[30] Ibid., p. 131bv
[31] Ibid., pp. n 131, 132.

highest ministries are reserved the temptations that correspond to them.'[32] John's trial, which consisted in the fact that Jesus's status as the Christ had ceased to be for him evident truth, is the Baptistine parallel to the sufferings of the Mother of God at the Cross of the Lord. It was a battering sustained by faith where John suffered but did not fall. Jesus's words to him, sent via his disciples, are therefore no criticism but quite the contrary. They are a 'salutation from the One who is coming to the one who is going away'.[33] This final farewell is an exultant proclamation ('*Blessed* is he!') which looks forward to John's death and glorification.

Death and glory

Bulgakov cannot envisage a life full of years for John the Baptist. What meaning would his life have on earth after the first Easter? How could the Friend of the Bridegroom find tolerable the Bridegroom's departure? The case of the Mother of God is entirely different. She was not involved in the public ministry of Jesus. She came into her own as the heart of the praying Church at Pentecost, in an intimacy that mirrored her life at Nazareth. John's mission by contrast is entirely public, and completely bound up with Jesus's preaching activity.

His death stands in sharp contrast to that of Jesus. It results from scheming by the civil powers, not the religious authorities. The teaching objected to is not theological but ethical. It was essentially the work of women, not men. Echoing the Marcan account, Bulgakov ascribes it to feminine malevolence triggered by the obsession of the sexually vicious with those who, while not virgins by temperament, have remained so by human effort. Not that John's 'integral chastity' is merely a natural affair. Bulgakov deflects any sense his analysis of the death narrative may create that this was a 'commonplace' martyrdom. He does so by re-emphasizing the role in John's life of special election of a universally significant salvation-historical kind. Following certain of the Fathers, he sees John as co-anointed with Jesus at the time of the Baptism, indeed as co-baptized with him – even if, before his martyrdom, and, more fundamentally still, before the saving death of the Lord himself, these actions could not fully bring about his future glory.

[32] Ibid., p. 140.
[33] Ibid., p. 144.

The 'glorification', *proslavlenie*, of John is Bulgakov's final theme in the body of his text. What Bulgakov intends to study under this title is the way the Church presents John in the glory of God through her icons. The icons house 'visions' of him, perceptions of the divine mysteries.[34] The iconography concerned may be of events in the sacred history, happenings in John's earthly life. His birth and execution, and above all the Baptism of the Lord at his hands, are obvious examples of these. Alternatively, they may be dogmatic or symbolic representations, where he may, for example, appear crowned or winged, or holding a cup with, in its interior, the Christ-Child, the Lamb of God. Some sophianic icons show beside him an angel all in flame. And finally of course he appears with the blessed Mother on the *Deesis* – the scheme that lies behind the entire Little Trilogy. The common factor in these icons, Bulgakov believes, is that they show John as a being apart: whether pairing him with the God-bearer or depicting him in some sense as an angel. As we shall see, the emblems of the latter have a peculiar interest for Bulgakov.

Quite commonly, John appears winged. This is, in the first instance, to indicate his 'angelomorph life', *evo angeloobraznoe zhitie*.[35] That phrase, though striking, is not especially surprising. The ascetic sources often speak of the the eremitical life in these terms, and owing to his desert period, John is a sort of proto-hermit. Bulgakov shows well enough that the Church makes much of the angel title for him in her liturgical poetry. In a text originally composed by St Andrew of Crete (*c.* 660–740), for example, the Liturgy hails him as 'earthly angel, heavenly man'.[36] Another chain of argument is not so convincing. Bulgakov claims that while the Liturgy, or hagiography, frequently calls various saints angelic, these other figures are never depicted on the icons with wings (except for the prophet Elijah, with whom John has, in Jesus's own admission, some sort of mysterious identifying bond). Actually, this claim – on which in a moment much is to be built – is not sustainable. In Ethiopian iconography, for instance, it is customary to depict ascetic saints, such as Tekle Haymanoth or Gabra Mantas Qeddus, in exactly this way. Unaware of such comparisons, Bulgakov draws the amazing conclusion that the wings added by the icon-painters cannot be intended in an 'allegorical' sense, but must be taken in 'all their reality'.[37] In a footnote, he brings to his

[34] Ibid., p. 179.
[35] Ibid., p. 180.
[36] Cited ibid., p. 181.
[37] Ibid., p. 182: *angel . . . po yestyestvu.*

readers' attention the inscription, on some of these icons, of the Malachi text (3: 1) 'Behold I send my messenger [in the Septuagint, *angelos*] before thy face'. Spelling out in unmistakeable terms what a non-allegorical sense might mean here, he asserts that the Church 'implicitly gives a literal interpretation of this prophecy', viz., that John is an angel by essence.[38]

More precisely, or at any rate in more nuanced fashion, Bulgakov proposes that the human and angelic worlds are hypo-statically united in John, just as the divine and human worlds are in Christ. Is this a pre-natal event? More probably it is a corollary of the Incarnation when in entering the world as one of his own creatures the Logos draws the angelic realm with him into the cosmos. John is more than a man, because he is an angel; he is also more than an angel, because he remains a human being – and it is humans, not angels, who are to be through the economy of Son and Spirit, lords of creation. But as the man-angel, *angelochelovek*,[39] that he should occupy the next place to the Mother of God – herself higher than all angels – becomes comprehensible. The proposal seems less bizarre when we recall Bulgakov's emphasis on the 'co-humanity' of the angels – which necessarily implies the 'co-angelhood' of men. Angels and humans have always been inter-dependent. Now in one instance their natures are held together in a perfect union.

One has the impression that the principal merit for Bulgakov of this doctrinal adjustment lies in the way it facilitates the claim that the Incarnation has had an effect in all worlds. It is also a testimony to the anthropocentric character of sophiology in its application to creation: an angel could not take on human nature which would be heterogeneous to it. But a human being could take on the angelic nature, such is the 'ontological plenitude of [man's] being'.[40]

Noting that John's portrayal holding his own head on its platter (and this in icons not directly concerned with his martyrdom) may also be a sign of his part-separation from the life of the body, Bulgakov passes to another motif of Baptistine iconography, the chalice with the Child. This he connects with its seeming opposite: images of John (and Mary) in the metalwork of the Byzantine-rite chalice itself. Through the iconostasis, and the prayers of the *proskomedia* or preparation of the Gifts, the Precursor is included in

[38] Ibid., note *
[39] Ibid., p. 184.
[40] Ibid., p. 188.

the Eucharistic celebration. Putting together these data of Tradition, then, must we not ascribe to him a special relation to the Holy Eucharist? Both as man and as angel he is present there, or, in Bulgakov's words:

> He who stood by Christ at the time of his earthly Theophany is eternally present in the everlasting mystery of his glorified Body, accomplished on the Holy Table; the Bridegroom's friend shares for ever in the wedding evening of the Lamb.[41]

That John should sometimes be depicted with a Cross, emblem of his pre-cognition of the redemptive mystery, is relatively unremarkable. More thought-provoking is the crowning scene, shared with the Mother of God, which appears on certain Russian icons of the sort most dear to Bulgakov because the Wisdom of God is also signified there. It takes him to the heart of the *Deesis*.

A theology of the 'Deesis'

In our explorations of Bulgakov's eschatology in *Nevesta Agntsa* we have already seen how for him both the Mother of God and the Precursor have a role in the Parousia – itself identical, materially speaking, with the Last Judgement. That is both an inference from the *Deesis* and a justification of it. But meanwhile, before the general resurrection, there is something of an incongruity about their proximity on the icon-screen. Mary is glorified body and soul, while John is still awaiting the full integrity of the risen life. Here again, the thesis of John's dual nature comes in useful. Insofar as he possesses the angelic nature, he can be utterly in glory already. Moreover his humanity *as embodied* does not have a comparable cosmic value to that of the Mother of the Lord, since of her flesh is the Logos, through whom all things were made. John's whole power belongs with the spiritual realm where the gifts to him as man, unspeakably augmented by gifts to him as angel, render him truly worthy to be closer to Christ than any mortal – saving always his holy Mother.

We have seen how in Bulgakov's ecclesiology Mary is the personal icon of the Church as Bride and Mother. But the Church, in her sophianic aspect, comprises not only humans but angels too. The conjunction on the *Deesis* of Mary and John has, accordingly,

---

[41] Ibid., pp. 191–192.

an ecclesial significance. Between them they express the Church's whole membership, Mary as its Mother, John as 'angel of the Church', *angel Tserkvi*.[42]

Nor does the *Deesis* lack Trinitarian meaning. It is not difficult to see how the Mother and the Precursor together testify to the divine Son. But they also witness to the Spirit, who descended on Mary at the Annunciation and whom John saw at the Jordan descending on Christ. And if Son and Spirit are implicit in the *Deesis*, so must be the Father who sent them. This explains how Bulgakov can call the *Deesis* itself a theophany.

There remains the simplest point of all. The Precursor, like the Mother of the Lord, is *praying* – not for himself but for the whole Church, which means potentially all humanity, indeed the entire cosmos. This is the Church in prayer, the Church praying for the Church, or, in a fuller formulation, 'the fullness of the love of the Church for God and for man'.[43] More especially, this is the prayer of the Church to the Lord in judgment, prayer for pardon for sinners.

A sophiological coda

In Jesus's encomium on John he remarks that Wisdom is 'justified in all her works' (Matthew [11: 19]) or 'children' (Luke [7: 35]). This is scarcely something a sophiologist can pass by. Of course Wisdom is justified in her *works*: the divine acts of creation and Incarnation. Naturally, John has his own place in both. A theodicy of Wisdom's *children* is more problematic. But the Lucan saying, like the Matthaean, has John in mind, and here for Bulgakov the Saviour is *praising* John for his sophianic quality as 'summit and representative of the whole human race'.[44] Either way, John is close to the Wisdom of God from which he 'receives radiance and glory'.[45] This can be confirmed iconographically, through the presence of John on (some, not all) icons of the divine Wisdom. In the name of humanity, the two elect ones, the Mother and the Baptist, represent the divine Wisdom in our nature, in conformity with their roles in the Incarnation of the Word. Wisdom, after all, is shown forth in man's plenitude – feminine and masculine together. These images, overwhelmingly Russian in provenance, leave us with that message.

---

[42] Ibid., p. 200.
[43] Ibid., p. 202.
[44] Ibid., p. 213.
[45] Ibid., p. 214.

16

The Angels

Bulgakov's angelology is more developed than that of any other modern theologian.[1] Not only is *Lestnitsa Yakovlya*, 'Jacob's Ladder', a fairly substantial treatise in its own right. More than this, angelological passages are scattered across Bulgakov's dogmatic writings – including at some crucial junctures already registered in the present survey. To his mind, the *doctrine* of the status and activity of the angels is well-established in Orthodoxy, and, as it happens, differs hardly at all from its presentation in Catholicism. But there remains much, on the basis of Scripture and the Fathers, the Liturgy and iconography, for *theology* to do in this domain. In his preface to *Jacob's Ladder*, dated the 'Synaxis of the Holy Commander of armies Michael and the other celestial powers, 1928', Bulgakov makes a personal confession of how great a spiritual 'consolation' writing this book has been. Its rich biblical texture and warm spiritual tone certainly contrast with the austere metaphysical investigations of *Die Tragödie der Philosophie*, also published in that year.

Introducing the guardian angels

He introduces his angelology by a theological essay on love. This is at first sight a strange *modus operandi*. It is made somewhat more intelligible when we discover his way into the world of the angels is through the notion of the guardian angel, the 'heavenly friend'. The goal divinely projected for human nature is, in the image of the trihypostatic Trinity: to 'raise oneself in humbling oneself', to 'find abundant riches in poverty of spirit', to 'accomplish oneself

---

[1] For an interpretative summary of his angelology, *see* L. A. Zander, *Bog i mir*, op. cit., II., pp. 247–274.

in exhausting oneself' – in a word, to 'become love'.[2] The one who
loves is wealthy since enriched by the God who is Love in a ceaseless 'dying and rising, *umiranie i voskresanie,* of the personal "I"'.[3] In
human beings, love does not abolish the hypostatic centre. Rather,
it makes that centre more sensitive and more 'exigent', multiplying
the possibilities of loving. The love-command of the Gospels is to
love not only God but also one's neighbour 'as oneself'. This
presumes that we have with our neighbour co-humanity not in the
First Adam (or the command would not be 'new', as the Jesus of St
John declares it to be), but in the Second. It belongs to the ontology both of nature and of grace that we cannot love ourself without
reflecting ourself in another, in an *alter ego* or 'friend'. Indeed, we
belong to ourselves only in such 'ecstasy'.

> The axiom of love is that the 'I' is not singular, solitary: it is dyadic,
> related, relative by conjunction, it only knows and possesses itself in
> connexion with its double, according to duality.[4]

Admittedly, there is an almost infinite number of ways in which
such 'doubling' can come about. And all of them are seen in their
limitation – their being relative *by value* – through awareness of the
one absolute love asked of us, love for God. Yet not the least
example of that duality is love for the guardian angel – introduced
here suddenly, indeed abruptly, and on the ground of the liturgical prayers of the Russian Orthodox Church.

   If Bulgakov's characterization of the guardian angel is chiefly
drawn from the Liturgy, he also makes some appeal to the untu-
tored language of popular Christian discourse. What is involved in
the spontaneous acclaim of a helpful human being as a 'guardian
angel'? We mean by that someone who is attentive, tender,
thoughtful and practically supportive, in a discreet, and almost
imperceptible fashion. In an indirect manner, the *sensus fidei*
reveals its understanding of angelic guardianship by the way it
leads people to identify that guardianship's human equivalent.

   On the basis of the Liturgy Bulgakov finds the guardian angel to
combine in an extraordinary way both delicacy and the willingness
to fight. These angels are not only 'sweetly silent'. They are also the

---

[2] LY, p. 7.
[3] Ibid., p. 9.
[4] Ibid., p. 14. The double-barrelled adjective contains the Valentinian Gnostic
term for pairing, 'syzygy', as reported by St Irenaeus. Bulgakov's effort to find
an orthodox meaning for the concept reflects that of Soloviev in an earlier
generation.

'protectors of our souls and bodies'. Through the depth and intimacy of the angel guardian's presence to us, he can draw out from us our best qualities, and make them predominate in some response or action. His is a 'heavenly pedagogy', tending to elicit from us wise initiatives as, under his tutelage, we marshall our powers for good from within and manifest them without. This is a sleepless presence, unconstraining yet ever prepared for our moral and spiritual correction. It is the incessant character of this vigilance which distinguishes it from human love, or any human behaviour. For Bulgakov, the guardian angel is not simply watching over us at the divine behest. It is indeed part of the divine creative will that these holy intelligences should function as God's instruments in our regard. But the relation of angel and human being is not an extrinsic one. It is by the angel's created essence that he is turned towards the human hypostasis he guards.

> His relation with us is determined not by an external mission but by the internal bond of love which already witnesses to an ontological union.[5]

The angel guardians experience both sorrow and joy in their relation with souls whose own dramas include sin and repentance. Their work in our regard is 'creative': they are not merely reactive but pro-active in our regard. Unlike God, their relation with beings immersed in temporal flux draws them into our mutability. The apostle's riddling prediction that 'we are to judge angels' (1 Corinthians 6: 3) suggests their creative labour can be done more or less well. On the other hand, the Church teaches their immutability in the eternal good which is the beatifying vision of God. 'Definitively affirmed' in their righteousness in the moment of the fall of the evil angels, the life of the holy angels is 'already illumined by eternity'.[6] Clearly, some explanation must be found for this capacity to prosecute a double existence. Bulgakov's explanation is that the 'energy of liaison between the two worlds is *love*'.[7] More specifically, the guardian angels' obedient acceptance of their bonding to carnal creatures is a kenotic love whereby they freely limit the serenity of their enjoyment of the vision of God so as to serve us. This is a 'kenosis of the angelic essence' which, from now on, becomes 'co-human'.[8] (And Bulgakov does not fail to

[5] Ibid., p. 25.
[6] Ibid., p. 28.
[7] Ibid.
[8] Ibid., p. 29.

mention that it has its analogue and foundation in the Incarnation of the Word.) We have no idea of what the patience of the guardian angels costs them as they suffer our obstinacy in evil, our inertia, indolence and (at the worst) bestial or even demonic thoughts and actions. The wounds one human being can inflict on another who loves them are the faint echo of the spiritual suffering of these bodiless 'friends'. Bulgakov singles out suicide as the action which most afflicts them. The suicide rejects the angel guardian in his being, and not merely in some aspect of his action.

The Russian liturgical text called the Canon of the Guardian Angel testifies that this friend, in its constancy, humility, abnegation, is with us from childhood – which Bulgakov interprets as from birth. This is divine philanthropy, invisible to us here but it will be visible hereafter. But in some personal 'notes' incorporated towards the end of the opening chapter of *Jacob's Ladder*, Bulgakov makes it plain that his angelology includes an element of autobiographical mystical experience. In the introduction to this book we have noted how his re-conversion to Orthodoxy appears to have been highly personal, not to say idiosyncratic, and owes little to anything like a classical 'preamble of faith'. So here too an experience of divine consolation, entering like a cool breeze into the sinful heart consumed in the flames of anguish, is interpreted as the special epiphany of his guardian angel. That angel is recognized as such by reference to the Old Testament text which provides much of the imagery of the passage: the account in the Book of Daniel, of one who walked with the Three Young Men in the burning fiery furnace (Daniel 3: 13–30). The curious structure of *Lestnitsa Yakovlya* is surely dictated by this powerfully remembered personal experience.

The *structure*, but not necessarily all the *content*. Bulgakov reports that for the wider Tradition the angelic mission is not confined to personalities. It embraces 'entire spheres of being, extends to the world, humanity, the universe'.[9] The angels, after all, compose the 'heavens' of Genesis 1: 1. They are the 'noetic' heaven, the heaven of the Incorporeals. It is to this wider relation between heaven and earth, the angelic realm and the cosmos, that Bulgakov now turns to contextualise his remarks on the role of the angels in human life.

---

[9] Ibid., p. 46.

The relation of heaven and earth

On the creation of the angels: invoking a liturgical hymn, Bulgakov presents it as ecclesial teaching that the angels were created before the definitive constitution of the world. The hymn writer was probably drawing an inference from the Book of Job (38: 7) which, in the version he uses and on his interpretation, speaks of the angels coming into being prior to the formation of stellar matter: the Hexaemeron's 'fourth day'. St Augustine, so Bulgakov reports, ascribes their creation to the 'first day' (they are aspects of the 'light' that was made then), while numerous Fathers, both Greek and Latin, consider that their making preceded the opening of the Six Day Account. Their creation is pre-mundane. This is the view to which Bulgakov inclines.

More consequential is the issue of the fundamental being that issues from the creative act. The angels are so made as to face in two directions: towards God, towards the world. On the one hand, they are, in the words of the Byzantine Office of the Incorporeal Powers, 'God-bearing coals, lit up by the dawn of [God's] being'. Their life in God consists in 'communicating with the Glory unspeakable', and in returning glory to Glory. On the other hand, they are indeed *angels*: 'those sent' (to the rest of the created world is understood). Remarkably, this is the only name under which, in revelation, we know them. They are created with a view to ministerial service. They are 'with' the earth, in essential relation to it. Except for sin, nothing is outside their providential watchfulness, nor accomplished without some degree of participation from their side. Once again, it is the hymns and icons of the Church that bear witness to this. But Bulgakov treats these relatively unsophisticated sources as expressing the deep mind of the ecclesial community – from which intellectual womb, so to speak, dogmatic consciousness can come forth, with Bulgakovian theology as midwife.

Bulgakov's proposal that pagan polytheism arises from a misreading of experience of the angels gains plausibility from the revealed datum of their relation to the natural elements as well as peoples and kingdoms. In explanation of both proposal and datum he holds that the angelic world possesses all the content of *our* world, albeit in a mode proper to angelic understanding. Were this not the case, the correlation that renders the angels co-cosmic and co-human would be unthinkable. And here Bulgakov deliberately introduces an ambiguity – or let us say, more kindly, a bivalency – into his reading of Genesis. When God created the heavens and the earth, did he create all things invisible as well as visible? (This is the assumption of Bulgakov's text hitherto, but on it no intrinsic relation of the angels to the cosmos is apparent, except through the detour of the divine mind and will.) So, by way of an alternative (complementary?) interpretation, did he create the ideal and the real universe? If so, since 'ideal' and 'real' are two aspects of the selfsame being, it is possible to hold that the entire content of the universe as 'real' is contained in immaterial mode within the principal 'embodiment' of the universe as 'ideal'. The angels can be described as endowed with inherent access to the contents of the human – and cosmic – world.

Needless to say by this stage in the exposition of Bulgakov's thought, all this is on the basis of a yet more primordial foundation, in comparison with which these divergences are merely distinctions: the Wisdom of God. It is generally agreed by students of the Canon of Scripture *in its total compass* that the opening text of Genesis, 'In the beginning God created the heavens and the earth', should be understood in the light of the initial affirmation of the Johannine Prologue, 'In the beginning was the Word'. On Bulgakov's reading – which proceeds by constant attention to Wisdom 8: 22, 'The Lord possessed me at the beginning of his ways', that gives to the phrase 'in the beginning' for both Old and New Testaments the combined sense of 'through', 'in conformity with', and 'on the basis of' that eternal principle which is the Wisdom of God.[10] What Bulgakov wants to commend in the perspective of angelology is a twofold expression of the archetypal ideas contained (in different senses) in the Wisdom and the Word of God. One of these expressions, entirely spiritual, is found in the angelic beings; the other is embodied in the visible world, including man. Angels and humans are united, therefore, by the 'community of theme of their ontology', *obshchinost' ontologicheskoi temi*.[11]

Angelic ontology

But the variations on that theme are considerable. For Bulgakov, the angels are sheer hypostases. There is, for him, no such thing as angelic nature as such. (He does not address the question, How then can we bring all the angels under the same concept?) Perhaps it might be said that the *function* of this claim is really to confirm

[10] Ibid., p. 35.
[11] Ibid., p. 48.

the – to him – more important assertion that every angel is formally different, being determined by its particular 'station' before the throne of God. (That is congruent with Aquinas's assertion that each angel constitutes its own species.[12]) But its *meaning* is difficult to reconcile with Bulgakov's succeeding statements that the angels do nonetheless have a 'world' – a stable, coherent approach to reality. As the early chapters of this study have shown, in Bulgakov's phenomenological ontology to have a nature is the same thing as to possess a world, so understood. Be this as it may, he now proposes that:

> All the plenitude, the *plêrôma*, of the universe is in a certain way proper to the angelic world. The latter is not a part of the world, it is the *entire* world, but under a particular, hypostatic-spiritual aspect.[13]

The angels have their wondrous existence. The hypostasis of each sums up in spiritual-personal mode one of the divine ideas. Yet the only created world in which their existence is meaningful is reality as shaped for human beings to inhabit. It is *our* world that by virtue of *their* being they serve.

The closest one can get to a literary expression of Bulgakov's angelology in this respect is the chapter entitled 'The descent of the gods' in C. S. Lewis's (1893–1963) *That Hideous Strength*, third and last member of his theological space fiction trilogy.[14] In that scene in the Director's house at St Anne's on the Hill, each descending angel of the planetary system is in his own hypostasis the quintessence of some aspect of the human world. (We can note in passing Lewis's source here in his explorations of Latin Neo-Platonism.) For Bulgakov, who consciously wishes to unify Christian Platonism with modern scientific evolutionism, the reality the angels contain in ideal form is, however, only the embryonic beginning of the world's development. Still, as executors of the will of the creative Word, their aboriginal guardianship of the human universe is a condition of possibility for its proceeding to sophianic term.

> The angelic choir is truly the *intermediary* between God and man, a ladder from earth to heaven, without which our world could not have suffered the proximity, otherwise immediate, of God. It unites, but it also separates.[15]

[12] Thomas Aquinas, *Summa theologiae* Ia., q. 50, a. 4.
[13] LY, p.50.
[14] C. S. Lewis, *That Hideous Strength* (London, 1955), pp. 197–205.
[15] LY. 52.

The world of ideas, which Plato rightly affirmed, but confused (thinks Bulgakov) with the divinity, is in reality the ladder of Jacob. It is the world of the angels in its relation to natural being.

Just as man is to a degree 'synangelic', insofar as the 'ladder', the ontological bond, between earthly and heavenly, has its 'foot' or resting-place in him, so the angels are – and to a heightened degree – 'synanthropic'. The 'conformity of the angels with man, *so-chelovechnost' angelov*, is the condition of their service'.[16] Bulgakov does not omit to cite the riddling comment of the author of the Apocalypse that the extent of the wall of the Holy City, the new Jerusalem, was calculated 'by a man's measure, that is, an angel's' (21: 17). Such reciprocity throws light on the witness of Scripture to the encounters of human beings with angels themselves in human likeness. And if, for Ezekiel and, after him, St John, they can also be presented theriomorphically, Bulgakov reminds us that the entire animal creation is summed up in man as microcosm, the one in whom all species are to cohere.

In their synanthropic activities, it is the angelic host *as a whole* that is turned towards humankind. The activity of the guardian angels is only the clearest and most immediate example of their concern. Intervening in a (mild) dispute among Fathers, Bulgakov inclines to say that the guardian given at birth is received in a new way at Baptism. He speculates that there is a resemblance between the hypostasis of the angel guarding and that of the human being guarded, to the point that the latter would be licensed in speaking of the former as his or her 'heavenly "I"'.[17] To the expected response that this is metaphysical exaggeration, Bulgakov replies that, after all:

> individuality consists only in a certain *quomodo* [how]: it is the mode of the assimilation of a universe common to all, of the Wisdom of God manifested there.[18]

Not that this intimate relation should be thought of as an *égoïsme à deux*. All human individuals are interwoven in the great cloth of humanity as a whole. And though the angels do not constitute a kind, they do make up a choir, with its own inter-relations. The

[16] Ibid., p. 55.
[17] Ibid., p. 64.
[18] Ibid., p. 62.

biblical data on angelic guardianship of peoples and indeed churches (compare the opening two chapters of the Apocalypse) show that atomic individualism would here be out of place. And in any case, the prayer of the Church is directed to all the angels, reflecting the testimony of Scripture to their presence as a *host* – whether at past high points of salvation history as in the Lucan birth narrative (Luke 2: 13), or in the future, in the eschatological scenario (e.g. Matthew 13: 41). In his glorious Parousia, the Son of Man will be escorted by *all* the angels (Matthew 25: 31).

The angels and the 'Deesis'

And yet the Bible does encourage us to individuate to some degree. Take for example Gabriel, the angel sent to Mary to announce the news of the Incarnation and 're-united with her forever on the Annunciation icon that crowns the royal gates [of the iconostasis]'.[19] The angel of the mystery of the Incarnation, who, thinks Bulgakov, must enjoy a special relation with the third Trinitarian person, is not, however, Mary's guardian. Without attempting to abstract Mary from the human family, that the Mother of God, more venerable than the Cherubim and incomparably more glorious than the Seraphim, should require a heavenly intercessor seems to Bulgakov unlikely. Her hypostasis, granted its exalted destiny, had no angelic prototype. None of this prevents Gabriel from being the personal servant of the Mother of the Lord and of her mission.

In effect, Bulgakov is exploring here the significance of the iconic relations shown in the *Deesis*, the intercession panel of the classical Russian iconostasis. Inevitably, then, he has to look also at the issue of angel guardianship and the Baptist. Like Jesus in Mary, John in Elizabeth has an angel to announce his conception and birth. (The presumption must be that for the Evangelist this also is Gabriel.) But the Friend of the Bridegroom is to be the 'angel-*anthrôpos*', head of the angelic as of the human world, insofar as a finite hypostasis can take such a role. Bulgakov thinks it more fitting to imagine the totality of the angelic realm, and not simply one figure within it, as engaged in John's providential protection.

A fortiori, one cannot speak of a guardian angel for Christ. That his human hypostasis *is* the very hypostasis of the Logos through whom all things were made renders such a role otiose in the

[19] Ibid., p. 67.

extreme. However, the Gospels speak of the angels who attend the Saviour at key moments in his drama. Bulgakov pauses to consider especially the 'angel from heaven' sent to strengthen him in his agony in the garden (Luke 22: 43), whom he rather confidently identifies with Michael. It would be appropriate for the *archistratê-gos*, the Commander of the heavenly armies, to appear at that point, in a twofold capacity as prince of the Hebrew people (a claim registered by the inter-Testamental text called *The Assumption of Moses*) and guardian of the human nature of Christ.

History as co-angelic

As Bulgakov points out, the Johannine Apocalypse goes further than any other biblical text in describing history as a collaborative enterprise of humans and the angelic powers – and not only history but also the issue of history in their conjoined humano-angelic worship of the Lamb.[20] Nor is this without anticipation in, above all, Old Testament apocalyptic. In the Book of Daniel, Gabriel makes it plain that he not only contemplates history but helps to make it, and, following some early twentieth-century exegesis, Bulgakov would identify him with the angel called 'the Strong One', *ho ischyros*, in Apocalypse 10: 1. Bulgakov comments:

> One might say that the archangel manifests the form of the relation of the angels to the human world and that their mission is not simple execution, but inspiration and creative activity.[21]

Considering the relatively small place Bulgakov's synergistic view of grace gives to prevenient grace – the grace that goes before and prepares human freedom for co-operation with God, it is quite a concession to the Catholic doctrine when, in a footnote, he suggests that what has been called *gratia praeveniens* may refer, at least in part, to angelic energies that are deployed in creative, inspirational action on earth.[22]

Moreover, their mission is also *sacrificial* activity. Unusually, Bulgakov links St John's remark that those who fought the great Dragon 'loved not their lives even unto death' (Apocalypse 12: 11) not to humans but to the angels who took the part of Michael in the war in heaven. He emphasizes the risk their engagement

---

[20] Ibid., pp. 78–85.
[21] Ibid., p. 92.
[22] Ibid., p. 96, note *.

entails. These are not omniscient beings, as the Liturgy underlines when it gives voice to their amazement at, for example, the Ascension or the Dormition. But the indefectibility of the divine plan, despite the setbacks and even ruptures that human liberty brings in its train, means that the harvest of angelic effort will one day be brought into the granary of God. Bulgakov associates the rather strange ending to the Parable of the Talents ('to everyone who has more will be given ... but from him who has not even what he has will be taken away' [Matthew 25: 29]) with the inheritance by the holy angels of the entire plenitude of the angelic realm, once shared with their fallen fellow-angels. He mentions in the same connexion the entrusting of the whole spiritual good of mankind to those humans who, owing not least to angelic influence, cooperate with grace. And what we can hope for corporately, in terms of the eschatological issue of history, we can also hope for individually, in terms of the end of our own lives at death. The guardian angel, whose delight it is to help us assimilate all the gifts of grace meant for us, will be with us at our death-bed, to receive our soul.

The angels and the Trinity

The synanthropic action of the angels should not deter us from contemplation of their essence and life in its God-directed aspect. In their doxological orientation (to give glory to Glory), the divine life becomes theirs by participation. Possibly in order to resolve the problem of those visionary experiences in the Hebrew Bible which seem to be ambivalently both theophanies – manifestations of God, and angelophanies – manifestations of the angels, Bulgakov wishes to say that the angelic hypostases are wholly transparent to God, mirrors of his Light, *having no nature of their own which could distract from this.* Theologically and philosophically, to say that the angels have no nature, that each is a 'who' without even being a 'what', is rather a high price to pay. How it can be ontologically justified is far from plain.

If the angels enjoy *sobornost'* , the togetherness of conciliarity, that is owed to no consubstantiality but to the ordered hierarchy in which each of the sophianic ideas at the root of their being is located. The nine angelic orders set forth in *The Celestial Hierarchy* by the 'mysterious pseudo-Denys' (*c.* 500), inasmuch as the notion of that 'ninefold' has been 'received' by the Church, suggests a peculiar relation of the angels to the Trinitarian persons.

Arithmetically, three is the square root of nine. The angels stand together before the indivisible Trinity. But does this exclude a differentiation whereby the diverse orders (or individuals) might 'bear the seal' of one or another of the divine Three? The Abrahamic tradition of a manifestation of the God of Israel in the form of three angels at the Oak of Mamre (Genesis 18: 1–15) suggests not. This is the scene which at the end of the fifteenth century became, in the celebrated painting by Andrei Rublev (c. 1370–1430), the classical Russian icon of the Holy Trinity. An older icon type of the choirs of archangels depicts Michael and Gabriel in a way that links them to, respectively, the second and third divine persons. To complete the scheme, Bulgakov makes the tentative proposal that a third archangel, generally unnamed, standing between the first two at a slightly higher level, may allude tacitly to the first Trinitarian person, the Father. Angels of the Father, though 'with' the world, are plunged into the abyss of his mystery as the 'divine Silence generating the Word and the divine Darkness irradiating the Spirit'. 'Speechless with the superabundance', they are the 'apophatic aspect of the heavenly world joined to the cataphatic being of the angels'.[23] It is in the angels of the Word that we find the angelic world to be the paradigm of our own. 'Making real the ideation of the world is anticipated in them.'[24] Contemplating the Son's works at the creation, it is these angels whose existence Plato seized by confused intuition in his doctrine of the Forms. What, then, of the angels of the Holy Spirit? They are servants of life, and most of all of the clothing of the work of the Word with beauty. The beauty of creation pre-exists in the angels of the Spirit, and they remain its guardians. (It is in this section of *Jacob's Ladder* that Bulgakov comes closest to ascribing to the 'noetic powers' a share in the creative act, even though it is most customary for him to assert that no creature, even by divine power, can *sensu stricto* create: this is the decided view, in Western Catholicism, of the Thomist school.)

If the angelic world is thus qualified according to the triunity of the divine persons, that must affect the forms of inter-relation of the members of its 'choir': that is to say, their mutual love. Though the angels are sexless, the distinction between angels of the Son and of the Spirit can be used discreetly, Bulgakov believes, so as to indicate an affinity with the masculine and feminine principles in the cosmos. There *is* a symbolic affinity between the truth of the

[23] Ibid., p. 116.
[24] Ibid., p. 117.

Son and the masculine principle, the beauty of the Spirit and the feminine principle. The angels of the first Trinitarian person, by contrast, are angels of the 'Father beyond all qualification yet qualified in the figures of the Second and the Third'.[25] The life of the angels of the Word and the Holy Spirit has its source in the perpetual light of those angels of the Father. (Here Bulgakov presupposes the Dionysian scheme of hierarchical communication between the angelic orders). There is an appropriateness in our inability to find for these angels an affinity in gender symbolics. In the sphere of human love, the spiritual complementarity of masculine and feminine, takes us back to 'that Principle of universal filiation and paternity', the One 'from every family in heaven and on earth is named' (Ephesians 3: 15). Unsentimentally, Bulgakov proposes that male human beings are more likely to have as guardians angels of the Spirit (they need the 'feminine' complement), female human beings to have as their angelic *alter ego* angels of the Logos (they need the 'masculine' complement). That Mary's angel is Gabriel (an angel of the third Trinitarian person) is the exception that proves the rule. Gabriel is not Mary's guardian but the servant of the Holy Spirit.

Of course, since for Bulgakov the angels have no nature, it is not difficult for him to remark that, while strictly speaking only what is *super*-natural is gracious, with the angels the gift of grace is coterminous with their hypostatic existence. Their being *is* a sharing in the divine nature. The angels are immortal hypostases 'sealed' by one of the Trinitarian persons. Their life towards God is their vision of him; their spiritual food is the Eucharist of the Son – not merely in the sense of their presence to the Church's Liturgy but in that of contemplation of the eternal Sacrifice whereby the Son offers himself to the Father for the world from the beginning. Of that Sacrifice – the Golgotha above, the Oblation of the Cross, and the Church's ritual offering, are the expression in space and time.

The angels, freedom, praise

The issue of angelic freedom worries Bulgakov. As personal spirits there can hardly be any doubt that they possess liberty. But, given his view that for angelic being existence and grace are indistinguishable, he is reluctant to allow a fully meritorious exercise of freedom which would appropriately be the occasion of their

---

[25] Ibid., p. 135.

transition from the order of creation to that of re-creation or supernatural righteousness. Indeed, he holds that angelic freedom is at first inchoate or immature. The angels had to 'become themselves' through realising by liberty all their possibilities.[26] They had to discover for themselves that they could live only by self-renouncing love towards God. Self-love is for them ontological suicide, leading not – to be sure – to the abolition but to the rupturing of their personal being. Lucifer discovered negatively what the holy angels found out in its positive sense. In each case, as our investigation of Bulgakov's theology of the two falls, angelic and human, in an earlier chapter indicated, angelic comprehension of the full bearings of an acceptance of egocentrism – unlike human – is 'unaccompanied by ignorance, error or misapprehension'.[27] The decision of the angels to favour kenotic love, once taken, abolishes their earlier 'immaturity', reducing any alternative course to the status of 'phantom-like potentiality'.[28] Bulgakov is willing to call this – by analogy with the redemption of human beings – the 'salvation' of the angels, seeing it as taking place synergistically by virtue of their love of God, itself empowered by the blood of the Lamb. As to the evil angels, they conserve the structure of their hypostatic life (will, intellect and so forth), but, desubstantiated by the malign act which contradicted their own essence, they now live parasitically on the evil passions of men. At the final Judgement, they will cease to be in the world, becoming bare subjectivity ceaselessly devouring itself. The question as to whether there can be for them any repentance, any hope, is one the Church is equipped neither to answer nor even to raise.

More rewarding for theological contemplation is the God-oriented activity of the holy angels, above all their praise. Their 'song' is the prototype of our hymnography, our worship. In the Temple vision of the prophet Isaiah, the seraphim proclaim the *Trisagion*, the hymn to the thrice-holy God, *to each other*:

> One called to another and said: 'Holy, holy, holy is the Lord of hosts; the whole earth is full of his glory. (Isaiah 6: 3)

This is something Bulgakov finds hugely suggestive. To his mind:

> It signifies that that praise does not consist only in a personal

[26] Ibid., p. 154.
[27] Ibid., p. 155.
[28] Ibid., p. 156.

address of each angel to God, but that it also forms the principle of their mutual relations, their common life, their *sobornost'*.[29]

This praise does not focus solely on the eternal Trinity in its unchanging actuality but also on the Incarnation and the Atonement: thus the Lucan angels at Christmas, and the 'four animals' of the Apocalypse, co-praising with the 'elders' the redeeming Lamb. In her Liturgy the Church has boldly added to these occasions when, it is held, the entire company of the angels sing praises – for instance, in connexion with Christ's Resurrection. Angelic praise is no mere jumping up and down. Bulgakov speaks of its monumentally intellectual quality. It is filled with what we could call – *very* humanly speaking:

> love of the wisdom of God, or *theology*; love of wisdom, or *philosophy*; and knowledge of the world, or *cosmology*.[30]

A grasp of the logic of things refers back to the Logos, as the sun's rays to the sun. Bulgakov thinks of it as an incessant, ever-deepening cognitive activity on the angels' part, though greatly differing from its human analogue by its intuitive and disinterested character. 'Greatly differing', but not differing *toto caelo*. Men too should have something of this loving, contemplative approach to knowledge. They should have the wings of angels.

Considered as the glorification of the divine truth and beauty, the praise of the angels can be considered the archetype of all art. Bulgakov would look in this perspective at poetry (understood as any rhythmic and – however austerely – ornamented speech). In any adequate poetics the beauty of words is treated as inseparable from their meaning, just as is, in a sound Trinitarian theology, the beauty of the Spirit is inseparable from the truth of the Logos. But the song of praise is not only words. It is music too. Bulgakov believed that musical sound originated in the modulations of heard speech. Instrumental music essentially *accompanies* the word. But music also has its analogies in the sounds of nature, notably among birds and certain insects. Though music proper occurs when sound that is independent of lexical meaning is deliberately given form and beauty, there is sufficient continuity here with the 'music' of nature to speak of not only man but the cosmos as uniting with the angels in song. Angelic praise is the paradigm of

[29] Ibid., p. 167.
[30] Ibid., p. 169.

music as it is of poetic art. What, then, of *visual* art? As 'second
lights' (God being the first), and pure forms, it is unthinkable that
the praise of the angels bears no relation at all to art that makes use
of colour (and therefore light) and line (and therefore form).
Form and colour, thinks Bulgakov, represent 'meta-matter in
matter'.[31] He uses an *a priori* argument to arrive at the conclusion
that visual art must also have its model in the praising activity of the
angels. That angelic glorification should be poorer than human is
unthinkable. Yet in her iconography the Church gives glory to God
in painterly art. It must therefore have *some* analogue among the
celestial powers. The angel guardians of the natural elements, who
are ideal anticipations of the real as found in those elements, could
be the locus where this speculation meets reality.

Angels and theophany

Before concluding his study, Bulgakov turns to two aspects of it
already touched on but so important that they need exposition,
however succinct, in their own right: the role of the angels in the
Old Testament theophanies, and their place vis-à-vis the
Incarnation in the New. In Genesis, Exodus, Numbers, Judges
(especially), the ambiguity attaching to angelic figures of whom it
can be said that with them the Lord spoke or was seen has often
been noted. Rationalists may treat these texts as evidence of a transition from polytheism to belief in one God. The faithful, says
Bulgakov, will hardly be content with so crude an evaluation. A
more nuanced appreciation will start from the recognition that
only the Word's incarnation is a perfect theophany, an immediate
revelation.

That does not mean, however, that Israel lacked veridical visionary experience, divinely originated theophanies. It denies nothing
save the immediacy – *neposredstvennost'* – of the revelation
concerned. Thus for instance Jacob did not actually know at the
time with whom he had wrestled. On the other hand, texts from
Exodus, Numbers, Deuteronomy, speak of the intimacy of Moses's
relations with God. Bulgakov takes this to be a literary device for
underlining the primacy of Moses compared with other prophets –
and contrasts it with the immediate revelation of the Word made
flesh to Elijah and Moses at the Transfiguration. Though Bulgakov
does not say so, the point was already well made by Irenaeus in the

[31] Ibid., p. 118.

second century. When the Lord tells Moses he may not stand on a
rock to see God openly but must take shelter in a cave in the rocks
while the glory passes by, this was a reminder of God's essential
invisibility to human beings and also a promise that perhaps things
might be different in the future. After all, God *had* let his glory
come close, albeit in an unseen way.

> By the wisdom of God, human beings will see him 'on the top of the
> rock'; that is, in his coming as a human being. And this is why Moses
> spoke with him, face to face, on the top of the mountain ... just as
> the Gospel records.[32]

Writing in this Irenaean spirit, Bulgakov divides the Old Testament
theophanies into two groups: epiphanies of glory, and manifestations of the angels. In the former, with, notes Bulgakov, a sensuous
element to the experience (a luminous cloud, a pillar of fire, the
changed atmosphere in the Jerusalem Temple in the theophany to
Isaiah), there is an anticipation of the Light of the Transfiguration,
but the divine presence is as yet anhypostatic. The angelophanies,
however, *are* hypostatic, though the hypostases involved are those
of the angels, through whom God manifests his divine power. The
Lord to whom, since the Fall, access was barred, as by the
Cherubim with a flaming sword (Genesis 3: 24), permitted man to
encounter him by the mediation of the angels. As fellow-creatures,
the angels were accessible to man. As theocentric beings, transparent to the divine life, they were capable of manifesting God to him.
Along with many exegetes, before and since, Bulgakov had registered the curious oscillation between singular and plural forms
when the Hebrew text speaks of these encounters. He has a nice
interpretation. By an act of the divine philanthropy, or loving-kind-
ness towards humankind:

> God hypostasizes his Wisdom-glory in the angels, in order to mani-
> fest himself to man until the moment when it will be revealed by the
> Word incarnate, his hypostatic Wisdom and Glory, the Christ.[33]

The angelic form is the only 'measure', *mera*, in which, before the
Incarnation, human beings can tolerate the 'unbearable fire' of
divinity. Yet when the Father sends on earth the Son, the Angel of
Great Counsel, these great lights fade, as the rising sun extin-
guishes the stars.

---

[32] Irenaeus, *Adversus haereses* IV. 20, 9.
[33] LY, p. 188.

But Bulgakov must somehow incorporate here the datum of the patristic tradition that it was the (pre-incarnate) *Logos* who showed himself in these epiphanies. Having established, to his own satisfaction at least, that all the angelic orders bear a special relation to one or another of the Trinitarian persons, he is in a position to do so. It was the angels of the Word who constituted the theophanic ladder between heaven and Israel. Once its premises are granted, this is an elegant solution. But in the upshot Bulgakov finds himself obliged to admit so many exceptions that it becomes unsustainable. Thus there is a Trinitarian angelophany to Abraham at the Oak of Mamre in Genesis 18: here angels linked to all three divine hypostases should be understood. Then there is the revelation of the divine Name to Moses in Exodus 3: here Bulgakov cannot suppose any other than an angel of the first divine hypostasis to be involved. In the episode of the Sacrifice of Isaac too, the typological link between Isaac and the Son – and therefore Abraham and the Father – makes it only congruent that the angel belong not to the Logos but to the Logos's Source.

The role of angels in mediating revelatory experience requires that there be adequate ways for them to enter the field of human perception. Bulgakov's idea of the 'co-humanity' of the angels, the esssentially 'synanthropic' nature of their existence, furnishes a basis for their appearance in human form which removes from the latter, at any rate in part, its rather unfortunate *Deus ex machina* associations. They already possess *chelovekoobraznost'*, a 'human configuration'.[34] Analogously, their capacity to enter the realm of human discourse is founded on the dual basis of the common provenance of angels and men in the Word, and the unity of heaven and earth as a single created order. They are 'others' but not 'strangers'.[35] There is, Bulgakov reports, no patristic consensus as to whether the angels are utterly immaterial or possess bodies of incomparable subtlety and translucency. For his part, he holds (with the Latin tradition, in fact) to their incorporeality. That they can express themselves in bodily form is explicable if we bear in mind the way angelic intelligences instantiate the ideal forms of things. Bodies are not utterly alien to them; they bear their ideal form within them. How, then, from our side does the angelic 'body' enter experience? While allowing that the angels can impact on elements of the cosmos, Bulgakov maintains that only by spiritual vision can they themselves be seen. Though human

[34] Ibid., p. 199.
[35] Ibid.

perception, as the knowing of ensouled animals, is, of course, normally mediated by the physical senses, we cannot say that non-sensuous perception is impossible. It must be possible if, after death, the separated soul is to learn (not to speak of the reports of those who have had 'near-death' or 'out of the body' experiences).

Bulgakov is hostile to the principled counterposing of spirit to body. In the Wisdom of God, the Blessed Trinity possesses, among other things, the perfect and comprehensive creative archetype of all corporeality. Indeed, how can the divine tripersonality be defined *over against bodiliness,* one of whose hypostases for our sake became incarnate? Our desire to avoid in the doctrine of God a false anthropomorphism, of the kind attacked by the fourth-century disciples of Origen in the Anthropomorphite controversy, should not lead us to suppress the true 'anthropologism', unshake-ably founded as this is on the Incarnation.[36]

The work of the angels in that Incarnation is Bulgakov's final theme. Though the integrity of creation continues to depend on angelic guardianship, with and after the Incarnation the role of the angels in divine-human relations cannot escape a certain relativi-sation. One need only think of the liturgical typology whereby Jacob's ladder, which gave its name to Bulgakov's treatise, becomes a title of the Mother of Jesus. On the other hand, the angels thirst for human salvation, not only because of their compassionate love but also because, in their synanthropy, they are destined to live in union with human kind. As divine saving action, the Incarnation crowns the aspirations of the angels as well as their propaedeutic work. The power of the redemption opens full angelic access to human beings: once fallen, now restored. (There is a gage of that in the enhanced significance of angelic guardianship for the baptized.) But more than this, when the Logos enters the human world he *brings with him the angelic order,* as the crucially sited angelophanies in the body of the Gospels indicates. Naturally, the words of Jesus to Nathanael in the fourth Gospel about how he will see the heavens open and the angels of God ascending and descending upon the Son of Man (John 1: 51) are key here. As Bulgakov writes, 'They have a capital importance for understand-ing the whole meaning of the Incarnation for relations between

---

[36] Light, both historical and doctrinal, is thrown on this by A. Golitzin, 'The Vision of God and the Form of Glory. More Reflections on the Anthropomorphite Controversy of 399', in J. Behr, A. Louth, D. Conomos (eds), *Abba. The Tradition of Orthodoxy in the West* (Crestwood, NY, 2003), pp. 273–298.

the angelic and human worlds.'[37] In Jacob's dream (Genesis 28:
12), as Bulgakov reads it, the Lord had stood at the top of the
ladder, sending down on the ancestor of Jesus angels that
descended the ladder and re-ascended again. In the Gospel, the
Lord stands on earth, at the ladder's foot. Towards him angels
descend and ascend again *while the heaven remains open*. In the God-
man the angels unite themselves as fully as can be with the human
race.

What then remains of the *Marian* symbolism of the ladder?
Through the coming of the Holy Spirit on Mary (her personal
Pentecost) and her bearing of the Word, she joins the purity and
plenitude of the angelic world with human nature. The Mother of
God 'received and reunited with the essence of man all that the
angels possess'.[38] That ultimate goal of the creation which the
angels serve is realized in her.

[37] LY, p. 221.
[38] Ibid., p. 223.

17

The Icons

Although Bulgakov's study of the icon and its veneration lies outside the trilogies which have provided the meat of this book, it seems appropriate to end with it. That is not merely because Bulgakov has frequently appealed to the icon, as also to the Liturgy, as a *locus theologicus* during his work. It is also because in a sense the whole idea of the Little Trilogy derives from an iconic consideration (it is based on an insight into the significance of the grouping of Mary, the Baptist and the angels on a particular level of the icon-screen). And then finally, the icon, owing to its special ontology, is well-placed, as we shall see, to form a summary conclusion for the study of a sophiological theology.

The value of the Nicaea II, the Council of the Icon

The opening of *The Icon and its Veneration* is abrupt. It begins with a brusque dismissal of the strictly theological (as distinct from either disciplinary or doctrinal) value of the conciliar teaching on the status of the icon at Nicaea II, the Seventh Ecumenical Council, 787, and of the work of the Iconodule doctors who prepared the way for the definition or defended the icon cult in their writings. Perhaps that account of his position is a little weak. Actually, Bulgakov does not think the *horos* of Nicaea II should count as a dogmatic decree in the full sense. It certainly canonized the veneration of the icon. It did not, he thinks, establish a dogmatic definition as such. Surprisingly, no reason is given for this summary statement other than the lack of directly attached anathemas. Among various general and individual judgments of the Council there *was* an anathema pronounced against those who reject the holy images, but only in the Council's first session. From his study we can infer, however, that Bulgakov found the *horos* insufficiently connected with the main corpus of Trinitarian and Christological doctrine reaching us from the earlier Councils for it to be in the fullest sense aggregated thereto. Hence his own judgement:

> Although the Church has justified the veneration of icons, she has not established the dogmatic foundation of this.[1]

So the whole matter is open to theological study. And while claiming to look at the work of the Iconodule theologians of the patristic epoch 'respectfully and seriously', Bulgakov's conclusion will be that, owing to accepting too much by way of initial premise from their Iconoclast opponents, they cannot in fact serve our turn.

The rise of the icon

Before presenting this remarkably negative conclusion – by way of a survey of such Fathers as Germanus of Constantinople (*c.* 640–*c.* 733) and John of Damascus, Nicephorus of Constantinople (758–828) and Theodore of Studion (759–826), Bulgakov offers us a brief account of the origin of iconodulia. He states baldly that the icon originates in paganism, from a world, both Greco-Syrian and Egypto-Mesopotamian, that was steeped in sacred images. This has implications at once negative and positive. *Negative,* because inasmuch as the religious art of the cultures surrounding Israel was specifically pagan, it was dedicated to false gods, and its icons were idols or even fetishes, turning people away from divine truth. *Positive,* because in the same way that pre-Christian Greek philosophy proved capable of furnishing what Bulgakov terms a 'natural language for Christian revelation and Christian theology', so the iconic cultures, and notably the Hellenic, proved able to contribute, at least to a limited degree, the prototypes of the Christian holy image.[2] How so? For Bulgakov, image-using paganism had already posed – and within its own framework resolved – the 'problem of the icon'. It had rejected the apophatic idea that the Divinity cannot be 'figured' or represented by images symbolically weighty if not fully adequate. And in the Hellenic context it had affirmed that the proper form in which to create such images was the human, bodily form. In other words, it had called to

[1] II, p. 7.
[2] Ibid., p. 9.

people's attention a 'human theomorphism, *bogopodobie chelovech-eskoe*', where the god appears in the form of a human.[3] The sheer beauty of these representations is for Bulgakov what led the Church to accept the content while changing the principle. Though some historians of the image would reject the term in this ancient context, the bridge between pagan iconography and Christian for him is the *splendour of art*. Despite not only the ambiguity but sometimes the sheer devilishness of the pagan iconography, it could nonetheless serve as a natural (that is, non-revealed) 'Old Testament' for the icons of the Church. It showed the Church the way of art as 'a particular mode of theognosis' – cognitive contact with the divine.[4] Gradually, so he wrote elsewhere, the realisation dawned that:

> Artistic work ... creates, out of what already exists, as a world of forms revealing Divine Beauty – something *given*, of which the artist need only discover the meaning.[5]

And the meaning is: 'the hand of God in the world'[6] – seen above all in man, as made to God's image, in his likeness, but more widely in all and sundry, 'every blessed thing', as the English idiom has it.

> The world, as it has been given to us, has remained as if covered by an outward shell through which art penetrates as if foreseeing the coming transfiguration of the world.[7]

Meanwhile, in the old dispensation, the divine prohibition on images (in the second of the Ten Commandments) was, thinks Bulgakov, *practically* justified by the tendency of Israel to slip into 'gross religious fetishism: a real cult of idols', even if the divine ordinance of sculpted cherubim for the desert Tabernacle and the Solomonic representational art in the Jerusalem temple 'abrogated the general rule, giving it only a conventional and pedagogic meaning'.[8] The temptation to 'deify the world', the temptation of 'aesthetic and mystical heathenism', was and is real and dangerous.[9]

---

[3] Ibid., p. 10.
[4] Ibid., p. 11.
[5] 'Revelation and Art', in E. L. Mascall (ed.), *The Church of God. An Anglo-Russian Symposium by Members of the Fellowship of St Alban and St Sergius* (London, 1934), pp. 175–191, and here at p. 178.
[6] Ibid., p. 183.
[7] Ibid., p. 178.
[8] II, p. 12.
[9] 'Revelation and Art', art. cit., pp. 181–182.

The Church inherited Israel's attitude to pagan images and never ceased to share it, as the examples of such Iconophile authors as Nicephorus and Theodore go to show. Yet the fact is that the idea of the icon, and the basic techniques of its manufacture, were received by the Church from paganism – something, however, which Bulgakov refuses to see as an example of pagan influence *on* Christianity. It was influence, rather, *in* Christianity, from the side of an influence which could readily – with significant transformations – find a home there owing to an inner affinity. Thus the icon took its *de facto* place in ecclesial life as an internal feature of the tradition. Only later was it noticed that the Church had in effect lifted the Old Testament interdiction – thus arousing a degree of dogmatic perplexity in which, Bulgakov willingly concedes, instances of superstitious practice by ill-formed Christians played their part. That at the first Iconoclast Council, Hiereia, in 754, as many as 348 bishops could have concluded against the icons shows the scale of the emerging problem for Iconodules. There was a 'legitimate theological perplexity' such that Iconoclasm constitutes to Bulgakov's mind:

> The expression of a necessary moment in the historical dialectics of the dogma of the veneration of icons.[10]

Iconophile limitations

Unfortunately, the Iconophile theology did not have the measure of its task. Iconophiles simplified unduly the doctrinal question behind the image-cult. Their attempts to convict Iconoclasts of Christological heresy – whether Nestorian or Monophysite – were unsuccessful. The Byzantine Iconoclasts were completely orthodox on such issues. Bulgakov notes that icons of figures other than Christ – the saints and angels – received disproportionately small attention in the quarrel. Iconoclasts hoped to impale their opponents on a fork whose prongs were, on one side, an apophatic argument from the theology of God and, on the other, a cataphatic argument from the theology of Christ. For Bulgakov they succeeded only too well. He does not accept as an adequate response to the Iconophobe challenge the claim – basic to Theodore's apologetic in his *First Refutation* – that if Christ is in two natures, he is at once indescribable in his divine being and describ-

---

[10] II., p. 17.

able in his human corporeity. How does this do more than license
icons of his humanity, or indeed of the mere external form of his
body? Despite the praise Theodore deserves as 'the great defender
of the icons and champion of their veneration, who was all his life
the servant by high deeds of his faith',[11] he left this crucial question
hanging in mid-air. From his premises one could just as well draw
an Iconoclast conclusion, and perhaps better. It remained to be
demonstrated that

> Christ was represented in the unity without either separation or
> confusion of his two natures, of which one can be figured and the
> other not.[12]

Nicephorus adds nothing Bulgakov regards as of substance. John
Damascene, writing before Nicaea II, puts forward an argument
Bulgakov will exploit brilliantly in a fashion all his own. For John,
it is owing to the weakness of people's understanding of either
the divine nature or the angelic that Scripture presents (literary)
images of divine or angelic being. Thus the Bible adapts itself to
our feeble condition. So likewise the Church, following suit,
licenses (visual) images to the same end and for the same
reason.[13] It was against precisely such concessions or adaptations
to human weakness that the Iconophobes raised their protest in
the name of true religion. Neither the Seventh Council nor subsequent Byzantine theology – much less that of the mediaeval West
where, says Bulgakov inaccurately, the question of the image was
neither examined nor even posed – gave a convincing answer to
the question the Iconoclasts had raised. His aim will be to show
that 'the dogma [of the legitimacy of venerating icons] is essentially a sophiological problem'.[14] If true, this would of course
explain why no adequate theological defence of the holy images
has emerged up to now. The Iconodules were barking up the
wrong tree.

The contribution of sophiology

Indeed, Bulgakov implies, we had better follow the line of enquiry
sophiology opens up because, on the premises taken for granted in

[11] Ibid., p. 34.
[12] Ibid.
[13] John of Damascus, *First Defence of the Holy Images*, xi.
[14] II, p. 40.

the controversy, dogmatic logic is, if anything, on the Iconoclast side. It is with the *basic premises* that the problem lies. Bulgakov contends that the fork on which the Iconoclasts would prong the Iconophiles is a false antinomy. It is falsely antinomic to contrast on the one hand a God who is essentially beyond representation and on the other the perfect depictability of the humanity of Christ. There is falsity here not because a true sense cannot be given to both of these principles but because the principles themselves *do not belong to the same logical – and even ontological – order*. In each case, we have half of a genuine antinomy. But these particular halves do not belong together. One belongs with theology, the other with cosmology. To try to join them is, in Bulgakov's comparison, like 'adding metres and grams on the pretext that both are measures'.[15] The thesis that God is essentially unrepresentable is a piece of apophatic theology, owed above all to the Pseudo-Denys and drawing attention to the way God is the Absolute, beyond all relation, and thus essentially alien to all correlation or definition – as the rich Greek vocabulary of alpha-privative adjectives indicates. To this thesis, the proper antinomic counter-thesis is not some claim about Christ's human nature. It is that God is in himself sheer relationship, the Holy Trinity, divine triune life. This does not bear on a 'history' of God – as if a primordial Godhead, an *Ur-Gottheit*, had 'become' the Trinity, as Jakob Boehme (1575–1624) and his German philosophical successors would have it. It is quite as original as the divine nature itself. In God there is in any case no process. There is only eternal act.

This God – and here we move toward a second antinomy where the humanity of Christ *does* play a part – is not only relationship in himself. He is also relationship with what he has created. In himself, God possesses the fullness of life and is all-blessed, all-sufficient. His perfect plenitude neither needs to be nor can be completed by anything beyond himself. And yet, so the second antinomy tells us, God enters into relation with another, with what is not himself, establishing what Bulgakov calls 'an absolutely relative relation in God which is that of Creator with created'. By virtue of the authenticity – the genuine reality – of the world and the world process, God joins himself to the becoming of the world.

Bulgakov insists that the first, theological antinomy has no relation to its second cosmological successor. 'No causal relation, *prichinno sootnosheniya*, can be established between them.'[16] From

<hr />

[15] Ibid., p. 44.
[16] Ibid., p. 49.

God as Absolute, no path leads to creation. But the way is now open to an account of God's self-revelation in the world, and following it we soon come across a third and final antinomy which this time is sophiological. Between God and the created world an unbridgeable gulf is fixed: 'You cannot see my face for no man shall see me and live' (Exodus 33: 20). And yet the created world has its being in God who by his creative relation with it is himself in the world. In his Wisdom, the life of the divine nature, God is turned toward the world. And the world itself is created in Wisdom and can have no other principle of being. The world is creaturely wisdom in becoming, in time. Creatures have their prototypes, what the Greek Fathers call their *proorismoi*, in the uncreated Wisdom – even if the world's life is also immersed in itself, in its own semi-being, and so is both sophianic and non-sophianic, or even anti-sophianic, at the same time.

As we have seen, this is for Bulgakov the background and condition of possibility for orthodox Christology, the Christology of Chalcedon, to which, in the struggle over the icons, both Iconoclasts and Iconophiles wished to remain faithful. The christological antinomy whereby Christ is both divine and human in a single person expresses 'with the greatest clarity' the general sophiological antinomy. As Bulgakov explains:

> The Creator and the creature, the eternal and the Temporal, uncreated divine Wisdom and created wisdom, are bound up in a single being and a single life, but in such a way that each of the two wisdoms keep its independence and its entire metaphysical distance from the other ('without confusion') at the same time as its liaison with the other ('without separation'), granted their ontological identity.[17]

The appropriate antinomy for a discussion of iconography is, accordingly, this: God cannot be figured for he is inaccessible to creaturely knowledge, *but* he can be for he reveals himself to the creature in the creation – as some celebrated words of Paul in Romans (1: 20) declare. God sets in the creation his image and his other traces – what the Latin Fathers call the *vestigia Dei*. The invisible things of God, *ta aorata tou Theou* in the Romans passage, have been made visible, indeed comprehensible, by God's creative work. The antinomy is one of theological cosmology not of theology in itself. Its specifically christological form is: God in himself is invisible *but* God in the cosmos is revealed by his Son. 'No one has

[17] Ibid., p. 53.

ever seen God; the only Son, who is in the bosom of the Father, has made him known' (John 1: 18).

Bulgakov emphasizes that both parts of the antinomy are necessary for gaining a true idea of revelation. 'In revelation, the inaccessibility of the mystery is correlative with the knowledge of it.'[18] Where there is no mysteric depth and the putative object of revelation can be sounded to its depths by a unilateral cognitive act, there is simply knowledge, and not revelation at all. But if the mystery does not in any way disclose itself, then it simply does not exist for man. For Bulgakov, apophatic theology, once brought into some attempted direct relation with iconology, spells death to the icon. This is the truth which the Iconodule Fathers failed to see and from whose evident implications they struggled vainly to escape. If the divine is absolutely beyond all images, it is plain that no image of Christ's humanity has any relation with his being as God, albeit God incarnate.

An ontology of the image

Given that Bulgakov has now shown how, negatively, he would deal with the Iconoclast divines, can he say how, positively, the icon is possible? He begins from the axiom that the icon is a work of art. (Quite apart from the question whether the term 'art' has the right connotations for a cult-image in antiquity, Bulgakov's statement that Iconoclasts were hostile to artistic representation *in general* is not one Byzantinists familiar with the eighth- and ninth-century sources would easily accept.) God reveals himself, so Bulgakov proposes, not only to human thinking in rational discourse but also to human vision in art. To Bulgakov's mind, the notion of art and the notion of image are inseparable. He offers in this context *a general ontology of the image.* Images depend on a first image, some sort of prototype with which in one sense they are identical but from which in another sense they are different. They are not repetitions of being. Reality does not in fact repeat itself. Rather, images are reality's ideal reproductions. What is thus reproduced is the *eidetic* image of being – that which enables things to have endless reproductions, as the modern photograph or even photocopying machine demonstrates.

Though an image belongs with the reality it images, it belongs *to*

18 Ibid., p. 60.

its possessor or what Bulgakov terms its 'creative bearer'.[19] In the world, the subject – as distinct from the object – of imagistic ideation is man. In this sense, all the images of being are human. *Pace* Damascene, this is not on account of human weakness and the need for ontological concession, but owing to 'the lordly power of man in the world as its eye, its ideal mirror'.[20] Man is the being who sees the images. He is *zôon eikonikon*, as well as the one who makes images, *zôon poiêtikon*. He receives and reflects images. He also acquires them creatively. He takes an active part in the iconisation of being, he discovers the icons of things in himself and through himself. All that is in the world has a reality that is representable for him. He is the 'pan-icon of the world', *vseikona mira*.[21] Where he is this in a creative sense, we have man the artist. Bulgakov declares himself strongly against a naturalism that is merely *trompe l'oeil* which 'replaces by a subterfuge the fundamental task of the iconisation of being, *ikoniatsii bitiy*'.[22] At the least, we should surely want to say that art aims through the surface of things to show their ideal form as manifested by the natural image in question. The artist tries to point to the authentic being of things by giving them a more fully iconic expression than they enjoy in nature. For Bulgakov, one just has to accept that there is in art a real *noêsis* (understanding) of form, that all genuine art grasps in one way or another the 'world of noetic beauty', the beauty of the primal ideal image of things. This is how Bulgakov would take Damascene's comment in his eighteenth oration that 'every image is a revelation and a witness of what is hidden'. Adapting a Kantian axiom, things without prototypes are blind (this is the mistake of naturalism); prototypes without things are empty and abstract (this is the error of all non-realist schematism). Thus Bulgakov reaches the important programmatic statement that:

> The creative act of art, by iconising a thing, consists first of all in perceiving by means of it its prototype; then, in expressing that protoype in appropriate media ... The icon is the expression of the true primal image which, by way of the thing represented, has a real being in the world.[23]

[19] Ibid., p. 65.
[20] Ibid.
[21] Ibid., p. 66.
[22] Ibid., p. 67.
[23] Ibid., pp. 71–72.

This takes Bulgakov into what is recognizably the world of Platonic ideas which he understands not, however, as with some inter-preters of Plato's corpus in quasi-logical terms but as

> existent noetic images, possessing an energy of being and realising themselves in being as the entelechies of things – their interior final causes.[24]

Put theologically, the philosophical theory of ideal protoypes of the world signifies the *sophianity of the created* which has as its own primal image and foundation the divine Wisdom, the pan-organi-sation of the ideas. At the basis of figurative art lies

> the objective and anthropocosmic foundation of the world, the sophianic prototypes according to which, created by Wisdom, it exists.[25]

There are, therefore, in Bulgakov's ontology of aesthetics three factors: the representation; the original of the representation; the noetic prototype of the original. The three come together in man inasmuch as all the eidetic images of being are seen in him accord-ing to their multiple unity. As the microcosm of the macrocosm, he sees them 'outside himself but by means of himself', and in this sense he 'finds them in himself and expresses them for himself'.[26] This will be pertinent when Bulgakov turns, as he now does, to the 'divine prototype'.

The Colossians hymn acclaims Christ as the 'image of the invisi-ble God, the first-born of all creation' (1: 15), or in the anti-Arian translation in Bulgakov's Russian Bible, 'born before all creation'. This, the Primary Image, is the pre-existent Son. The Son images the Father 'visibly' because in the Word, whom Bulgakov calls 'Word of all words and Image of all images', appears the content of the divine life and of all that enters created being, the ideal noetic figures of which the Word holds for the world. This Image expresses the Father's Word but unlike other images it has as its bearer a divine hypostasis, the second trinitarian Person. The third

---

[24] Ibid., p. 72.

[25] Ibid., p. 74. Notable by its absence in Bulgakov's account is the crucial theme of Pavel Florensky's cognate account, namely that in the case of the icons these 'hyper-empirical ideas' are the saints as bearing witness to God in Christ – whether by their mystical visions or in their 'holy countenances that sacred significance has permeated'. Thus P. Florensky, *Iconostasis* (Et Crestwood, NY, 1996), pp. 67–69.

[26] II, p. 76.

Person too is involved here. Patristic literature sometimes calls the Holy Spirit 'the Image of the Son', and this for Bulgakov is because the Spirit accomplishes the image of the Father in the Son, realizing the iconic character of the Son in relation to the prototypical Father.

From the bi-unity of the Image of God by which the Father reveals himself in the Son and the Holy Spirit, it is appropriate to pass to the single figuration or content of that Image in the Holy Trinity. Summing up his entire sophiological account of Christian revelation and a biblically resourced metaphysics, Bulgakov writes that the content of that Image in the Holy Trinity is nothing other than the Wisdom of God. This is 'the living and life-giving Idea of all the ideas in their perfect unity and reality',[27] as attested by no less an authority than sacred Scripture itself: 'The Lord possessed me at the beginning of his ways' (Proverbs 8: 22). Wisdom is the Prototype of the world created by Wisdom. The world is thus a created icon of divinity. By its ontological theme, the created is identical with its prototype. By now, these notions are highly familiar to us. What is new is their pressing into service as the real basis of visual art.

> This relation between the trihypostatic God and his Idea, the divine Wisdom as Prototype of the world, and the relation between this Prototype and the world, its created image, constitutes in general the foundation of all iconicity, *oskovanie vsyakoi ikonnosti*.[28]

Iconology needs as its starting-point the sophiological principle by which God is figurable and the world configured in his image.

Now we know from Bulgakov's account of the Godmanhood of the Word, and the related theme of the image of God in man, that the divine Wisdom is also the eternal humanity of God. The Word of God is the heavenly Adam, the Prototype of a world centred in man. This conformity between God and man is why the Word could become incarnate as human. Seen from below up: humanity in its theanthropic character is the living image of the divinity – the created image of the uncreated Image hypostatized in the all-creative Word. An obscure feeling for this theomorphism is what made possible the pagan art of the divine-in-human-form – the form of a human body considered as disclosure of the human spirit as itself bearing a divine likeness. This is the aboriginal image of the kind Greek Christian piety called *acheiropoiêtos*, 'not made by

27 Ibid., p. 81.
28 Ibid., p. 82.

human hands'. Alas, owing to original sin theomorphic man is now decomposed by the fallen passions, bestialized, no longer able to show forth the image of God. For Bulgakov, then, the Old Testament prohibition on anthropomorphic images of God is explicable by the inauthenticity of the image now that man has lost the purity or integrity of his humanity.

This leads Bulgakov, incidentally, to his subtle explanation of the great exception to the aniconicism of the First and Second Temples, the image of the Cherubim. *Positively*: inasmuch as the angels have features in common with humanity (we have seen how for Bulgakov they are 'synanthropic'), the Cherubim *could* be represented in human form. But *negatively*, that *only* the angels should thus be represented indicates the 'occultation of the theomorphic character of man, which is now obscured by sin'.

The Incarnation of the Word as Jesus changes all this.

> The one Christ, without sin, the new Adam, has re-established in his humanity the authentic image of man which is that of God. The Lord has shown himself truly man and in him has appeared the true man, the new Adam. He bears the true image of man, the icon of divinity, living and 'not made by human hands'.29

That is clearly expressed by the 'secret' prayer in the rite of the blessing of icons of the saints in the *Trebnik*, the Slavonic ritual. The Incarnation restores man's iconic quality – that is its real significance for iconodulia. In his Godhead, Christ is Image of the Father as Prototype of man (cf. 1 Corinthians 15: 47 and 49), while 'the man' in Christ is the direct image of Jesus's divinity, which itself has a human figure. The image, then, belongs to Christ's hypostasis *in its unity*. His image reveals itself in a dyadic way: invisibly according to the spirit, visibly according to the body. But this visible human image is nonetheless identicals with his invisible divine image. This the *perichôrêsis* of the natures in the single hypostasis tells us, and the Transfiguration on Mount Thabor demonstrates it.

Icon and portrait

Bulgakov does not deny that the painterly icon of Christ has its limits. A portrait is always a *pars pro toto*, 'fixing' only one of the

29 Ibid., p. 90.

'manifestations of the phenomenology of the spirit'.[30] Hence its merely relative value – and the possibility of supplementing it by others. Still, the entire spirit, being indivisible, appears in each manifestation. That is the significance of the act of naming the portrait, which establishes a relation not only with the prototype (the sitter) but with other portraits (of the same person).

One difference between an icon of Christ and a merely human portrait is that, as New Adam, the Saviour is a super- or pan-individual. In some sense his face 'contains' all particular individuals. Or, conversely, each human face has something of that of Christ about it. That is why there can be portraits of him painted by unbelievers, and why ancient religious art can be said to have created, all unconsciously, a pre-Christian icon. But to represent the God-man the painter must have not only art but an appropriate vision, and this is only possible on the soil of ecclesiality where the 'creative demands of art are joined with ecclesial experience'.[31] Painting an icon is a theurgic act, requiring prayer and *askêsis*. The iconic canon expresses objectively the tradition of the Church. The Church's iconography is a 'treasury of the Church's living memory of the visions and representations' by which her artists have imaged the divine world in form and colour as testimony to her own 'creative, common activity'.[32] The iconic canon should not be seen, then, as an 'external rule', requiring a servility of mere copying. This was the mistake of the Russian Old Believers from the late seventeenth century onwards.[33] Colour photography, though practically useful, cannot replace authentic iconography. That the canonization of new saints requires new icons should alone suffice to dispel this misunderstanding. And just as the life of the Church is inexhaustible thanks to the Holy Spirit, so novel

---

[30] Ibid., p. 101.

[31] Ibid., p. 107. In a letter of 11/24 August 1929 to the icon-painter Julia Reitlinger (1898–1988), later Sister Johanna, Bulgakov speaks of this devout woman 'training' him in the sophiological significance of the colours in which Christ's humanity is depicted. Partly indebted to the *Ateliers d'Art sacré* of the former 'Nabi' but later pious Catholic Maurice Denis, Reitlinger went on in the last years of her turbulent life to play a role in the pastoral ministry of the well-known Orthodox priest Alexander Men' (1935–1990). Prior to his murder, Fr Men' frequently commissioned her clandestinely to make tiny icons for the people he baptized. I am grateful for this information to an as yet unpublished lecture by Elizabeth Roberts, 'Sister Johanna (Reitlinger)'s Iconography and her Letters to Father Aleksandr Men´', given at Soesterberg, The Netherlands, on 22 June 2004.

[32] II, p. 108.

[33] See O. Tarasov, *Icon and Devotion*, op. cit., pp. 23–24.

icons appear: the Rublev Trinity, the Novgorod icons of Wisdom, the various 'cosmic' images of the Mother of God. But ancient icon-types should themselves be painted – and inevitably are – in a fresh manner, by an accumulation of tiny changes. True copying is properly creative.

Icon and blessing

That icons belong to ecclesial tradition is attested by their *consecration* through a liturgical act. The inscribing of a name is also an essential element of the act of representing the icon performs. It seals the icon with the copula: this representation '*is* Christ; it belongs to him'.[34] Here iconology belongs with 'onomatology', the veneration of the icon with the glorification of the divine Name (in Greek, *to onoma*). The name is the verbal icon of the hypostasis. Hence to name the image is already in some wise to consecrate it to the prototype, to actualize the representation. But only the Church can do this, by the power of the Spirit. In giving an icon a name she consecrates it and only then does the icon become truly itself.[35] The Church's sacramental act consists precisely in naming. It signifies that the image is assimilated ecclesially to the Primal Image. (In his footnotes, Bulgakov rejects the modern Greek Orthodox notion that consecration of an icon is unnecessary, a false accommodation to Latin practice – even if, as he accepts, the need for such consecration was only felt comparatively late in the consciousness of the Church.)

What are, then, the limits of veneration of such an icon, if any? For Bulgakov, consecration makes an icon communicate in the being of its prototype as a 'special place of the presence [of that prototype] by grace'.[36] Praying before an icon of Christ we pray to him directly, salute him, kiss him. And here the Iconoclasts were right to raise the question of comparison (and contrast) with the Eucharistic Gifts. The Lord appears in the icon for a prayer presence; he appears in the sacramental mystery of the Holy Gifts for communion. There his presence is substantial but without image (Bulgakov feels that the Latin Church treats the Elements as if they were an icon of Christ, evidently so in the Elevation at Mass but also in Eucharistic devotions). The icon is Christ's image, but not his

[34] II, p. 117.
[35] The same point is made by Florensky in *Iconostasis*, op. cit., p. 91.
[36] II, pp. 124–125.

substantial being. However, though the materials of the icon are not transubstantiated, as are the bread and wine of the Eucharist, Bulgakov allows a transfiguration of the painterly image into the true image of the Prototype. Once consecrated, the image:

> becomes 'not made by hands', it is like the figure of the Saviour which, by his own will, was imprinted on a cloth for king Agar.[37]

Every consecrated icon is thus miraculous since the divine power is present here even if this is only actively expressed in certain of their number. Nicaea II, not knowing consecration as a rite, has no doctrine of the power of icons – only of their being a commemoration of the primal images, to arouse love for them. Trent, so Bulgakov believes, through ill-advised concession to Protestantism, underlined even more strongly the merely commemorative aspect. But it is as Christ's ideal presence and in this sense his living image that the icon merits veneration. After the Ascension, Christ keeps a bond with the world in two modes – substantially in the Eucharist, ideally in the holy icons. Both of these enjoy eschatological significance. Just as, by transforming this world's substance into Christ's Body and Blood the Eucharist has a cosmic significance that points to this world's final transfiguration, just so, through the iconic assimilation of images to the primal Image, Christ traces his figure in the world that it may shine out there when 'the times are accomplished'.[38]

Non-Christological imagess

So far, Bulgakov has concentrated almost exclusively on icons of Christ. But these are by no means the only icons known to the Byzantine tradition. Nicaea II itself spoke of images of Our Lady, the angels, the saints. What types, then, does he admit? As sixteenth-century disputes in the Church of Russia might lead us to expect, Bulgakov begins with the difficult question of iconic representation of the first trinitarian hypostasis, the divine Father. Perhaps surprisingly, he has no objection to the portrayal of the *Creator* in human form – the human aspect of *Elohim* corresponds to the eternal humanity in the Wisdom of God. He has more qualms about the *Father* portrayed as a venerable human figure,

[37] Ibid., p. 130.
[38] Ibid., p. 136.

along with the Son, in images of the *Trinity*. To signify the Son's
likeness to the Father, the Father's iconography has 'attracted' to
itself the human iconology of the incarnate Son. Bulgakov prefers
to think that what is shown in such icons is an image of the human-
ity-in-divinity of the pre-incarnate Lord – only by virtue of which
could the Father of the Son be humanly portrayed. (We have seen
how his views evolved to the point of accepting, in *Agnets Bozhii*,
icons of the Father compassionating the suffering Son.) The Holy
Spirit has no icon of his own – Bulgakov would add *directly*. But *indirectly*, images of the Mother of God, the *Pneumatophora*, after the
Annunciation, act as such. Still, the prohibition of a direct image
of the Holy Spirit remains instructive. It shows that the revelation
of his hypostasis, as distinct from his gifts, belongs to the Age to
Come. What of the Trinity as the theophany of three angels at the
Oak of Mamre, made famous in the version by Rublev? Again, this
is an anthropomorphic representation, even if the emphasis lies
not on the personal character of each 'angel' but on their trinitarian correlation.

The angels properly so called can be iconised in human form
owing to their 'co-humanity' – though an additional set of, purely
symbolic, aspects of their iconography is founded on the prophetic
visions in Isaiah, Ezekiel and the Apocalypse. Such symbolism
enters into various 'dogmatic' icons – above all, those of Holy
Wisdom of the Novgorod variety. Such icons are as instructive to
Bulgakov's eye as they were (in all probability) the inspirational
source of Soloviev's original sophiological scheme. Here a central
figure of a fiery angel on an altar, with the Saviour and the noetic
heaven above, the Mother of the Lord and John the Baptist on
either side, symbolizes the eternal Humanity of the Godhead
revealing itself in the created world. That 'Wisdom' reveals itself
first and foremost in the God-man but also in Mary and John who
embody the summits of spiritual humanity, and finally in the world
of the angels themselves. Such dogmatic icons derive for Bulgakov
from mystical or prophetic illumination: rare but possible as a
source for amplifying the iconographic canon.

Images of the saints are easier to deal with. Since Christ is
'formed' in them (cf. Galatians 4: 19), they represent his multi-
faceted visage. Unlike Israel of old (the chronology of the
archaeological digs suggests Bulgakov did not know in time of the
synagogue art of Dura-Europos[39]), the Church portrays the saints

---

[39] C. Hopkins, *The Discovery of Dura-Europos* (New Haven and London, 1979), pp.
    140–177; A. Perkins, *The Art of Dura-Europos* (Oxford, 1973), pp. 55–65.

of the ancient Covenant as well as those of the New. This she does, says Bulgakov, because:

> *their* human figure too began to shine in the light of the resurrection of Christ and thanks to the energy of his Incarnation.[40]

As always, the icon portrays the face of the holy person as glorified, not as on earth, even though certain traits of the individual's likeness may be preserved. This puts Bulgakov in mind of the topic of *relics* which are at once *less* than an icon, since they do not bear the ideal image of the saint, and yet *more*, because in their uniqueness, they are 'grasped' by the holy person who even in death keeps this link with the poor remains of his or her body. Those remains, even in obscurity and corruption, have the promise of future glory.

The icon and the Mother of God

In traditional Christian art, icons of the Mother of God are especially numerous, varied, beloved and beautiful. This does not astonish Bulgakov. He considers them first in relation to Christ. The Mother and Child is the primary image of the Incarnation: earthly humanity united to heavenly and so a sophianic image *par excellence*. He also views them in relation to the Spirit: when Mary appears without the Child it is as the woman who became perfectly transparent to the Comforter. (As already mentioned, the image of the Mother of God venerated by St Seraphim was of this type: but some Orthodox consider it Latinizing and an embarrassment.)

Bulgakov treats the image of the *Theotokos* in relation to the Church as well. This is something best expressed in the Kievan image of Wisdom where Wisdom's 'temple' is represented by a Mary surrounded by prophets and apostles. Finally, he deals with Marian images in their relation to the cosmos. Through Mary – so such icons as the *All creation rejoices* tells us, the sophianity of the entire created realm finds voice. In all this the Mother of God remains herself, Mary of Nazareth. She is not shown as 'a lovely lady', as in much Western sacred art, even in its best examples. Rather, the icons portray her now beyond her earthly fate as well as formed by it. The result is no less tender a beauty. It strikes Bulgakov that her 'miraculous' or 'revealed' icons are more numerous than those of Christ himself who, after all, gives himself

---

[40] II, p. 147.

to us in the Holy Eucharist as well as in the Gospels, his verbal icons, and indeed in his holy Name. The sheer quantity of the Marian icons also speaks of Mary's closeness to the world whose life and suffering she shares. She is 'the Protecting Veil'. Her motherly love leads her to weep for the world from which, as a glorified creature, she is differentiated but not distanced.

Narrative and Cross

Bulgakov affirms the descriptive or didactic role of the icon, but he associates this more with the fresco which so often takes as its subject wider biblical themes or motifs of Church history or even, in the entrance to church buildings at least, the pagan philosophers and sibyls seen as Christians before Christ. (But the fullest exemplars of this are Western.) He notes how in the way landscape is shown on icons, the division between nature and humanity seems to vanish. For Bulgakov, nature has acquired an undue independence – even apartheid – from humanity owing to the Fall. In such icons as those of the Transfiguration of the Lord, we see non-human nature in its destiny of participating in the transfiguration of all things.

   Finally, there is the Cross, which even Iconoclasts did not touch. It can be seen as, quite simply, the image of the Crucified, or in more complex fashion as signifying the sacrificial kenotic love of the Trinity, as well as the suffering love of God for the world. The sign of the Cross, traced by the hand in the air, and joined with the Trinitarian Name, already has a power of sanctification. Bulgakov calls it the seed from which the icon grew, the original indissoluble union of power and image, the heavenly and the earthly. In this sense the Cross too is a sophianic image – an image of the Church as the union of heaven and earth – hence the Cross's place above every church building. It is 'the type of every iconic quality, the icon of the icon', *ikona ikoni*.[41] This reminds us of the true centre of all Bulgakov's sophiological speculations: the kenosis of the Trinity on the glorious Cross.

---

[41] Ibid., p. 164.

Conclusion

I hope that this study will have convinced readers of how much there is to learn from Bulgakov's under-appreciated dogmatic thought. So far as Catholic students are concerned, I do not believe the doctrinal difficulties this corpus of writing represents has much to do with sophiology. Sophiology is one version of how to combine the metaphysics of the Old Testament's sapiential books with Christian Platonism, and this is a general formula with which the Fathers of the Church and the later tradition lived happily for centuries. At times, it is true, I have offered a 'benign' reading of the verbal remnants of a more gnostically coloured religious philosophy as found in Bulgakov's early writings. But 'remnants' is the word. In the mature dogmatics, as Archbishop Rowan Williams has written,

> Sophia is definitely not any kind of person but a characterisation of divine action itself as realized in all three persons of the Trinity.[1]

The problems Catholic theology finds with Bulgakov are chiefly concerned with some of the classical disputed issues, the articles that separate Greek East and Latin West. Notable among them are the *Filioque*, the Papacy and – a more recent addendum, the theology of grace lying behind the Immaculate Conception dogma of 1854. On one of the ancient – well, mediaeval – issues, that of Purgatory, Bulgakov (ironically, we might think) reversed the direction of much Greek criticism of Latins. With largely token reservations, he espouses a universalism reminiscent of Origen of Alexandria and St Gregory of Nyssa – just the outcome that not very well informed Byzantine objectors to the Western eschatology of the Middle Ages most feared! These are certainly neuralgic

[1] R. Williams, 'Russian Theology: Challenge and Innovation', *The Saint Austen Review* 2, 2 (2002), p. 11.

spots. To them may be added the influence of historic Modernism (Protestant and Catholic) in Bulgakov's treatment of the origins of the episcopate – for which I have ventured to suggest a biographical explanation in terms of his (mixed) experience of hierarchs. His animus against the term 'transubstantiation', by no means generally shared in early modern and modern Orthodoxy, is unfortunate. The eccentric teaching on the dual nature of St John the Baptist could raise an eyebrow, but maybe also a kindly smile. It arises from fervour of devotion, not a failure to think with the Church.

In Bulgakov's doctrinal corpus, not only are there long passages indebted to the consonant sound of Orthodox and Catholic in the common faith. There are also moments where the distinctive music of Bulgakov's mind and heart leaves one surprised by joy. But this itself is unsurprising. Great theology is always fertile in fresh illuminations of natural and revealed truth.

In the body of the text I made a comparison with the work of Hans Urs von Balthasar. Both men believed in the necessity for Christian intellectuality of a confident metaphysic, for which they drew elements not only from Hellenic but also from Germanist thought, tutored in their choice of materials and themes by the biblical revelation. Each was a thoroughgoingly Trinitarian thinker in his approach to modern theology, finding the Trinity most fully displayed in the Cross and Resurrection of Christ. Both writers combined an Chalcedonian Christology with a moderated kenoticism. They were equally concerned to integrate nature and grace, not least in the form of eros and agape. Implicitly, they sought to negotiate a *via media* between tradition and modernity, notably by emphasizing the value of the creative receptivity (with equal weight on adjective and noun) of the human subject. Explicitly, their overall project was comprehensive, and into its service they pressed a large variety of sources from Scripture and patristics, the Liturgy and other poetic texts. Despite their Christian humanism they were remarkably eschatological in outlook. Both leaned heavily on Scripture's last book, the Apocalypse of St John. Each was tempted by universalism; yet neither found optimistic humanism convincing in the slightest degree.

Some Orthodox would like to see Father Sergii 'glorified'

(=canonized). Some Catholics regard Hans Urs von Balthasar as an unofficial 'doctor of the Church'. In each case there are some doctrinal questions to be raised, but by the standards of here-siarchs – ancient and modern – these are severely circumscribed in kind. There is much they could have shared on earth. May they sit adjacently in the heavenly choir.

Select Bibliography

1. Works by Sergei Bulgakov

O rynkakh pri kapitalisticheskom proizvodstve (On Markets in the Capitalist System of Production, Moscow, 1897).

Kapitalizm i zemledelie (Capitalism and Agriculture, St Petersburg, 1900; two volumes).

Ivan Karamazov kak filosofskii tip (Ivan Karamazov as a Philosophical Type, Moscow, 1902).

Ot marksizma k idealizmu (From Marxism to Idealism, St Petersburg, 1903).

Istoriia politicheskoi ekonomii (A History of Political Economy, Moscow, 1907).

Dva grada (Two Cities, Moscow, 1911).

Filosofiia khozyaistva (The Philosophy of Economic Activity, Moscow, 1912).

Tserkov' i demokratiia (Church and Democracy, Moscow, 1917).

Svet nevechernii (The Unfading Light, Moscow, 1917).

Khristianstvo i sotsializm (Christianity and Socialism, Moscow, 1917).

Svyatie Petr i Ioann. Dva pervoapostola (Saints Peter and John. Two Prime Apostles, Paris, 1926).

Die Tragödie der Philosophie (The Tragedy of Philosophy, Darmstadt, 1927).

Drug zhenikha (The Friend of the Bridegroom, Paris, 1927; Et *The Friend of the Bridegroom. On the Orthodox Veneration of the Forerunner*, Grand Rapids, Mich., 2003).

Kupina neopalimaya (The Burning Bush, Paris, 1927).

Lestnitsa Yakovlya (Jacob's Ladder, Paris, 1929).

Ikona i ikonopochitanie (The Icon and its Veneration, Paris, 1931).

Agnets Bozhii: O bogochelovechestve, I (The Lamb of God, On Godmanhood, I, Paris, 1933).

The Orthodox Church (London 1935; 2nd edition Crestwood, NY, 1988).

Uteshitel': O bogochelovechestve, II (The Comforter, On Godmanhood, II, Paris, 1936).

The Wisdom of God. A Brief Outline of Sophiology (London, 1937). Republished as *Sophia. The Wisdom of God: an Outline of Sophiology* (Hudson, NY, 1993).

Nevesta agntsa: O bogochelovechestve, III (The Bride of the Lamb, on Godmanhood, III, Paris, 1945; Et *The Bride of the Lamb,* New York, 2002).

Avtobiograficheskie zametki (Autobiographical Notebooks, Paris, 1946; 1991),

Filosofiia imeni (The Philosophy of the Name, Paris, 1953).

L'Orthodoxie (Paris, 1965).

A Bulgakov Anthology, ed. J. Pain and N. Zernov (London, 1976).

Sergii Bulgakov. Towards a Russian Political Theology, texts edited and introduced by R. Williams (Edinburgh, 1999).

2. Secondary works

W. F. Crum, 'S. N. Bulgakov: From Marxism to Sophiology', *Saint Vladimir's Seminary Quarterly* 22 (1978), pp. 3–26.

C. Evtuhov, *The Cross and the Sickle: Sergei Bulgakov and the Fate of Russian Religious Philosophy, 1890–1920* (Ithaca, NY, and London, 1997).

C. Graves, *The Holy Spirit in the Theology of Sergius Bulgakov* (Geneva, 1972).

B. Jakim (ed.), *Sergius Bulgakov: Apocatastasis and Transfiguration* (New Haven, 1995).

C. Lialine, 'Le Débat sophiologique', *Irénikon* 13 (1936), pp. 168–205.

V. Lossky, *Spor o Sofii. Dokladnaya zapiska Prot. S. Bulgakova i smisl' ukaza Moskovskoi Patriarchii* (The Question about Wisdom. A Report on the Case of the Archpriest Sergii Bulgakov and the Meaning of the Decree of the Patriarch of Moscow, Paris, 1936).

A. Nichols, O. P., *Light from the East. Authors and Themes in Orthodox Theology* (London, 1995), Chapter IV.

P. Valliere, *Modern Russian Theology. Bukharev, Soloviev, Bulgakov. Orthodox Theology in a New Key* (Edinburgh, 2000), Chapters 10 to 14.

L. A. Zander, *Bog i mir. Mirosozertsanie ottsa Sergiia Bulgakova* (God and the World. The World-view of Father S. Bulgakov, Paris, 1948, 2 volumes).

3. General background

A. Kniazeff, *L'Institut Saint-Serge de Paris. De l'Académie d'autrefois au rayonnement d'aujourd'hui* (Paris, 1974).

A. Nichols, O. P., *Theology in the Russian Diaspora. Church, Fathers, Eucharist in Nikolai Afanas'ev, 1893–1966* (Cambridge, 1989), Chapter 1.

M. Raeff, *Russia Abroad: A Cultural History of the Russian Emigration, 1919–1939* (Oxford, 1990).

C. Read, *Religion, Revolution and the Russian Intelligentsia, 1900–1912* (London, 1979).

J. Scherrer, *Die Petersbürger Religiös-Philosophischen Vereinigungen* (Berlin, 1973).

V. Shevzov, *Russian Orthodoxy on the Eve of Revolution* (Oxford 2004).

C. E. Timberlake (ed.), *Religious and Secular Forces in Late Tsarist Russia. Essays in Honor of Donald W. Treadgold* (Seattle and London, 1992).

N. Zernov, *The Russian Religious Renaissance of the Twentieth Century* (London, 1963).

Index

Lightning Source UK Ltd.
Milton Keynes UK
UKOW05f1021060217
293702UK00001B/21/P